**THE TRUMAN
ADMINISTRATION
AND BOLIVIA**

GLENN J. DORN

THE TRUMAN ADMINISTRATION AND BOLIVIA

MAKING THE WORLD SAFE FOR LIBERAL CONSTITUTIONAL OLIGARCHY

THE PENNSYLVANIA STATE UNIVERSITY PRESS
UNIVERSITY PARK, PENNSYLVANIA

Earlier versions of parts of chapters 3, 4, 5, and 6 appeared in
Glenn J. Dorn, "Pushing Tin: U.S.-Bolivian Relations and the Coming
of the National Revolution," *Diplomatic History* 35 (April 2011): 203–28
(first published online 6 March 2011).

Library of Congress Cataloging-in-Publication Data

Dorn, Glenn J.
  The Truman administration and Bolivia : making the world safe for
liberal constitutional oligarchy / Glen J. Dorn.
    p.   cm.
  Includes bibliographical references and index.
  Summary "Examines the interaction of the Truman administration in
U.S. and five Bolivian governments in years leading up to Victor Paz
Estenssoro's National Revolution, focusing on negotiations over the price
of tin"—Provided by the publisher.
  ISBN 978-0-271-05015-7 (cloth : alk. paper)
  ISBN 978-0-271-05016-4 (pbk. : alk paper)
  1. United States—Foreign relations—Bolivia.
  2. Bolivia—Foreign relations—United States.
  3. United States—Foreign relations—1945–1953.
  4. Bolivia—Foreign relations—20th century.
  5. Tin—Prices—Bolivia—History—20th century.
  6. Tin industry—Bolivia—Government policy—History—20th
century.
    I. Title.

E183.8.B6D67 2011
327.73084—dc 23
2011023350

Copyright © 2011 The Pennsylvania State University
All rights reserved
Printed in the United States of America
Published by The Pennsylvania State University Press,
University Park, PA 16802-1003

It is the policy of The Pennsylvania State University Press to use acid-free
paper. Publications on uncoated stock satisfy the minimum requirements
of American National Standard for Information Sciences—Permanence
of Paper for Printed Library Material, ANSI Z39.48–1992.

The Pennsylvania State University Press is a member of the Association
of American Universty Presses.

FOR *Cassandra*

CONTENTS

Acknowledgments   ix

List of Abbreviations   xi

Introduction   1

1 Villarroel: April 1945–July 1946   27

2 Junta: July 1946–March 1947   49

3 Hertzog: March 1947–May 1949   71

4 Urriolagoitia: May 1949–June 1950   95

5 To the Mamertazo: July 1950–May 1951   117

6 Ballivián: May 1951–April 1952   137

7 Paz Estenssoro: April 1952–January 1953   163

Conclusion   185

Epilogue   197

Notes   211

Selected Bibliography   242

Index   248

ACKNOWLEDGMENTS

In writing *The Truman Administration and Bolivia*, I have enjoyed the support of more friends, family members, mentors, and colleagues than I could ever deserve. Without them, this project could never have been realized.

I would like to begin by thanking the teachers and historians who taught me what I know of the historian's craft. I owe my career in this profession to Michael Hogan, whose patience and skill as a mentor cannot be overstated. The lessons that he, Peter Hahn, Warren Van Tine, and my other professors at Ohio State University taught me were invaluable. William O. Walker III has, quite literally, been there for me from my first day as an undergraduate. As a freshman chemistry major, I was blessed to attend his 8 A.M. U.S. history class. His passion and skill as a teacher, along with that of David Steigerwald and Richard Spall, drew me to the field of history and convinced me to make a career of it. I have continued to call upon Bill's wisdom and advice ever since. My first day of teaching was as a one-year replacement for him, and I took it as my mission to do for my students what he had done for me. I remind myself of that every semester and attempt to rise to that near-impossible challenge each year.

This project presented new challenges for me, and I am grateful for all of those who lent me their expertise. The archivists at the U.S. National Archives, the Harry S. Truman Presidential Library, the Franklin Delano Roosevelt Presidential Library, and the George Meany Memorial Archives in Washington, D.C., were, as always, invaluable in my research and a credit to their great profession. Martha Paredes in La Paz and Carlos Dellapiane in Buenos Aires had the more challenging task of helping me find what I needed in their archives. Both showed more patience and dedication than I had any right to ask for. Before and during my trip to La Paz, James Siekmeier and Thomas Field provided insight and assistance that added much to the venture. Donald Burge at the University of New Mexico went far above and beyond the call of duty to ensure that I was able to access Senator Chavez's records. The staff at Penn State University Press deserve special recognition for their skill, professionalism, and patience. I cannot thank enough Sanford Thatcher, Kendra Boileau, Laura Reed-Morrisson, Stephanie Grace, and the rest of the PSUP staff, as well as copy editor Jeffrey H. Lockridge, for the time and effort they spent to improve my work and shepherd it to publication.

I also want to thank my colleagues at Embry-Riddle Aeronautical University (ERAU). James Libbey has been a mentor since I arrived in Daytona Beach and has been my model for how to balance teaching and research. I aspire to excel at each, as he did. Steve Craft contributed to this work more than he can know. Whenever I reached a difficult point in the research and writing, Steve's suggestions and comments unfailingly pointed me in the right direction. Lynnette Porter has been not only a great friend but also the toughest, most diligent editor I have ever run across. Donna Barbie of the Humanities and Social Sciences Department, Dean Bill Grams, Chief Academic Officer Richard Heist, and President John Johnson ensured that I had the time and money I needed to fulfill some ambitious research and travel goals. That they did so in difficult financial times only adds to the debt I owe them. My colleagues and students at ERAU have made it nothing less than a home for me, and for that I am deeply grateful.

And, finally, my special thanks to Jeff, Kathy, and Gary Dorn and my eternal gratitude and sincerest apologies to Mary and Cassandra for enduring this project over the last several years. Without their patience, love, and support throughout, nothing would have been possible.

ABBREVIATIONS

COB	Central Obrera Boliviana
COMIBOL	Corporación Minera de Bolivia
CTC	Combined Tin Committee
DPA	Defense Production Agency
FDA	Frente Democrático Antifascista
FEA	Foreign Economic Administration
FSTMB	Federación Sindical de Trabajadores Mineros de Bolivia
ITA	International Tin Agreement
ITC	International Tin Committee; International Tin Council (after 1956)
ITO	International Trade Organization
MNR	Movimiento Nacionalista Revolucionario
OAS	Organization of American States
PIR	Partido de la Izquierda Revolucionaria
POR	Partido Obrero Revolucionario
PURS	Partido de la Unión Republicana Socialista
RADEPA	Razón de Patria
RFC	Reconstruction Finance Corporation

INTRODUCTION

The use of the word "democratic" throughout this dispatch, as applied to the present government of Bolivia, should be construed in its limited sense as distinguishing the type of government, i.e., as against a dictatorship, communist regime, et cetera, rather than that it embraces all other generally accepted concepts in the meaning of the adjective "democratic." It might otherwise be described as a liberal constitutional oligarchy.
—*James Espy, 10 February 1950*

The Bolivian case, in schematic definition, is one of three and a half million inhabitants, dominated and exploited by a minority who utilizes the visible forms of a democratic regime to give the patent of legality and perpetuate essentially undemocratic privileges.
—*Víctor Paz Estenssoro, March 1951*

On 16 October 2003, truckloads of workers descended on La Paz, Bolivia, to help unseat an unpopular, corrupt, decadent regime, break the back of the free market economy it espoused, broaden Bolivian democracy, and seize control of the nation's subsoil riches. It was not the first time they had done so. In April 1952, tin miners rallied to the defense of Víctor Paz Estenssoro, his Movimiento Nacionalista Revolucionario (MNR), and their National Revolution against "liberal constitutional oligarchy." Whereas what has been called the "Third Bolivian Revolution" of 2000 to 2006 paved the way for Evo Morales's landslide presidential victory, however, the National Revolution put an end to the *sexenio*—the Bolivian elites' unsuccessful six-year battle to preserve the established order against a rising tide of popular unrest. That the United States, the International Monetary Fund, and the World Bank helped set the stage for the latest revolution—by encouraging the Bolivian adoption of neoliberalism and the "Washington consensus" and by militarizing the eradication of coca as part of the War on Drugs—is well documented.[1] Much less studied was Washington's role in events leading to the National Revolution of 1952.

The story of U.S.-Bolivian relations in the years after World War II represents a unique convergence of three major factors. The first was the efforts of President Harry S. Truman to forge a global liberal capitalist order by overcoming South American nationalists who threatened to derail those plans. The second was the efforts of the Bolivian *rosca* to preserve its hold on power in the face of a fierce revolutionary challenge from 1946 to 1952 (the sexenio). A third factor was decisive, however, in shaping this all-too-familiar clash between South American nationalism and U.S. hegemony: the determination of U.S. national security planners to secure a more or less permanent source of cheap tin vital for defense industries at the onset of the Cold War. As Bolivian leaders fought to stave off revolution, they anticipated resistance from the forces of populist nationalism but had every right to expect U.S. support. What they did not anticipate was that they would be undercut at almost every turn by the Reconstruction Finance Corporation (RFC), a U.S. agency given exceptional authority to secure a tin stockpile and dismantle an international tin cartel that had vexed Washington for decades.

For six years, four Bolivian governments desperately sought U.S. support as they battled on every front to forestall the ascension of Paz Estenssoro's MNR. Truman's State Department, hoping that the governments of Tomás Monje Gutiérrez, Enrique Hertzog Garaizábal, Mamerto Urrioagoitia Harriague, and General Hugo Ballivián Rojas could succeed in that venture, sought to provide what aid it could. U.S. diplomats, however, found themselves time and time again at loggerheads with the RFC, an independent government agency created by Herbert Hoover to assist in domestic recovery at the height of the Great Depression. With the outbreak of war, Franklin Roosevelt had turned the procurement of critical imports like tin and rubber over to the technocrats, whose primary mandate was to purchase as much Bolivian tin as possible at the least cost to U.S. taxpayers. Each year of the sexenio, an increasingly acrimonious ritual played out in Washington as RFC functionaries entered negotiations with the tin barons and representatives of the Bolivian government. For the Bolivians, the goal was always to secure as high a price as possible to finance modest reforms that might at least stave off an apparently inevitable revolutionary transformation of the country. Despite the efforts of a sympathetic but largely powerless State Department, they enjoyed little success, and in April 1952, the National Revolution finally occurred. Not entirely coincidentally, it occurred in a bankrupted nation as nearly a year and a half of tin shipments sat on Chilean docks awaiting a tin contract that never came.

Although it is impossible to know with certainty—despite Assistant Secretary of State Spruille Braden's firm assertion to the contrary—whether RFC "bungling" was responsible for the National Revolution and the triumph of the MNR, even Secretary of State Dean Acheson conceded that the agency's policies contributed to the weakening of four Bolivian governments at a time when they could ill afford it. The tin crisis may not have caused the National Revolution, but, as historian James Dunkerley has eloquently put it, "it was a decided mess within which the status quo was unraveling as fast as its opponents were consolidating."[2] Caught between the revolutionary plotters of the MNR and the thoroughly reactionary tin barons and landlords who dominated almost all facets of Bolivian society, the Monje, Hertzog, Urriolagoitia, and Ballivián regimes faced almost impossible challenges. Not the least of these was their own disunity, incompetence, and inability to understand just how precarious their control over the nation truly was. Still, the role of the Truman administration must not be underestimated. For six years, President Truman permitted the Reconstruction Finance Corporation to exploit a monopolistic position to punish not only the tin barons, but also the Bolivian governments that parasitically survived off the taxes they paid. If a middle course between stagnation and revolution had even been possible, then the RFC eliminated that small chance.

Postwar U.S. Policy in South America

The Truman administration, dominated by the final stages of World War II, reconversion to a peacetime economy, the onset of the Cold War in Europe and Asia, and the battle to create a new global economic order based on liberal capitalism, had few resources to dedicate to Latin America. Although the Western Hemisphere had once been the central preoccupation of U.S. diplomats, the emergence of the United States as a superpower stretched U.S. economic, military, and diplomatic assets to their limit at a moment when revolutionary nationalism was being galvanized across South America. Occurring in tandem, these developments created a confusing panorama that has impeded formation of any real historiographical consensus regarding the diplomacy of postwar inter-American relations.

The onset of the Cold War has probably been the foremost contributor to this confusion. As Stephen Rabe has noted, "historians of Inter-American relations frequently lump the years between 1945 and 1960 together as an unhappy, dull, and insignificant interregnum between the Good Neighbor and the Alliance for Progress."[3] Most historians attribute to the Truman presidency an anti-Communist zeal in Latin America that was far more prevalent in later presidencies. The Truman Doctrine may have called for increased anti-Communist interventionism in Europe and Asia, but, if anything, it reduced

U.S. interest in Latin America, an area where there was no major Communist threat, without otherwise altering fundamental U.S. goals and tactics there.

Although there can be little doubt that U.S. policy makers at the highest levels had been preoccupied with the Soviet Union and the spread of Communism since at least 1945, there is very little evidence that this extended in any meaningful way into South America during the Truman years. Truman's diplomats wisely paid little heed to the incessant efforts of J. Edgar Hoover and his Federal Bureau of Investigation to track Communism's rather feeble spread in South America through the 1940s. Nor did they pay much heed when South American leaders accused their rivals of "Communism," understanding that such accusations were a routine, almost meaningless feature of many nations' political discourse or, at most, a transparent ploy to attract U.S. attention and support.[4]

Instead, the State Department understood quite well that the Soviets had no significant interest in the Western Hemisphere and that a foreign ideology like Soviet-style Communism had little appeal in nations where fierce nationalism, Roman Catholicism, and jealously guarded independence predominated. Truman's critics may have assailed him for failing to fight global Communism with sufficient zeal, but in South America, his diplomats consistently refused to be duped into a pointless red-baiting campaign against a virtually nonexistent enemy. A meeting of Latin American specialists within the intelligence community in the Panama Canal Zone in January 1947 simply noted: "Communism has not become numerically important (i.e., controlling more than 10 percent or more of the voters) as yet except in a few countries" where "special factors have contributed to its growth." As late as 1950, the U.S. government could identify just 150 "Stalinists" and 2,000 "fellow travelers" in all of Bolivia and did so only by stretching the definitions of both terms to the limit. Communism was so weak in Bolivia in 1953 that leftists did not even attempt to "set up a united front with the Stalinists because they were not worth the trouble." Robert Alexander, perhaps the most well-informed student of labor unions in the Western Hemisphere, considered the Bolivian Partido Comunista to be "the most naïve Communist party" in the Americas.[5]

Still, scholars have perceived a Cold War shift in U.S. policy in 1947 or 1948 as U.S. anti-Communist rhetoric escalated and tensions with the Soviet Union grew. In perhaps the finest example of such scholarship, Leslie Bethell and Ian Roxborough illustrate how most nations in the hemisphere experienced greater democratization at the end of World War II, only to see those gains erased by 1950. They explain the trend by identifying a variety of domestic and international, economic, political, and social factors, but their analysis breaks down when it assumes that the U.S. commitment to democratization, development, and reform was motivated, to any significant degree, by anti-Communism. Indeed, Bethell and Roxborough show how domestic elites throughout Latin

America opposed any mass movement that threatened their control, just as the United States did any movement that threatened foreign investment or the cheap raw materials it coveted. U.S. policy makers came to understand that increased democratization would increase the power of nationalist groups whose goals were, in most cases, antithetical to those of the United States.⁶ Whereas "communism proper has so far had little popular appeal," what U.S. diplomats called "native socialist or semi-socialist parties" were flourishing. As Alexander has explained: "The Communists do not make headway" in countries where there is another "popular social and political movement which has captured the imagination of the rank-and-file citizen."⁷ Truman's diplomats in South America, despite their ever-vigilant efforts to ferret out Communists, simply could not find all that many. What they did find, however, was a disturbing number of homegrown nationalist movements.

Those movements were characterized by later generations of historians as "revolutionary nationalist" or "populist" and constituted, for Truman's lieutenants, the true menace. Thus State Department officers found themselves constantly at odds with revolutionary nationalists who were, in most cases, even more committed to anti-Communism than they were. Indeed, nationalist organizations such as the Alianza Popular Revolucionaria Americana in Peru, the Acción Democrática in Venezuela, the MNR in Bolivia, and the Peronists in Argentina were the most effective bulwarks against Communism.⁸ These often multiclass organizations and movements competed with (and regularly triumphed over) the anemic Stalinist, and more prevalent Trotskyite, Communist parties in the all-important battle for the loyalty of working- and lower-class constituencies. Had President Truman attached any real significance to anti-Communism in South America, any of these nationalist groups would have been natural partners for Cold War Washington, as the MNR later became for President Eisenhower. Instead, the State Department spent five years destabilizing Juan Perón's regime in Argentina, committed itself to blocking the MNR's ascension in Bolivia, and formed quite satisfactory partnerships with the military regimes that ousted, outlawed, and violently persecuted both the Alianza Popular Revolucionaria Americana and the Acción Democrática.⁹

Scholars following in the footsteps of pioneering historian David Green have illustrated well that, for Truman's State Department, the revolutionary nationalists were far more menacing to U.S. economic interests than the Communists they had so thoroughly supplanted. Michael Grow's *The Good Neighbor Policy and Authoritarianism in Paraguay* uses a case study to refine and expand Green's central thesis that U.S. interests were primarily economic and dedicated to aggressively expanding what later generations would call the "Washington consensus." James Siekmeier, however, offers the most persuasive and comprehensive illustration of U.S. efforts to derail economic nationalism across the hemisphere through case studies of Bolivia and Guatemala. Although Siekmeier's *The Containment of Latin America* focuses primarily on the Eisenhower presidency, his chapter on Truman is perhaps the most cogent and effective analysis of those efforts to date.[10] Thus, even though U.S. policy makers rebuilding Europe and Asia may have found their greatest obstacles in local Communist parties, the geostrategic reality of the Soviet Union, or some combination of the two, U.S. plans for South America were impeded primarily by all-too-independent nationalism epitomized by Peronism in Argentina.

The focal point for the U.S. campaign to establish an order of liberal capitalism and multilateral commerce in South America under the aegis of U.S. hegemony was, of course, Peronist Argentina. Perón had swept to power, in U.S. minds, like a fascist phoenix rising from the ashes of World War II, advocating a particularly statist brand of developmental nationalism, autarchy, and economic independence entirely antithetical to the U.S. vision. That he had done so through an unprecedented broadening of democratic institutions and had shattered the Argentine oligarchy in the process only made the perils of democratization more apparent. For the Truman administration, it was clear that Perón was the harbinger of the newest round of revolutionary nationalism in South America, economically committed to statist development and fully capable of triumphing through the same democratic processes that U.S. policy makers, at least in theory, had advocated for decades.[11]

But Perón was hardly alone. Across South America, U.S. diplomats faced movements—some directly inspired or funded by Perón, but most entirely independent—committed to many of these nationalist goals, invigorated by the triumph of the Allies, and dedicated to the increased democratization and economic renovation of their nations against entrenched oligarchies. Time after time, Truman's diplomats found themselves embroiled in battles between the agents of revolutionary change and elite representatives of old "liberal constitutionalist oligarchy." Although U.S. envoys were often disgusted by the façade of democracy, the repression of the masses, and the stagnation that regularly characterized the old order in many South American nations, they saw little choice but to embrace and support that order. The oligarchies, at least, maintained stability, welcomed U.S. capital by and large, and had a vested interest in preserving the economic order U.S. policy makers hoped to extend.

In Colombia, Jorge Gaitán's efforts to transform the Liberal Party into a mass organization for reform struck fear into the State Department, and dissident *febreristas* and Natalicio González's Guión Rojo wing of the Colorado Party called U.S. attention briefly to Paraguay. In Uruguay, Jorge Herrera's *colorados* threatened the pro-U.S. *blancos*, at times with Perón's assistance. In Chile, the Communist Party, periodically in league with nationalists whom Ambassador Claude Bowers branded "Peronists," worked to subvert the coalition of Radical President Gabriel González Videla. Although U.S. policy makers could tolerate both the Acción Democrática in Venezuela and the Alianza Popular Revolucionaria Americana in Peru, they could never entirely reconcile themselves with the nationalist agenda of either party.[12] More important, the State Department found it far more comfortable to work with the despotic military regimes that drove both parties from power in late 1948. Whereas, in Europe and Asia, the Truman administration fought tirelessly to build a new and lasting democratic order through the reconstruction of Germany and Japan and the restoration of prosperity in Western Europe, in South America, it found itself battling merely to preserve an old order against the onslaught of nationalist alternatives and challenges.

Siekmeier's study of Bolivia reveals that this was the case on the Altiplano as well, and the stakes for the U.S. vision were high. Not only was Víctor Paz Estenssoro's MNR, like Peronism, mistakenly considered an offshoot of European Fascism, but also Bolivian tin was critical for both the U.S. economy and the new demands of the national security state. Scholars such as John Child, Chester Pach, and Roger Trask have explored how the Truman administration militarized its diplomatic relations with Latin America through the Rio Conference, arms standardization, and military cooperation. The desperate need for Bolivian tin added yet another dimension and an element of urgency to U.S.-Bolivian relations.[13] As Dwight Eisenhower put it later, "it would be much better to have tin in Fort Knox than gold." Because the United States produced almost no tin for its own military or civilian needs and World War II had disrupted the global tin industry, Bolivia suddenly acquired an importance for Washington that it had never had, nor would ever have again.[14] The global tin shortage of the postwar years also guaranteed that U.S. diplomacy would be conducted not only by the State Department, but also by the wartime and postwar procurement agencies, whose agendas were far different. The results were little short of disastrous for the governments of Bolivia as their nation's security and stability were subordinated to the demands of U.S. reconversion and European reconstruction.

Instead of acting to undo or at least mitigate the damage, the Truman administration, not perceiving a major Communist menace, simply braced for the consequences of what it saw as an inevitable "coming depression" in South America. Most Latin American nations had enjoyed the benefits of exporting large quantities of raw materials to the Allies at good prices during the war, but the war was now drawing to a close. Assuming that Asian and European production would soon be restored, U.S. policy makers understood that the "cessation" of U.S. purchases would "result in our being blamed in large part for the ensuing depression." Naturally, "friendliness toward the United States [might] be expected to wane."[15] In other words, at the exact moment that radical nationalism was reaching its peak, the postwar economic order espoused by Washington was poised to create a climate in which it would flourish to the detriment of U.S. diplomacy. The State Department would be facing a wave of nationalist challenges aimed explicitly at the economic order the Truman administration was hoping to build; it would be shackled by its inability to completely control U.S. foreign policy. Bolivia offered perhaps the most striking example.

The Bolivian Political Economy

Whereas the United States stood alone as the most stable and prosperous nation in the Western Hemisphere, if not the world, prewar Bolivia had long been among the most unstable and impoverished. Landlocked since the War of the Pacific in 1879, Bolivia had endured more than sixty separate governments in its first 125 years as a nation. Its land, however, was a treasure trove of mineral wealth. The silver mines of Potosí had inexorably drawn the Spanish to the heart of South America and become graves for millions of Native Americans. The Spanish had been content to plunder what would become Bolivia, heedless of the consequences of their actions, and after independence, their successors had not deviated too far from that unfortunate example. In short, Bolivia's social and economic patterns remained disturbingly close to their colonial antecedents, with the rosca replacing Spaniards as feudal overlords, ruthlessly exploiting the indigenous masses to tear profit from the land.[16]

The two distinct groups making up the rosca, the landed *hacendado* aristocracy and the enormously wealthy tin barons, had dominated all facets of the Bolivian political economy for decades. The white rural elite enjoyed almost completely unchallenged rule throughout much of the nation, dominating local politics in most *departamentos* and rarely needing to join the national political fray. They paid "ludicrously light" taxes (less than one-fifth of a percent) based on their own undervalued assessments of their lands and built fortunes on the backs of their indigenous workforce with tools and practices that had changed little, if at all, in more than three centuries. Sharecropping *colonos*, almost indistinguishable from serfs, had scant incentive or opportunity to produce more. Landowners, with almost no expenses and a virtually guaranteed income, had even less incentive to risk upsetting their lucrative but stagnant system.[17] They simply rented parcels to the colonos in exchange for three to four days a week of free labor on their land, the "rent-in-labor" system, and demanded additional personal service through *pongueaje* and *mitanaje*. The indigenous masses, most of whom spoke Aymara or Quechua rather than Spanish, were so isolated from the national political economy that, when defining the terms "Bolivia" and "Bolivian," U.S. diplomat James Espy clarified that he was referring only to "the literate, dominant classes of people" and not to "the toiling Indian or other manual workers," whose primitive, subsistence agriculture combined the most onerous aspects of feudalism and slavery.[18]

Still, according to political scientist James M. Malloy, the "dominant culture saw the city as the repository of civilization and the hacienda, its rural outpost" against the indigenous masses. What remained outside the control of the hacendados was what Malloy has called the "national system," centered in the capital, La Paz, and extending to Cochabamba, Oruro, Potosí, Sucre, and the tin mining camps. As absolutely as the landed elite ruled the countryside, mining executives, most notably the tin barons Carlos Aramayo, Mauricio Hochschild, and Simón Patiño—the "Big Three"—ruled the cities and mining camps. Because the tin ore and other minerals they pried from the Altiplano constituted more than 80 percent of Bolivian exports, they were the economic backbone of the nation.[19]

The influence of these men extended far beyond economics, however. For example, Aramayo owned *La Razón*, the largest and most influential newspaper in the country, Hochschild had partial control over *Ultima Hora*, while Patiño owned one-third of *El Diario*. Through their wealth, power, and control over most of the news outlets, the tin barons constituted nothing less than what their critics claimed was a "superstate" that far overshadowed the national government. Nonetheless, because their wealth made them the most visible target of reformers, the barons were forced to pay the lion's share of taxes to support the state; their partners in the rosca, the landed aristocracy, paid next to nothing.[20]

Although Mauricio Hochschild was generally considered to be the most politically active of the tin barons, and Carlos Aramayo the most ruthless, Simón Patiño, one of the ten richest men in the world and the "King of Tin (Rey del Estaño)," was without a doubt the most formidable. Starting with one tin mine, "La Salvadora," which for a time produced 10 percent of all the world's tin, Patiño had built a globe-spanning empire by 1930. He controlled the richest tin veins in Bolivia and used his profits to purchase controlling interest in the 95,000-ton capacity Williams, Harvey tin smelter in England, establishing the Consolidated Tin Smelters, Ltd., in 1929. Within five years, his General Tin Industries, incorporated in Delaware and allied with the National Lead Company, had gained control of more than fifteen British and German tin smelters and mines across Southeast Asia. His name became as synonymous with tin as Henry Ford's was with the automobile.[21] Although Patiño died in 1947, his son, Antenor, followed closely in his father's footsteps, ensuring that Simón Patiño's legacy would persist through the sexenio.

Still, the tin barons by and large remained above most Bolivian politics. An urban petit bourgeoisie, directly or indirectly dependent on the barons for its financial well-being, constituted what passed for the Bolivian political class. Composed largely of mine company employees, bureaucrats, lawyers, doctors, and other professionals, this mostly urban middle class created political parties, managed government, regularly contested elections, intrigued for power, and periodically rebelled within carefully prescribed limits on behalf of the 80 percent of the nation disenfranchised by literacy, property, and wealth requirements imposed on those seeking to vote. For decades, various factions and alliances of Liberals, Republicans, Socialists, and soldiers had jockeyed for control of the national government and periodically attempted cosmetic reform, but underlying their petty disputes was the enduring, virtually omnipotent old order of the rosca.

In essence, the broad power of the tin barons economically and politically stifled the nation. Because Patiño and his fellow tin barons remitted their profits to shareholders overseas or channeled them into lucrative foreign investments, Bolivian tin had an exceptionally low retained value for the nation. And because Bolivian tin concentrates were processed, smelted, and rolled at facilities in Great Britain, Holland, and eventually the United States, the role of Bolivian tin workers was reduced to simple extraction. Although this model suited Patiño, who owned most of the world's smelting facilities, it did little to stimulate growth or investment in other industries on the Altiplano. Moreover, the subsistence wages paid to miners were insufficient to, as John Thoburn puts it, "generate a market for local consumer goods, and thereby spread development."[22] Even worse, finding no worthwhile investments within Bolivia, the tin barons continued to export as much of their surplus capital as they could. Bolivian politics was strictly confined to intra-elite battles within carefully prescribed rules. The taxation of tin provided enough revenue for the oligarchy to forswear meaningful changes in the political economy, particularly if such changes risked unleashing a social revolution. Although some within the white and mestizo political class understood that the old order was deeply flawed, virtually all shared the assumption that they owed it every privilege they enjoyed.[23]

For those not among the privileged classes, however, the tin barons' empire had come at "the inhuman cost of tuberculosis, misery, and backwardness" in a nation whose per capita income was the second lowest in the hemisphere. Put simply, U.S. officials found it "difficult to comprehend how the Altiplano Indian manage[d] to stay alive" under the brutal conditions he was forced to endure.[24] The Bolivian tin mines, one U.S. ambassador asserted, "make Russia's Siberian labor camps look like Labor Day picnics." This was not much of an exaggeration: overcrowded, unhygienic mining camps produced malnourished children and an "exceedingly high" though unmeasured infant mortality rate. Earning at most $8.00 a week, miners routinely spent entire twelve-hour shifts underground, and at the Hochschild mine in Pulacayo, they were expected to work a forty-eight-hour shift once every month.[25]

For most observers, the conditions in the mines defied description. Temperatures could reach 135 degrees as "rock dust fill[ed] the air and lungs," and "carbon dioxide bubble[d] from the freezing water that drip[ped] from the ceiling." Thousands of miners, "clad only in a G-string and rubber boots," toiled until mine accident or disease claimed their lives. A 1951 study revealed that 20 percent of miners suffered from silicosis, 7 percent from tuberculosis, and fully one-third from other respiratory maladies. Indeed, a member of a United Nations survey team asserted that "after five or six years, virtually every worker" fell victim to silicosis. Not surprisingly, a miner's life expectancy was less than forty years, and by the end of World War II, almost half the workers in Patiño's mines had been forced to work there by the *enganche* (conscription) system.[26]

The two component groups of the rosca had created two distinct economies that intertwined in a bizarre pattern of underdevelopment. The shortcomings of life on the Altiplano only exacerbated the problems of the tin miners, who supported their families at an altitude of more than fourteen thousand feet, sustained by incessant coca chewing, Cuban sugar, Argentine meat and fats, U.S. wheat, Chilean rice, and Peruvian clothing.[27] Even with the vast majority of the population dedicated to agriculture, the nation was critically dependent on foreign products (and thus on the foreign exchange generated by tin sales abroad). Large areas of northern and eastern Bolivia represented, according to one U.S. diplomat, "immense virgin resources" that remained untapped due to the inability or unwillingness of the "Altiplano Indian to adjust physically to conditions at or near sea level." Yet, even in 1952, there was no reliable highway or rail line connecting the cities and mines of the Altiplano with the eastern lowlands. Whereas the demands of the tin economy had made it essential to have easy and reliable access to Chilean ports for the export of minerals and the import of European and North American finished goods and machinery, there was no apparent incentive to connect the areas of Bolivia that lay outside the "national system."[28]

More than three-fifths of the nation was covered in rich tropical lowlands that would have been ideal for a lumber industry, agriculture, or ranching, if only the labor and transportation issues could be resolved. Without transportation, however, there was little market for lowlands agriculture or incentive for the indigenous peoples of the highlands to abandon their homes to work in hot, disease-infested jungles to which they were not acclimated. Indeed, a UN mission in 1951 concluded that only 2 percent of Bolivian soil was actually being cultivated; the 1950 census noted that more than 70 percent of the population derived their income from agriculture.[29] With most of the population politically inert and engaged in subsistence agriculture on plots scattered throughout the Altiplano, the nation was forced to import most of its food, machinery, and consumer goods. The resulting drain on foreign exchange placed an entirely unnecessary burden on a population that could ill sustain it and exerted a constant pressure on government to extort more foreign exchange from the tin barons. In short, according to Carter Goodrich, "the economy of Bolivia is that of a mining camp": it "sells what a mine sells, and like a mining camp, buys everything else." Thus the average resident of La Paz consumed just eighteen hundred calories per day at an altitude that demanded three thousand in a nation where three-quarters of the population engaged in agriculture, and where tin had made Patiño one of the wealthiest men on earth.[30]

The rosca had for decades used repression, propaganda, and armed force to keep the indigenous masses and the miners under their control, but the disparities in wealth and racial inequities had not gone unnoticed. In the 1930s, a new generation of critics emerged within the political class; they were soon joined by tin miners, railroad employees, and other workers in Bolivia's nascent industries. The fervor of these critics was spurred by two disasters during the 1930s: the Great Depression and Bolivia's humbling, catastrophic defeat by Paraguay in the Chaco War (1932–35). Although the Depression collapsed the economy and provoked political crises in Bolivia as in most nations, the 1932 border dispute that escalated into war between South America's two poorest nations was possibly even more significant. Despite advantages in manpower and weaponry, the Bolivians were defeated time and time again by the Paraguayans. Indecisive civilian leadership, "inept, corrupt, and cowardly" officers, and internal political disputes all hamstrung the Bolivian war effort and eventually led La Paz to cede one hundred and seventy thousand square miles of territory to Paraguay. In the end, the war exposed what historian Waltraud Quieser Morales has called the "extremes of ineptitude and inequality of the traditional and social system" and gave new impetus for radical reform, if not revolution. Feeding on this discontent, at least four major new political parties emerged over the next few years, ranging from the Falange Socialista Boliviana to the Trotskyite Partido Obrero Revolucionario.[31]

Foremost among the new radicals were José Antonio Arze, Ricardo Anaya, and their Partido de la Izquierda Revolucionaria (PIR). Drawing its leaders from the schools and universities, the PIR was a bourgeois organization that aimed to radicalize miners and industrial workers and to mobilize them behind a socialist vision of a modernized Bolivia. Professing independence from the Comintern, but support for the Soviet Union and Marxist-Leninist ideals, PIR leaders sought to guide the growth of the Bolivian proletariat through their enlightened leadership. The PIR extended its tendrils into many of Bolivia's fledgling labor organizations and grew rapidly by calling for industrialization and land reform, yet it managed to maintain ties with the rosca by promising to channel and moderate working-class nationalism. By the 1940s, the PIR was Bolivia's largest political party, one of very few with anything resembling a mass base, although hardly the only emerging challenge to the old order.[32]

Formed in 1941, Víctor Paz Estenssoro's Movimiento Nacionalista Revolucionario (MNR) brought together young ex-Socialists from the upper and middle classes, disenchanted Chaco War veterans, and labor militants in a "patriotic movement of socialist orientation directed toward the defense and affirmation of Bolivian nationalism." The party's message was a vague but emphatic attack on the rosca's "antinational superstate" and an appeal to "incorporate into national life the millions of peasants." Whereas the PIR sought to gradually consolidate its strength within the working classes, the impatient leaders of the MNR hoped for an immediate entry into power to purge the nation of "false, betraying," and "bankrupt" "pseudo-democracy."[33] The opportunistic urban intellectuals of the MNR tied themselves to the growing discontent in the mining camps through a loose alliance with Juan Lechín Oquendo, a one-time soccer star who would eventually become the secretary general of the powerful Federación Sindical de Trabajadores Mineros de Bolivia (FSTMB). The MNR critique initially said little about conditions in the countryside or the hacendados' domination of indigenous Bolivians that was the cornerstone of Bolivian society but focused instead on the rapacious tin barons and their crimes. Although the MNR hoped for a multiclass alliance and gradual reforms, it also cultivated unlikely allies among the army officer corps.[34]

Arze and Paz Estenssoro both headed promising civilian movements, but a third force emerged within the ranks of the junior officers in the army in the 1940s. Whereas the PIR and MNR both sought some form of expanded democratization of Bolivian society and hoped to ally themselves with the nation's rapidly growing labor unions, the third emerging faction, semisecret military lodges such as Iron Star and Razón de Patria (RADEPA; formerly Santa Cruz), sought for the most part authoritarian solutions to Bolivia's many problems. Founded in a Paraguayan POW camp at the end of the Chaco War, RADEPA brought together disenchanted junior officers who were disgusted by the incompetence of their civilian leaders and military superiors. It was dedicated to nothing less than the renovation of the country and the elimination of the rosca's stranglehold on the national polity. Fighting in the trenches, these junior officers had risked their lives with their troops while white, elite generals sat safely behind the lines and spent their time cultivating "politicians fishing for opportunities" and engaging in other political intrigues. Strongly influenced by European corporatist thought of the 1930s and bolstered by a strong sense of patriotism, RADEPA sought to revitalize the nation through a familiar mix of hierarchical statism and a vague brand of syndicalism. Although the military had long been the most formidable tool of the rosca, the officers of RADEPA saw their struggle as equal to Bolivia's wars of independence; they proclaimed their willingness to die "for the noble ideal of forging our nationality."[35]

Despite the increased call for radical reform from the working classes, the PIR, the MNR, RADEPA, and the other new parties and factions, the old order remained firmly in control during the early stages of World War II. General Enrique Peñaranda del Castillo, the chief of the army in the last year of the Chaco War, easily won election to the presidency in 1940, opposed only by José Antonio Arze and his PIR. Elected explicitly to maintain the status quo, Peñaranda did little to stave off the coming radical challenges and filled his cabinet with members of the traditional Liberal, Socialist, and Republican Parties. World War II, however, forced difficult choices on the regime when Japanese expansion in Southeast Asia cut off the United States and Great Britain from their traditional sources of tin.[36]

Peñaranda bowed to necessity by opting for virtually total cooperation with Washington. In 1937, "military socialists" had, as part of the post-Chaco wave of nationalism, expropriated Standard Oil's properties in Bolivia, driving a wedge between the United States and Bolivia. With war looming, U.S. policy makers hoped to unite the hemisphere against the Axis and to secure a reliable source of tin for war industries by working toward rapprochement with Peñaranda's government. Eager to partake of U.S. economic and military aid, Peñaranda was quick to respond. He welcomed a team led by State Department officer Merwin Bohan to develop a program for economic diversification of the Bolivian economy, agreed to a number of "denazification" measures, and signed a military assistance pact. Most important, he settled with Standard Oil soon after Pearl Harbor and agreed to pay the company $1.5 million for its expropriated properties. He was rewarded with Lend-Lease aid and financial assistance to start implementing the Bohan Mission's findings. In short, the war brought the two nations into an unprecedented partnership and seemed to offer the promise of future cooperation.[37] The only dark cloud on the horizon was the undecided price for Bolivia's tin.

Peñaranda eventually agreed to sell the nation's entire tin production to the Allies for a price well below what most Bolivians expected. Even worse, the tin barons, with at least tacit U.S. support, squeezed their labor force to maximize production and profits. The deteriorating working conditions in the mines and the restrictive contracts with the United States, which, nationalists claimed, cost Bolivia as much as $650 million in lost revenues throughout the war, provided easy fodder for dissidents.[38] The "unfavorable contracts over raw materials, the commitments to contribute to the democratic cause, the inhuman persecution of Japanese and Germans[, who had] settled for many years in the country"—persecution undertaken at the behest of the United States—brought nothing but "pain, grieving, and impoverishment" to the Bolivian people. As the foremost standard-bearers of this critique, which melded xenophobia, outrage toward Peñaranda's subjugation of the national interest, and traditional *antirosquismo*, Paz Estenssoro and the MNR rapidly emerged as the foremost opposition group.[39]

Although Malloy describes the wartime MNR as a "small group of intellectuals stirring up what fuss they could," the Roosevelt administration considered it the most dangerous element in Bolivian politics. In late 1941, British agents, presumably hoping to cement Peñaranda's support for the Allied cause, had forged letters incriminating elements of the MNR and the officer corps in a conspiracy with the Germans to overthrow him. The MNR accused Peñaranda's cabinet of forging the letters, but the State Department, alarmed over the apparent Nazi threat to the Western Hemisphere, unquestioningly accepted the forgeries as real.[40] As a result, no U.S. diplomat could view the MNR as anything less than Nazi tainted for years. This was not an entirely unjustified view. In 1941, on the anniversary of Hitler's ascension to power, one MNR newspaper editorialized that "the lesson of Hitler and the New Germany is a lesson of optimism" and that Bolivia, with its history of territorial loss to all of its neighbors, had "much to learn from Lebensraum." U.S. diplomats, already predisposed to view every event in Latin America through the prism of the war, became fixated on the "anti–United States and anti-Jewish" MNR.[41]

On 21 December 1942, a violent incident at Patiño's Siglo XX tin mine in Catavi created the opportunity the MNR had long sought. When miners assembled to protest for improved conditions and higher wages—they were earning less than $1.50 a day—Peñaranda's troops fired upon them, killing dozens, if not hundreds. The MNR and the PIR immediately escalated their efforts against the government; the leaders of the MNR branded Peñaranda a tool of the rosca in general and of Patiño in particular. For its part, Aramayo's *La Razón* condemned the workers for seeking wages of $1.50 a day and lauded the president for his decisive action.

The Catavi Massacre exposed the hypocrisy and brutality of the old order for all to see and thoroughly discredited the government, even in the eyes of its U.S. patrons. Peñaranda clung to power for another year, but his fate was sealed. The PIR worked toward a popular revolt, several generals plotted their own coups, and the MNR forged alliances with the RADEPA and Iron Star lodges. The MNR and RADEPA won the race to unseat Peñaranda, and their "Revolution of the Majors" seized power almost a year to the day after the massacre.[42]

According to Paz Estenssoro, the MNR had been involved in several plots that had been brewing for months and had even attempted to seize Peñaranda weeks earlier in Cochabamba. At one point, Peñaranda's chief of the General Staff offered his loyalty to the MNR in exchange for its support, and another general, Angel Rodríguez, apparently approached Paz Estenssoro to enlist the MNR's participation in a plot financed by Mauricio Hochschild. Paz Estenssoro "terminated this conversation" by telling the general that "he would be delighted to [participate] if Rodríguez would promise to execute Hochschild the day after they took power." Allying himself instead with junior officers such as Major Gualberto Villarroel López and the members of RADEPA, Paz Estenssoro understood that he had to move quickly: Peñaranda planned a crackdown on the MNR immediately after Christmas 1943.[43]

The president apparently remained ignorant of the plots against him, despite a number of mistakes by the MNR and RADEPA. The Ecuadoran Embassy in

La Paz somehow acquired details of the coup the day before it occurred, Villarroel had hinted to friends on 18 December that a revolution was coming, and Paz Estenssoro himself had all but announced it in a session of Congress. At the last moment, Majors Villarroel, Edmundo Nogales, and Antonio Ponce even sought what Nogales called a "patriotic understanding" in "defense of national interests" with Peñaranda. They hoped to convince him to abandon the "the Great Tin Barons and North American Imperialism," to whom he had "surrendered" a price of tin "as a gift" in the name "of continental unity, the good neighborhood of peoples, and the defense of democracy."[44] When Peñaranda rejected their demands, RADEPA and the traffic police effected an almost bloodless coup, installing Villarroel as president on December 23, 1943.

The British believed that the revolution was a "good thing for Bolivia and the United Nations," brought about by "left-center" nationalists disgusted by the "corruption and inefficiency of the previous government." The chief of the U.S. Military Mission in La Paz considered the revolutionaries "sincere patriots, to the point of idealism," and many in the State Department were reluctant to label them "totalitarian" or "pro-Nazi." As Philip Bonsal tried to explain to Secretary of State Cordell Hull, the "unfriendly" statements and acts by MNR members or military officers detailed in his memorandum were "only a very small proportion" of their activities and were more or less an "automatic" response to anything Peñaranda did. The MNR and RADEPA, Bonsal said, actually represented the "legitimate and respectable, if perhaps unattainable, aspirations of certain sectors of the Bolivian people." Laurence Duggan went further, comparing the MNR to Louisiana populist Huey Long. He argued that the MNR was genuine in its call for the uplift of the masses and indeed might lead Bolivia to "evolve peacefully and gradually from semi-feudalism to something approaching twentieth century civilization."[45]

For President Roosevelt, however, this was no time to be "wishy-washy." And Secretary Hull, though no great supporter of Peñaranda, was outraged by the emergence of a cabinet featuring five majors, Paz Estenssoro, and two other supposedly pro-Nazi MNR members. Convinced that the MNR and the military were "connected with Nazi groups in Germany and Argentina" and "received financial support from pro-Nazi sources," Hull inaugurated a policy of nonrecognition against Villarroel's government in the hopes of provoking a counterrevolution or at least the removal of the MNR. The United States was joined by the other nations of the hemisphere (except Argentina), but Hull refused to tell Villarroel what he had to do to secure U.S. recognition. Through veiled hints and suggestive conversations, it eventually became clear that Hull sought the expulsion of German and Japanese nationals from Bolivia and the elimination of the MNR from the cabinet.[46]

In April, Villarroel removed the MNR ministers from his cabinet and replaced MNR prefects with nonpartisan army officers. In May, he complied with a U.S. demand to turn over eighty-one German and Japanese nationals. Although U.S. diplomats were barraged with "for-God's-sake-don't-recognize" pleas from Aramayo and other oligarchs, by June, every other nation in the hemisphere except Uruguay supported recognition of the regime. With congressional elections pending, the U.S. recognized Villarroel in the hope that this would strengthen his hand against the MNR and encourage other parties to join the government. Within months, however, Villarroel formalized his alliance with the MNR by appointing Paz Estenssoro to the post of finance minister and other party members to other cabinet posts. The MNR had won a share of power but had also earned the enmity of the rosca, the PIR, and the United States.[47]

Villarroel is best seen as a harbinger of the National Revolution of 1952. When Harry S. Truman became president in April 1945, Villarroel had been entrenched in the Palacio Quemado for more than a year and a half. The tentative steps Villarroel had undertaken toward changing the status quo were a clear warning to the rosca and the political classes. Patiño, Aramayo, Hochschild, and the hacendados may have been content to preside over the hopelessly warped economy of Bolivia, but more astute observers understood that, without reform, revolution was inevitable. For the next seven years, Villarroel and his more traditional successors sought to achieve national development without dismantling the centuries-old foundation of the Bolivian political economy. They faced the almost impossible task of finding a middle road between Paz Estenssoro's promised National Revolution and the intransigent stonewalling of the rosca.

World War II Tin Diplomacy

Although Washington's drive for a global capitalist order and Bolivia's struggle for national development were obviously critical elements in the diplomacy of the sexenio, perhaps the most decisive aspect was the postwar destruction of the international tin cartel and the establishment of an Anglo-American tin purchasing monopoly. If the governments of the sexenio hoped to bankroll modest reforms with tin export revenue, they required high tin prices to, if nothing else, prevent a disastrous economic downturn. Because World War II had left Bolivia as the sole major producer of tin concentrates for the Allies and the State Department did indeed fully support efforts to block the MNR, there was cause for optimism. However, developments in the international tin trade quickly overshadowed all other aspects of the U.S.-Bolivian relationship.

Before the war, Bolivia produced roughly one-sixth of the world's tin concentrates. Two-thirds came from the Malay Straits, especially the Dutch East Indies and Malaya, and one-ninth from Nigeria, the Belgian Congo, Siam, and China. The United States, which had only produced two thousand tons of tin in the previous sixty years, consumed more than 40 percent of the world's total, and European nations, led by Great Britain, another 45. In 1927, Patiño's Consolidated Tin Smelters and John Howeson's London Tin Corporation formed a producers' cartel, the International Tin Committee (ITC), to stabilize the world tin market, protect themselves from the devastating fluctuations that periodically wracked the industry, and guarantee their profits. By 1931, they were joined by representatives from all the major tin producers—Bolivia, Nigeria, Malaya, and the Dutch East Indies.[48] Government officials and private tin producers united to set quotas, restrict output, and at one point even launch a two-month "tin holiday" by suspending all shipments to raise prices. Consuming nations were eventually given access to the proceedings but, much to the consternation of Washington, were denied any vote.[49]

For Bolivian miners, this "prescient cartelisation," to use Dunkerley's phrase, had been nothing short of a godsend. Alluvial tin concentrates from the Malay Straits, far purer than Bolivian ones, were dredged from easily accessible rivers by cheap labor and would have otherwise doomed Bolivian producers. Simply put, the Bolivians could not compete. Their tin, generally of low quality, had to be extracted from the dizzying heights of the Andes hundreds of miles from the nearest port. Moreover, Bolivian workers, though poorly paid, were still better compensated than their Far Eastern counterparts. Finally, the tin barons bore the bulk of the nation's tax burden. In all, U.S. experts estimated that that the cost of production in Bolivia was almost double that of Malay Straits producers. The cartel remained the only means by which Bolivian tin could remain competitive with English and Dutch producers in the Far East.[50]

In June 1940, U.S. planners, weary of the decades they had spent at the mercy of the ITC, set in motion a series of events that culminated in the United States seizing control of the international tin trade in the postwar period and placing Bolivia at Washington's mercy. The U.S. military consumed massive quantities of tin, primarily for canned food and solder. Anticipating war and economic dislocations, Undersecretary of State Sumner Welles proposed creation of a fifty-thousand-ton tin stockpile and construction of a U.S. tin smelter designed to accommodate low-grade Bolivian tin concentrates. A smelter and stockpile, in conjunction with a massive recycling campaign, would insulate U.S. industry from the conflicts in Europe and East Asia and possibly shatter the ITC once and for all. Roosevelt agreed and authorized the Reconstruction Finance Corporation's Metals Reserve Company to construct a U.S. tin smelter.[51]

Ostensibly in response to the German seizure of the Dutch Arnhem smelter and to fears that the Luftwaffe might at some point put British smelters out of commission, the Longhorn Tin Smelter was built in Texas City, near the port of Galveston. It cost the U.S. government $8 million but more than paid for itself during the war. It was the potentially the world's largest and most versatile smelter, capable of processing any type of tin concentrate from any part of the world. The RFC contracted with the Dutch smelting giant Billiton Mastschappij, known for its experience with both Bolivian hard-rock and Far Eastern alluvial concentrates, to construct and operate the Longhorn smelter. Because the urgency of its construction had mandated against using innovative but still relatively unproven techniques, the smelter itself was not the world's most modern, but it was capable of processing the entire Bolivian tin output and perhaps meeting U.S. demand. Although high labor costs and outdated techniques hurt the Longhorn smelter's efficiency, it was hoped that plentiful fuel and acid, combined with cheaper transportation costs from Bolivia, might make it competitive with European commercial smelters.[52]

Still, the Longhorn smelter's construction was not entirely a response to the war. Indeed, the smelter was established explicitly to "eliminate this country's dependence on the foreign tin cartel." The British, who along with Patiño dominated the International Tin Committee, hoped to first dissuade the Roosevelt administration from building the smelter. Failing that, they sought to secure a commitment that the Longhorn smelter would be closed at the end of the war. Needless to say, the State and War Departments refused both requests, adamant that the United States never again be held hostage by the ITC. Indeed, when State Department analyst Herbert Feis negotiated the first contract with the Bolivians in 1940, he sought a twenty-five-year commitment of all Bolivian tin—a clear indication of U.S. long-term goals. Although the British were horrified by the prospect of the U.S. government entering the field of tin processing, Feis coolly reminded them that the discrimination and restrictions of the previous half century made this move inevitable. When the British complained that a U.S. smelter could not be operated profitably, Feis retorted that, although this was "probably true," underhanded British tactics and the cartel had never permitted that thesis to be tested. Indeed, U.S. corporations had, on several occasions, attempted to open smelters on U.S. soil in the past, only to have the British drive them into bankruptcy.[53]

The State Department sought more than one thousand tons of tin concentrates per month to supply the Longhorn smelter, but this requirement ran afoul of existing contracts that sent almost all Bolivian tin to Great Britain. Because the British smelted nearly all of their Far Eastern tin in Malaya, smelters in England were almost entirely dependent on Patiño's Bolivian production. Still, after the fall of Holland, where the Arnhem smelter had traditionally processed Hochschild's and Aramayo's tin, Peñaranda and Hochschild encouraged construction of the Longhorn smelter. Not only might U.S. competition break Bolivia's dependence on the British smelting monopoly, but it would also permit the tin barons and the government to acquire dollars rather than blocked sterling. The first U.S. offer was for 42¢ per pound, slightly more than London was currently paying, and the Japanese made their own offer soon thereafter. Within weeks, Peñaranda and the tin barons were presiding over a bidding war among the three rival nations.[54]

Although Patiño saw the Longhorn smelter as a means to "extricate" himself from restrictive British sterling contracts, and other tin barons viewed it as a way to weaken Patiño's dominant position in smelting, they soon found that the sword cut both ways.[55] The Bolivians sought 45¢ per pound for all grades of tin concentrates, but the United States hoped to pay just 42¢ for only the highest grade. For the tin barons, the U.S. contract was a unique opportunity: neither the British nor the Dutch smelters had been willing to process their lowest-grade concentrates, and if they could secure a fixed price, they would now be able to export their lower grades. Washington attempted to break the deadlock by increasing the amount of tin it would purchase to eighteen thousand tons per year, but the Bolivians demanded even more concessions regarding smelting charges. After months of negotiation, the State Department, eager to begin operations at Texas City, finally agreed to pay a fixed price of 48½¢ per pound, to match low British smelting charges for five years, and to take responsibility for the ores in the Chilean ports of Arica or Antofagasta. Through hard bargaining that even the RFC's own historian conceded meant "not standing as a neighborly supporter of Bolivia in its hour of economic distress," U.S. planners were purchasing a good percentage of the tin available to the Allies at less than half of the World War I price.[56]

For Great Britain, this arrangement was little short of a catastrophe on a number of levels. Patiño now argued that unless the British matched the U.S. price, he would break his long-term contract with them and sell to the RFC. At one point, he even threatened to enter the bidding to construct the U.S. smelter himself. Although the British were unable to forestall the U.S. contract with Bolivia, they attempted to end U.S. involvement by agreeing to purchase all Bolivian tin production for the five years after the U.S. deal expired.[57] Naturally, Peñaranda and the tin barons refused, hoping to keep Anglo-American competition alive for the foreseeable future.

Pearl Harbor and the Japanese offensive in Southeast Asia changed everything. As Japanese forces overran British Malaya and the Dutch East Indies, world tin markets were thrown into chaos. Both the Allies' main sources of tin concentrates and much of the world's smelting capacity were captured. The British and Dutch, anticipating Hitler's onslaught in Europe, had shifted much of their smelting capacity to Malaya and the East Indies, placing it directly in the path of the advancing Japanese. More than 70 percent of the world's tin production (and an even higher percentage of its smelting capacity) rapidly fell into Axis hands, and U.S. leaders faced the unhappy prospect of entering the war with no viable source of either raw tin concentrates or processed tin plate. As precarious as the situation was for the Allies, Peñaranda and the tin barons seemed to have an unprecedented opportunity to become virtually the only source of tin for the Allied war machine.[58]

It did not take long for Patiño to recognize the implications. With the ITC's production control schedule set to expire at the end of 1941, the British requested a renewal on favorable terms. For the Bolivians, letting Great Britain, which would remain almost exclusively a consumer for the duration of the war, use the ITC to establish a low tin price seemed foolish. Instead, the Bolivian government and tin producers sought the freedom to negotiate major price increases with the United States and Great Britain in 1942. Therefore, Patiño, chafing under British sterling exchange restrictions, refused to sign the ITC renewal. What he apparently did not consider was that by spurning the ITC, he was removing the only impediment to the creation of an Anglo-American alliance based on their mutual interest in suppressing the price of the tin they consumed. Whitehall, now demonstrating "exceptional bitterness," proposed a "common policy" to Washington to "prevent any attempt at blackmailing tactics." Although Patiño eventually did sign the renewal (only to see it voided soon thereafter by the Japanese invasion of Malaya and the Dutch East Indies), the damage had been done, and the cartel would never again exert the authority it once had. In the view of political scientist Laurence Whitehead, by facilitating an alliance between Great Britain and the United States, Patiño and the tin barons had, however inadvertently, "shifted" market control "decisively" from the "rosca to the U.S. government."[59]

This was not immediately apparent, however. Peñaranda, Aramayo, and Hochschild wasted no time in requesting that the 1942 base price for tin concentrates be set at 65¢ per pound. Hochschild, whom U.S. diplomats described as "no shrinking violet in negotiations," claimed that all of his mines except Colquiri were operating at a loss at the 1941 price and noted that the RFC had more than doubled its purchase price for lead imports.[60] Nonetheless, the British, who were committed to pay Patiño whatever rate Washington agreed to pay Aramayo and Hochschild, could not "see why Americans or we should submit to Bolivian blackmail" since "the Bolivians are entirely dependent on U.S. and UK markets for their one vital export." Whitehall urged the Roosevelt administration not to increase the price at all. Ultimately, the tin barons agreed to accept 60¢ per pound until the middle of 1943, and Peñaranda agreed not to place new taxes or restrictions on the tin barons.[61]

When the tin contract came up for renewal in June 1943, the Bolivians demanded no less than 70¢ per pound but found their U.S. counterparts intransigent. Not only had the "shortsighted and avaricious" Peñaranda, in clear violation of the old contract, imposed new taxes on the tin producers and demanded a higher percentage of their foreign exchange, but the producers themselves had also violated the contract, by shipping the United States excessive amounts of low-grade ores and concentrates. U.S. planners therefore insisted on maintaining the current price for another year. The stalemate dragged on until December 1943, when Villarroel ousted Peñaranda from power. Because the United States now possessed a tin stockpile "adequate" for the next two years of war and the army was "not greatly concerned [about the supply of tin] at this time," the Department of State recommended that negotiations be suspended.[62]

Villarroel and the tin barons had to live with the 60¢ price until December 1944, when Washington agreed to a 2½¢ increase. Any benefit to the tin barons was then quickly negated, however, when Villarroel mandated a series of wage increases for workers and Paz Estenssoro, reinstalled in the cabinet, this time as minister of finance, decreed that 60 percent of all foreign exchange would be retained by the government. When Washington resumed negotiations for a new tin contract in July 1945, it again insisted that the Bolivian government enact no new restrictions on the tin barons and that the barons pay severe penalties for shipping exceptionally low-grade tin. Although the tin price did increase several cents per pound, the new contract called for it to decrease over the next year. With Japan nearing defeat and U.S. planners envisioning the return of the Malay Straits to the colonial powers, whatever leverage Patiño and Peñaranda may have had in 1940 was rapidly disappearing.

Still, there would be inevitable tin shortages until Malay Straits production became available again. Thanks to the Longhorn smelter, aggressive recycling campaigns, and the Bolivian contract, the War Production Board had been able to meet the needs of the U.S. war effort, but with the end of the war in Europe, "the situation materially changed for the worse." The navy still demanded massive amounts of tin, liberated nations also demanded it for reconstruction, and domestic industries embarking on reconversion clamored for their share. These factors were only accentuated when, even after the Japanese surrender in August 1945, Malay Straits tin was still unavailable to meet the new demand; Director Erwin Vogelsang of the War Production Board's Tin, Lead, and Zinc Division speculated that it might forever remain so.[63]

After a British scorched-earth retreat at the onset of the war, four years of fighting, and intense anti-Japanese guerrilla campaigns, no dredges and only forty-five mines remained in operation in Malaya. Hundreds of small European and Chinese mining companies there and in China might not ever be able to finance a full restoration of the facilities destroyed during the war. Moreover, imperial policy and the lack of foreign exchange made it unlikely that the British would request U.S. assistance to help restore tin productivity in Malaya. And, even though the Dutch government and Billiton Mastschappij (in which the government held five-eighths control) had at war's end immediately ordered replacement equipment for their tin operations in the Dutch East Indies, it did not matter, Director Vogelsang argued, because production would ultimately be determined by a restored ITC, which would "not be enthusiastic about undertaking prompt and effective, yet costly, action" to restore tin mining in Southeast Asia that might lead to overproduction.⁶⁴

For U.S. planners, it was therefore imperative that the ITC never be allowed to reconstitute. World War II had struck a decisive blow against the tin cartel; the International Trade Organization (ITO) and the United States would now finish it off. Chapter VI of the ITO Charter mandated that producers and consumers have an equal voice in any international commodity agreement, in effect banning price-fixing, government-ordered production restrictions, quota systems, or other stabilization schemes. That being the case, State Department functionary Donald Kennedy proclaimed that the ITC no longer served any "valid function." Not surprisingly, Bolivian diplomats argued that the ITC should be restored and "revitalized with the goodwill and concurrence of the consumers to secure the harmonious development of the industry beneficial to all nations." They soon learned, however, that Malayan producers, under pressure from the British government (itself coerced by Washington), were opting out. Although delegates from Bolivia and the Dutch East Indies desperately sought a formula that would salvage the ITC, they had to tread lightly "at all times," so as "to not antagonize" the Anglo-American alliance.⁶⁵ When the Bolivian ambassador asked for leeway to continue the ITC until the postwar transition was completed, the U.S. response was an "unequivocal" no. In November 1946, at the "suggestion of the United States" (although Bolivian ambassador Ricardo Martínez Vargas believed "the term 'pressure' would be more appropriate"), the only institution that had permitted long-term Bolivian competitiveness was formally dissolved.⁶⁶

In the place of the ITC, Anglo-American planners formed the Tin Study Group and the Combined Tin Board as an "experimental" "first stage" in achieving an ITO-compliant commodity agreement in what they hoped would be an "atmosphere of mutual goodwill." It quickly became clear that the study group was "not concerned with the arrangements governing the immediate supplies of tin" but was instead a toothless "opportunity" for "a broad exchange of views and information" and "purely routine" statistical compilations. The RFC considered it little more than a pointless and "continuous round of secret meetings, veiled threats, and open accusations of bad faith."⁶⁷

The true authority over tin production and pricing was vested in the Combined Tin Committee (CTC) in Washington. One of many emergency planning measures designed to efficiently allocate scarce resources during and after the war, the CTC exercised almost complete control over the commodity it monitored through firm national quotas. The Anglo-American technocrats of the CTC determined that all Bolivian tin, other than Patiño's, which was committed to Great Britain was to be sold to the United States. For the RFC, the CTC represented nothing less than a unique opportunity to acquire for the United States and Great Britain the leverage the ITC had once wielded. Once either nation negotiated a price with its suppliers, usually after months of brutal negotiations, that price became the "world price," which other producers would be obligated to accept. The ITC producers' cartel was thus replaced by an "Anglo-American purchasing cartel" so domineering that some Bolivian tin producers found it preferable to negotiate with the potentially "gigantic market" of the Soviet Union.[68]

The implications went even further: U.S. planners considered the destruction of the ITC to be only the first step in dismantling trade restrictions on the tin industry imposed by the tin-producing states. The ITC was far from alone in imposing such restrictions. Through export duties on Malayan tin in 1903 and 1924, the British government had derailed U.S. plans to establish smelters before World War II. Even so, in the opinion of U.S. experts, Bolivia's restrictions were the most onerous in the world. Because only an "infinitesimal number" of Bolivians paid any tax at all on real estate or income, the national government was funded almost entirely by a Byzantine system of taxes on the production and sale of tin. Through literally hundreds of national export taxes, local taxes, indirect excise taxes, income taxes, mining transfer taxes, dividend taxes, and a burdensome foreign exchange surrender scheme to finance imports, the Bolivian government extracted, by U.S. estimates, 15¢ of tax revenue from each pound of tin. Moreover, this list did not include regularly decreed ("often retroactive") wage increases or other social benefits for workers or new taxes like one commemorating the four hundredth anniversary of the founding of Potosí. The obvious next step for the United States as it entered the postwar period was the elimination of this maddeningly unpredictable taxation scheme, in which La Paz alone had 468 different taxes and the national government another 366 taxes and duties.[69]

Ironically, the U.S. drive for "free markets" through the ITO could well have worked to the advantage of the Bolivians, at least for a few years, had these been regulated equitably. Although Bolivian tin was ordinarily unable to compete with alluvial tin from the East Indies and Malaya, the war and the Japanese occupation had crippled tin production in both these regions. Restoration of normal production in the Malay Straits was at least years away, and the soaring demand for tin created by postwar reconstruction gave rise to a tin shortage that augured well for the tin barons and any Bolivian government that subsisted off them. The U.S. decision to maintain smelting operations at Texas City, which the RFC considered the "most effective means of securing for the United States its share of limited world production," should have guaranteed competition that would benefit Bolivian producers.[70]

Instead, as tin became, under the RFC regime, "the most controlled of all commodities" in the world, Bolivian diplomats entered annual negotiations with the ruthless technocrats of the RFC having little or no leverage. The

Table 1 Presidents of the Republic of Bolivia

	Beginning of term	End of term
Enrique Peñaranda del Castillo	15 April 1940	20 December 1943
Gualberto Villarroel López	20 December 1943	21 July 1946
Néstor Guillén Olmos[a]	21 July 1946	15 August 1946
Tomás Monje Gutiérrez[a]	15 August 1946	10 March 1947
José Enrique Hertzog Garaizábal	10 March 1947	22 October 1949
Mamerto Urriolagoitia Harriague	22 October 1949	16 May 1951
Hugo Ballivián Rojas[b]	16 May 1951	11 April 1952
Hernán Siles Zuazo	11 April 1952	15 April 1952
Ángel Víctor Paz Estenssoro	15 April 1952	6 August 1956

[a] President of the Provisional Junta of Government.

[b] President of the Military Junta of Government.

Reconstruction Finance Corporation, the British Ministry of Supply, and private Dutch smelters all benefited from Combined Tin Committee collusion that forced Malayans, Bolivians, Nigerians, and Indonesians to sell their primary exports to a sole bidder. Although the RFC justified its monopoly by asserting that the world's three largest producers were chronically unstable and that a crisis in any one would "mean a serious world shortage," it clearly worked to U.S. advantage.[71]

For the Bolivians, the primary diplomatic task of the postwar period was to somehow circumvent this cunning system calculated to bring the combined might of the great industrial powers "almost exclusively against the tin industry of Bolivia." Failure, they correctly predicted, would inexorably lead to the "decline and ruin" of the private tin industry in Bolivia, if not the political order it undergirded.[72] Bolivia found itself at a critical juncture. The old political and economic order was deteriorating rapidly, and the next several years would either see collapse, a smooth transformation of the nation into a somewhat more modernized, more egalitarian society, or revolution. Patiño and the tin barons had welcomed and encouraged the U.S. intrusion into the tin markets, but these masters of manipulation soon found their would-be saviors to be as self-interested as they themselves were.

What emerges from this complex interplay of powerful forces is the realization that U.S. diplomacy was unable to coherently address the coming of the National Revolution, contributed to the demise of three successive governments that it sought to bolster, and inadvertently provided assistance to a movement it considered, at various points, to be "Nazi," "Peronist," and "Communist." The needs of the national security apparatus, embodied in the Reconstruction Finance Corporation and the creation of the tin stockpile, completely overrode

U.S. diplomatic priorities and, through a convoluted process, actually hastened an anticapitalist revolution that threatened to destabilize a major supplier of the U.S. defense industries, if not the entire Andean Cordillera.

The chapters that follow examine the Truman administration's dealings with six distinct and quite different governments of Bolivia in some detail (see table 1). Chapter 1 focuses on the supposedly "fascist" regime of Gualberto Villarroel and his MNR allies, whose first effort at societal reform ended in the lynching of the president. Chapter 2 details attempts by the junta of Tomás Monje and the Bolivian elites to regain control of the nation and to rebuild liberal constitutional oligarchy at the beginning of the sexenio. Chapter 3 deals with the presidency of Enrique Hertzog and his failed diplomatic initiatives in Buenos Aires and Washington; chapters 4 and 5, with Mamerto Urriolagoitia's efforts to suppress the MNR, rein in the tin barons, and secure a tin contract that might stave off the coming revolution. Chapter 6 tells of General Hugo Ballivián's desperate attempts to reach agreement with the RFC. Chapter 7 begins with the National Revolution of 1952 and the regime of Víctor Paz Estenssoro and ends with Truman's departure from the presidency in 1953. The conclusion briefly discusses the early days of the Eisenhower administration, when a more sophisticated, if not effective, U.S. approach to Bolivia finally emerged.

1

VILLARROEL

April 1945–July 1946

We have, of course, certain practices of party discipline and order, but the difference between them and the goosestep is as great as from La Paz to New Orleans. This is a government of essentially nationalist tendencies—let us say clearly, an eminently democratic government.
—*Víctor Paz Estenssoro, 24 December 1943*

One is led to suspect that though the MNR may have absorbed Fascist argot and Fascist ideology during its formative years, faced with the actual task of governing it will not be prepared to apply Fascist methods as thoroughly as they have been applied in Europe, if for no other reason than that the social climate of Bolivia and that continent are so different that first, the MNR could not effectively absorb European Fascism and second, Fascism as known in Europe is not fully applicable to Bolivian society, especially not at the present stage of its economic development.
—*Walter Thurston, 13 February 1945*

When Harry S. Truman assumed the presidency at the close of World War II, the final defeat of the Axis in Europe and Asia obviously preoccupied every branch of the U.S. government. For the heirs of Franklin Roosevelt's Good Neighbor policy, however, that valiant struggle extended deep into the heart of South America as well. Since 20 December 1943, when Major Gualberto Villarroel López had risen from the barracks to seize control of Bolivia, U.S. policy makers had viewed issues on the Altiplano almost entirely through the prism of the war against Hitler's Germany. That fateful perspective paved the way for seven years of misconception, misunderstanding, and deeply flawed policy making because it impeded U.S. efforts to formulate an effective response or even to fully understand events in the region. Nonetheless, by the end of the war, the State Department had discovered a far more realistic rationale for its opposition to both the Villarroel government and its MNR backers.

Simply put, Villarroel's government was the harbinger and Paz Estenssoro's Movimiento Nacionalista Revolucionario (MNR) the driving force behind an urgently needed populist transformation of Bolivia that postwar Washington could not endorse. U.S. statesmen spent much of their time attempting to discern obscure links between the Bolivian regime and Juan Perón's Argentina, not just because both shared some imagined link with now-defunct Nazism, but also because the nationalistic underpinnings of both Peronism and the MNR threatened U.S. conceptions of liberal capitalism in South America. Villarroel and Paz Estenssoro were working assiduously, if somewhat haphazardly, to break the back of "the old and ruthless exploitation" practiced by the rosca, to "fight for economic liberation against the tin oligarchy" and its "history of abuse, violence, and corruption," to end the virtual enslavement of indigenous Bolivians, and to lay the foundations of a wider democracy in which most, if not all, Bolivians would have at least some voice in government.[1] Although the Truman administration professed its support for most of these objectives, it simply could not countenance a mass movement based on the primacy of labor, statist intervention in the national economy, and the eventual nationalization of the tin mines.

The Villarroel Government

Despite their initial opposition to the Villarroel regime, by 1945, U.S. diplomats had, for the most part, arrived at a more realistic assessment of events on the Altiplano. The Movimiento Nacionalista Revolucionario had once been "very much in accord with the principles of the Nazi Party," U.S. chargé Hector Adam stated, "but the character of the party had changed considerably" over the previous year. Functionaries at all levels of the State Department could find little fault in Villarroel's wartime record of cooperation with Washington. Indeed, as the department's Division of North and West Coast Affairs concluded, Villarroel's "cooperation with the United States," though not "all we could wish it to be" and "forthcoming for reasons other than those of affection," was far superior to General Peñaranda's. U.S. Embassy personnel agreed that the members of the revolutionary government were "much more accessible, receptive, and much less obstructionist than their predecessors."[2] Secretary of State Edward Stettinius bluntly proclaimed that Villarroel's government "is cooperating in the war effort to a very full extent, as its predecessor was not" and had shown no sign of "collaboration or particular affinity" with "either the Nazis or the Colonels' Clique in Argentina." Even if the Villarroel government did share with other "primitive and unstable American republics" a tendency toward "arbitrary action," and was "inept, demagogic, dishonest," and corrupt, at least it was not "terroristic and totalitarian." As Ambassador Walter Thurston, no friend of the regime, grudgingly acknowledged, "regardless of its insincerity and venality," its "war record is not bad."[3]

By the end of the war, the State Department had abandoned its claim that Villarroel was emulating European Fascists by running a brutal police state. Although the regime had "at certain times been bloody and tyrannical," the "devil must be given his due." In 1945, there had been, the U.S. Embassy claimed, "only one death as a result of a political measure," no "political murders or kidnappings," and fewer than a dozen political prisoners incarcerated without justification. Although the documented killing of several opponents by "hot-headed elements of the Government" in Oruro in November 1944 and rumors of arbitrary arrests continued to taint Villarroel's government, most U.S. leaders had to concede that these paled before the actions of virtually any previous Bolivian government. Ambassador Thurston himself acknowledged a "tendency toward moderation" and conceded that the "abuses" of 1945 were "mere pranks by comparison with earlier outrages" and far from atypical of South American politics. But, even though Villarroel had managed to partially rehabilitate himself in the eyes of most U.S. diplomats, the State Department still remained quite uncomfortable with Paz Estenssoro's MNR—a nationalistic party possessed of an "irrational anti-capitalistic and anti-upper-class bias."[4]

Indeed, it was most likely at the urging of the MNR that Villarroel had enacted a wide range of explicitly prolabor, antibusiness policies. "National unity," the *movimientistas* had insisted, "cannot be achieved under the regime of free competition since those who are strong, the owners, always vanquish the workers and Indians in the economic struggle to the death between the two classes."[5] Villarroel decreed that workers could not be fired without cause and that the heirs of workers killed on the job be paid two years of the decedents' wages; he implemented severance bonuses, pay increases, and a minimum wage and mandated improved sanitation and health facilities in mining camps. The Ministry of Labor appointed legal advisors to counsel workers and report violations of the new decrees. The MNR even contemplated a bill barring foreigners from holding managerial positions in some industries. When the Banco Minero mandated that the tin barons nearly double the price they paid *ckacchas,* self-employed "private contractors," for the ore they mined on company land, it paved the way for the eventual elimination of this exploitative practice. The tin barons faced not only a barrage of decrees that radically increased their labor costs, but others mandating tax hikes and the seizure of their precious foreign exchange. Moreover, Villarroel's backers amended the Constitution to permit the national government to monopolize all tin exports and decreed that the government had the right to seize and operate any mine closed by its owners. In short, according to one U.S. diplomat, Villarroel and the MNR had "severely punished the mining industry"—a "stronghold of malefactors, perhaps, but the country's principal source of income" to "uphold [the MNR's] demagogic slogans."[6]

The most critical development, however, was the emergence of the Federación Sindical de Trabajadores Mineros de Bolivia (FSTMB), the country's first national mining union. Created with the support of the MNR and at least the acquiescence of Villarroel and the *radepistas* of the Razón de Patria, the FSTMB, under Juan Lechín Oquendo's leadership, eventually supplanted weak company unions and the PIR-dominated Confederación Sindical de Trabajadores Bolivianos with an invigorated, politicized organization. For the MNR, perhaps driven by the understanding that it was doomed to remain a junior partner to the officer corps in the government and recognizing the need for mass support, the emergence of the FSTMB, in which the middle-class intellectuals formally pledged their allegiance to the working class, was nothing less than a milestone. Although the MNR's vision of a multiclass alliance ran contrary to the call for class conflict by the Partido Obrero Revolucionario (POR), Lechín was able to paper over this serious difference for the time being. Allying with the FSTMB was, for the movimientistas, a critical first step because they began to assemble a loose coalition of groups and factions from different regions and classes under its banner. Their efforts to this end, as Christopher Mitchell has noted, were exceptionally well suited to the physically and socially fragmented nation and even extended to the forgotten countryside.[7]

The MNR's agenda outside the cities and mining camps was more ambiguous and less revolutionary. The MNR platform supported suffrage and basic rights for indigenous Bolivians but stopped short of calling for full-fledged revolution and land reform. Instead, it hoped to gradually modernize agriculture to increase production and, most important, to draw indigenous subsistence farmers into the cash economy. The white and mestizo members of the MNR, like their counterparts in the old political parties, feared they might be overwhelmed by the indigenous masses and determined to move slowly. The labor system would be reformed, but the large fincas and haciendas would remain in the hands of the rosca. In May 1945, the MNR convened an "Indian Congress" as a cautious first step toward fundamental change in rural Bolivia. The Congress proposed an end to the traditional agrarian system of debt servitude, pongueaje, the establishment of schools in indigenous communities, the creation of a rural police force to stop hacendado depredations, and the formation of modernized rural cooperatives. Even if implemented fully, however, the proposals of the Congress would not have eliminated the rent-in-labor system or threatened the dominance of the landlord classes in the countryside. Still, as Laura Gotkowitz has shown, it was a vital step in the addressing, if not redressing, centuries-old race- and class-based grievances.[8]

Ambassador Thurston found some aspects of the MNR program laudable but was quick to point out that, "for all the talk of the importance of the Indian," even MNR leaders could not overcome their "ingrained feeling of superiority" and conducted their policies with a paternalism that only reinforced a "sense of inferiority" among indigenous Bolivians. Moreover, Thurston shared the rosca's fear that the MNR was taking a senseless "gamble" by lifting indigenous aspirations, one that could easily unleash lawlessness and violence across the Altiplano. "As the Department knows," he wrote, "the Bolivian Indian is still very much a savage" quite capable of "overwhelm[ing] the white population and their half-breed farm managers."[9] For U.S. policy makers, even a pro-fascist regime might have been preferable to the unpredictable social upheaval that Thurston believed the MNR was courting.

In short, Villarroel and the MNR promised nothing less than the fundamental reshaping of Bolivian labor relations and society. Their ultimate goal was to eliminate the nation's dependence on tin through economic diversification and self-sufficiency. Recognizing that the country could not continue to subsist off the tin mines forever, they aimed for a statist solution similar to Roosevelt's New Deal and Truman's reconversion plans. Paz Estenssoro called for the eventual nationalization of the tin mines but understood that the lack of Bolivian technical expertise made such a step unfeasible in the short term. Instead, to spur economic growth and sustain the nation in the longer term, the Bolivian government would purchase agricultural equipment and build a modern transportation network by increasing taxes on tin exports and by limiting the foreign exchange the tin barons could funnel offshore. Time was of the essence, for if this was not done before Malay Straits tin became available and depressed the value of Bolivian exports, the country would soon "become a nation of ghosts haunting abandoned pits" across the Altiplano. Paz Estenssoro's diversification and industrialization program even extended to a plan to "destroy" the "taboo" against the domestic smelting of Bolivian tin by constructing a Bolivian smelter. If all went according to plan, the foundations for a new, modern, economically independent Bolivia would be entirely laid by 1948.[10]

Washington found these developments anything but innocuous. Although finally convinced that MNR leaders were not Nazi puppets (or that, with Hitler's defeat, it mattered little whether they were), the State Department lamented that they could neither "keep their hands off large enterprises," which they incessantly "soaked" for tax revenue, nor stop "conceding to mine labor practical immunity from legal action for illegal violence." Regardless of their party's antecedents or international position, that the MNR leaders relied on working-class support and were dedicated to breaking the rosca stranglehold on power guaranteed that their program was antithetical to the U.S. goal of promoting capitalism through liberalized trade, despite Villarroel's oft-stated pledge to be "more a friend to the poor, without being the enemy of the rich."[11]

More important, MNR nationalism was explicitly antiforeign and implicitly anti–United States. In Mitchell's words, the MNR critique "pictured the entire nation as subject to international capitalist exploitation, which made it possible and necessary to postpone any class conflicts until after the winning of full national autonomy." As a later MNR handbill put it, "the criminal rosca must be considered and combated as a foreign invader, because it is foreign!" But, for the short term, Carmenza Gallo suggests, the MNR exempted the landed aristocracy from its antiforeign critique of those responsible for Bolivian underdevelopment so that it could direct its efforts and outrage almost exclusively against the rapacious tin barons.[12] Moreover, Paz Estenssoro publicly acknowledged that, because any government in Bolivia was effectively at Washington's mercy, prudence dictated a pro-U.S. policy, unless, he joked, that government could somehow find a way to ship Bolivian tin to "Germany by submarine from Lake Titicaca." Although he claimed to have no quarrel with the U.S. government and even stated that the United States was the only nation that could assist in his endeavors for Bolivian self-sufficiency, MNR propaganda did regularly feature anti-U.S. messages.[13]

Most Bolivians' only direct experience and contact with the United States was through their dealings with white-collar employees of the tin companies. The tin barons regularly hired Europeans or U.S. citizens as engineers, overseers, technicians, and managers. In the drive to radicalize the mining camps, it was all too easy for pro-MNR labor leaders to infuse demands for wages with a racially charged *antiyanquismo* that already existed among the indigenous and mestizo miners. One MNR newspaper serving the miners of Potosí depicted North American managers as "ignorant, gluttonous" despoilers, while another, *Revolución* (whose credo was "Bolivia for the Bolivians"), described a U.S. engineer as a "dirty exploiting Gringo" who goes "to the doors of the mine to abuse the workers who really work without daring to enter the concavities of the earth" himself.[14]

By permitting, if not actually encouraging, anti-U.S. propaganda, the U.S. Embassy argued, the MNR was creating an environment in which "Americans coming to work in Bolivian mines [were] gambling with their lives." Living in small enclaves in and around the isolated mining camps, U.S. personnel and their families were easy and natural targets for intimidation, harassment, and even assault during periods of labor unrest. When Thurston toured the mining camps, he found among the workers a pervasive "anti-foreign" resentment against the "white bosses" either "inspired" or "tolerated" by the MNR that had been "not heretofore witnessed by the American personnel." In short, with inadequate police protection and labor representatives "inciting the unlettered laborers against the 'gringos,'" the "labor situation is shaping up for an explosion in which United States nationals are going to be hurt."[15]

Ambassador Thurston regularly took Villarroel to task over the danger posed by MNR propaganda and warned that "should an American be killed," it would resurrect the perception that the Bolivian government was a "camouflaged Nazi regime." Indeed, Thurston considered the threat to U.S. citizens to be so serious that he urged his superiors to make the "discontinuance of incitement of the Bolivian mine workers against Americans by members of the Ministry of Labor" a sine qua non for any new tin contract.[16] Because of the need for Bolivian tin, however, his superiors refused; instead, they ordered him to prevail on U.S. employees to remain in Bolivia even though, "as the Department knows, their lives are daily in very real danger."[17] To prevent an exodus that might cripple the tin mines and thereby hinder the war effort, U.S. civilians were to be left in harm's way.

MNR leaders understood the danger posed by shop floor anti-Americanism and sought to reassure U.S. Embassy officials on several occasions. Continued incidents in the mines, however, only served to illustrate how little control the MNR leadership actually had over the unions or the PIR and POR elements within the rank and file. When MNR leaders Hernán Siles Zuazo and Rafael Otazo argued that the United States did not understand their efforts on behalf of the poor, U.S. chargé Adam vehemently asserted that "no government in the world was more anxious to see the welfare of the proletariat improved than mine"; he discounted the leaders' claims that the MNR desired amity with Washington. Indeed, when Adam had urged them to purge a militant anti-U.S. agitator from the party's ranks, they had refused because doing so would "indicate that the MNR was knuckling under to the 'interests.'" Even worse, FSTMB leader Lechín had sent a provocative open letter to Ambassador Thurston.[18]

In it, Lechín had denounced Thurston, the United States, the rosca, and the capitalists' "conquering and enslaving" imperialism in the strongest terms. Ambassador Thurston, who had criticized Lechín and the FSTMB on several occasions, came under particular fire as a "trafficker in public opinion" serving U.S. and rosca "imperialism" in the "unequal battle between the exploiters and the exploited." Thurston's criticism of Villarroel and the MNR only gave them "strength to fight against oppressors" and illustrated that "American 'democracy' each day advance[d] more resolutely on the road to Fascism." If the MNR sought to become "more popular abroad," gestures like these were, Chargé Adam retorted, "a hell of a way to do it."[19] Clearly, Paz Estenssoro was harnessing the power of working-class radicalism and nationalism by linking the MNR to the mine workers and did not dare to alienate those constituencies in the name of better relations with the yanqui colossus. No amount of diplomacy or amicable reassurances could reconcile MNR aspirations with the U.S. commitment to liberal capitalism.

Villarroel, the MNR, and the Blue Book

Despite misgivings about the MNR and the social upheaval it was threatening to provoke, U.S. policy makers soon realized that the *villarroelista* government "would not permit itself to be overthrown without plunging the country into [another revolution]," which might bring on worse instead of better conditions. Even ousting the MNR was dangerous, U.S. officials noted, because "MNR leaders have stated . . . publicly that they will not relinquish power without a fight and will bathe the country in blood if an attempt is made to oust them."[20] Therefore, the best hope rested with Villarroel himself and the more conservative elements of RADEPA, who might eventually cast out the MNR and govern as a more conventional military regime dedicated to stability, rather than reform. This was no idle hope. Indeed, the U.S. Embassy reported in late 1945 that, since the overwhelming MNR victory in the 1944 congressional elections, "a cleavage has existed in the cabinet" between the "too aggressively radical" MNR and the military. Paz Estenssoro considered himself to be a member of the "slightly crazy" ("poco loco") faction within Villarroel's cabinet, whose task it was to rein in the "crazy" and "half-crazy" military factions who were "all out for taking the wild point of view on almost any topic," but U.S. policy makers saw a more ominous split.[21]

On at least two occasions, Villarroel's military backers had demanded that the president eliminate the MNR from his cabinet. On the first, when the MNR's Rafael Otazo placed the entire blame for the 1944 Oruro killings on the army, Villarroel had barely been able to turn back their demands. The second occasion involved Foreign Minister Gustavo Chacón. In October 1945, MNR deputies launched censure proceedings against Chacón in the hopes that Villarroel would replace him with one of their own. The ploy succeeded to the extent that the foreign minister stepped down, but the president temporarily replaced him with Lieutenant Colonel José Celestino Pinto, an officer "linked by family to the rosca," rather than a movimientista. Villarroel never did name a permanent replacement: doing so would have either infuriated or emboldened the MNR. The officer corps understood all too well that the MNR was "strategically placing" its members in office across the nation and strengthening the FSTMB to secure an independent base.[22]

When Villarroel proposed a cabinet shuffle to bring in other civilian elements, presumably as a counterweight to the MNR, outraged movimientistas threatened to abandon the government and move into opposition. They called for a massive rally in the Plaza Murillo, one that Villarroel apparently told Pinto was "against you and against me." Unimpressed, Pinto responded that he could fill the plaza with fourteen thousand troops the next day if the president so desired and asked which group's support he would rather enjoy. Whereas Paz Estenssoro had once proclaimed that the army and the MNR must "hang together or they would hang separately" because "they would all be shot" if the "traditional parties should return to power," Villarroel, like the State Department, understood that differences between the two groups were becoming "practically irreconcilable." In Chacón's words, "it is either them or us."[23]

Thurston did nothing to discourage Villarroel's disenchantment. When Villarroel asked Thurston for his assessment of the MNR, the ambassador reminded him of the old "pro-Nazi" accusations and cited more recent "disparaging references to democracy, pan-Americanism, etc." by movimientistas. He was pleased to report that Villarroel "was not particularly interested in defending" the MNR. For Thurston, an open rupture with the MNR (generally cast as the "elimination of totalitarian influences") would erase "stigmata that have blemished the regime and which might eventually draw to it unwelcome attention of the kind to which Argentina has recently been subjected."[24] Thurston regularly lectured Villarroel about protecting U.S. citizens and warned him that if he did not "use his influence to stop the abuse of political and civil liberties," he risked "falling into the bad graces of the United States." Whereas Thurston employed some subtlety in his efforts to convince Villarroel to abandon the MNR's "brass-voiced casuists," other U.S. diplomats were more blunt. Adam, for example, simply explained to Foreign Minister Pinto that "relations between the U.S. and Bolivia would be facilitated by the elimination from the government of the MNR" and its "Nazi nucleus."[25]

Although Villarroel had clearly soured on his alliance with the MNR, he dared not purge the movimientistas from his cabinet. Whether he feared retribution from the MNR, approved of its agenda, was using the party as a counterweight to military factions, or was simply vacillating, as some critics claimed, Villarroel made no overt move against Paz Estenssoro's organization. One cabinet member openly informed U.S. officials that RADEPA members were afraid the MNR would accuse them of being allied with the rosca and "unleash disorders and bloodshed" if they made any move to oust Paz Estenssoro.[26] If the State Department had any realistic hope of engineering a break between the MNR and RADEPA, however, the traditional political parties of Bolivia soon made that unlikely. At the end of December, leaders of the Liberal, Republican Socialist, Socialist, and Genuine Republican Parties joined with the Unión Cívica Femenina and the Partido de la Izquierda Revolucionaria to forge the Frente Democrático Antifascista (FDA) against the Villarroel government.

Denounced by the MNR as a "rosca-pirista," Communist-plutocrat alliance, the FDA united almost all of the nation's significant political parties, PIR's mass base, and the wealth of the tin barons and landed elite into one organization comprising as much as 80 percent of the "politically conscious populace." Committed to the restoration of democratic government, it explicitly demanded that the military return to the barracks and, much to the chagrin of U.S. diplomats, rejected any compromise with Villarroel. Even more important, however, the FDA announced that, once it took power, it would convene special "People's Courts" to put on trial and punish those who had served in or collaborated with the Villarroel government. José Arze even spoke about emulating the war crimes tribunals of Nuremburg. With these pronouncements, the FDA discouraged any civilians that Villarroel might invite into the government as a counterbalance to the MNR and, indeed, ensured that no such invitations could be made. Although Pinto considered the military-MNR alliance to be a "marriage that turned out badly," he and fellow officers were not inclined to give the opposition an "entering wedge" that might lead to their death sentences.[27]

Nonetheless, if efforts by the United States to drive Villarroel and the MNR apart had at first been ineffectual, in February 1946, they became actually counterproductive, when the Frente Democrático Antifascista took an aggressive turn just as Assistant Secretary of State Spruille Braden mounted a new offensive. Having served as ambassador to Argentina during the formative stages of *peronismo*, Braden—whom Bolivian ambassador Victor Andrade called "the embodiment of the conscience of the American people as a champion of principles and ideals against authoritarian regimes"—had waged an embarrassingly activist campaign to derail Perón and his followers. From Braden's new post, he opted to continue a crusade that had repercussions across South America.[28] Embassy personnel like Adam and State Department officials like Joseph Flack and James Espy from the Division of North and West Coast Affairs were Braden appointees who wholeheartedly endorsed his belief that Villarroel was little more than an Argentine proxy. If the destruction of Nazi Germany seemed to eliminate the threat posed by a "pro-fascist" regime in Bolivia, the MNR and, to a lesser extent, Villarroel were now deemed to be, at best, symptomatic of the spread of Perón's brand of "totalitarian" populism across South America and, at worst, pawns in an Argentine drive to forge a "southern bloc." Laurence Whitehead has suggested that it is easy (if "depressing") to trace the U.S. "reclassification" of the MNR from "Nazis" to "Communists" during the Truman presidency, but an important, if largely overlooked, stage in that reclassification was "Peronists."[29]

Assistant Secretary Braden and his staff had spent six months sorting and compiling German archival records into the infamous "Blue Book" to use against Perón in his bid for the presidency. Braden released the Blue Book, formally but deceptively entitled *Consultation Among the American Republics with Respect to the Argentine Situation*, weeks before the election in an effort to paint the Peronists in Argentina as Nazi sympathizers and totalitarian puppets.

He included sections that purported to show links between the Nazis, the MNR, and RADEPA in an effort to resurrect the old accusations and, for the first time, to directly and formally "implicate" Paz Estenssoro in "collusion with the Argentines and Nazis."[30] Although the MNR was able to shake off the flimsy U.S. accusations of pro-Nazi behavior rather easily, allegations of collaboration with Peronist Argentina were more persistent and haunted the party throughout the Truman presidency.

In fact, there is little if anything to suggest any meaningful Argentine role in the coup that brought Villarroel to power beyond the usual accusations of interference by neighboring states that accompanied almost every South American revolution. The best evidence anyone could procure was that Paz Estenssoro had visited Buenos Aires in June 1943 as part of an academic exchange. Still, U.S. secretaries of state from Cordell Hull to Dean Acheson remained convinced that the MNR leaders, if not Villarroel himself, owed their position, at least in part, to an alliance with Argentine nationalists. Indeed, the "Revolution of the Majors," coming as it did just months after the Argentine "Colonels' Revolt" ousted a moderately pro-Allied government in 1943, invited comparisons. Both revolutions had been led by secret military lodges and officers somewhat sympathetic to, if not actually trained by, Germany. Both embarked on nationalistic campaigns to industrialize the nation, demonize a *vendepatria* elite that had dominated the nation for decades, and achieve economic self-sufficiency. Both forged alliances with the working class to carry out what the State Department considered to be a "totalitarian" agenda. Moreover, at the height of the 1944 nonrecognition crisis, Bolivian Foreign Minister José Tamayo had proposed the formation of an "austral bloc" of Argentina, Bolivia, and Chile. Although Tamayo's memorandum was denounced by all sides and he was immediately dropped from the cabinet, it added fuel to the fire.[31]

The State Department was not alone in its suspicions: even Villarroel's first ambassador to Argentina apparently warned his president that "if I find any evidence of Peronist involvement in your coup, I'll resign."[32] Evidently, he did not. The State Department never really found much, either. "So far as the Embassy is aware, it has never been proved that the Revolution of December 20, 1943, received any financial assistance from Argentina," one foreign service officer observed, but "of course the charge was made by the Department of State" nonetheless. The U.S. Embassy in Buenos Aires could find no evidence, either, except for a highly suspect report from Mauricio Hochschild, whose "penchant for stirring up trouble is well known," as was his desire to see a government in La Paz more responsive to his interests.[33] None of this, of course, deterred Braden from his course.

For their part, the Peronists did, to some extent, see the MNR as a potential ally. Both movements were, the Argentines believed, the targets of an unholy "Communist-oligarch" alliance that had been hammered together in Braden's office in 1944 between José Arze and Mauricio Hochschild. Braden had supposedly told the tin baron and the PIR leader that "we shall kill the dog and then the fleas will die," suggesting that his campaign against Perón would eventually lead to Villarroel's demise. Whether the story was true or not, Peronists viewed the U.S. campaign against Villarroel as an effort to diplomatically "isolate the Argentine Republic." In the view of the Argentine Embassy in La Paz, if Argentina could acquire "substantial quantities of tin" from Bolivia, "the economy of [that] country [would] change its center of influence" from Washington to Buenos Aires. Villarroel had entered discussions with Peronists to have the iron fields of Mutún opened up to Argentine capital, and in a matter of "greatest importance" to Bolivia, the Argentine Banco Central was offering him loans that Washington and Wall Street refused to consider.[34]

Despite, however, the Argentine courting of a prolabor government "unprecedented in the institutional history of [Bolivia]," U.S. diplomats reported that "the Bolivian Government has appeared to give the Argentine considerable reason for annoyance." Bolivian diplomats concurred and even admitted privately that the Argentines had legitimate reasons for a certain mistrust of Villarroel. Disputes arose from Bolivia's "misuse" of Argentine rolling stock and "its inefficiency in railway matters in general"; they had escalated to the extent that the Argentines had, at one point, recalled their ambassador from La Paz.[35]

Far more serious, however, was Villarroel's willing participation in Assistant Secretary Braden's embargo against Argentina. The Reconstruction Finance Corporation had purchased the entire Bolivian rubber production throughout the war and allocated it to the Allies. As a neutral, Argentina had received no rubber quota and, despite widespread smuggling, was suffering from serious shortages in late 1945. With the end of the war in Europe and the reopening of their traditional markets, the Argentines claimed that the Bolivians were charging exorbitant prices for rubber and then compounding their crime by not delivering it. Argentina retaliated by simply cutting off food shipments to Bolivia. In fact, almost all Bolivian rubber was still committed to be sold to the United States, and Braden refused to permit any sales to Argentina that would lead to a resumption of grain shipments. To avert disaster, the State Department arranged an emergency shipment of ten thousand tons of Australian wheat to Bolivia. Even when the Argentines resumed grain shipments, they had raised the price of their wheat by more than 50 percent, and the absence of Argentine-Bolivian amity should have been obvious.[36]

In light of episodes such as this, in March 1946, after insisting "for the dozenth time" that "he was no special friend of Argentina," Villarroel explained to U.S. chargé Adam that he had to give his "avaricious and more powerful" neighbor "every courtesy because of Bolivia's dependence on it for food." Although the *peronistas* may have shared some ideological sympathies with Villarroel and the MNR, there was little hope for long-term cooperation. Paz Estenssoro tried to explain that, because his program for economic diversification was directly aimed at reducing Bolivian dependence on Argentine food imports, Argentina was "not disposed to assist" in his quest for "self-sufficiency." Indeed, should the MNR achieve its goals of radically increasing the agricultural production of Bolivia, it would be directly at the expense of Argentine exporters.[37] In the end, peronistas certainly hoped for some sort of anti-U.S. solidarity with their Bolivian counterparts, but there was little basis for it, despite Braden's fervent belief that there was.

The Bolivian ambassador in Washington, Victor Andrade, showed a remarkable understanding of Assistant Secretary Braden, the Blue Book, and the strange persistence of the myth of Argentine complicity in Bolivia's 1943 revolution. Because President Truman and Secretary of State James Byrnes were preoccupied with reconversion and the European Cold War, Andrade argued that Braden had an "unprecedented" free hand in assailing Perón's Argentina. Bolivia had been drawn into Braden's campaign by faulty evidence (which could, of course, never be refuted) and his need to "convince the American people of the danger" posed by the Argentine government. "It was not sufficient to tell of [Argentina's] supposed totalitarian ideology or speak of its failure to take action against subjects of Axis nations," Ambassador Andrade explained, so Braden needed to find or fabricate an example of Argentine "imperialism" that would "constitute an immediate international threat." Accusing the Argentines of fomenting the Bolivian revolution accomplished that goal, but, the ambassador was quick to point out, the Blue Book had never really been intended to influence events in Bolivia. Indeed, Andrade believed that Braden had been extremely supportive of Bolivian arguments regarding the tin contract, and he noted that State Department officers had barely mentioned the Blue Book to him. Although silence was part of the State Department's calculated strategy to let the Bolivians "stew" over the accusations, Andrade was essentially correct in his analysis.[38]

Still, State Department officials did initially hold out some small hope that, when the Blue Book fell "like a bombshell on Bolivian politics," it might inspire a revolution against Villarroel. It would give both the FDA and anti-MNR officers "powerful ammunition" to use against Paz Estenssoro and possibly bring about a formal split. Even if this did not occur, U.S. diplomats hoped it might also provide an impetus or a pretext for Villarroel to remove the MNR from his government and to invite the FDA in, providing for an "orderly transition" of power back to the traditional parties and the "moneyed class." Foreign Minister Pinto was rumored to support that option, and at least one other cabinet member told U.S. chargé Adam that he very much wanted to do just that but could not yet act on his desires. The third and most undesirable possibility was that Villarroel and Paz Estenssoro would retrench, mend their differences, and "hang together" in the face of Braden's and the FDA's uncompromising assaults.[39]

Within days after the release of the Blue Book in February 1946, that third possibility had come to pass. "By strengthening and solidifying the opposition," Adam explained, "the Blue [Book] has postponed the possibility of the military members of the Government throwing out the MNR and substituting some other civilian group." Prior to the release, Villarroel and Pinto had shown clear signs that they were "ready to throw all those accused to the wolves," with the exception of Paz Estenssoro, who, Villarroel assured embassy personnel, was innocent of the charges against him. However, the Blue Book spawned "resentment that [sprang] from patriotic motives," apparently across the political spectrum as Bolivians believed that their "honor and dignity [had] been impugned" by foreign intervention. It did not help that the MNR and RADEPA were able to preemptively refute much of the evidence against them even before the Blue Book had been made public.[40] Rather than weakening Villarroel and the MNR, Braden's assault had apparently bolstered their nationalist appeal.

The Argentines agreed with U.S. diplomats that the Blue Book had shifted Bolivian public opinion in favor of Perón and "against foreign interference." Indeed, Argentine diplomats now believed that Bolivian "men of Government and general opinion look upon Argentina with special sympathy" as fellow victims of U.S. aggression. That reaction seemed to be fairly pervasive across Latin America: the Blue Book generated more complaints about U.S. interventionism than alleged Argentine or Bolivian fascism. Because Braden's efforts lacked international support, Ambassador Andrade argued, they were no longer of any "importance or danger" to either the Bolivian government or the MNR, although Braden's "state of mind and position" remained a cause for concern.[41] There was, in short, "no likelihood at all of any governmental change being effected in Bolivia" as a result of the Blue Book revelations. Although the Blue Book did not fail as miserably in Bolivia as it did in Argentina, like the FDA's assaults, it only furthered the "fortress" mentality that now pervaded the Villarroel regime.[42]

Duly chastised, the State Department declined to take further opportunities to influence events, in part out of fear that more overt U.S. opposition might drive Villarroel completely into the "camp of Argentina." Evidently speaking for the Frente Democrático Antifascista and anticipating that the Blue Book augured a more aggressive U.S. position, a Liberal leader approached the U.S. Embassy in May, requesting a pledge of U.S. aid should his party succeed in toppling Villarroel from power. The Liberals sought to guarantee wheat and meat supplies should Perón cut off shipments in retaliation for the removal of his supposed ally. Despite the U.S. Embassy's support for a measure that would "counteract Perón's victory in Argentina," Secretary Acheson bluntly warned Adam that, to preserve the policy of nonintervention, "you should refrain from any discussion whatever of the matter." Wanting to pursue a policy of "discreet and patient pressure," some State Department officials hoped to use the tin contract to obtain a quid pro quo should Villarroel "go ahead with his undemocratic Nazi-Fascist totalitarian program in league with the Perón Government and against all the principles and tenets of the Inter-American System." But this was not to be.[43]

The 1946 Tin Contract

Had Assistant Secretary Braden truly sought the fall of the Villarroel government, the tin contract would have been his best means to bring it about. In late 1945, Ambassador Andrade, Mauricio Hochschild, State Department officers, and representatives of the Foreign Economic Administration (FEA) assembled in Washington to negotiate the first postwar contract. Although the intrigue that permeated these negotiations gave Braden the perfect opportunity to deal a significant blow to the Villarroel government, to the surprise of many, he remained largely neutral and, at times, even supported Ambassador Andrade. The Bolivian government needed all the support it could get as it faced off with the technocrats of the FEA and found itself under assault by Hochschild as well.

The Bolivians had initially hoped that the end of the war would lead to a relaxation of the wartime controls and a three-year tin contract that started at 63½¢ per pound. Instead, the FEA opted to deploy a "revolver to the head" policy, as Hochschild called it. Arguing that, with the end of hostilities in the Pacific, Malay Straits tin would soon become available and depress the market price, the FEA's "sharks of Wall Street" demanded a price decrease over six months from 63½ to 55¢ per pound. This phased reduction, they claimed, would allow the Bolivian economy time to adjust to the lower prices they believed would prevail in the postwar period. That said, the FEA announced that there were to be no negotiations: Villarroel and the tin barons could simply "take it or leave it." In short, the "honeymoon [was] over." Because the FEA had already stockpiled one hundred and twenty thousand tons of tin metal and thirty-three thousand tons of concentrates, this was no bluff, and in Ambassador Andrade's words, "we Bolivians couldn't eat our tin."[44]

For its part, the State Department viewed the FEA position with alarm, believing it threatened to "seriously jeopardize the economic and social stability of Bolivia." According to Ambassador Thurston, although Patiño could continue to produce tin for Great Britain profitably at FEA prices, it was "likely" that all "Aramayo production would be suspended" and Hochschild would be forced to follow suit. In effect, "our principal current production sources of supply would be terminated" if FEA's "untenable" proposal was implemented. There was little chance, if any, that Villarroel might roll back wage increases or taxes to allow the mines to remain profitable and even less chance that he might "relinquish his power to more conservative civilian groups."⁴⁵

Assistant Secretary Braden's diplomats argued that the FEA should not even suggest "slashing wages or depriving the workmen of the benefits of recent social legislation." Doing so would only "increase the rift between the Government and the miners and involve us in a very messy domestic situation." Indeed, the most likely consequence of the FEA's approach seemed to be nationalization of the mines. If Aramayo and Hochschild ceased or even reduced their operations, Villarroel would be compelled to seize and reopen the mines, if only to ensure the flow of foreign exchange. It did not help that elements of the RADEPA and the MNR were already ideologically disposed to do so. Any or all of these steps would at best only "delay a return of sound, democratic government." Instead, Undersecretary of State Will Clayton suggested his own price schedule, which would keep the tin price at 60¢ per pound for a year.⁴⁶

Ambassador Andrade and the tin barons naturally found the FEA proposal unthinkable and Undersecretary Clayton's alternative only marginally less so. Outraged by the FEA's uncompromising stand, Andrade argued that the U.S. position was "unjust," "unwise," and based on unrealistic assumptions. It was unjust because it punished the Bolivian producers who had dramatically increased their production during the war to support the U.S. war effort and unwise because it would almost certainly force Villarroel to nationalize the mines to sustain the national economy. The ambassador had no illusions that the government could operate the mines for more than two years before tapping out the best veins; moreover, he knew that nationalization would scare off desperately needed foreign investment and eliminate any possibility of his nation receiving foreign loans for the foreseeable future. On the other hand, he saw little reason why the price of tin should be reduced at all before Asian production facilities were in Allied hands, and he doubted FEA claims that significant quantities of Malay Straits tin would be available within three years. It made little sense to assert, as the FEA did, that it was to the benefit of Bolivians to deny them a fair price for a year to prepare them for an even lower one the next. Indeed, if his country did not receive 70¢ per pound, "Bolivia [might] have to be written off as a casualty of war." If, however, the United States would maintain the tin price for several years, Paz Estenssoro could realize his program and Bolivia would "emerge as a diversified and largely self-sufficient economy."⁴⁷

Although Mauricio Hochschild derided this "dream" of self-sufficiency, he agreed entirely with Ambassador Andrade that U.S. policies were "unfair and unjust" and that the Bolivian government would "exhaust and ruin" any nationalized mines. Not surprisingly, he believed that the tin price should be "at least" 80¢ per pound and "very probably" $1.00. He also claimed that he and Carlos Aramayo were already "losing money" at the current price and "had not made any money" during the war because his labor costs had, thanks to the 1943 revolution, increased from eighty-five to five hundred dollars per ton. If the United States government would not pay him what he believed his tin was worth, it should at least pressure the Villarroel government to "cut out labor agitation" and "revise the tax system." When told that this would violate Good Neighbor nonintervention pledges, Hochschild cited Braden's campaign against Perón, claiming that "although [the United States] talked the doctrine of nonintervention, [it] did not follow it." He was quick to point out, however, that this was "exactly the right thing" to do. Indeed, because the U.S. tin contracts explicitly stipulated that the Bolivian government not impose taxes or other charges that might impede production, he argued that the State Department was obligated to intervene on his behalf. Sidestepping his argument, the Truman administration countered that, because the Bolivian tin industry had been more productive under Villarroel than ever before, there was no basis for a U.S. protest.[48]

Ignoring Hochschild's appeals, the State Department initially left negotiations to the Foreign Economic Administration. According to Ambassador Andrade, FEA representative Alan Bateman told the Bolivians that he had set up three chairs outside for those who "wished to dispute" his terms. He then assured them that "I will not occupy one of those chairs." When Hochschild claimed that Bolivia could obtain a higher price in an open market, Bateman made three counterarguments. The third and most compelling was simply that the U.S. and British governments had no intention of easing their controls over tin purchases, so further discussion was pointless. The Bolivians still did not understand the lengths that the Truman administration was willing to go to guarantee tin imports to the United States and its stockpile. At the same time the FEA's Bateman was browbeating Ambassador Andrade, State Department officers were using a proposed loan to quietly blackmail the Dutch government into giving the Reconstruction Finance Corporation a ten-year option to purchase East Indian production despite its negative impact on Dutch interests.[49]

Bateman did, however, take up and support Hochschild's complaints regarding Villarroel's tax and labor policies. Dismayed State Department officers were stunned by the FEA's willingness to place "our Government, before the public both at home and abroad, in the position of protesting wage increases to Bolivia's impoverished workers." When Ambassador Andrade and the State Department lodged protests against Bateman's "brusque" approach, Bateman had, according to Andrade, "disappeared suddenly from the Washington scene." The FEA then reversed course and agreed on a schedule that would reduce the price of Bolivian tin concentrates to only 58½¢ per pound. Although the State Department was "very happy" with how the matter had been resolved and Andrade later boasted that his efforts had held the price steady against heavy odds, U.S. diplomats warned that Bolivia had nine months to prepare "to meet the situation whereby the best price she could hope to get for tin would be 52 cents."[50]

The signing of the tin contract, however, was only the prelude to further developments. In January 1946, Foreign Minister Pinto, believing rumors that the British were paying the Malaysians 72¢ per pound, informed U.S. chargé Adam that he desired a revision of the contract. Adam responded, without consulting his superiors, that his government was hesitant to pay more because the profits from "increased prices would be frittered away in further salary increases and social benefits." Though crassly put, this was a real concern in Washington and one that the State Department had shared for years. The Bolivian export taxes on tin were the highest in the world and further impeded tin firms already handicapped by unfavorable geography. Moreover, it fell hardest on small and medium-sized companies, which would have much preferred a tax on profits that would have targeted the Big Three. Because the tin contracts imposed a flat price on all producers in the nation, owners with particularly rich veins (like Patiño) could reap exceptional profits at prices that would bankrupt smaller or less efficient ones. Finally, the government's reliance on the export tax permitted the agricultural elite to pay almost no taxes whatsoever because tin quite literally sustained the Bolivian economy.[51]

The solution was for the Bolivian government to join with U.S. officials and private experts in a "technical commission" to examine and rewrite the tax codes in a way that would more equitably distribute the tax burden, encourage tin production, and permit Bolivian tin to compete with Malay Straits tin in the long term. This, Undersecretary Clayton and Ambassador Andrade agreed, would result in replacing the production tax with one on profits that would, at the very least, shift the burden onto the shoulders of the tin barons and assist the small and medium producers.[52] Although Hochschild also agreed, at least in the abstract, he and the tin barons were, in fact, the major impediment to what could have been a productive and effective cooperation. Indeed, the export tax system existed primarily because the Big Three refused to grant government officials access to financial records that would permit them to even guess at the tin barons' profits. "If the government is able to obtain actual cost figures from the producers," Thurston argued, "a valuable advance will have been made." Paz Estenssoro and Villarroel could push the rosca only so far, however, and they never requested the technical commission that Ambassador Andrade sought and the State Department very much hoped to send.[53]

Nonetheless, before the Bolivians could renegotiate the tin contract, they had to first present evidence that a price adjustment was necessary. Having smoothed the way with numerous U.S. officials, Andrade asked the tin producers to draft a memorandum that emphasized "the injustice of the present contract" and its "effects ... on Bolivian mining," as well as those of postwar inflation and rumored British offers of 64 to 66¢ per pound to Malaya.⁵⁴ Whereas Hochschild had, up to this point, quietly complained to the State Department about Bolivian tax policies, he now took this opportunity to openly assail the Villarroel regime. The memorandum he and his fellow "political enemies of the Government" sent to Washington focused almost exclusively on the Bolivian tax structure and clearly aimed to draw the Truman administration into their struggle against Villarroel. Although the Bolivians did, with State Department support, receive permission to renegotiate, internal Bolivian policies would be on the table, and Andrade would stand almost alone against the combined might of Hochschild, his government's "mortal enemy," and the U.S. technocrats.⁵⁵

When negotiations began in earnest in March 1946, the RFC's George Jewett and Jesse Johnson, standing in for the Foreign Economic Administration, immediately asserted that their agency would be willing to hold the price at 60½¢ per pound, but only if the Bolivians would "make concessions" of their own through a reduction of export taxes. Still claiming to be operating at a loss, Hochschild demanded a price of 68¢ from the RFC and a tax cut from Andrade, retroactive to 1945. Although the State Department, using data that Hochschild had provided earlier, was able to expose this claim as a lie, his complaints about significantly higher labor costs may have had some merit.⁵⁶ The tin barons asserted that their labor costs had increased by more than 20¢ per pound during the war, and even Patiño had been forced to close a mine that could not produce a profit at less than 72¢ per pound. Doing so had, under Villarroel's revised labor codes, cost the "Rey del Estaño" more than four hundred thousand dollars in indemnification payments to the workers he had laid off. Moreover, the tin barons were unable to understand why tin was apparently the only product on the planet whose price had declined in the previous year.⁵⁷

By April, the RFC's Jewett had increased his offer twice, but now it was "up to the Bolivian Government" to also "lend a hand" by reducing taxes and exchange restrictions. Paz Estenssoro's representative in Washington claimed that this would amount to "political suicide for his government," which would be "immediately accused of selling out to the *rosca*." When Jewett, following State Department recommendations, did present an offer of 63½¢ per pound, Hochschild refused to budge from 67¢. Bolivian chargé German Rovira then suggested an adjournment for the producers to prepare a counterproposal; Hochschild replied that he "had just finished making one" and Jewett should consider his offer rejected.⁵⁸

The State Department apparently did at one point briefly take up the tin barons' cause. At one of the sessions, Braden's assistant, James Wright, took the floor and proposed that the RFC pay 63½¢ per pound and that the Bolivians "modify their tax schedules and exchange rates" to essentially grant the tin producers another 4¢ per pound of pure profit. Although Ambassador Andrade's superiors were apparently "ready to make some concessions in taxation" and to "express the sacrifices that we are willing to make," Andrade was not. Stunned that the State Department was now openly endorsing Hochschild's position, Andrade immediately sought out Senators Arthur Vandenberg and Tom Connally, leaders of the Senate Foreign Relations Committee, who had long been critical of Braden's penchant for intervention. With the senators' support, he approached Braden and politely but firmly threatened to publicize this most recent "intervention." Because Andrade had not yet told Senators Vandenburg and Connally the substance of his complaint or sent word of Special Assistant Wright's "suggestion" to La Paz, he offered Assistant Secretary Braden the opportunity to retract it quietly. To Hochschild's amazement and displeasure, the assistant secretary reconvened the meeting, and Wright disavowed his statement.[59] The next time Hochschild claimed that "the Government of Bolivia should do something" about its tax policy, State Department officer Sam Lipkowitz bluntly replied, "That is your problem, I am not working there." The RFC quickly confirmed that Bolivian fiscal policy was "not involved in our present negotiations."[60]

During a conversation with Ambassador Andrade in May, Assistant Secretary Braden apparently said that "others here had asked him to insist that the Bolivian Government for its part help to reduce the high costs of production in Bolivia by decreasing taxes, the exchange rates, etc.," but he had replied that "he could not do so." He explained to Andrade that "he had been strongly criticized for the very staunch support he had given the Bolivian side" at various meetings. He was certainly remembered for years as a man "known to feel the RFC treated Bolivia rather shabbily." On several occasions, Braden had argued for an increase in price on behalf of a regime he despised against a branch of his own government and even seems to have taken a personal liking to Andrade.[61] Moreover, if Special Assistant Wright had suggested internal policy changes, he had done so with the blessing of Undersecretary Clayton, who believed that, since the Bolivians were using production costs as the basis for their arguments, "all cost factors became a matter of interest." Though Braden personally believed Villarroel could easily reduce export taxes without harming social welfare measures by trimming his nation's exorbitant military budget, he appears never to have made this suggestion. Remarkably, even at the peak of the Blue Book hysteria he had unleashed, Braden remained at least neutral toward and at most supportive of Villarroel's government during the tin negotiations, if only to ensure that tin continued to flow.[62]

Meanwhile, Ambassador Andrade continued his tireless efforts to secure 67¢ per pound by stonewalling and by darkening the door of every remotely influential U.S. senator, congressman, cabinet member, or journalist he could find. In mid-July, he finally made headway by demanding that, unless the RFC met his price or lifted all restrictions blocking Bolivian sales to European nations, he planned to bring this "discriminatory practice" before the United Nations. Even though Assistant Secretary Braden supported the Bolivian desire to sell its tin on an open market, because of quotas set by the Combined Tin Committee, no nation would permitted to purchase it.[63] Still, Andrade's threat appears to have been effective. A day after his ultimatum, the RFC gave its approval to a formula that essentially granted the Bolivians their coveted 67¢ per pound. Villarroel and Andrade had reluctantly agreed, "more or less as an indirect result" of U.S. protests, not to tax the tin producers on more than 62½¢ per pound, but this bittersweet concession was soon dwarfed by political catastrophe. Villarroel's government was toppled just three days later, and in Andrade's words, "as a result of a painful paradox, the fruit of all of our efforts served, in the end, to benefit our enemies."[64]

The Blue Book may not have inspired a revolution against Villarroel, but it seems that opponents of the regime were not lacking for inspiration of their own. Fearing that the Machiavellian tin baron was plotting and financing a new counterrevolution, overzealous radepistas had kidnapped Hochschild in 1944. Only Villarroel's personal intercession had brought about his release. When a revolutionary plot was discovered and foiled, however, the government violently repressed the PIR and very likely sanctioned an attempt to assassinate *pirista* leader José Arze. And when an insurrection broke out in Cochabamba and Oruro, government officials executed ten conspirators. This escalating repression by the government provoked outrage from both large sectors of the country and the State Department and, according to historian Carlos Mesa Gisbert, marked the "beginning of the end" for Villarroel, as the Catavi Massacre had for Peñaranda.[65]

Responding to an upsurge in FDA agitation within the middle and upper classes, Villarroel declared a state of siege at the end of May 1946. FDA leaders, teachers, professors, anti-MNR labor leaders, and other "Democrats and decent people" were arrested en masse, torture was reported, and the major La Paz newspapers were seized as "organs of sedition." Because, however, the United Press and Associated Press employed representatives of these papers as their primary correspondents in Bolivia, this did not put a stop to criticism of Villarroel. When army and air force units (possibly funded by Carlos Aramayo) rebelled in June, they were met, not by military units, but by armed MNR militias. Although the stage was set for a revolution, the FDA, "poorly organized and united only in hate of the present regime," was ill equipped to start one, much less carry it off.[66]

Instead, the revolution began in mid-July with a student strike at the universities of La Paz, backed by PIR labor agitators.[67] When Villarroel ordered its suppression, fighting broke out in the heart of the city, and several students were killed. As marches and protests led by casket-bearing students sprang up across La Paz, PIR unionists called a general strike, paralyzing the city. Students and piristas armed themselves to battle for La Paz and the nation. Within days, both the military and the MNR had abandoned Villarroel, who now faced an insurgent mob almost alone. On 23 July 1946, the president was dragged into the Plaza Murillo, beaten, mutilated, and hanged from a lamppost "a la Mussolini."[68] Newly appointed U.S. ambassador Joseph Flack, who had arrived just in time to witness the lynching and the fall of what he called "one of the most noxious governments the country had ever experienced," was awestruck by the spectacle. The opposition had, according to Flack and other State Department officers, "with their bare hands alone" triggered a "volcano of popular discontent" to oust a "Nazi-tainted dictatorship" "a la French Revolution."[69]

As movimientistas scattered into exile and sought refuge in the embassies of La Paz, the MNR's tentative experiment in populist reform came to an abrupt halt. Contrary to movimientista and peronista propaganda, Braden's State Department seems to have done nothing to provoke or support the revolution, although it rejoiced when the old order and liberal constitutional oligarchy were restored. For the next six years, the MNR plotted its return in union halls, mining camps, clandestine party meetings, and the streets of Buenos Aires, while the tin barons worked to reestablish their control over Bolivian society. Whereas the MNR considered the sexenio to be nothing more than the naked restoration of the rosca to full power, conservative reformers, ever wary of counterrevolution, tried their best to steer a middle course between the radicalism of the MNR and the revanchism of the old elite. Their efforts, despite the full support of the U.S. State Department, were doomed to failure.

2

JUNTA

July 1946–March 1947

This is one of the profound constitutional contradictions of Bolivian democracy. It cannot have majoritarian government, first because the majority of the Bolivian population is alien to the political life, and second because inside the nucleus of the minority that has political awareness, the majority is in violent divergence with the interests that have in their hands the vital responsibilities of the nation.
—*Demetrio Canelas, 5 January 1952*

It is true that the salaries and wages that are paid [in Bolivia] cannot furnish employees and workers a standard of living like that of the United States or Argentina because neither from England nor from the United States . . . have we been able to obtain prices that permit adequate increases in these salaries and wages.
—*Gabriel Gosálvez, 3 September 1949*

In the aftermath of the revolution of 21 July 1946, both the Truman administration and Bolivia's Provisional Junta of Government optimistically looked forward to a new era of cooperation and mutual understanding. Relief, exuberance, and satisfaction characterized the mood at the State Department. Members of the new junta made the astonishing and extremely unlikely claim that, at the time of the revolution, Major Villarroel "had a mission in Buenos Aires prepared to give way to Perón's desires, arrange elimination of customs barriers, and assure 'Anschluss' with Argentina." Although more sanguine observers like U.S. diplomat George Messersmith suggested that "anyone who knows the Bolivian attitude on sovereignty realizes that even Villarroel would not have bartered on this point," U.S. chargé Hector Adam had nonetheless concluded that "there can no longer be any doubt that Bolivia, either through fear of reprisals or genuine willingness," had "signed up" in a "southern bloc" with Argentina.[1] If nothing else, Villarroel's lynching put to rest any fears that Perón had a puppet in La Paz.

Those fears were replaced with jubilant optimism on the part of newly appointed ambassador Joseph Flack. When a junta headed by former judge Tomás Monje Gutiérrez eventually took control of Bolivia, promising a restoration of democracy, Flack took it upon himself to shepherd that process. The new regime faced impressive obstacles, including revolutionaries it could not control, fear of a MNR counterrevolution, and an Argentine food embargo that threatened to further destabilize an already unstable situation. Although Flack and his superiors did everything in their power to protect and assist the junta, the Reconstruction Finance Corporation was not so charitable. Picking up where it had left off, the RFC was determined to undo Bolivian ambassador Victor Andrade's victory. In other words, the greatest threat to the new regime came not from vengeful peronistas or movimientistas, who were painting the names of the junta's leaders on lampposts in anticipation of their counterrevolution, but from representatives of the same U.S. government that had pledged its full support.

Restoring Order to Revolutionary Bolivia

Villarroel's sudden demise and the complete collapse of his government caught the established parties and the political class entirely off guard. In the wake of the army's complete abandonment of Villarroel, chaos reigned in the streets of La Paz. Although an informal Tripartite Committee of students, teachers, and workers attempted to restore order to the city, it failed to curb the mob violence: hordes of vengeful *paceños* descended on the foreign embassies where members of the old regime had taken refuge. Gangs of students besieged the Argentine and Ecuadoran embassies, firing guns into the air and hurling insults at those who were sheltering movimientistas and pro-Villarroel military officers. They even stopped and searched the car of the Peruvian ambassador, whose wife was related to the MNR ex-mayor.[2]

With the army discredited and confined to the barracks and the police unwilling to take to the streets, the hastily assembled new junta found it impossible to establish control of the nation. Composed largely of men employed directly or indirectly by the tin barons and former officials of the Peñaranda government who had not taken part in the uprising, it had an uphill battle restoring order to La Paz. Respected judge Tomás Monje Gutiérrez was named head of the junta but, for almost a month, was too ill to take charge. Néstor Guillén Olmos and Monje Gutiérrez took limited steps to reestablish control but could not risk either putting uniformed soldiers on the streets or attempting to disarm the revolutionaries. New police officers were issued badges stamped "21" to symbolize their support for the 21 July uprising and to give proof that any semblance of *villarroelismo* had been purged.³ Responding to a pervasive fear within the diplomatic corps that MNR members would be killed by mobs or arrested rather than exiled, a fear that precluded any prospect of immediate international recognition of the new government, the junta made restoring order and protecting members of the old regime seeking asylum its highest priorities.

For U.S. policy makers, especially Ambassador Flack, the threat of further bloodletting was the only shadow to darken what was otherwise a shining triumph. Flack had arrived in La Paz on the eve of the revolution and had narrowly missed being hit by a stray bullet. This did little to dampen his spirits, however: he immediately proclaimed the revolution to be "an act of pure democracy emanating from the people and accomplished almost entirely with their bare hands," and believed that it could well produce the "first democratic government in Bolivian history." He lauded the revolutionaries in the highest terms and believed that the refusal of the masses to turn in their guns actually "had a salutary effect on any ideas which the military may still cherish surreptitiously of eventually trying to retake the government."⁴ In short, Flack argued that "democracy's first steps are apt to be faltering" but "should be supported in every reasonable and decent way by our country." The tin barons rejoiced as well, expecting "relief from the troublesome labor problems" of the recent past and an end to what they called Villarroel's "odious labor laws."⁵

Still, Ambassador Flack agreed with his diplomatic colleagues in La Paz that recognition had to be withheld until the government allowed MNR members an "unmolested departure to another country" because this would "present a test of Bolivian adherence to existing treaties and the junta's authority to maintain order." Despite U.S. hostility toward the MNR, the entire diplomatic corps hoped to avoid the "serious international incident" that the La Paz press seemed to be encouraging through its vilification of Paz Estenssoro and his followers. Although Flack understood that the State Department sought the "gain in good-will" that would accompany swift recognition, he could not "conscientiously recommend" it. The embassies that had granted asylum were depending on the United States for "moral support"; if it granted recognition unconditionally, Flack believed, there would be little reason for the junta to protect those embassies from vigilante justice or to permit the safe departure of MNR members.⁶

Early in August, Assistant Secretary of State Braden candidly explained the U.S. position to the new Bolivian ambassador, Ricardo Martínez Vargas, his longtime friend and a former member of Patiño's board of directors: the State Department, though "favorably impressed by the composition and declared objectives of the junta" and desiring to aid and extend recognition to it, could not do so until both "adequate police control in La Paz" was established and the asylum situation was resolved. Martínez Vargas countered by suggesting that any "genuine, unanimous popular uprising of the people" was bound to "result in a strong demand that 'criminals be brought to justice'" but agreed to impress upon the junta that "its good name abroad" and recognition could not be "disconnected" from the treatment of those seeking asylum.[7] Monje eventually relented despite his desire to see the supporters of Villarroel tried and punished. Under pressure from both Buenos Aires and Washington, members of the junta approached the Tripartite Committee and apparently asked that it respect the sanctity of embassies. The students agreed and went so far as to act as embassy guards; they were even given soldiers to command.[8]

For Ambassador Flack and the State Department, this was "unequivocal evidence" of the junta's authority and a "great credit" to its members. Indeed, Flack believed that this "commendable demonstration of authority" was also a sufficient pretext for the United States to accord immediate recognition, which would create a "distinctly favorable psychological moment... beneficial to the junta in the maintenance of public order." President Truman agreed. Monje and the junta continued to pleasantly surprise the Truman administration, by allowing MNR members to go into exile, by calling elections for the beginning of 1947, and what was perhaps most significant, by announcing on 11 October that none of their number would run for office, guaranteeing at least a modicum of impartiality.[9]

To support the new regime, U.S. diplomats found themselves at odds with their counterparts in La Paz, especially the Brazilians, who "had asked that we go slow, mainly for the purpose of not encouraging revolutions and the spilling of so much blood." Indeed, weeks after U.S. recognition was secured, it became clear the junta's control over even La Paz was far from complete. On 27 September, Luis Oblitas, a deranged young ex–army officer, burst into the Palacio Quemado brandishing a gun and threatened to kill Monje. According to *Time*, "the President, unbuttoning his vest and spreading his arms," told Oblitas, "Fire. I am here by the will of the people." When Oblitas hesitated, he was immediately arrested by the police. A mob quickly formed, seized the soldier, and hanged him from a lamppost in the Plaza Murillo; Monje and his compatriots were reduced to the role of "spectators." Not content, the mob then stormed a prison and seized Major Jorge Enguino and Captain José Escobar, the officers accused of perpetrating the 1944 Oruro executions. After each being given a bottle of Coca-Cola, they were shot and then also hanged from the lampposts. In the words of Mesa Gisbert, "no authority impeded this new aberration."[10] In seeking quick recognition to bolster the return of liberal constitutional oligarchy, the State Department had, in the end, cared little about the degree of control the junta actually had.

Nonetheless, recognition did pave the way for emergency food shipments, military sales, and the final ratification of Ambassador Andrade's tin contract—all of which would strengthen the authority of the new government. Ambassador Flack had done what he could to ensure that the oligarchs of the junta and not the popular forces of the Tripartite Committee gained legitimacy and control over La Paz and the nation. While he was exuberantly hailing the newly recognized government as an "irreparable blow" to the "formation of an anti–United States bloc so dear to Perón's heart," his superiors were acting to ensure that postrevolutionary Bolivia did not succumb to counterrevolution or Argentine pressure.[11]

Although U.S. nonrecognition of the new government had been as benign, supportive, and short as it could be, initial signs suggested that the Argentines were taking advantage of the transition period "by creating a food crisis" and "general economic chaos," either to foment a counterrevolution or simply to avenge Villarroel. Immediately after the revolution, Bolivian diplomats in Buenos Aires reported rumors that Peronists might "besiege" Bolivia "through hunger." In the next weeks, Argentine food shipments to Bolivia did indeed drop "off sharply" and ceased altogether on 7 August, for fear of "uprisings of miners and Indians," according to Argentine diplomats, but there was far more to the story.[12] Later in August, Peronists closed the border with Bolivia entirely and stopped issuing export permits; this created a "critical situation" that was "worsen[ing] by the day." In the most notorious case, Argentine customs officials turned back twelve rail cars of wheat bound for Bolivia. Bolivian diplomats first concluded that these steps were part of a concerted Argentine policy until Perón's foreign minister convinced at least some of them that Argentina was simply following the U.S. lead on nonrecognition.[13]

As the situation became "much more grave" by the day, however, the Bolivian chargé in Buenos Aires, Ernesto Daza Ondarza, seems to have spent every waking moment trying to ascertain the real reason critically needed food was not crossing the border. Periodic shortfalls in Argentine grain and meat shipments to Bolivia were nothing new; these had grown more pronounced toward the end of the war. Now, however, Argentine diplomats were placing blame for the recent "suspension of transport to Bolivia ... exclusively [on] the grave transportation problem from which Argentina suffer[ed]." Several officials pointed to a shortage of rolling stock; others suggested that a recent sixty-day campaign to reduce the cost of living in Argentina was draining off food originally destined for export to other South American nations. One railway official taking this view told the chargé that nothing could be done without a direct order from Perón's cabinet. The director general of transportation explained that Argentine railways had deteriorated and that the line into Bolivia was in "the poorest condition of all the rail lines in Argentina." He assured Daza Ondarza, however, that he would contact Perón to obtain permission to ship "all that Bolivia needs." Perón apparently responded with an order that "special preference" was to be given to rail shipments bound, not for Bolivia, but for export overseas to Europe.[14]

When Chargé Daza Ondarza approached Argentine customs officials, they expressed surprise that wheat and meat were being held up at the border, noting that only certain minor products were subject to export prohibitions. They directed him to Minister of Industry and Commerce Rolando Lagomarsino, who could reopen the border with a stroke of the pen. Lagomarsino, in a manner Daza Ondarza described as "Florentine," claimed to be "very surprised" at this "new development" and directly contradicted the customs officials. Such contradictions and apparently deliberate obfuscations supported the thesis that the Argentines were simply applying pressure on the junta, but it remained unclear toward what end. As the State Department noted wryly: Perón had "Bolivia over a barrel" but was "nimble" and "adroit enough to put on, from all outward appearances, an irreproachable front."[15]

After weeks of bureaucratic runaround and deepening shortages, Chargé Daza Ondarza believed he had finally discovered the real source of the problem. Well aware of Peronist "sympathy with the fallen government" and the daily "attacks on the Bolivian revolution" that appeared in the peronista press organs, he had long suspected "political factors." And, indeed, after giving him yet another recitation of the sad state of Argentine railways and yet another round of "assurances and promises," a deputy minister of foreign affairs asked Daza Ondarza "about those seeking asylum." When the Bolivian responded by asking whether this was not the "essence of the question" and the "cause of his nation's difficulties," the Argentine diplomat "could not conceal a rather suggestive smile."[16] Although the State Department's sudden decision to recognize the new government had forced the Argentines to abandon nonrecognition as a tool to guarantee the safe evacuation of MNR members, they had apparently opted for another form of pressure.

In all likelihood, the Peronists' concern for the MNR refugees went well beyond simple humanitarianism or respect for international law; they considered them to be the only Bolivian faction who "could respond to our overtures for the formation of a bloc" against the "Yanqui and Brazilian imperialisms aligned against us." Because most MNR members, including Paz Estenssoro himself, were seeking refuge in Buenos Aires, the potential for intrigue was virtually unlimited. Although other Bolivian diplomats attributed at least some blame for the food crisis to the inefficiency of the new Peronist trade monopoly and noted that other nations had suffered from it as well, this did nothing to change the fact that the "normalization of exports" from Argentina would "not be possible in the short term."[17]

What the Peronists failed to take into account, however, was the State Department's strong desire to see the Monje junta prosper. Over the course of 1945 and 1946, U.S. diplomats had discovered that "Argentina normally eases its policies on supplies quite readily after it discovers that we are willing to take care of its neighbors' food needs." Because U.S. diplomats urgently sought to strengthen the new government and Braden was receptive to any means by which any Argentine venture could be countered, this was the perfect opportunity. Indeed, State Department officers had been planning for this contingency since before the revolution, and Assistant Secretary Braden pledged that he would meet Bolivia's "minimum requirements" of food. In fact, he "was already making arrangements to do so" in mid-August, when the first Bolivian request arrived.[18] His superiors immediately authorized the shipment of twenty-four thousand tons of flour, and promised more to come. In October, the United States shipped eight thousand tons of wheat as well as an additional nine thousand tons of flour by rail from Chile; Ambassador Martínez Vargas confidently informed his superiors that he could obtain another eight thousand tons of U.S. wheat in November. For the Bolivians, the lesson was clear, and one they would exploit for years. Because the United States would provide wheat and flour to counter a Peronist embargo and ease a "critical and dangerous economic and political situation," Bolivian diplomats could use the promise of U.S. aid to secure lower prices from the Argentines and, in turn, lower prices from the North Americans as well.[19]

Once the State Department announced that it would meet Bolivia's needs and Monje declared that the MNR exiles would be given safe transit out of Bolivia, the Argentines lifted their "virtual blockade" almost immediately.[20] Although the new Bolivian chargé in Buenos Aires was obliged to run almost exactly the same gauntlet of Argentine functionaries in October that Daza Ondarza had run in August, he was greeted with "a spirit of cooperation that translated into the immediate dispatch of export permits." When queried by U.S. diplomats, Bolivian statesmen reported no complaints at the end of October and attributed the "reversal of Argentina's position solely to United States expressions of aid, which have, in effect, nullified Argentina's economic pressure."[21] At least one U.S. official was convinced that Daza Ondarza had for months "failed to bring Bolivia's problems to the attention of the proper Argentine representatives," but this had clearly not been the case. Although the Peronist motivations remained somewhat unclear, one MNR leader suggested that the Argentines had been "pointing a gun at the head of Bolivia" to remind it that "it could not afford the luxury of an anti-Argentine policy" at a time when mobs in La Paz were chanting, "Perón, to the lamppost!"[22]

In the end, both U.S. and Argentine diplomats had applied pressure, albeit of a much different character, to protect Paz Estenssoro and the MNR refugees.

When Paz Estenssoro finally arrived in Argentina in November, he admitted that "he owed his life" to the leaders of Argentina, Paraguay, and Mexico, who had insisted on Bolivia's "firm" adherence to the principles of political asylum. He did not include Ambassador Flack or the Truman administration among his saviors, for swift U.S. recognition of the junta had, if anything, endangered him and his colleagues. Thoroughly unrepentant, Paz Estenssoro reaffirmed his support for Villarroel, whose work had been "so barbarously interrupted by the Bradenist plutocracy," denounced Monje as a figurehead for "vampires who suck the blood of the Bolivian people," and lamented that his homeland was now "completely asphyxiated by the overwhelming pressure of the oligarchic and plutocratic tentacles."[23] As MNR members dispersed, some fleeing to Argentina and others going underground in Bolivia, to plot their response and to reorganize in the mines, Monje and the junta had passed their first test and survived their first challenges.

With Bolivia's international relations reestablished and normalized, the junta's primary task was to pave the way for a restoration of constitutional rule by holding elections for the presidency, the Senate, and the Chamber of Deputies. The MNR was naturally prohibited from participating, which ensured that the competition would be among the various parties making up the Frente Democrático Antifascista. Although the election of March 1947 was, on one level, notable for the civility and relative harmony that accompanied it, on another, it was a harbinger of the factional infighting that would cripple the governments of the sexenio. Unified only by hatred and fear of the movimientistas, the FDA had brought together the Marxist Partido de la Izquierda Revolucionaria, the rightist Liberal Party, bastion of the landed aristocracy, and the more moderate Socialist Republican, Genuine Republican, and Socialist Parties into a united front against Villarroel. Dropping "Antifascista" from its name, the Frente Democrático hoped to present a single slate of candidates who would restore unity to Bolivia. This hope would be dashed, however, by the ambitions of José Antonio Arze and his PIR.

The piristas seem to have believed, with some merit, that the moment had finally arrived for them to ascend to power. Theirs was the one remaining party that, through its influence in the mining, industrial, and railway unions, had anything resembling a mass constituency. Indeed, what organized support the 21 July revolution had enjoyed had come almost exclusively from PIR cells in the student federations and unions in La Paz. With the MNR being driven out of the mining camps, the piristas had every reason to believe they would be able to fill the void and finally achieve a dominant position among the working class. Explicitly Marxist in orientation since its founding in 1940, the PIR advocated a reasonably thorough reform of Bolivian society through a "12 Point" agenda that called for a centralized economy, women's suffrage, education reform, the elimination of illiteracy, and "action against imperialism, feudalism, and Nazi-Fascism." Notably, it was able to coexist with the landed elite because it did not call for immediate land reform or liberation of the indigenous masses and with the tin barons because it did not call for immediate nationalization of their properties.[24] Confident in its own strength, however, the PIR was unwilling to sacrifice its agenda to the more conservative parties of the Frente Democrático: its defection destroyed whatever consensus may have existed in the postwar period.

Pan-American Union official Ernesto Galarza offered a different version of the breakup of the Frente. According to Galarza, the PIR was effectively purged from the FDA when the "political marriage of the Rosca and the PIR proved to be a shot-gun wedding with a hangman's honeymoon." Although the piristas had great strength in the Tripartite Committee, the junta quickly supplanted and then disbanded the committee. Further, Monje's success in disarming the newly armed paceños dealt a direct blow to the PIR's ability to threaten the regime or launch a "second workers' revolution." José Arze and his followers were gradually eliminated from their positions in the junta and denied the representation they believed they deserved on councils and electoral slates; they came under increasing fire from the tin barons' newspapers.[25] Even though the other parties blamed the dissolution of the Frente Democrático on the PIR, Galarza's version of events has considerable merit.

The PIR was not the only party to defect from the Frente Democrático: other defections quickly followed. When the Republicans and Socialists forged a coalition, the Partido de la Unión Republicana Socialista (PURS), to fill the void left by the PIR's departure, the Liberals made a bold move to block their old rivals, suggesting that Monje be named president by acclamation. And when Monje turned down the nomination, the Liberal Party announced its intention to run its own slate of candidates against the PURS. Ironically, this most reactionary and elitist of the major parties found itself thrust into an anti-PURS coalition with the Marxist PIR, a coalition that chose the politically moderate Luis Guachalla to be its presidential candidate.[26]

For its part, the PURS nominated physician Enrique Hertzog Garaizábal, one of the original founders of the FDA, a Chaco War veteran, and a bureaucrat who had held a variety of cabinet posts throughout the 1930s. His Genuine Republicans, generally regarded as the most conservative and pro-rosca of the parties making up the PURS, also boasted the largest membership. The Socialists and Waldo Belmonte Pool's Socialist Republicans introduced a spirit of tentative reform to the PURS platform. With the MNR outlawed and the PIR taking a backseat in the presidential campaign, the election of 1947 bore a distinct resemblance to the old intra-elite contests of the 1920s and 1930s between the Liberals and Republicans. Just months after what "experienced observers" considered the "bloodiest" revolution in the nation's history, Bolivian politics had degenerated to little more than prewar personalism.[27]

Although deemed to be a clean election by almost all sides, the contest could be considered democratic only in the loosest possible sense of the word. The electorate was composed of fewer than one hundred thousand upper- and middle-class men of European or mestizo descent. That this 3 percent of the population was also the group with the least interest in meaningful reform or any major transformation of the status quo virtually guaranteed a bland campaign. Indeed, both Guachalla and Hertzog clearly represented the old, stagnant order, and both promised only modest reform. So similar were the candidates in their political views that they published a number of joint statements during the campaign on the major issues confronting postrevolutionary Bolivia. Indeed, Guachalla would later become an instrumental member of several of Hertzog's cabinets.[28] The only party that could have interjected anything resembling a genuine call for national rejuvenation, the Partido de la Izquierda Revolucionaria, inexplicably refused to enter the fray.

Why the PIR, at the apparent apogee of its political popularity, chose to adopt such a low profile remains something of a mystery. U.S. diplomats suggested several explanations for José Arze's tentative approach. On the one hand, the piristas were occupied by the formidable task of recapturing the "consciences of the mine workers put to sleep by the Nazi Villarroel demagoguery." On the other, Arze might also have determined that a concerted move for the presidency by the PIR would bring the violently anti-Communist and historically anti-PIR army out of its barracks in response. Until the party had consolidated its position fully within the working class, such a move might be premature, not only because of the military's hostility, but also because the oligarchy might easily extend its repression of the MNR to the "Communists" of the PIR. Even as Arze concentrated on winning over junior officers and securing a majority in Congress, he understood all too well that the entrenched leadership of the military would not countenance a pirista government and that his best hope lay in supporting and working through Guachalla and the Liberals, whose government the piristas could presumably dominate.[29]

The United States and the Cold War might also have been on Arze's mind. The PIR leadership was nervous, unjustifiably it turned out, about the U.S. reaction to a pirista government. Indeed, Arze's lieutenant, Ricardo Anaya, approached Ambassador Flack in early August to broach this very subject. Anaya believed that there was "strong feeling against the PIR in the United States" because of the party's "presumed Leftist orientation" and feared that U.S. aid would be "cut off" if it came to power. Even though opponents of the PIR routinely branded it "Communist," however, Flack did not; for him, the party was, at worst, "perhaps slightly tinged with pink."[30] After poring through countless FBI reports, the ambassador had concluded that Arze, Anaya, and their fellow piristas, despite effusive praise for Soviet Communism and frequent rhetoric denouncing imperialistic capitalism, were "generally friendly to the United States." Indeed, Arze, who had worked for Nelson Rockefeller's Office of Inter-American Affairs while in exile during the war, publicly professed his "admiration and affection" for the United States and understood that, "without the frank aid of the U.S., Bolivia could not raise its economic level."[31] Flack estimated that the PIR had the support of more than 80 percent of the electorate and predicted that, in the coming elections, "the PIR will get a working majority" in Congress and "the next President of the Republic will be a man who takes Arze's orders." Confident that the PIR was neither "a Communist organization" nor "likely to develop into one," Flack welcomed the party's ascension to power. Indeed, he reassured his superiors that a PIR victory would "presage a period of harmonious United States–Bolivian relations."[32]

Ultimately, lukewarm PIR support was not enough to carry Guachalla to the presidency on 5 January. Of the nearly ninety-three thousand total votes cast, Hertzog won by a margin of fewer than four hundred votes, and with that tenuous mandate, the PURS coalition assumed national leadership. Although Paz Estenssoro predictably denounced the elections as "fixed," most U.S. and Latin American witnesses could only laud them as the "purest and most extraordinary in the memory of the country." The incoming president immediately sought to assemble a government of national unity by inviting not only Guachalla but also the PIR into his cabinet.[33]

As the traditional parties divided the spoils of their victory, the MNR was forced into a major reassessment. One faction, led by Rafael Otazo, argued for moderation and an eventual peaceful reentry into Bolivian politics. Paz Estenssoro, however, argued that only through revolution could the old order be overturned, and, if anything, the example of Villarroel proved that a barracks coup would not suffice. Paz Estenssoro's path required a more militant agenda and a much closer alliance with radicalized mine workers. If the MNR saw alliance with the unions as a means to co-opt them, the unions viewed it as an opportunity to infiltrate a political party. Juan Lechín became, at this point, an even more important figure than Paz Estenssoro. With one foot in the MNR and the other in the FSTMB, Lechín was in many ways the link between the intellectuals in exile and the masses in the mines and streets. While the MNR brought organization and a path to power to the workers, the workers transformed the party from a small, tightly knit upper-class venture into a true multiclass mass organization. It would be years, however, before this strategy bore fruit, and, until then, the old parties and the PIR would have national politics to themselves.[34]

In the end, U.S. policy makers could hardly have been more pleased with Bolivian developments since the 1946 revolution. The State Department's highest priority was the elimination of MNR influence, and every party now meaningfully represented in the executive and legislative branches of government was thoroughly committed to keeping Paz Estenssoro in Buenos Aires, or at least out of La Paz. Moreover, the Liberals, spearheading the opposition, had a vested interest in eradicating the economic nationalism that characterized the MNR. Not even the inclusion of the PIR in Hertzog's cabinet soured Cold War Washington on the new government. Ambassador Flack reminded his superiors that, despite the PIR's "clenched fist symbol" and a program that "at least roughly parallel[ed] that of the Communists," there was "no evidence to prove any direct connection between the PIR and Soviet Communism." Indeed, he asserted, "at the present time there is no Soviet Communism in Bolivia worthy of serious consideration."[35] Because the PIR had more to lose than any other party if the MNR did return to power, the State Department was easily able to find common ground with the closest thing Bolivia had to Communism. Liberal constitutional oligarchy was alive and well.

The 1947 Tin Contract

That said, the success or failure of both the junta and President Hertzog's government ultimately rested in their ability to negotiate favorable tin contracts that would bolster the PURS and enable it to enact whatever modest reform agenda it envisioned. Manuel Mier y León of the Banco Minero and Raúl Canedo Reyes, director of mines, presented the State Department with an excellent brief of the Bolivian position in February. They started by preemptively refuting any arguments the tin barons might make for reducing taxes or curtailing state-mandated social welfare measures for tin miners. The subsistence wages paid to tin miners could not be reduced because even "the native, as well as the white man, requires a minimum of nutrition and warmth to survive," even if he "cannot aspire to better things." Moreover, because inflation had increased the price of clothing by 190 percent and the price of beef and coffee by almost 80 percent in the last half of 1946 alone, wages needed to be increased significantly to offset these increases. In the end, "the members of the RFC may judge for themselves if the salaries of the workers who live under these conditions can be reduced."[36]

The export tax, which represented by far the largest tax the tin producers paid, was, after government subsidies, an average of 9.27¢ per pound of tin. Any further reduction in this tax would necessitate the virtual disbanding of Bolivia's "tiny army," the closing of schools, universities, and health clinics, and the end of most public development projects. And any such "reduction of public services" would, in turn, "create disorder and discontent" that "would end by affecting mine production itself." Although the junta was no mere puppet of the rosca, neither was it unsympathetic to the needs of the tin barons. Because their ability to purchase the equipment and to make the technological improvements they needed to maintain production and to lower costs was dependent on what the barons were paid, paying them the lowest possible price would effectively doom the Bolivian tin industry. Mier y León and Canedo Reyes insisted that 76¢ per pound was the "minimum price necessary to stay the progressive paralyzation of the Bolivian tin industry" and far lower than the nation deserved. Using the price of zinc, copper, and lead since the beginning of the war as a baseline, the Bolivians concluded that had tin not come under the control of the Reconstruction Finance Corporation, its price would now be between $0.97 and $1.06 per pound.[37]

For the Truman administration, the fundamental issue in the tin negotiations of 1947 was whether it would support the junta by offering a higher price for tin or insist that the contract was an "exclusively commercial" transaction to be negotiated dispassionately. All Bolivians desperately hoped it would be the former. Before the election, candidates Hertzog and Guachalla had laid aside their partisan differences to approach Ambassador Flack personally and enlist State Department support for a higher tin price. They reminded the ambassador of the "high moral duty of the United States towards Bolivia" and its restored democratic institutions. When Flack reported this highly unusual overture, he reminded his superiors that these were the two most important political figures in Bolivia at the moment. He fully endorsed their appeal and informed his superiors that "all of the men of influence in Bolivia" will have a "very strong feeling of having been let down" if "the United States is unable to come to her assistance at this time in this matter." To "prevent the return" of the "forces uprooted in July by the Bolivian people," U.S. policy should not be "guided solely by commercial factors in concluding the tin contract" but should support the "young Bolivian democracy" through direct or indirect financial assistance.[38]

Assistant Secretary Braden "sympathized" with the Bolivian position, promised Ambassador Martínez Vargas he would "lend ... his support," and offered advice. After reiterating that the State Department "wished to do all it possibly could to help Bolivia," however, he claimed he was in no position to "ask another Agency" to "spend an additional $5 million to $15 million of our public moneys." In theory, it should have cost the U.S. government only $5 million to meet the Bolivian demand of 76¢ per pound, but because of "most favored nation" clauses in contracts with other producers, the actual cost was nearly $15 million. Martínez Vargas asked whether it might be possible to arrange "some sort of concealed payments" to tin producers, and one business leader even asked Braden to "command" the RFC to "grant a higher price," but to no avail. Citing congressional prohibitions, Braden was forced to rebuff both requests. Although the assistant secretary seemed to share Martínez Vargas's belief that a free market should be reestablished, Braden could do nothing until Congress rescinded the agency's purchasing monopoly.[39]

For its part, the RFC had no intention of relaxing its restrictions and made clear its determination to keep the negotiations "purely commercial." After preliminary discussions with the agency, State Department economic specialists handed Ambassador Martínez Vargas a memorandum "discouraging the hope of a higher price" with the stunning observation that "it does not seem that any real benefit would accrue to Bolivia from an increase in the price of tin." Although Martínez Vargas's "most violent objection" to this "slamming the door in Bolivia's face" at least forced the RFC to negotiate, U.S. diplomat James Espy, still smarting from Bolivian ambassador Andrade's triumph in 1946, warned that "this just cannot go on forever." The RFC's Jesse Johnson then declared that a higher price would only "make the situation worse" for Bolivians by making "more difficult the inevitable adjustment which may have to take place before the end of 1947," when East Asian production was expected to return to prewar levels. In a stark reversal of his statements to Martínez Vargas, Braden agreed that "there was no justification for this government to pay a higher price for Bolivian tin concentrates"; Johnson was pleased to note that the State Department would take a "hands off" approach. Although Ambassador Flack continued to press the Bolivian case, his superiors and the RFC had concluded that the price should remain at the levels negotiated by Andrade in 1946. All they offered President Hertzog was a cosmetic victory: the RFC "might be willing to make some adjustments in the price which might make it appear that a more favorable price" had been won, but of course "the actual price would be the same." In short, the United States "would not accede to an increase in price to be paid."[40]

Even if the negotiations were kept "purely commercial," the Bolivians had every right to expect a significant increase in price. In late 1946, the International Tin Conference estimated that the world's tin producers could sell one hundred forty-one thousand, six hundred tons in 1947. It quickly became clear that this estimate was at least twenty thousand tons too high, and there would, in fact, be a global shortfall of twenty-nine thousand tons. Even if the Bolivians could produce the forty thousand tons per year they had during the war, and even if all went perfectly in Asia, production would still fall twenty-one thousand tons short of demand. However, all was going far from perfectly in Asia. In Malaya and Indonesia, strikes and shortages in coal, food, equipment, and labor combined with wartime damage to impede restoration of normal production. Whereas the Far East had once produced one hundred ten thousand tons of tin per year, it was now producing just sixteen thousand. Eight replacement dredges ordered from Holland were delayed by postwar economic dislocations, a fierce European winter, and storms in the Bay of Biscay. The situation in Nigeria and the Congo was little better and was not expected to improve until 1949.[41] The RFC estimated that the United States required sixty thousand to seventy thousand tons of tin to "meet only the most essential uses" and one hundred ten thousand tons to supply normal productivity. Indeed, on a "purely commercial" basis, the tin barons and the Bolivian government had every reason to expect a significant price increase that would permit all of Bolivia's mines to remain open and profitable.⁴²

Johnson and Espy were not entirely blind to the inconsistencies and consequences of their position and understood that a low price for tin might well provoke "political disturbances" that could affect Bolivian tin production. Having claimed that "we are paying a very high and fair price," Espy nevertheless agreed that the Bolivians could, in all likelihood, sell their tin for far more than the current price if only the RFC would permit an open market. Indeed, he understood that "in the eyes of the Bolivian public and possibly even the world at large" the RFC monopoly "amounted to a purchasing cartel." Even as the State Department tentatively pressed for a restoration of the free market, Johnson privately conceded that his agency would be willing to grant the Bolivians up to 72¢ per pound.⁴³

None of this manifested itself in the early negotiations, however, when the RFC presented what Bolivians considered to be an "unfriendly and unjustified" offer of 67¢ per pound. Ambassador Martínez Vargas pledged to Braden that he would enlist the secretary of state to ensure that "political" factors were included and the price set at no less than 76¢ per pound. The ambassador understood fully that this would be an uphill battle: the RFC had just purchased ten thousand tons of Dutch East Indies tin for just 70¢ per pound and clearly expected the Bolivians to accept a lower price. He therefore urged the tin barons to prepare to cut off tin shipments altogether until the price was settled and suggested to his superiors that they explore other markets or press for the return to a free market.⁴⁴

Martínez Vargas's advice was heeded. With the full financial and moral support of the junta, the tin barons cut off shipments to the United States and Great Britain and launched a press offensive. Within weeks, nearly every media outlet in Bolivia was decrying how "the United States [had] exploited Bolivia and its mine workers during the war and wishe[d] to continue to do so." Embassy personnel reported sadly that there was "almost no indication of any appreciation for the merits" of the U.S. position. For his part, Espy argued that if Hertzog and his officials were feeling pressure from the Bolivian public to press for a higher price, as Martínez Vargas claimed, "it is unfortunately their own fault." The Bolivians were counting on State Department support and the fear of a return of the MNR to secure a better price. Espy "strongly" suspected the "fine hand of one Mauricio Hochschild" in this ploy because it was one Hochschild had successfully used before. Although he believed that the State Department should "quietly stand aside" and "let Bolivia work out of it by itself," Espy feared that, this time, Hochschild, Canedo Reyes, and Martínez Vargas had "stirred up a hornet's nest" by elevating the hopes of mine workers for raises that would "bode no good for Bolivia economically and politically."⁴⁵

Even though Espy and the State Department's economists supported the RFC's hard line, Assistant Secretary Braden did eventually come around to the view that "refusing [the] Bolivians a free market and price raise" could be interpreted as an "intervention in their economy" that "we should avoid." Whether the RFC was persuaded by Braden or by worsening global tin production forecasts, it increased its offer to 71¢ per pound on the last day of February. That same day, disappointed Bolivian diplomats opted to explore other markets, especially the British Ministry of Supply. When Bolivian ambassador Napoleón Solares approached British private smelters, he found them "greatly interested in purchasing additional ores." Unfortunately, they received orders from the Board of Trade "forbidding any dealings with Bolivian producers of tin until such a time as a new contract was signed with the United States." Solares claimed that British officials feared "repercussions of a political character" if they defied Washington and lamented the "state of quasi-dependency that Great Britain finds itself [in] with respect to the United States."[46] Ambassador Martínez Vargas believed he was more successful: a week after he secured newly appointed Secretary of State George Marshall's "intervention," the RFC increased its offer to 74¢ per pound for all non-Patiño Bolivian tin. The ambassador reported on 7 March that he planned to accept it "with much satisfaction" but was stunned to learn that his superiors would not.[47] Unbeknownst to him, the same day he reached his compromise in Washington, the Bolivian Foreign Ministry had reached its own intriguing one with the Argentines.

Perón had agreed to purchase four thousand tons of tin concentrates over the next five years at a price of 76¢ per pound. Although Argentina, whose canning industry was a major consumer of finished tin plate, had almost no smelting capacity and therefore no obvious use for Bolivian tin concentrates, since the election of Perón, Argentine foreign and domestic policy had taken a radical turn that made the importation of Bolivian tin desirable for a number of reasons. For one, such importation would further the ends of Peronist "economic czar" Miguel Miranda, who was determined to assemble an economic "southern bloc" in South America through a series of bilateral treaties. Miranda saw "economic unity between Argentina, Bolivia, Chile, Uruguay, and Paraguay" as the "only means" by which those nations could avoid "an economic life of a distinctly colonial character."[48]

For another reason, as Argentine ambassador Mariano Buitrago bluntly stated, Bolivian tin concentrates were an essential part of the Peronist industrialization scheme. Miranda envisioned minerals from Bolivia, Chile, and Peru flowing into Argentina, where government smelters and plants would process them into finished goods and transform Argentina. For yet another, Bolivia was the "easiest place for the infiltration of Yanqui imperialism, which had to be combated in defense of South America." Although the battle would be difficult because "there was a prejudice in favor of the United States" under the new regime (which was "nothing more than a variant of the old regime of the mining empire that has dominated Bolivia for fifty years"), the Peronists believed they could prevail in the end. It was, in fact, an "exceptionally favorable moment" to "economically penetrate" Bolivia and deal a blow to the United States and its plans to "obtain economic control of" the nations of South America and to "subordinate them to the interests of [U.S.] foreign policy." Perón grandly proclaimed that it was the "spirit of San Martín" that had "inspired his policy of economic emancipation" for Argentina, but he could not consolidate those gains without "the equal emancipation of neighboring brother nations."[49] Chile had signed the first bilateral treaty with Argentina in December 1946, and Peronist envoys had approached the Bolivian junta soon thereafter, offering a 300-million-peso loan, a customs union, and an exchange of Bolivian raw materials (including three hundred tons of tin concentrates per year) for guaranteed food shipments. The junta initially rebuffed the Peronists, claiming that it preferred to wait until constitutional government was restored.[50]

In March, shortly after Washington had decided to ignore the small Argentine request for tin, a new Argentine mission arrived in La Paz offering to purchase eight thousand tons of tin concentrates per year at a price of 76¢ per pound. The new offer had been artfully engineered by Bolivian ambassador David Alvéstegui, who had moved decisively to draw the Peronists into what would become known as the "battle for tin." Although the idea of revising the treaty to incorporate a major tin sale had been, in no small part, Alvéstegui's, he wanted the initiative to appear to have come from the Argentines, so that any U.S. retribution would be aimed at Buenos Aires, rather than at La Paz. Miranda, in particular, found the idea enticing and obliged Alvéstegui, secretly dispatching his minions to make the new offer. The Bolivians feigned shock and claimed to have had "no advance notice" of the peronistas' visit "until the day of [their] arrival." Miranda believed that the element of "surprise would contribute to success" and, according to Alvéstegui, "he completely achieved it."[51] Indeed, Ambassador Flack reported that the Argentines had "arrived at a most inopportune moment from the standpoint of the Bolivians" and were using "blitz tactics." That the negotiations took less than a week and proceeded until 3 A.M. for days on end suggested to Flack that "it is scarcely possible that a carefully crafted document could have been produced."[52]

The peronistas had a multifaceted agenda. They understood that, on the one hand, the "United States [would] have great influence in the new government" but that, on the other hand, the RFC was alienating its would-be partners in La Paz. Furthermore, an economic entente with the PURS would guarantee Perón a friendly government in La Paz—always a priority in Argentina's constant jockeying for position with Brazil. By providing loans and financial aid, he could expect Bolivians to contrast Argentine amity with the RFC's arrogance.

Indeed, Ambassador Martínez Vargas did just that to embarrassed State Department officers, denouncing the RFC for its "take-it-or-leave-it attitude" and "willingness to take advantage of price controls to drive a one-sided bargain" while praising the Argentines for their far more accommodating attitude: they had "arrived at La Paz to do business, not to bargain over price." Even President Hertzog was not shy about comparing the Argentine willingness to pay a "fair" price for tin and to ship Bolivia "wholesome, abundant and cheap" food with the RFC's mercenary approach.[53]

Ever eager to mete out punishment to Washington, Miguel Miranda gleefully told his Bolivian counterpart that "now we are going to squeeze" the United States, fully comprehending the impossible hand he was dealing the State Department and the RFC. What the Argentines intended to do with the Bolivian tin was unclear but disquieting. Miranda was working with private corporations to construct a smelter in Argentina and might have hoped to permanently reorient Bolivian exports toward Buenos Aires. More likely, however, he intended to resell the tin concentrates at a profit abroad, to private smelters, to the major consuming nations, or even to the Soviet Union. Depending on how Miranda fared as a middleman, his meddling in tin markets would have, at best, driven the price for the Anglo-Americans much higher. At worst, it might have shattered the international tin control system the RFC and Ministry of Supply maintained and opened the door for a possible restoration of the International Tin Committee. Secretary of State Marshall therefore deemed it "undesirable from every standpoint" for the Argentines to gain any foothold in the tin industry.[54]

Ambassador Alvéstegui believed the Argentine offer would ultimately lead to a "triumph in our game" to "obtain from the Republic of the North a more just treatment for our tin," and he happily claimed full credit when it did. A higher price for Bolivian tin was only the first of many benefits the bilateral treaty promised. These most notably included financial assistance and loans and securing a cheaper food supply as one of Perón's preferred trading partners, which would be a major step toward Bolivia's economic stability. Although the informal grain embargo had ended, the Bolivians were currently forced to pay the Argentines' "elevated prices" for food sales, to endure shortages, and to depend on U.S. emergency shipments. The exchange envisioned by the treaty would both resolve these problems and "open an interesting market" for other Bolivian exports. Alvéstegui took great pride in engineering the pact and adroitly manipulating both Argentines and Americans to his nation's benefit without "estranging" either Buenos Aires or Washington.[55]

The Bolivian ambassador admired Perón's ability to circumvent the Combined Food Board and unilaterally raise the price of Argentine food exports, believing that it was an excellent model for his nation in its struggle to thwart the Combined Tin Committee. He was careful to warn, however, that U.S.

and British "resentment" over Perón's methods, and especially over his treaty with Bolivia, would have detrimental consequences for Argentina in the long run. Other Bolivian diplomats were more blunt in their criticism, arguing that the Argentine goal was to turn their nation into an "economic slave" and the Brazilians, fearing any Argentine overture to a neighboring state, lodged the "strongest protest." A later Bolivian foreign minister went so far as to label Miguel Miranda an "archfiend."[56] The oligarchs understood well that hitching their wagon to Perón's revolutionary movement was dangerous, but desperation over the price of tin had led them to contemplate it nonetheless.

For President Hertzog, there was one additional benefit to the proposed treaty. If Perón could gain the cooperation of the oligarchs currently ruling the Altiplano, he would have no reason to provide assistance to the MNR exiles plotting in Buenos Aires. Indeed, Paz Estenssoro was quick to point out, "in the beginning, Perón had received" the MNR refugees "with open arms," whereas, after the negotiations began, "it was almost impossible for any of the MNR exiles to get in touch with any important Argentine official." Indeed, the Argentine Embassy in La Paz initially saw little reason to cooperate with Hertzog and his "Yanqui supporters," believing that a treaty with Hertzog was "delivering a weapon into the hand of our enemies" against the MNR, which "echoes our ideals."[57]

The treaty was particularly important, Ambassador Alvéstegui explained, because the MNR exiles, with "systematic perversity," were attempting to poison Perón's government and the Argentine people against the new junta. Indeed, the Peronist press, which still claimed Assistant Secretary Braden had engineered the 21 July revolution, launched "crude and slanderous" assaults upon the junta almost daily. This, Alvéstegui claimed, created an "atmosphere of distrust and suspicion" that the junta could ill afford at this "exceptionally delicate and difficult" time—especially since Perón's economic centralization allowed his government to "undertake works of extraordinary breadth and sustain without vacillation a defiant foreign policy." In addition to acquiring leverage against the Reconstruction Finance Corporation and securing badly needed financial support for development projects, the junta was buying Argentine neutrality in its battle with the MNR and discouraging any peronistas who might have openly or clandestinely backed Paz Estenssoro's revolutionary ambitions. For this reason alone, Ambassador Martínez Vargas believed, the treaty "should substantially improve the domestic situation."[58]

Nevertheless, the pact did put Martínez Vargas "on the spot" by forcing him to reopen discussions for twelve thousand tons of Bolivian tin, instead of the twenty thousand tons the RFC expected. The State Department and the RFC had not been concerned in January, when it appeared the Argentines were only seeking minimal purchases; as Espy then declared: "Under *no* circumstances need a higher Argentine offer for a small quantity be taken into account in determining our offer."⁵⁹ Suddenly, however, Truman's government, which had only a week before believed that "we can afford to outwait" the Bolivians "for an indefinite period of time," recognized its error. Not only was the RFC "doing immense harm to the Good Neighbor policy," but it was also allowing Argentina to make "political capital for herself" at the expense of the United States.⁶⁰ Furthermore, it had driven the Bolivians closer to entering into a customs union with Perón—the very thing Villarroel had been accused of seeking. Now certain that "Argentina is not bluffing and is pursuing political motives inimical to us" and that, in Ambassador Flack's words, Bolivians "with few exceptions" were now "convinced" that the treaty offered the "best promise" for their nation's future, Assistant Secretary Braden's underlings pressed the RFC to settle with the Bolivians immediately.⁶¹

Ambassador Martínez Vargas quickly seized the initiative and promised that if the Reconstruction Finance Corporation would match the Argentine offer, he would work to reduce the amount of tin sold to Argentina to five thousand tons. The RFC reluctantly complied, understanding that there was "little purpose in attempting to hold the Bolivian Ambassador to the seventy-four-cent price." Nonetheless, Martínez Vargas remained cautious. Despite his victory, he feared that Bolivia's sale to Argentina and the "alarm it produced in the Secretary of State" would "cause us serious difficulties" in the long run. At worst, it might even jeopardize the continuing operation of the Texas City smelter, which needed large quantities of Bolivian tin to stay financially viable. The most the Bolivian government could promise was that, should the higher price stimulate production, all excess would be sold to the United States.⁶²

While hoping that the amount of tin concentrates sold to Argentina might be reduced later, Ambassador Martínez Vargas confidentially promised the State Department he would work to have at least one-half of the Argentine share taken from Patiño's sales to Great Britain. When, however, over Hochschild's objection, the tin barons and the Bolivian government settled on a price of 76¢ per pound, State Department officer Espy summed up this turn of events succinctly: "The price was increased 9 cents over last year's contract to meet the higher offer of Argentina." If there was any silver lining to the negotiations, it could be found in the Bolivian assertion that, at that price, the tin barons could be expected to produce at least forty thousand tons of tin concentrates per year until at least 1951.⁶³

In the end, the tin contract of 1947 must be seen as a defeat for the State Department. The Truman administration, which had been calling for the dismantling of trade barriers, had spent three months attempting and ultimately failing to exploit an "Anglo-American purchasing cartel" to the detriment of the Bolivian producers and government. Ill will on both sides was inevitable as a result of such acrimonious dealings. In June, Director of Mines Canedo Reyes published his report on the episode, entitled "The Battle of Tin." He apologized for his "quite strong" denunciations "of various situations and persons in the United States" and eventually requested that U.S. diplomats "help him eliminate anything that might contain anti-American feelings" from the report. His account was widely circulated, appearing in Aramayo's *La Razón* in serial form.[64]

Even though the Truman administration and the junta had every reason for diplomatic cooperation and harmony, the RFC's handling of the tin contract was poisoning relations and allowing Perón to earn "political capital" in Bolivia. Ambassador Flack had believed that, with Villarroel's fall, the prospect of an Argentine-Bolivian entente was "ancient history," but the RFC had, in effect, done all it could to drive the new government into Perón's arms. Flack was incensed that Perón had received "the credit for a spontaneous friendly and cooperative attitude toward the Bolivian government in the minds of the public," whereas the junta's true benefactors in Washington were almost universally criticized. Flack was certain that the RFC had engineered a "detour" in State Department efforts to aid the new government and managed to "abridge the execution of our policy for a considerable time, long enough to impair our relations with Bolivia" and "encourage the penetration of Argentine interests."[65]

"If the junta had not conducted itself" as well as it had, Ambassador Flack would write in his eloquent postmortem, Bolivian democracy "would not have withstood" the crises to come. It had acted to "hold the country together" after the revolution of 21 July 1946, it had presided over "honest elections providing for a permanent government," and, in short, it had performed "essential work" not "brilliantly, as it is not competent either to confront or solve outstanding basic problems, but satisfactorily." Indeed, composed of "business and professional men who out of a high sense of patriotic duty consented with reluctance to serve their country," the junta had not done badly. Unable to rely upon the army (which needed reorganization) and desperately afraid of "another Catavi incident," it had been forced to use a relatively light hand to restore order and had done so "satisfactorily."[66]

That said, the greatest threat to the junta came not from the MNR and Peronists in Buenos Aires, but from the Reconstruction Finance Corporation in Washington. In less than a month, the RFC had managed to transform Bolivian hostility toward Argentina into an extraordinarily broad and comprehensive treaty that would, if implemented, forge permanent links between the two nations. In its zeal for frugality and its willingness to exploit its dominant position, the RFC was jeopardizing the State Department's program to contain Peronist nationalism in South America. The Bolivians had artfully wielded a "weapon of the weak" to secure a victory, but their Argentine gamble would not pay off a second time and would have consequences.

3

HERTZOG

March 1947–May 1949

It seems to me the Department should not toss aside too lightly the grave misgivings expressed by the Bolivian Ambassador in regard to the attitude of the RFC. . . . If we do not at least inform the RFC of the serious concern of the Bolivian Government, and the reasons therefore, it means that the Bolivian Government through its Ambassador here approaches us on this important matter, gives us its views and arguments, requests our help, and then nothing happens except that one of us drafts a memorandum which is filed.
—Paul Daniels, 22 December 1947

It is easy to be brave when attacking a democratic government respectful of human lives. I will take no repressive measures and will let public opinion decide on 1 May.
—Enrique Hertzog, April 1949

When Enrique Hertzog Garaizábal finally assumed the presidency in March 1947, it was a cause for almost unbridled optimism in Washington. Ambassador Flack viewed Enrique Hertzog's ascension and the seating of a new Congress as nothing less than "the rebirth of democratic government" in Bolivia and a "concrete expression of the freely expressed will of the people."[1] Hertzog's Partido de la Unión Republicana Socialista articulated a moderate reform agenda that initially reunited almost all remaining major political parties in Bolivia and led to their inclusion in his first cabinet. Throughout his nearly two years in office, Hertzog attempted to establish control over the political factions within his government, to meet the demands of labor, and to repress the Movimiento Nacionalista Revolucionario. Unfortunately, he would fail almost completely in all three of these monumental tasks. Not long after he took office, the coalition he had assembled to defeat the Villarroel government and the MNR was beset by partisan wrangling, which would destroy his cabinet, paralyze Congress, and prevent the implementation of any significant program.

Still, at least on the diplomatic front, there were grounds for hope. The recently signed commercial treaty with Argentina promised significant developmental loans and credits and a guarantee of Argentine neutrality, critical to the success of the new president's campaign against the MNR. Moreover, friendly relations with the United States offered the prospect of U.S. financial support, either through loans or, more likely, an increase in the tin price, which might revitalize the industry and dramatically improve the nation's finances. But if diplomacy seemed to offer Hertzog the greatest hope, it turned out to be perhaps his greatest disappointment. The treaty with Argentina was never ratified, much less implemented, badly prejudicing Ambassador Martínez Vargas's next round of negotiations with the Reconstruction Finance Corporation. Worse yet, the State Department, despite its eagerness to support the new government, proved helpless to assist in any meaningful way.

Politics and Policies of the Hertzog Government

On 10 March 1947, a forty-nine-year-old paceño doctor with decades of government service became Bolivia's forty-eighth president with an exceptionally narrow margin of victory and no clear mandate beyond purging the nation of the MNR and the army of villarroelistas. Hertzog's PURS had won 14 of 27 seats in the Senate—the barest of absolute majorities—but only 45 of 111 seats in the Chamber of Deputies. There, in a startlingly lackluster showing, the Partido de la Izquierda Revolucionaria had won just 36 seats; and the ultra-conservative Liberal Party, 16 of the remaining 30 seats, to hold the balance of power between the two. Still, because of the fluid nature of Bolivian politics, even those numbers were not exact: individual deputies regularly switched party allegiance and "shifts from one party to another are the rule." Indeed, several deputies made no public declaration of party allegiance at all. In the end, however, the Liberals and the piristas did permit Hertzog to assume the presidency "without either overt disorders or covert sabotage."[2]

Hertzog made it clear that his all-PURS cabinet was only a stopgap measure until he could form a "Cabinet of National Conciliation." By May, the PURS, the PIR, and the Liberal Party had agreed to an acceptable formula. The PURS received five portfolios; the Liberal Party and the PIR, two each. The coalition ministers were joined by a lone independent. From Washington, it seemed clear that "unless the various elements get to squabbling among themselves, the prospects are reasonably good for a fairly stable administration." Unfortunately, the "spirit of 21 July" and the Cabinet of National Conciliation swiftly foundered on the rocks of partisan politics. Hertzog's PURS first split over whether two MNR deputies should be allowed to take their seats and whether the MNR should be permanently outlawed. Ultimately, one MNR deputy was denied a seat by a vote of 84 to 2, due to his failure to comply with military service requirements. The other was seated by a vote of 45 to 41, but his opponents blocked his taking the oath of office by withholding a quorum. Moreover, when a petty internal dispute between the local leaders and national directors of the Liberal Party caused a rift, its leadership resigned en masse, and the Liberal ministers lost whatever guidance they had.[3] As Hertzog battled with chronic poor health, his "Cabinet of National Conciliation" crumbled around him.

The final member of the coalition, the PIR, was in no better shape. Given the systematic decimation of the MNR, the PIR and José Arze, as the new president of the Senate, should have been the major beneficiaries of the coalition's victory. With an existing mass base, control of a number of unions, international recognition, and a strong presence in the mines, the PIR seemed poised to absorb the increasingly radicalized working class. But the party faced an impossible choice. If it cooperated with a government that critics routinely labeled a puppet of the rosca, it would lose the revolutionary credentials that were vital to success in the mining camps. Moreover, it would be held at least partly responsible for any antilabor activity Hertzog undertook, thereby validating MNR denunciations of "PIR-rosquismo." On the other hand, if the PIR defected from the government of "National Conciliation," it would be widely accused of betraying the 21 July revolution and, once again, suspected of supporting Communism over the national interest. Finally, if the PIR renounced the power it would wield as part of the dominant coalition to preserve its radical appeal, it might easily join the MNR as a target of both the government and the army.[4]

Early indications boded ill for Arze both as a legislative and as a party leader. April sessions of the Chamber of Deputies were regularly disrupted by spectators in the galleries. The vast majority of the catcalling was "directed against the PIR by name" and took the form of "Down with Communism!" Arze felt compelled to ask Hertzog to increase the number of guards in the Congress to at least one hundred as debate in both houses degenerated into a "series of ignominious personal charges and countercharges." With the parties and both houses in chaos, no legislation of substance reached Hertzog's desk, and, by June, the backlog of projects awaiting implementation had grown to more than five hundred.[5]

In the early days of "National Conciliation," it seemed that the PIR was trying to have its cake and eat it, too. With control of the Labor Ministry, the party could strengthen and extend its influence in the unions, but pirista leaders were clearly veering toward opposition and a more extreme leftism. José Arze and Ricardo Anaya launched a new magazine, *Camarada*, that U.S. officials believed pursued "a clear-cut anti-American communist-oriented line." *Camarada* featured articles such as "Hitler Is Dead but Truman Lives" and "Truman Wishes to Make of the Continent a Colony of North American Imperialism" as well as a commentary on Josef Stalin: "The Builder of World Peace." In stark contrast to the preelection rhetoric, the PIR organ now denounced the "tyrannical dictatorship of Wall Street" and warned that "in Bolivia, cradle of great historic precedents and tomb of ambitions, we also wait for those who try to convert us into slaves of Wall Street gold." When asked if the PIR was now Communist, Anaya's noncommittal reply, that it was not the time "to discuss whether we [are or] are not Communist," reassured no one.[6]

Expressing sympathy with the "anti-imperialistic position of democratic North America," Arze explained that the people of the United States despised the "reactionary and warlike" elements that dominated the Truman administration. At a PIR rally in Cochabamba, Anaya compared Truman's anti-Communism with Hitler's, and a pirista deputy even claimed that the FBI was "more frightful than the SS troops of Germany."[7] Apparently, by adopting an anti-U.S. line, the PIR was hoping to undo some of the damage to its radical image caused by its affiliation with Hertzog and the rosca; in the process, however, it was only confirming suspicions that it was, after all, a Communist organization. Although U.S. diplomats flatly insisted that "there is no Communist Party in Bolivia," they had to concede that the PIR agenda now "at least roughly parallels that of the Communists." The "ferocity and viciousness" of the party's rhetorical anti-Americanism caught even a number of "ardent Pirists" off guard and only exacerbated existing divisions within both the party and Hertzog's coalition. Even worse, the PIR had no success in winning mine workers away from the resourceful Juan Lechín and his Federación Sindical de Trabajadores Mineros de Bolivia. When PIR Minister of Labor Alfredo Mendizabal addressed the FSTMB in June, the miners shouted him down with "Glory to Villarroel!" and "Death to the murderers of La Paz!"[8]

Arze nonetheless pledged that he would continue to support Hertzog in the "spirit of high patriotism" so long as the president continued to implement elements of the PIR program. A strike at Catavi Siglo XX in August 1947, however, doomed PIR efforts to mold the Hertzog government into one it could support, much less dominate. When the PURS and Liberals united behind Patiño's efforts to break the strike and Hertzog declared a state of siege, the PIR was torn. Holding the Labor Ministry, it was obligated to support the government's repressive move. For piristas in the Chamber of Deputies, however, this was the last straw, and they sided with the remaining pro-MNR elements in a futile attempt to deny Hertzog the authority for the state of siege.[9] In defiance of Hertzog, PURS deputies then united with the Liberals to completely exclude piristas from the leadership positions the party's numerical strength entitled it to. Rather than come down on the wrong side of a bitter labor dispute, Arze's two ministers resigned in protest, departing the "Cabinet of National Conciliation" after only three months, and joined the opposition in the Senate and the Chamber of Deputies. The controversy climaxed when, after a particularly contentious session of Congress, a pirista shot and killed a high-ranking member of the PURS. Perhaps the most troubling sign was that the PURS deputies had gone behind Hertzog's back to exclude the PIR, and although Arze had nothing but praise for the president, neither seemed to have much control over his own partisans.[10]

Nevertheless, the municipal elections of December 1947 seemed to indicate widespread support for President Hertzog and the PURS's break with the PIR. A Liberal-PURS alliance won the bulk of the elections, and the PIR was mauled, but the MNR made a reasonably strong showing. Hertzog announced that Bolivians had, by choosing his "moderate" coalition of Liberal Party and the PURS, repudiated the extremes of the "Left or Right," the PIR, the Falange, and the MNR. He attributed the piristas' defeat at the polls to "a series of errors" and the "moderate tendency of the world to eliminate the influence of the doctrines of the extreme Left." Between "Democracy and Communism," Bolivians had made the right choice. Still, some commentators ominously suggested that the PURS's "constant hammering" of the PIR had given the MNR, now truly the only major party with a legitimate claim to the miners' support, an opening to exploit.[11]

Hertzog's PURS and the Liberals soon created a new cabinet, but it barely survived until January 1948, when petty partisanship and a "political blunder that could have been avoided by the exercise of elemental political tact" again divided the coalition. Apparently, the PURS, jockeying with the Liberals for dominance in the city of Santa Cruz, appointed a number of their partisans to key posts in the surrounding departamento in defiance of the *cruceño* minister of health, Melchor Pinto Parada. When Pinto and his three fellow Liberals withdrew from the cabinet and joined the opposition, the PURS stood alone and partisanship escalated even further.[12] Instead of recognizing that its control over the nation was slipping away and that it needed to tighten ranks, the PURS became embroiled in internecine battling among its three component parties over cabinet positions. At the end of Hertzog's first year in office, his fifth cabinet consisted of three Genuine Republicans, two Republican Socialists, two Socialists, and three independents. To complicate matters even further, dissident Socialists, unwilling to cooperate with the PURS, formed a new Socialist Party, which immediately joined the Liberals and the PIR in opposition.[13]

Warning against "unmitigated pessimism," Ambassador Flack observed that the situation, "unsatisfactory as it is at present, is fluid" and that "growing pains must be expected." He likened the embattled Bolivian government to a "not too seaworthy ship advancing slowly over a relatively calm sea." But, he reminded his superiors, this "ship of state," though not yet prepared to "weather the difficult seas which must be anticipated or the real storms which may develop," remained afloat for the time being.[14] It was clear to other U.S. officials, however, that Hertzog's government was growing "progressively weaker," with only the president's "personal prestige" holding it together. It was not that Hertzog had a "delirious following," but that he was "not blamed personally" for the many failings of his government. Perhaps his greatest asset was the business community's "unquestioned" belief in "his personal integrity and sincerity." More important, the rosca, whatever its reservations about Hertzog's approach to the labor disputes that racked the nation, understood that "any conceivable revolutionary government would have been worse than the existing one."[15] That at least ensured that the tin barons would not be financing a coup against Hertzog, as they had against past presidents.

Enrique Hertzog is probably best seen as a tentative reformer who hoped, on the one hand, to stamp out the MNR, which he genuinely saw as a totalitarian menace, and, on the other, to eliminate the worst of the tin barons' excesses and abuses, which fed radicalism. In short, he hoped to stabilize Bolivia's "liberal capitalist oligarchy" by steering a relatively moderate course that would preserve elite dominance against the threats posed by revolutionaries, on the one hand, and by reactionaries, on the other.[16]

For the first six months of his presidency, Hertzog faced an upsurge in working-class radicalism and a wave of strikes that climaxed in the Siglo XX strike of August 1947. Postwar inflation on imported necessities strained workers already subjected to some of the most brutal working conditions in the world. The miners and other workers who had come to expect the support of the Villarroel government and the expansion of social benefits (especially in the wake of the favorable tin contract) continued to demand an improvement of their lot and were therefore receptive to what the U.S. Embassy called "chronic troublemakers" and "professional agitators" like Juan Lechín. Having survived the MNR purge, Lechín's FSTMB had been the driving force behind the strike at Siglo XX, called when Antenor Patiño, heir to his father's empire, attempted to lay off a number of miners, including key union leaders. Although Patiño sought Hertzog's assistance in crushing the strike, the government did not want another Catavi Massacre and, for a time, had even handed control over the mine to the FSTMB.[17]

However, when the strike dragged on, jeopardizing government export tax revenue, and the PIR left the cabinet, Hertzog was forced to act. Although unwilling to "provoke a situation that might once again bring the country into the field of bloodshed," the president came down fully on the side of Patiño by authorizing the tin baron to shut down the mines and fire the entire labor force—in what would later be called the "white massacre"—so long as he paid full indemnity to the workers. Lechín then called for a nationwide general strike, but few answered his call. When the miners at Siglo XX were, in essence, offered an average of $250 apiece for agreeing to the elimination of the FSTMB at the Siglo XX mines, the U.S. Embassy reported, with some exaggeration, that support for Lechín "ceased to exist." But, as embassy personnel who traveled to Catavi to protect U.S. citizens would soon learn, Hertzog's government now had no authority in the mines. "Armed workers are at complete liberty to use these arms," they reported, and constituted the "only effective police" force, in open defiance of all government authority and complete contempt of the "gringo" managers. Although the "white massacre" had, in U.S. eyes at least, ended satisfactorily, and Patiño's general manager had even claimed to have been inspired by the Taft-Hartley legislation in the United States, the limits of Hertzog's authority had never been more starkly revealed.[18]

The president's handling of the Siglo XX strike nonetheless typified the approach he was compelled to take. By undermining MNR influence wherever he could but offering significant bread-and-butter reform to workers at the tin barons' expense to soften the blow, Hertzog hoped to steer a middle course that would strengthen his government. Indeed, in several areas, he enacted and implemented Villarroel's policies. Although not willing to go forward with agricultural reform, he granted industrial workers both a *prima* (profit sharing) and an *aguinaldo* (Christmas bonus) retroactive to 1945. When the railroads insisted that they had not turned a profit during 1945 and therefore owed their workers nothing, Hertzog assembled a committee to investigate that dubious claim. If the committee found that a company had indeed turned a profit, it was to pay the prima. If not, it was to pay a 12-million-boliviano "voluntary bonus" to its workers. The companies immediately agreed to pay the "voluntary bonus," reasoning that they could not afford a general strike, even though it would likely result in the ouster of Hertzog, who never looked less like the rosca's puppet or the "tool of the mining industry."[19]

Thus President Hertzog was attempting to buy a measure of labor peace, maintain wages in the face of the postwar inflationary spiral, and assuage workers who, Ambassador Flack conceded, had "never earned what would be considered a mere living wage in most countries of the world." Hertzog's government regularly acceded to workers' demands "even though," the U.S. Embassy lamented, "these were at times illegal." When Patiño closed the Araca mine, Hertzog's government demanded that he pay the workers full indemnity, even though only 50 percent was mandated by law. When Hochschild closed the San José mine in August 1947 because he could not turn a profit there, the Banco Minero essentially nationalized it and "increased production to an amazing degree," thanks to tax exemptions. Moreover, Hertzog decreed that all miners working as *pirquineros* (independent contractors) receive all social welfare benefits accorded ordinary wage earners, essentially rendering the pirqinero system obsolete. The Hertzog government granted no favors to the tin barons on the issue of foreign exchange, and by 1948, they were entitled to keep only 36.4 percent of their export revenue.[20]

Although Hertzog clearly had little compunction about soaking the tin barons, he had almost none about repressing the MNR. He attributed every disturbance or abortive indigenous uprising to Víctor Paz Estenssoro's organization and suppressed it quickly and decisively. Though determined to avoid at all costs a reprise of the 1942 Catavi Massacre, he authorized the detention of Juan Lechín several times in the course of labor disputes, and twice proclaimed a state of siege in his first year, during which hundreds of MNR members were imprisoned or exiled. He met Indian uprisings supposedly fomented by the MNR with fierce repression and a "pacification" campaign that relocated rebellious groups from the Altiplano to the Chaco lowlands. Although Hertzog was genuinely preoccupied with the threat of a MNR resurgence, his campaign against the organization was the one aspect of his program that Liberals, PURS members, and even Falangists and piristas could all support. On the other hand, James Malloy suggests that Hertzog's vocal and sometimes violent campaign against the MNR actually elevated the organization in the minds of many in the working class and created the perception that Paz Estenssoro's movimientistas were far more widespread and numerous than they actually were. In other words, every repressive step or denunciation by Hertzog strengthened the MNR's appeal and helped solidify its position as the sole true opposition to the PURS and the old order.[21] Though not entirely consistent, Hertzog's approach was neither the rudderless vacillation nor the blind subservience to the rosca that its critics claimed.

Still, having decisively defeated the FSTMB at Siglo XX but, in U.S. eyes, generally siding with workers in a number of other disputes, Hertzog managed to buy himself a rare period of relative labor peace after November 1947.[22] With the FSTMB at least temporarily cowed, labor's demands being addressed, if not fully met, and a measure of stability returning to the mining camps, Hertzog and his cabinets passed their first tests and succeeded in at least establishing a measure of control over the nation. The newfound stability Hertzog bought would, however, face an even more pressing test at the end of 1947 when the tin contract came up for renewal.

The 1948 Tin Contract

Ambassador Martínez Vargas opened discussions over the tin negotiations with a plea that the State Department avoid a "recrudescence of the difficulties that had been witnessed last winter" when the "very unsatisfactory and inconsiderate manner" and "miserly and uncooperative" attitude of the Reconstruction Finance Corporation had forced his nation to turn to Perón. The Bolivians hoped that the United States would eliminate the RFC monopoly in the summer of 1947, but the U.S. Congress, acknowledging the persistence of critical shortages, renewed the RFC mandate for another year. Moreover, the RFC showed every sign of being as intransigent as ever on every conceivable issue. Newly appointed RFC Chairman John Goodloe even turned down the ambassador's suggestion that negotiations be held in La Paz, claiming that "acceptance of the Bolivian invitation would imply a willingness" to bend on the issue of price. If there was any good news, it was that the United States would be continuing to add to its stockpile of tin and would keep the Longhorn smelter at Texas City operating for at least another year. Martínez Vargas hoped to open negotiations early so that a price could be determined before 1948, and he aimed for no less than $1.00 per pound.[23]

Aside from the Bolivian aspirations for a major price increase, there was one highly significant complication in need of immediate attention—the Treaty of Economic, Financial, and Cultural Cooperation with Argentina. Although the treaty had been drafted in December 1946 and modified heavily in March 1947, the Bolivians had consistently pressed for further modifications. Despite Miguel Miranda's request that they "not ask us for that which we cannot give you," he agreed to offer Bolivia a new public works loan in August. However, he also insisted that his government had the right to purchase twenty thousand tons of tin concentrates per year, and neither Bolivian diplomats nor an economic team sent by Hertzog could dissuade him.[24]

The impasse arose from Article 15 of the March 1947 version of the treaty, which stated that, beyond the mutually agreed eight thousand tons per year, "the Argentine Government commits itself to purchase from Bolivia up to an additional quantity of 12,000 tons per year of fine tin in concentrates which might be uncommitted by existing contracts or negotiations under way." On 9 September, Miranda's agents "suddenly put forth the contention" that Hertzog's government was "not free to sell 12,000 tons" to the United States. Moreover, they "demanded (and that is the exact term)" that Argentina be granted the right "to acquire the quantity of tin that *was customarily sold to the United Kingdom*" and informed the Bolivians "point blank" that they intended to purchase all tin concentrates but Patiño's.[25] The Argentines went even further, insisting that Bolivia was obligated to sell them twenty thousand tons per year until 1951, when it would be obligated to ship its entire tin production—all forty thousand tons—to Argentina. In the words of the new Bolivian ambassador in Buenos Aires, Gabriel Gosálvez, once the "Anglo-American buyer's monopoly passed" away, the "Argentine monopoly will remain." Article 15, Hertzog's diplomats claimed, had been included solely to protect Bolivia as "insurance" in case the RFC negotiations had broken down entirely, but the Argentine interpretation threatened to put their nation's economy "under the complete control" of Perón and Miranda.[26]

What the Argentines wanted with the entire tin production of Bolivia remains a mystery. Miranda's plans to erect a tin smelter in Argentina had not advanced appreciably in the previous year, and Bolivia's director of mines, Raúl Canedo Reyes, was convinced that they would never amount to much. Nor had Miranda made any real progress on his announced plans for Bolivian coal and iron. Canedo Reyes suspected that the Argentines were actually hoping to get the Bolivian tin processed in Great Britain and returned to Argentina until World War III broke out, when the "stockpiles of tin would be worth far more to Argentina than gold." The director of mines had not been particularly concerned over this development when it looked like Argentina would only be purchasing eight thousand tons at whatever price the United States was willing to pay.[27] If, however, there was no U.S. purchase, the Bolivians would be forced into direct negotiations with the ruthless Miranda, who had once told Bolivians to "buy wheat at today's price" or risk "death by starvation." They feared that Miranda would use his control over the Bolivian food supply to force down the price he paid the Bolivians for tin, and then resell the tin abroad at a much higher price. Perón claimed that he was merely continuing to work "loyally with Bolivia in breaking the buyer's monopoly," but Canedo Reyes interpreted his actions as calculated to reduce Bolivia to "scarcely more than a province of Argentina."[28]

President Hertzog's dilemma was clear. If the Peronists had their way, the United States would receive no Bolivian tin concentrates for the year—a circumstance that might well lead to the closing of the Texas City smelter. Moreover, maintaining the flow of tin concentrates into the United States was the only real incentive the Bolivians had to offer for the U.S. financial aid they so desperately needed. Still, ignoring the Argentine demands also carried its own risk. The Bolivian public had been "led to believe that the Argentine treaty [would] act as a 'cure-all' for all of the country's ills," and there would be "political repercussions" if that pact should "break down." If the Argentines could claim that Hertzog violated Article 15, they would likely have a "change of heart" about offering the loans, which had grown in size to nearly 800 million pesos, and Hertzog and the tin barons would be left to face a "storm of protest" from the Bolivian public. The tin barons, in particular, would be accused of "sabotaging" the treaty. For fear of the potentially devastating "political repercussions" should it "become necessary to disillusion the public at large," the Bolivian government kept the controversy a closely guarded secret—even from the RFC. Hertzog, "sincerely alarmed at the possibilities of destroying the treaty with Argentina or losing the United States as the chief customer for the country's tin production," had been stockpiling foodstuffs from other countries for a year to reduce Bolivia's economic dependence on Argentina, but these alarming possibilities threatened to make that dependency complete.[29]

For Hertzog's economists and Ambassador Martínez Vargas, the best solution was to reach an agreement with the United States before 1 January 1948, when the old U.S. contract expired and Bolivia's tin became officially "uncommitted." Unfortunately, even opening negotiations entailed some risk of alienating the Peronists: indeed, at least one Bolivian diplomat concluded that Buenos Aires could interpret this as a Bolivian attempt to abrogate the commercial treaty. Ultimately, however, the Bolivian diplomats followed Canedo Reyes's advice and simply opened negotiations with the RFC in November 1947 without consulting the Argentines. Miranda did not complain.[30]

For the RFC, it was clear that "the Bolivians were more interested in pressing their advantage in a period of scarcity" and building upon the "exorbitant terms of the 1947 contract" than in "cementing a lasting relationship" with the United States. Not surprisingly, the agency was determined to pay neither the $1.20 per pound that Hochschild wanted nor even the $1.00 that Martínez Vargas sought. Indeed, the Argentine-Bolivian treaty and the anticipated recovery of tin production in the Malay Straits allowed the RFC to take a relatively cavalier stand. Because the agency believed it was only negotiating for twelve thousand tons, just one-sixth of U.S. needs and one-seventeenth of world production, there was "no justification for the United States again, in effect," to set "the world price" through its dealings with Bolivia." Instead, for 1948, the RFC planned to allow the Ministry of Supply's negotiations with Malayan producers to do so, then follow the British lead. On the other hand, "considerable agitation" in Malaya and Great Britain's need for dollar exchange led the RFC's Jesse Johnson to anticipate that Whitehall would "undoubtedly" increase the price significantly, at the expense of British consumers. But Johnson also believed that, even if the RFC purchased no Bolivian tin in 1948, the United States would be as "well off" as it had been the year before because of the anticipated Far East rebound.[31]

The RFC's cavalier attitude boded particularly ill at a moment when Bolivian passions were running high. In yet another memorandum to the U.S. Embassy, Canedo Reyes began by asking forgiveness for the "vehemence" of his "overly antagonistic" criticisms of the RFC and reiterated that he could "do no less than be absolutely frank" with his U.S. friends. As a veteran of the tin negotiations, he was quite familiar with and hostile toward the RFC determination to keep the negotiations a "purely commercial matter" once it had closed all of the world's markets through its "strange but effective" monopoly. Although his government requested only a "narrow margin of profit necessary to avoid a progressive deterioration of production and the productive capacity of the nation," "no one would heed the seriousness of our arguments nor the anxious pleas of my country for equity and justice." Faced with a choice of an "immediate and violent death" or "a prolonged agony," the producers had no choice but to accept the RFC's "progressive strangulation" and "disgraceful and pitiful economic imperialism."[32]

The RFC, Canedo Reyes continued, was doing nothing less than dooming his nation to "suffer an unprecedented collapse in the face of Asiatic and African competition." RFC officials clearly were forcing Bolivian tin prices down during the production shortages of the postwar period but would restore the open market once Malay Straits production was "sufficient to cover their demands" and "destroy us with their low costs." It pained the director that, in the face of this "grave injustice," the RFC had pushed "his nation into the signing of the [commercial treaty] with Argentina," but this had been the only way for the Bolivians to receive "equity and justice." He concluded with a plea for the "upright and great men of the American government" to eliminate the "narrow-minded policies followed up to now by the purchasing agencies" and break the "chains which have bound" Bolivia "in a state of complete prostration." "If it happens that the United States is truly disinterested" in Bolivia's future, he wrote, "I must confess that the situation in my country at the moment appears truly desolate."[33]

State Department officers now found themselves concurring with this latest of Canedo Reyes's annual appeals. Ambassador Flack, diplomat James Espy, and Undersecretary of State Paul Daniels were especially dubious of the notion that the tin price should be determined on a "purely commercial basis," which, Daniels contended, now meant that "a monopolistic United States Government buyer in a foreign country sets as low a price as it can by taking full advantage of its strong bargaining position." Proclaiming that such behavior "is unfair to the Bolivian Government (which incidentally is a friendly one and one of the best they have had in many years)," Daniels wanted U.S. diplomats to take a hand in the upcoming negotiations.[34]

Even Espy agreed that there was "a great deal of justification for the Bolivian arguments" that their producers were "receiving the short end of the stick." For his part, Ambassador Flack declared that the highest priority was "economic cooperation to aid in maintaining the democratic institutions in Bolivia." Embassy personnel who had studied the issue closely concluded that if "Bolivian production is to go above 25,000 tons in the coming year," the price would have to be "about $1.00 per pound." Espy expressed his hope to Johnson that the RFC could "without further wrangling and undue delay" see "its way clear to agreeing to pay the Bolivians a much higher price for tin." It was, after all, "pretty hard to explain why prices for everything else in the world" were "soaring upward" in an open market. That said, State Department officers were still unwilling to "express in writing" or "go on the record as urging another agency of this government to pay an increased price for a commercial commodity for political considerations."³⁵

The Bolivians nonetheless barraged the State Department with transparent appeals for "political considerations." President Hertzog started with an anti-Communist argument he thought would play well in Cold War Washington. "Bolivia is fertile ground for Communist growth," he informed Ambassador Flack, due to the poverty, ignorance, and illiteracy of the masses. He apparently convinced Flack that a Communist revolution might occur in just six months unless Washington negotiated a major price increase for 1948. "Since we are handing out so much money in Europe to check the advance of Communism," Flack wrote, the Truman administration should base its policy in Latin America on "bolstering struggling democracies, rather than on the basis of a few cents per pound." Mauricio Hochschild tried a variation on this ploy, claiming that Iron Curtain nations were expressing interest in Bolivian tin in the hopes that this "could be used as a lever in discussions with the United States." Ambassador Martínez Vargas went further, asserting that the fate of the entire tin industry was at stake. Because of low prices, he claimed, production in the Patiño mines had fallen to less than half its usual level in May, and June promised to "be even worse." Flack may have been duped by the president's anti-Communist argument but quickly discounted the ambassador's ruse. The Patiño mines had suffered a major strike throughout most of May, and June production was "exactly the average of 1946."³⁶

Still, Martínez Vargas continued to plead his case in Washington with familiar and equally futile "moral" arguments. He asked, "What would have been the situation of the essential Allied industries during the war without the important contribution of Bolivian tin?" He reminded U.S. policy makers of the cost to his nation. To increase production, Bolivian producers had mined the richest and most accessible veins. As old equipment had deteriorated and the price of all Bolivian imports had increased, the nation's economy had grown weaker and weaker; it was now in dire straits. If Bolivia was to remain the "great tin reserve of the Americas," it required a "reasonable price" and the cooperation of the United States. Finally, Martínez Vargas pleaded for the Truman administration to honor the spirit of the International Trade Organization, which it claimed to champion, by putting an end to the RFC-CTC monopoly.³⁷

Martínez Vargas believed that production shortfalls in the Malay Straits meant that it should "be possible" to "obtain a relatively high price" for the next "two or three years." This was necessary not only to maintain the Bolivian government, but for the tin producers to "accumulate the reserves necessary" to endure the "coming depression of prices" once Asian tin production was restored. He even enlisted his old friend Spruille Braden, now retired from the State Department, to plead the Bolivian case and explain to his former colleagues "the danger with which this situation is fraught."³⁸

The ambassador eventually overplayed his hand, however. When he had quietly presented the controversy over Article 15 to the State Department in October, Espy had made it clear to the RFC that the department objected on "economic and political grounds" to any Argentine purchase of Bolivian tin, and the technocrats had agreed wholeheartedly, although U.S. diplomats feared that, for want of another market, RFC intransigence might well force the Bolivians to sell their tin concentrates to Perón.[39] Then, in early December, two days after informing Espy that the dispute over Article 15 "had cleared up and he looked for no more trouble," the ambassador requested an interview with senior State Department officials to discuss "Argentine pressure on Bolivia for an option to take all Bolivian tin." Espy reacted strongly to this latest maneuver and argued that "we should be very cautious in our attitude toward it." Even Flack believed that Martínez Vargas was "resorting to tactics in the hope of bringing pressure to bear on us" and agreed with Espy's assessment that it was "one thing for us to support on economic and political grounds Bolivia's hope to obtain from the RFC a high price for its tin"; it was "quite another" to get "mixed up in a 'squeeze play'" such as this one.[40]

Indeed, for months, the State Department had been quietly working to dissuade the Argentines from following through on their plans to purchase Bolivian tin. The department had made it clear to the British and Dutch governments that any nation that processed Argentine tin would be guilty of a violation of its commitments to the CTC and would make "effective international allocation" of tin "impossible." The Ministry of Supply informed the owners of the Capper Pass and Williams, Harvey smelters of the "delicate situation" and secured their agreement not to process tin coming from Argentina. Billiton was warned off as well and feared that acceding to an Argentine request would eventually put it in a "disadvantageous position" with the other CTC members.[41] Knowing that U.S. secretary of state Marshall considered it "undesirable from every standpoint" for the Argentines to have any hand in the Bolivian tin industry was enough to scare off the other European processors. Two Argentine officials even approached the White House, the Department of Commerce, and the Reconstruction Finance Corporation but received a predictable response.[42] The State Department thus managed to prevent the Argentines from making use of any tin they might acquire from Bolivia and, in so doing, eliminated their interest in Bolivian tin.

Ambassador Martínez Vargas was thereby denied the beneficial leverage the Argentines had once provided. Nor could he officially offer all of Bolivia's tin to the RFC. Since the RFC had agreed to negotiate for only twelve thousand tons, Johnson declared that his agency was "not justified in offering a higher price for the relatively small amount of tin that it would buy." Then, when it became clear that the Malayans were going to receive less than 90¢ per pound from the Ministry of Supply, he offered the Bolivians, not the $1.00 per pound

Martínez Vargas had asked for, but 88¢ per pound to bring them "back into the realm of realities." Despite his claims to be "most sympathetic" to the Bolivians' position, Johnson intended to pay them no more than the British were paying the Malayans.[43] The Ministry of Supply then fixed the price of tin at 88¢ per pound, making it impossible for either Malayans or Bolivians to obtain anything higher than that "unjust" and "uneconomic" price. Worse yet, the minister of supply informed Bolivian ambassador Solares that, even if Martínez Vargas could somehow get the RFC to agree to a higher price, the British would pay no more than 88¢ per pound for Patiño tin. With no leverage, Martínez Vargas saw hopes for $1.00 per pound, let alone $1.07, vanish before his eyes.[44]

Unfortunately, the ambassador had received orders to sign the new tin contract before year's end, presumably to avoid opening the door to further Argentine intrigue. On New Year's Eve, just before the old contract expired, he agreed to 90¢ per pound—2¢ higher than the price the RFC had first offered—for the next two years.[45] That the Bolivians, after less than three weeks of haggling, had accepted a price so far below what they had wanted illustrates the importance they attached to the Peronist threat. A tremendous asset in March, Miguel Miranda had become an albatross around President Hertzog's neck in December. Not surprisingly, Martínez Vargas was unable to secure a provision that would allow for renegotiating the tin price when a free market was reestablished. Instead, he contented himself with the knowledge that 90¢ per pound was "simply a basic price subject to modifications negotiated between the RFC and the producers" later. Though a significant increase over the 1947 tin contract price, the new price still did not match the pace of postwar inflation.[46]

President Hertzog's diplomats faced nearly impossible odds against a well-coordinated Anglo-American alliance dedicated to imposing its will upon his nation, but the peronistas had eliminated whatever chance they might have had. Though the State Department could console itself that the price of Bolivian tin had increased by 14¢ per pound over its 1947 level, the department had again proven helpless to assist its Bolivian allies: it had only once tried to sway the Reconstruction Finance Corporation and then only tentatively, hoping to "take the opportunity to express our views" without stepping on the toes of "the commercial operations" of the agency. For the RFC, the tin negotiations became a double victory: the agency was able to acquire not only the twelve thousand tons of tin concentrates it planned to purchase but, eventually, also the eight thousand tons allocated to Argentina.[47]

The 90¢ price was hardly a disaster for Hertzog, however. At the very least, it was enough to stimulate Bolivian production and to justify reopening the Araca and Oploca mines. Although U.S. officials feared that the "forced draft" production of "Bolivian tin over the next two years might well cause a "sudden and severe drop in output" afterward and that the Bolivian government would not take proper advantage of the momentary price increase, they soon had more immediate concerns.⁴⁸ Within months, Ambassador Martínez Vargas was denouncing the 90¢ price as "inadequate and prejudicial" not only to Bolivia but also to the restoration of the world's tin industry. Adopting a "moderate and conciliatory but firm tone," he and Foreign Minister Adolfo Costa du Rels approached Assistant Secretary of State Norman Armour and Ambassador Flack to request an increase. The State Department response was quick and decisive. Because the two nations had signed a binding contract that the Bolivian price would match that of Malay Straits tin, no adjustment was possible. Although the Bolivians were free to provide any information about their production costs, which would "of course" be most "useful for the RFC" and "always appreciated," it would not result in any "revision of the price." Rebuffed again, Martínez Vargas responded by making one final appeal to resurrect the International Tin Committee.⁴⁹

Hertzog desperately needed a victory, whether through an increase in the tin price in 1948, the restoration of the ITC, or the return to a free market before the global production shortage ended. With the support of the Nigerian and Malayan producers, the Bolivian diplomats and Hochschild himself made their appeal to the Tin Study Group for the restoration of the ITC for five years. They also sought either the establishment of a world tin price of at least $1.07 or the removal of RFC, CTC, and Ministry of Supply controls. All the producers understood that "the results depended upon the equanimity of the U.S. representatives." The delegates from Belgium, the British colonies, and Bolivia were disappointed, but not surprised, when the U.S. delegation again invoked the ITO charter and the principles of free trade to defeat the producers and defend the Combined Tin Committee's monopolistic practices.⁵⁰ State Department economist Donald Kennedy argued that the CTC and quota systems, as well as the U.S. determination to pay the "minimum price," were necessary for the U.S. defense of the Western Hemisphere. Kennedy's "intransigence" ensured the collapse of the conference after three fruitless days of debate, and the U.S. Congress's renewal of tin controls in May ensured that the Bolivians would get no relief for at least another year. The RFC did agree to increase the price of tin to 99¢ per pound in April 1948, probably to assuage incensed producers, but this was little more than a Band-Aid for Hertzog.⁵¹

Hertzog's Decline and Fall

Although Hertzog and the tin barons were able to declare a minor victory in the tin negotiations at the start of 1948, they did so quietly, having vowed to hold out for a price of $1.07 per pound. Moreover, the 14¢ increase in the tin price virtually guaranteed another round of labor disputes since workers were certain to demand their share. The new tin price, Bolivian diplomats argued, was not enough either to halt the deterioration of the mines or to provide sufficient government revenue for new programs or projects.[52] For the State Department, Hertzog's government was fast becoming a major disappointment. The president had failed "to heed what should have been obvious warning signs," although if he could "eradicate internal dissension," there was still "a chance" his government could "survive." Nevertheless, Ambassador Flack's rosy optimism had faded as Hertzog charted what looked more and more like a "highly interventionist and nationalistic" rather than a middle course, one that divided even his own coalition.[53]

Although the PURS's three parties had long battled for dominance within the coalition and had periodically broken with one another over regional issues, in mid-1948, a new schism emerged. Older, more conservative PURS members tied most closely to the tin barons and the agropastoral elite urged Hertzog to slow his modest push for reform and to take a harder line against labor. They called for a restoration of the old alliance with the Liberals against the radical forces represented by the PIR and the MNR. This plan fell victim to petty disputes that led the head of the Liberal party to proclaim that "the PURS is kicking us in the pants and expecting us to help them." Challenging the old guard in the PURS was what the State Department called a "younger, aggressive" faction committed to a "more dynamic and more progressive" reform agenda. To overcome the stagnation and stalemate in Congress, these radicals pushed for an alliance with the PIR.[54]

Unfortunately for the more progressive elements, José Arze and the PIR had taken a suicidal turn to the left that would ultimately doom the party. The PIR's rhetorical shift to demonizing the United States and praising Stalin had seemed to confirm the old suspicions that the party was indeed Communist. At least partly because of its relentless obstructionism in Congress, the PIR suffered a humiliating defeat in the municipal elections of December 1947. Although President Hertzog attributed this to the good sense and inherent conservatism of the Bolivian electorate, the State Department speculated that the PIR might simply be lying low until Arze returned from an extended trip abroad.[55]

Late in 1947, Arze had left for Europe, allegedly for medical reasons, and the State Department lost track of him for six months. Hearing rumors that Arze was forging ties with Soviet agents in Europe, the U.S. Embassy staff in La Paz requested that the department determine his exact whereabouts, lest he return to Bolivia "as a full-fledged agent of Soviet Communism with orders to start an aggressive Communist campaign here." Reportedly rebuffed by French Communists, Arze apparently had more success in Rome in July, where he visited the Soviet Embassy "almost daily" and was driven around the city in an embassy vehicle.[56] Upon his return to La Paz, he used the PIR's eighth anniversary celebration to unveil his new direction. Although the PIR would not follow the Communist Party line, it "must model its political line in agreement with all the authentic Marxist parties of the world" and "continue its sympathy toward the Soviet Union," the "indisputable vanguard of the world proletariat." He now demanded nationalization of the mines, agrarian reform, "unification of the syndicalist movement," and a policy of strict opposition to the MNR.[57]

Although Ambassador Martínez Vargas insisted that the piristas' new attacks on U.S. imperialism and their open support for the Soviet Union were "purely for propaganda purposes in Bolivia" and that Arze was "at heart a friend of" the United States, this did little to reassure U.S. diplomats, who feared that the PIR leader had returned to La Paz "imbued with Communism" and was prepared to act as "the Communist wedge into Bolivia" if not the "Communist spearhead into central South America." Neither were they encouraged by the revelation that the Soviets had denied Arze a visa to visit Moscow. Offsetting this supposed proof that the PIR chief was "not accepted" as "one of their own" by the true Communists, Ricardo Anaya admitted in the Senate that he had ties with the Soviet Embassy in Mexico City.[58] Arze and Anaya could hardly have found a more self-destructive path for the PIR. Ambassador Flack suspected that, having been seduced by promises of Soviet aid, they were now at least "fellow travelers." Open endorsement of the Soviet Union and Communism did not play well in the staunchly Roman Catholic nation of Bolivia: potential supporters and long-standing party members alike soon found themselves ostracized. Ironically, by denying that the PIR, "whose pro-Soviet position is well known," had anything to do with the Paz Estenssoro's "pro-fascist" organization, Arze actually increased the MNR's prestige.[59]

Moreover, the publicity that Hertzog's campaign of repression gave to the MNR ensured that Paz Estenssoro's movimientistas, not the piristas, were perceived as the true standard-bearers for radical, if not revolutionary, change. Although Lechín and the FSTMB could claim at least some credit for many of the concessions that labor won, the PIR had only its obstructionism in Congress to show for itself. Espy reported that the PIR's "anti-nationalistic and anti-religious doctrines" were daily "proving to be a deterrent to its finding any large popular following" and leading the party into "disrepute." Still, President Hertzog was apparently desperate enough to open conversations with the PIR in October 1947. When the Liberals demanded too much power in exchange for reentering his government, Hertzog apparently decided that he could not alone "fight two enemies (the MNR and PIR) at once" and therefore attempted to come to an entente with Arze and the PIR. The discussions went nowhere, but the fact that the president was willing to even entertain the idea of a coalition with an open advocate for Communism clearly illustrated his desperation.[60]

Among the foremost of Hertzog's problems was the MNR's resurgence. The party had officially resumed its operations in April 1947 and had made huge strides in reconstituting itself. Lechín's FSTMB remained a potent force and, despite the abortive Siglo XX strike, had proven its ability to wrest some concessions from management in numerous actions across the country. Moreover, Paz Estenssoro was still giving orders and instructions to MNR cadres by sending coded letters from Buenos Aires. Although officially committed to coming to power through elections, according to one MNR source, cadres were signing up paceño recruits at a "rate of about twenty persons per day," purchasing arms and ammunition on the black market, and promising land reform to Altiplano Indians in exchange for their support. In the same December 1947 elections that led to the PIR's humiliation, the MNR won decisive victories in Potosí and Santa Cruz. Even though Hertzog attributed the MNR victories to "deceit," "deception," and "strong-arm methods," it was clear that a year and a half after the fall of Villarroel, the president had neither won over the working classes nor crippled the MNR.[61]

Nor could President Hertzog point to any great diplomatic victories. He had hoped to use U.S. investment in Bolivia's petroleum reserves to stimulate the economy but again suffered from his political weakness. The national petroleum company, Yacimientos Petrolíferos Fiscales Bolivianos, was actively working to drill wells in Camiri and set up a pipeline to Cochabamba, where a refinery was being built. Unfortunately, regional factionalism again manifested itself, and officials from Sucre demanded their own refinery. Both Hertzog and U.S. diplomats believed there was absolutely no justification for the project. Nonetheless, Hertzog did hope for an even more ambitious program and signed a contract with Superior Oil of California in October that would have led to far greater and broader investment in Bolivian petroleum. Unfortunately, the contract was savaged by a congressional subcommittee as a "violation of national sovereignty" and a "surrender of Bolivia's wealth to foreigners." Although the U.S. Embassy did not hold Hertzog responsible for this upwelling of nationalism, neither was it reassured by his inability to "improve the chances of congressional ratification."[62] Considering the animosity that had developed over the tin contract, it is hardly a surprise that Hertzog would not risk further inflaming nationalist sentiment through a public concession to a U.S. corporation.

With the prospects for Argentine financial assistance fading by the day, President Hertzog needed U.S. economic support more than ever. The State Department repeatedly advised Hertzog that the likelihood of Bolivia receiving Export-Import loans or other U.S. assistance hinged on the restoration of Bolivian credit through a resumption of payments on the nation's defaulted debt of $130 million. In July 1948, Hertzog's government informed Secretary of State Marshall that it was going to reach a settlement with the Foreign Bondholders' Association. The president proclaimed his desire that Bolivia no longer be considered a "deadbeat," and Secretary Marshall deemed the promised resumption of debt service to be "most satisfactory." The deal provided for the Bolivians to pay $1.5 million per year to the U.S. bondholders, but, to no one's surprise, the deadlocked Bolivian Congress could not even bring the matter to a vote.[63]

The commercial treaty with Argentina, which remained unratified, was not going to rescue President Hertzog, either. Despite almost constant negotiations, the two sides were unable to finalize the deal for a 750-million-peso loan. Not only did tin pose a problem, but so did the repayment schedule and the deterioration of the Argentine economy. As a result, for all of the fanfare and controversy that the treaty had inspired, not one centavo had flowed into Bolivia and not one ounce of tin had gone to Argentina.[64] For Hertzog, the failed treaty was a disaster on two different levels. Having weakened the Bolivian bargaining position with the United States and compelled the Bolivians to settle on a less than satisfactory price before New Year's Day, the treaty with Argentina was now dragging down what remained of the president's popularity. Initially lauded by the Bolivian public for the massive loans it promised, the still unratified treaty became a source of massive disappointment. Every day that passed without Bolivian ratification only served to heighten the growing perception that the Hertzog government and its diplomats were ineffectual, if not puppets of the rosca. The Peronists, on the other hand, could content themselves that "every day" more Bolivians declared themselves in "favor of our country," hoping that the treaty might "contribute to lifting Bolivia from the state of misery in which it lives." Hertzog had begun his presidency buoyed by twin diplomatic victories in Buenos Aires and Washington, but any goodwill he had won had dissipated in less than a year.[65]

There was little he could do to remedy it. As Bolivian and Argentine diplomats wrangled over the disposition of the loans, exchange rates, and the quantities of tin and wheat that would be exchanged, Perón grew frustrated. In mid-1948, he put forward the accusation that "foreign interests" (presumably the United States) had "secretly interfered" to sabotage his treaties with Bolivia and Chile. President Hertzog personally refuted the accusation. "My government has [been subject to] no foreign influence," he asserted, adding that it would not have yielded to such influence even if there had been any. He reminded the Argentines that he was "only awaiting the Argentine response" to the latest Bolivian proposal. Unfortunately for Perón, his former ambassador in La Paz echoed Hertzog's denial of "the presence of foreign interests."[66]

Meanwhile, Miguel Miranda had grown impatient, warning in July that "either there is a complete treaty or there is no treaty" and urging the Bolivians to cease their efforts to modify its terms. Gosálvez still believed that the treaty, when implemented, might well alleviate the "difficult economic situation of our nation and the incongruous social situation," but its implementation remained improbable.[67] By January 1949, with the total collapse of the Argentine economy, it became impossible. Economic czar Miranda was ousted, and Perón was forced to abandon the most ambitious of his plans in favor of austerity. The small hope of Argentine financial assistance evaporated entirely.[68]

Ambassador Gosálvez and President Hertzog were now forced to defend themselves against Argentine and opposition accusations that they were responsible for the failure of the treaty negotiations. The president of the Bolivian Central Bank began to publish articles in Argentine newspapers full of what Gosálvez labeled "falsehoods and insidious suggestions" blaming Hertzog's diplomats for the failure to implement the pact. Gosálvez, "for many and obvious reasons," could not "polemicize" against another member of his government, but privately he blamed both the Central Bank and the tin barons for the failure. Once hailed as promising national salvation, the would-be treaty had hurt the nation during the last tin negotiations with the RFC and was now providing Hertzog's opponents with still more ammunition to use against him. The treaty fiasco even led Espy to wonder whether Bolivian foreign policy was "insincere or merely stupid." He concluded it was "probably ... a combination of both." This was not the last setback the president would experience, but it had hurt him on all levels.[69]

By the end of 1948, Hertzog had still failed to pull his coalition partners together and found himself "unequal to precipitating a showdown with mining labor," although he had, in U.S. eyes, presided over "general tranquility and economic prosperity." Facing a series of labor disputes and an MNR-PIR effort to censure his labor minister in the Chamber of Deputies, Hertzog suggested to PURS leaders that he needed a month-long vacation from office. Although he was eventually talked out of the vacation, Ambassador Flack conjectured that the president was suffering from "complete discouragement as the result of the apparent failure of his attempts to govern the country successfully democratically." The Argentine Embassy in La Paz agreed that Hertzog was "morally tired and physically fatigued by the futile" battles he was waging.[70]

When the president declared yet another anti-MNR state of siege in October, the Liberals, "jockeying for increased party strength," suddenly reversed course and joined the piristas and movimientistas in opposing this and other policies. In what the State Department described as a "moment of rather childish petulance," Hertzog vowed to resign in protest but, at the last moment, was apparently convinced by his PURS supporters to stay on. Not that the PURS was doing him any great favors in Congress. With the Liberal Party, the PIR, and even sometimes the MNR united against them, several PURS ministers were forced to resign their posts and take seats in the Senate so the coalition could retain its majority. Hoping to achieve a dominant majority in the next election, PURS deputies refused compromises and even provoked a brawl on the floor of the Chamber of Deputies, which led to open fighting and gunplay, taking the body "to the brink of mob chaos."[71] With a hopelessly deadlocked

Congress unable to pass any meaningful legislation and Hertzog's helplessness highlighted by his resignation bluff, the PURS could not muster the strength either to implement a genuine reform program or to mount a consistent campaign against the MNR.

Oddly enough, at the height of government ineptitude, President Hertzog made what the State Department considered to be his "firmest pronouncement" and most decisive stand against the MNR by arresting and deporting fifty of its leaders. Taking advantage of a temporary ceasefire with his legislative opponents, he used the four hundredth anniversary of the founding of La Paz to denounce the "MNR-Communist radicals who were preparing to plunge the country into a bloody revolution in order to establish a dictatorship of a Soviet kind."[72] Still, despite this bold move, legislative bickering immediately resumed after the end of the holiday. Unable to control even his own party and unwilling or unable to seize dictatorial power for himself, Hertzog continued to preside over an irreconcilably divided government.

In January 1949, the president assembled his seventh, and most mediocre, cabinet, composed of all PURS members and one noteworthy independent, Guillermo "Willie" Gutiérrez, a hero of both the Chaco War and the 21 July revolution. Any hope that this appointment might halt the decline of Hertzog's prestige quickly vanished in February when the new labor minister, Fernando Loaiza Beltrán, attempted to mediate the most recent FSTMB strike in Catavi. Loaiza was forced from his hotel by miners, who dragged him into the public square chanting, "Death to Hertzog!" and "Glory to Villarroel!" Under duress, the minister allegedly proclaimed his support for the strikers. Ultimately, Lechín and other labor leaders "rescued him from the fury of the crowd," but the damage was done. The national press assailed Loaiza for his bad judgment and his "weak and undignified deportment in the face of insults to the government" and criticized the government in general for its failure to eradicate the MNR.[73]

President Hertzog characteristically placed blame for the incident on a "dozen professional agitators," but the episode epitomized his dilemma. If he sacked Loaiza, it might well infuriate labor and upset the internal balance within the PURS, but if he did not, it might well "embolden" the radicals. Forced to assemble his eighth cabinet, in desperation, he again invited the PIR to participate in his government. Arze, whose own party was disintegrating around him, flatly refused to board the sinking ship. The U.S. Embassy now saw "no signs that the Bolivian political parties and politicians have submerged party and personal ambitions and jealousies in the interest of the nation."[74]

In April 1949, President Hertzog made what turned out to be his final appeal to the United States, asking Flack to arrange a "small Marshall Plan" for Bolivia before the MNR and PIR were able to "clasp hands in a common totalitarian move" and "have the country by the throat." He raised the specter of Communism and again tried to stir U.S. fears of Peronism by providing evidence of Argentine links to the MNR. The implication was clear. If the United States did not offer immediate and significant aid, the Bolivian democratic experiment would fall prey to the dual menaces of Communism and Peronist nationalism.[75] Needless to say, this request was dismissed as the desperate ploy it was.

Hertzog's presidency unofficially ended less than a month later. At the beginning of May, new congressional elections somehow produced a major PURS victory and a stunning defeat for the piristas and the Liberals. Although Arze and Anaya retained their seats in Congress for the PIR, this election was the party's death knell, as it was for the Liberals, who failed to elect a single deputy. If the PURS had, almost by default, been the primary beneficiary of public disgust with Liberal obstructionism, the MNR could also claim victory by electing ten new deputies and a senator, most likely at the expense of the PIR. Despite the countless failures of the past two years, Hertzog had finally secured solid majorities in both houses of Congress. Apparently suffering from a medical condition aggravated by La Paz's high altitude (some twelve thousand feet above sea level), he was now determined to take the leave of absence he had sought since mid-1948. Whether the president ever intended to return is unclear, but he "temporarily" turned power over to Vice President Mamerto Urriolagoitia on 7 May 1949.[76]

Although U.S. policy makers had first viewed Enrique Hertzog's ascension as the dawning of a new and glorious era of democracy for Bolivia, by the time he left office two years later, they had become thoroughly disillusioned. The president had lacked the political acumen to hold together a fragile coalition and the decisiveness to take a bold stance. He had repressed the MNR, as the tin barons and landlords had hoped he would, but he had done so ineffectively and inconsistently. As a result, MNR strength in the mining camps and union halls had grown almost unchecked. By 1949, U.S. diplomats could barely contain their disgust at his government's failure to act and at the Congress that hamstrung him. One embassy official suggested that the time was right for an aggressive campaign against the MNR but sarcastically added that was unlikely since Hertzog's "traditional policy of procrastination, postponement and evasion appears to have worked well to date."[77]

In Hertzog's defense, temperamentally, he was far more an administrator than a leader, and Ambassador Flack credited him with presiding over a "period of relative economic general prosperity unparalleled in [Bolivian] history," characterized by "more democracy and political freedom than ever before." Nevertheless, he was completely ensnared by the larger forces around him. He could not turn back the clock and resort to the repression that the reactionary tin barons and the Liberals sought, without risking a reprise of the Catavi Massacre or the 21 July revolution. Neither could he win labor away from Juan Lechín or the MNR by acceding fully to its demands without enraging the tin barons and guaranteeing his ouster at their hands. He could not even rely on the PURS or the other traditional parties, which seemed quite content to ignore the coming storm and squander this final opportunity to preserve the essence of the old order by indulging in what Flack called their "singularly abject" "petty party wranglings and bickerings."[78] To carry off his plan to cripple the Movimiento Nacionalista Revolucionario and the Federación Sindical de Trabajadores Mineros de Bolivia through selective repression and modest but concrete reform would have required political adroitness the president simply did not have. Hertzog had hoped that a diplomatic success in either Washington or Buenos Aires might win him both the prestige to rise above the political squabbling and the funds he would need to enact any meaningful reform. Needless to say, his failure in the international arena was as complete as in the domestic one.

The State Department sought time and again to help Hertzog but failed to do so in any meaningful way. It infuriated U.S. diplomats that the Argentines had "not taken a pound of Bolivian tin" from the unimplemented treaty but still "got the credit for a spontaneous friendly and cooperative attitude." Still, on the critical issue of the tin contract, the State Department stood aside as the Reconstruction Finance Corporation imposed its will and, even worse, torpedoed the one Bolivian opportunity to rally the international community toward a resurrection of the International Tin Committee. Evidently, a producers' cartel would have been a gross violation of the principles of liberalized trade, whereas a consumers' monopoly was perfectly acceptable. President Hertzog's dalliance with Perón had won Bolivia a price increase of 2¢ per pound and promised "the Hertzog government a [new] lease on life" but at a far greater cost in the long term.[79] Even as the Partido de la Izquierda Revolucionaria finally became the Communist Party its critics had long accused it of being, U.S. policy makers did not come to Hertzog's defense, nor, on the other hand, did they express any concern when he tried to bring the PIR into his government. Instead, they understood that the PIR's open embrace of Communism would destroy it more effectively than anything they could do and that a Communist Party could not prosper in an environment where the MNR's brand of nationalism was flourishing. Unfortunately for the State Department, the MNR showed no signs of undergoing such a convenient self-destruction.

4

URRIOLAGOITIA

May 1949–June 1950

The strategic interests of this country would appear to be served fully as well if Bolivian tin remains in the ground as if mine production is maintained.
—*Willard Barber, 9 March 1950*

A collapse of the tin industry, which supplies about 70 percent of Bolivian foreign exchange receipts and accounts for roughly half of government revenues, supporting directly or indirectly about one third of the population, would of necessity result in economic and financial chaos, probably ending in violent political and social upheaval. . . . In addition, our general policy objectives in Bolivia would be threatened seriously since that country would be expected to become a festering sore in the heart of the continent, the subject of penetration and rivalry by its neighbors, given over to strife and violence and receptive to the spread of totalitarianism of the left and/or right.
—*Willard Barber, 10 April 1950*

On 7 May 1949, Mamerto Urriolagoitia Harriague, a Sorbonne-educated lawyer and diplomat from Sucre, became acting president as something of a mystery to many in both Bolivia and the U.S. diplomatic corps. It did not take long for U.S. officials to learn that fierce determination was his defining quality. He wore a goatee to cover the scars he had gained in battles with the opposition years earlier, and his right arm was shorter than his left—apparently the result of torture he had once endured. His approach was a far more aggressive variation on Enrique Hertzog's program of appeasing labor in general while repressing its more militant elements. Within weeks, the acting president had purged most of the leaders of the Movimiento Nacionalista Revolucionario from the mining unions and pressed forward with Herzog's tentative reforms. As the tin crisis worsened, however, Urriolagoitia's government would suffer from the same debilitating political conflicts that had paralyzed his predecessor's.

Like Hertzog, Urriolagoitia enjoyed the full support of the State Department during his first year in office, but this offered him little solace when East Asian tin production finally rebounded and the price of tin plummeted throughout that year. As Director of Mines Raúl Canedo Reyes had predicted, the Reconstruction Finance Corporation and the Ministry of Supply relaxed their price controls and permitted open competition just in time to cripple the Bolivian economy. By mid-1950, the State Department all but gave up on the efforts of the Partido de la Unión Socialista to salvage liberal constitutional oligarchy. Then, in July, just weeks after the outbreak of the Korean War, speculation and stockpiling drove the price of tin to new heights, throwing Urriolagoitia a desperately needed life preserver by saving the Bolivian economy from total collapse. This, however, turned out to be merely a reprieve.

The Civil War of 1949

Although Urriolagoitia entered office with a seemingly stable political situation and a newly united and reinvigorated PURS, he had also inherited a MNR poised to make its own bold move for power. On congressional election day, 1 May 1949, movimientistas in La Paz had staged a march and protest that had degenerated into a bloody riot, killing ten and injuring dozens. President Hertzog had managed to quell the unrest in the short term, but the long-term solution fell to Urriolagoitia, who showed himself to be more decisive from the start.

Since February 1949, Juan Lechín and the Federación Sindical de Trabajadores Mineros Bolivianos had been on strike against Antenor Patiño at Catavi, but the dispute had escalated. Miners had beaten journalists and company personnel, destroyed company property, held Hertzog's labor minister hostage for a time, and even killed two U.S. engineers. In May 1949, the government proclaimed a settlement in the miners' favor that Patiño agreed to accept so long as he could fire 20 percent of the workforce. On 27 May, as discussions were proceeding with both unions and management, Urriolagoitia made his move. He ordered the detention and exile of more than two hundred labor leaders, villarroelista ex-army officers, and other MNR militants. Foremost among these was Lechín, who was exiled to Chile. Other deportations without trial followed. For the State Department, these steps, which appeared "somewhat reprehensible" and "cannot be termed 'democratic measures,'" were "nonetheless necessary" and beneficial. As one State Department functionary explained, "the Government had no other recourse" when faced with "criminally dangerous, power-seeking labor leaders" like Lechín. Not surprisingly, violence erupted across the mining camps.[1]

Now enjoying government support and disturbed by a recent decline in the price of tin, Patiño refused to implement the wage increases mandated by the May 1949 settlement, and an emboldened Carlos Aramayo took the opportunity to cut his workforce by almost 25 percent. Mauricio Hochschild would wait until December to lay off 40 percent of his workforce at the Unificada mine, when the International Mining Company would close its Tunapaca mine altogether, laying off another 210 workers. In July, Urriolagoitia launched a campaign to limit labor unrest through a further crackdown on union militancy, a six-month wage freeze, and the registration and investigation of unions. Unions accepted their "new circumstances in a surprisingly resigned manner," the U.S. Embassy reported, probably because of the earlier repression and the removal of firebrands like Lechín. The president matched his repression, however, with a new burst of social legislation, including a tax of one cent per pound on tin for social security, a paid maternity leave program, and pension increases for railroad workers.[2]

Neither Urriolagoitia's repression nor his social reforms deterred the MNR from rallying its forces for a new and far wider uprising, however. On 27 August 1949, MNR militias rose up in the major cities and immediately seized control of Santa Cruz and Camiri. The government, somehow forewarned, suppressed the La Paz outbreak with ease, but lost ground quickly elsewhere. In Cochabamba, two hundred government soldiers and part of the air force joined the MNR, depriving Urriolagoitia of most of his air power and at least raising the prospect that Víctor Paz Estenssoro and other MNR leaders might return to the country by air. Fortunately for Urriolagoitia, what remained of the Partido de la Izquierda Revolucionaria stayed out of the struggle. The MNR and PIR had periodically collaborated to impede the PURS in Congress; in early August, the two parties had reportedly agreed to "fight together against the imperialism and privileged interests." When, however, rebels in Potosí had hanged two prominent piristas (including the ex-mayor) to avenge an old wrong, José Arze had declared his party's neutrality in the conflict. As battles raged across the Altiplano, the government could get no word from its troops in Sucre.[3]

Urriolagoitia quickly rallied his military and diplomatic forces against what he called a "totalitarian, antidemocratic, and anti-Bolivian" revolution. On the day of the uprising, he asked that Paz Estenssoro, deported to Uruguay a month earlier, and his fellow MNR leaders be placed under surveillance to prevent their return to Bolivia. Uruguayan President Luis Batlle Berres gladly isolated the MNR leaders and agreed to support any "suggestion proposed to [the] Democratic Governments of America to collaborate with the Bolivian Government to defend it in its cruel struggle," tacitly endorsing open U.S. involvement. For his part, Chilean President Gabriel González Videla ordered the exiled Lechín to report to the police daily to prevent his taking a hand in the revolt and even contemplated relocating the FSTMB leader to Patagonia to deny him access to the border with Bolivia. In Peru, General Manuel Odría, theoretically an ally of Juan Perón at the time, proclaimed a "hands-off" policy, which was probably the best Urriolagoitia could hope for.[4] The Bolivian president's best prospects for material aid, however, were in Washington.

Urriolagoitia summoned James Espy, now U.S. chargé in La Paz, and presented him with two urgent requests. The rebels had managed to capture ten of the nation's twenty-one transport planes and had used them to bomb La Paz and to move their troops around the nation. To counter the rebel advantage, Urriolagoitia asked that the United States lend his government warplanes attached to the U.S. air mission in Bolivia to transport oil and gasoline, if not troops. The use of U.S. warplanes, even for transport, would have introduced an element of U.S. "imperialism" into the conflict that might have cost Urriolagoitia dearly. Espy had neither the authority nor any inclination to approve such a blatant and potentially disastrous intervention and "strongly" urged Secretary of State Dean Acheson to turn the president down. Acheson concurred and ordered Espy to formally refuse the request.[5]

Urriolagoitia's second request was even more problematic. The president asked that the United States immediately transfer "ten fighter planes and ten bombers" to his government, although Ambassador Ricardo Martínez Vargas later explained to Secretary Acheson that any warplanes at all would be of "inestimable value." Because Bolivia had not yet ratified the Rio de Janeiro Inter-American Defense Treaty (at least in part due to the enmity that developed between Bolivia and the United States during the last several tin contract negotiations), Espy explained that "there was no legal authority for the transfer of such equipment."[6] Urriolagoitia asked Espy to pursue the matter nonetheless. Secretary Acheson again refused but informed the Bolivian ambassador that the State Department "would do all it [could]" to assist his government. Ambassador Martínez Vargas took up the cause with his usual vigor, arguing that, if he returned to Bolivia empty-handed, the rebellion would be strengthened: "The rebels would no doubt make much of the fact" that his government "could not get from the United States the necessary backing and material aid." The ambassador concluded by saying that "the promises of United States support and [Secretary Acheson's] own assurances ... would be meaningless" if he could not secure U.S. military aid.[7]

Because the matter was considered an internal Bolivian one, the State Department was obligated to remain neutral. Urriolagoitia and his diplomats therefore attempted to persuade Washington that this uprising was in fact an international conflict inspired by Perón as part of an "overall scheme of Argentina to dominate South America." Martínez Vargas worked his way up the State Department's hierarchy "expounding" the thesis that the MNR was actually the cat's-paw of "Argentina and international communists" in their "plot to embroil all of South America." How, the Bolivians asked, could the MNR have massed seventy armed men in Quiaca on the Argentine border with Bolivia without the Peronists' knowledge or assistance? Where else could the MNR have obtained weapons bearing the "official Argentine seal" or the money to fund such a well-coordinated revolt? The U.S. Embassy did suspect that arms had been smuggled in from Argentina through private channels but found no evidence that Perón's government had played any role.[8]

Ambassador Martínez Vargas was not alone in accusing Argentina of intrigue against Bolivia. According to U.S. ambassador Claude Bowers in Chile, "all public men with whom I have conversed" have "no doubt whatsoever that events in Bolivia have been inspired and supported from Argentina." Indeed, when Urriolagoitia had requested warplanes from Chile, in declining his request, González Videla had told him that any overt Chilean aid would only "be seized upon by Perón" as a pretext to send his own planes to the Bolivian rebels. The Chilean ambassador in Washington met with Secretary Acheson to officially inform him of the Bolivian request for aid and to ask "very bluntly" what the United States was planning to do about the MNR and its supposed Argentine patrons. The Chilean ambassador in La Paz claimed to possess "documentary proof" of Argentine involvement but would not produce it because President Urriolagoitia feared that it might "bring an open intensification" of Argentine involvement. The Chileans had "no evidence which could be submitted to a court" but "forecast gloomily" that, unless Washington acted, "Communists" would triumph in Bolivia, if not all of South America.[9] Sensing the escalation of the Cold War in Asia and Europe, Urriolagoitia and his allies were attempting to capitalize on U.S. anti-Communism, but their transparent efforts fooled no one in Washington.

When State Department officers discussed the issue with Perón in Buenos Aires in the presence of Bolivian ambassador Gabriel Gosálvez, they found "Argentina's Number One Worker" "vehemently" resentful of being cast in the "role of whipping boy." According to Gosálvez, rebels in Santa Cruz had announced that they would be receiving Argentine planes, weapons, and ammunition, and other MNR factions were "trying to impress the popular masses by invoking the name of Argentina, and at times, Perón himself." Perón agreed to stiffen security at border crossings and airports; his frontier police had already stopped at least one "movimientista column" from crossing into Bolivia. He pointed out, however, that he had been blamed for every disturbance in South America for the past five years and could hardly control what revolutionaries in other countries said. Even though U.S. diplomats denied the existence of a Bolivian-Chilean campaign against him, Perón warned that he "might be forced to take measures" and "adopt more severe arrangements" (which had already been "conceived and planned") if the governments of these nations and Uruguay continued their "bad faith" campaign against him. The State Department conceded that "at this point," there was "little basis" to prove Perón's "complicity" with the MNR.[10] As Assistant Secretary of State Edward Miller told the Argentine ambassador in Washington: the United States had found "no evidence of any Argentine activity in support of the Bolivian revolutionaries." One State Department officer noted that Perón appeared to be guilty only of using "surveillance almost as loose as that in the U.S. on exiles from other countries" and wryly suggested that if Urriolagoitia kept sending his opponents into exile, he should expect plotting from outside the country.[11]

This did not, of course, stop Ambassador Martínez Vargas from presenting his case directly to President Truman. When the president invoked the Good Neighbor principle of nonintervention, the ambassador responded by likening Bolivia's situation to that of Greece; he warned that Argentine "money, war matériel, propaganda, and other measures" were as "dangerous as an armed invasion." Truman "made no commitment at all" other than "moral support." Indeed, he chose to address the Bolivian civil war only indirectly, through a press release issued on 9 September at the weekly State Department press conference: the United States could not "fail to be disturbed when a minority political group in any country attempts by force of arms to overthrow a government which has gained its right to authority through a genuine elective process."[12]

This vague statement actually reflected careful consideration. Anything more specific would be construed as intervention in the internal affairs of Bolivia, and "anti-American interests" would "be likely to seize upon such statements for propaganda purposes." Furthermore, supporting Urriolagoitia "might be regarded as a precedent" that could prove embarrassing in the future and force the State Department into taking sides in future conflicts across the hemisphere. Indeed, specific comments and statements had to be avoided at all costs, lest the presence or absence of a U.S. statement become expected or embroil the State Department in difficult conflicts.[13] Any government in South America besieged by revolutionaries would come to expect verbal U.S. support and would denounce the United States if none was forthcoming. Much as the State Department dreaded an MNR victory, it was not willing to set a dangerous precedent that would have ramifications across the hemisphere for years.

Even when told that Sucre had fallen to a band of MNR rebels, the State Department refused to rise to the bait, ultimately concluding, as Chargé Espy did, that Urriolagoitia and the Chileans were employing "deliberate tendentious exaggeration of reports" designed to induce Washington to "come forward with further political and economic assistance." Although State Department officers had "no information" substantiating the Bolivian claims of Argentine interference, they admitted, however, that "it is sometimes difficult to refute the Bolivian arguments." After meeting with the fourth "special emissary" from

Urriolagoitia, and put off by "the kind of tactics" the Bolivians were now employing, Assistant Secretary Miller told Ambassador Martínez Vargas that "we have already done as much as we possibly can to help" and that the United States resented having Bolivian "cooperation with us conditioned upon additional cooperation from us."[14]

Unconvinced of any Argentine involvement, the State Department still hoped for a government victory and was willing to expedite export licenses for Bolivian weapon purchases from private suppliers in the United States, in particular, AT-6 aircraft from the North American Aviation Corporation and machine guns and ammunition from Colt and Remington. Although the U.S. government would not provide the Bolivians with credits to buy the planes, Ambassador Martínez Vargas was confident that his government had the money for any necessary purchases. By 6 September, Bolivia had purchased eleven aircraft at a reduced cost but still had not secured the guns or ammunition it sought from Colt.[15]

As events unfolded, however, Urriolagoitia did not need either U.S. weapons or support: his government forces succeeded in breaking the back of the rebellion within weeks, although the revolt dragged on when the government failed to quickly redeploy its troops to the eastern lowlands. Once the rebels were finally defeated in late September, nearly one hundred thousand paceños turned out for a massive progovernment rally to celebrate. All told, the civil war had killed almost six hundred Bolivians, with six hundred rebels captured and imprisoned. For Urriolagoitia, the most positive sign was not only that the people of La Paz had shown their "strong support" but also that, in much of the rest of the nation, the public was "either sympathetic to the Government or indifferent." The army, by and large, had proven loyal—a testament to the success of government efforts in the previous two years in purging it of pro-MNR or villarroelista elements. Whereas President Hertzog had been loath to put the army to the test, in Chargé Espy's opinion, the army was now the trusted "backbone" of President Urriolagoitia's regime. The State Department found it most encouraging that both Urriolagoitia and the army had "emerged from the [civil war] with enhanced prestige and strength."[16]

Perhaps the most surprising aspect of the revolt was the "general apathy of the individual miner" and the rebels' failure to rally him to the MNR cause. Chargé Espy offered several possible explanations. First, the exile of prominent MNR leaders like Lechín had deprived the MNR of much of its ability to organize effectively in the mining camps. Second, fearful of any "adverse publicity" that would be generated by the "murdering and torturing of foreigners," the MNR had made "every effort in their propaganda to hold down violence" that might endanger recognition and popular support should the MNR emerge victorious. Third, President Hertzog's labor policies had most likely also played a role in ensuring workers' neutrality. And, finally, by standing aloof, the PIR had ensured the failure of the revolt. Although PIR leaders had discussed entering a "National Liberation Front" with the MNR, in the end, they had opted to "wait and see." The State Department could not have been happier to see the MNR routed at last, even if it did leave the admittedly "Communist" PIR as the sole "remaining champion of labor" with "almost a clear field to itself." Ambassador Joseph Flack, soon to be replaced, gave a final warning that Arze's PIR would now be free to "make every effort to spread its doctrine" to the indigenous masses who "can readily be influenced by able leaders." His superiors were unconcerned.[17]

Still, the revolt could hardly have turned out better for Urriolagoitia. Because the MNR's deputies and senators were ousted and replaced by PURS, Socialist, and Liberal partisans, the PIR was virtually the only opposition remaining in Congress. Moreover, the remaining MNR supporters in the army had been exposed and purged, enabling Urriolagoitia to rely far more heavily on it than Hertzog had ever dared. The new president had been transformed from a relative unknown into what Ambassador Flack hailed as "a nucleus around which a stronger future Bolivian state can be built," and as Chargé Espy put it, a "good politician," who had showed "bravery and determination." With his crackdown on labor militancy and the successful prosecution of the civil war, Urriolagoitia effectively ended Hertzog's presidency and began his own. On 22 October 1949, less than a month after the end of hostilities, Hertzog tendered his formal resignation, and Urriolagoitia was inaugurated to serve out the remainder of Hertzog's term. The uncertainty regarding Hertzog, which had caused delays in long-range plans and even in "day-to-day administrative decisions," was now at an end; Urriolagoitia had the reins of government firmly in his hands.[18]

All in all, the State Department was quite pleased with the results of the civil war. It commended Chargé Espy, in particular, for forestalling "future embarrassment and unpleasantness stemming from the Bolivian request for U.S. arms" by steadfastly opposing a step that "would have been tantamount to recognition of the belligerency of the revolutionists."[19] Moreover, the fighting had, by and large, neither spread to the mining camps nor endangered U.S. citizens, except at Cochabamba, where U.S. air mission personnel had been forced to hole up in a hotel and maintain radio silence until the threat passed. Espy believed that withholding aid had taught President Urriolagoitia and the PURS that "they would have to stand on their own" and "to take the measures that were required to meet the situation rather than to wait on us to do it for them." He also believed that the PURS needed to be shown that "the handout good times of the war period and to some extent the postwar period have come to an end."[20] Bolivians of any political stripe would have been surprised to learn there had ever been "handout good times" or any times when the United States had solved a problem for them. But worse things were yet to come.

Ambassador Martínez Vargas and the tin barons were about to learn just how ruthless the Reconstruction Finance Corporation could be.

Mamerto Urriolagoitia, Irving Florman, and the Decline of the Tin Price

Urriolagoitia had taken office just as the long-dreaded decline in the world tin price had set in. From a high of $1.03 per pound in late 1948, the price had begun to fall by May 1949 and would continue to fall in the months ahead. In the wake of the most recent devaluation of British sterling, the Ministry of Supply had unilaterally cut the price of Malay Straits tin to 95¢, and the RFC was planning to respond in kind in September. Moreover, rumors were now circulating that the British were on the verge of discontinuing their bulk purchases of tin and permitting the operation of a free, competitive market. Representatives of the Reconstruction Finance Corporation, Commerce Department, and State Department had actually been prepared to decontrol tin as early as June or July 1949 but had agreed to maintain the RFC monopoly at least until the end of the year in case the Movimiento Nacionalista Revolucionario won the civil war.[21] With Urriolagoitia firmly in the saddle, the Ministry of Supply and RFC loosened restrictions at the end of 1949 and allowed the tin exchanges in Singapore, London, and New York to reopen for the first time since the start of World War II. Although this announcement would once have been greeted with celebrations and parades in La Paz, it now heralded a financial disaster and social upheaval.

As the world price of tin fell, Bolivian production also fell, by 10 percent during 1949, and all indications were that both trends would continue. The RFC was again at the heart of Bolivian difficulties: because it would take months for private contractors to purchase and deliver any new shipments of tin from Africa, Asia, or Latin America, the agency elected to pick up the slack by disposing of the surplus tin it had accumulated throughout the year. With the world tin price at 95¢ per pound, the RFC set its selling price of tin at 96¢ "to encourage importation from private sources" and to keep the price of tin in New York significantly higher than that prevailing in the Singapore and London markets. Anticipating increased production in the Malay Straits and a corresponding decline in tin prices, the British Ministry of Supply began to dump its supplies in New York to capitalize on the opportunity and garner dollar exchange. Because RFC policy was to "follow the market down as rapidly as possible" and to encourage a "downward price trend," every time the British undersold the RFC, the agency "would then lower [its] price to the same level and thereby cause another reduction by the Ministry of Supply." The British continued to dump their surpluses until March, when the RFC announced that it would bring its selling price down to the world market level. By June, the British had depleted their holdings almost completely, and the world price of tin finally stabilized at just 78½¢ per pound after temporarily bottoming out at 73¢.[22] Although the Bolivians and other producers sought an international accord to stabilize the price in the Tin Study Group, being quite satisfied with recent developments, the State Department continued to block any move in that direction. For Ambassador Martínez Vargas, the highest priority at the 1948 Bogotá Conference had been to adopt a clause blocking "unilateral measures that limit or damage the production of raw materials," but there as well the United States had been able to stymie any effort to do so.[23]

For the tin producers, the lower prices decreased profits and forced them to close the more inefficient mines, increasing unemployment and discontent and fueling MNR recruitment. True to all predictions, in December, Mauricio Hochschild laid off 40 percent of the workforce at his largest mine, abandoned the lowest grades of tin, and reduced production by 20 percent. Although Antenor Patiño had no plans to reduce his workforce, three medium-sized mine owners announced that they would be forced to close down operations unless the government could provide some relief. If the tin barons continued to lay off their workers, this would bring an end to the relative labor peace that the PURS had worked so hard to achieve. Still, according to the State Department, unemployment among mine workers was only part of the problem. Most of the miners laid off would simply drift back to the fincas and disappear from James Malloy's "national system" altogether, as the civil war had shown. On the other hand, without the foreign exchange garnered by tin sales, industries in the cities would founder, raising unemployment among urban workers, who might then overthrow any government, as they had all too well demonstrated in the case of Villarroel. Moreover, without the tax revenue generated by tin exports, the government would be forced to reduce the civil service and cut social welfare, provoking even more discontent in the urban centers, especially in all-important La Paz. Espy predicted that any further decline in the price of tin would prompt "a complete economic collapse" that would "bring serious political disturbances in its train."[24]

By the end of 1949, the situation had deteriorated across the Altiplano. In his New Year's Eve message to the nation, President Urriolagoitia warned of the coming depression, but, "rather unfortunately" in Espy's eyes, "tempered his warning by adding that there was no cause for alarm, as the Government was taking all necessary measures to cushion the shock." It was not. Assistant Secretary Miller informed Secretary Acheson that "Bolivia can look forward to serious political and social repercussions from the existing economic chaos." The U.S. Embassy and the representatives of all three tin barons agreed wholeheartedly, expressing "extreme pessimism" and warning that "the present government is doomed" to be ousted by the military in "six months, if not earlier."[25]

Like Hertzog's before him, Urriolagoitia's government was hamstrung by wrangling within the Partido de la Unión Republicana Socialista and between it and the traditional parties. Despite majorities in both houses of Congress, the "woefully weak" leaders of the PURS proved unable to legislate effectively in 1949 and, in the words of U.S. Embassy personnel, had "done less, if possible, than the fruitless 1948 session." The economic decline was, in part, to blame. President Urriolagoitia endeavored on three separate occasions to build a "Democratic Front" that would bring the Liberals and Social Democrats back into the government but was rebuffed each time. Chargé Espy concluded that the other parties were motivated not only by their typical "petty" and "selfish" maneuvering, but also by an unwillingness to associate themselves with the impending economic collapse.[26] Urriolagoitia's failure to form an effective coalition led to a brief resurgence of the Partido de la Izquierda Revolucionaria, which won municipal elections in Potosí and Cochabamba on 27 December and forced the PURS to ride "roughshod over the civil rights of the opposition" in order to eke out a win in Santa Cruz. In February 1950, to block the opposition, PURS deputies and senators were compelled to boycott Congress and thus prevent a quorum: if they could do nothing productive to assist their government, at least, they could prevent its opponents from doing it harm during the session.[27]

When Congress attempted to reconvene later in February, many PURS deputies did not even bother to return to La Paz, guaranteeing there would be no action on any issue until at least August. Accusations of graft and torture leveled against the government distracted and divided the PURS at a moment when more than ever it needed to be united; even worse, a hunger strike among prisoners of the civil war highlighted the unsanitary conditions, brutality, and mistreatment they were forced to endure. Viewing the political paralysis of Congress and President Urriolagoitia's cabinet, Chargé Espy again pointed out that both were dominated by the "same landed and commercial interests" that had always "selfishly opposed major efforts at reform," pursued their own pet projects to the detriment of the nation, and "bickered endlessly over trivialities." The economic crisis forced Urriolagoitia into ever more frantic and counterproductive policies. When U.S. technical experts and the tin barons sought to mechanize their mines in an attempt to increase efficiency, Urriolagoitia, already nervous about the impact of his decree freezing wages for the last half of 1949 and the recent layoffs in the mines, blocked their efforts for fear of the increased unemployment that mechanization would bring.[28]

Though the State Department still held President Urriolagoitia in high regard, he clearly could not count on receiving any U.S. assistance. Indeed, a series of events during his first months in office had given rise to "an uneasy feeling of apprehension that possibly the United States cannot be relied upon." The failure of the United States to come to Urriolagoitia's aid during the civil war had provoked "disappointment, if not dissatisfaction" among many in the army and government. As Chargé Espy explained, since Urriolagoitia was "representing and upholding democracy in a life and death struggle against totalitarian dictatorial attack," his backers believed that "they had every right to appeal to us for immediate support."[29] In October 1949, Ambassador Martínez Vargas, ever the consummate diplomat, tried to smooth over the growing rift between his country and the United States by maintaining he "did not know where so many Bolivians received the false impression that the U.S. had done nothing to help them face the recent crisis," but he could not deny that many did. Urriolagoitia's special envoy to President Truman, Alberto Ostria Gutiérrez, was far more candid, frankly stating that "the U.S. had let them down in their hour of trial" during the civil war.[30]

Despite Ostria Gutiérrez's warnings that, unless Bolivia received "moral and material aid in this crucial moment," democratic government would be replaced by a "totalitarian regime," Chargé Espy argued in early February 1950 that "it is hardly conceivable that a Russian-orientated communist oasis could be set up here" and that, if indeed the PIR and Communism did triumph in Bolivia, it would only be because of a "global holocaust" so severe that "whether [they] did or not would little matter." Therefore, he went on to add, despite PIR control of several key cities, "the consensus here is that neither communism nor the PIR is to be considered a very serious danger for the moment" and there was "absolutely no justification for any financial assistance due to the threat of communism."[31]

That said, President Urriolagoitia and Ambassador Martínez Vargas were not about to abandon their anti-Communist appeals. As Espy also noted, both men knew the "international propaganda value" of taking a "strong position" against Communism. Indeed, well aware that Western Europe was receiving massive aid from Washington because of its proximity to the Soviet Union, Martínez Vargas duly reported later in February that Bolivia was now the "center of the Communist movement in South America" and that "the entire hemisphere" would be at risk unless U.S. aid was forthcoming. In March, Bolivian police raided a supposed Communist cell, arrested twenty-five people, and proclaimed that they had "smashed yet another communist plot to overthrow the Government." Fantastic rumors quickly spread like wildfire. Several claimed that either a Russian military officer or the Brazilian Communist leader Luis Prestes had organized the cell's well-advanced plans for a national revolution to unleash the "Stalinist hosts." The Chilean ambassador in La Paz predictably warned that the Communists had forged an alliance with Perón and that Urriolagoitia's fall was "imminent."[32]

Within days, however, it became clear that whatever "threat" existed had been tremendously overblown. Most of the "Communists" were high school or university students, who were handed over to university officials for punishment—hardly the expected treatment for dangerous international conspirators. Secretary Acheson and the U.S. press had picked up the story about the Soviet general, but newly appointed ambassador Irving Florman reported that the only Russian the embassy knew about in the entire nation of Bolivia was the owner of a "borscht emporium" in Cochabamba. It became clear even to Florman that Urriolagoitia was just "crying wolf." The charade was far from over, however. The police reported that the Communists had chosen Cochabamba as the site of their "headquarters" for the overthrow of the Argentine, Bolivian, Brazilian, Chilean, and Peruvian governments.[33]

Not long after receiving these reports, Ambassador Florman apparently had a radical change of heart. He now declared that a "deplorable Communist condition is developing in Bolivia" and that the Communists possessed a "cunning" and "concrete" plan to "use Bolivia as their field of operations to conquer all of the South and Central American republics," with "world-shaking repercussions." This, Florman stressed, was a threat of epic importance since a totalitarian Bolivia would then serve "as an offensive springboard for an airborne assault" on either Florida or the Panama Canal.[34] The rest of the State Department remained unconvinced, however, especially since, just days before the supposed Communist menace emerged, Ambassador Martínez Vargas had been told that "South America could expect little assistance from the U.S. unless a real threat developed there." U.S. officials, though not ignoring "the dangers to Bolivia and the continent from Communist activities," nonetheless concluded that this scare had been little more than a pretext for Martínez Vargas to make yet another plea for a "Marshall Plan for Latin America" in general and for Bolivia in particular. Desperate for any news he might turn to diplomatic advantage, President Urriolagoitia soon declared that his government had broken up two MNR conspiracies and a Communist one in less than two months. So far as the U.S. Embassy could determine, however, only the second of the MNR plots might have posed a legitimate threat, and then only a slight one. Moreover, as Chargé Espy reported, "even the anti-communist press [had begun] to complain of the constant misrepresentations and exaggerations" coming from the Palacio Quemado. Espy concluded that Urriolagoitia's rather pathetic attempts to sound an anti-Communist alarm were the result of "either naïveté, hysteria, or possibly the belief that a good communist scare may be used to obtain further economic assistance from the United States."[35]

It quickly became clear that the U.S. ambassador, a Broadway lyricist and inventor from New York, was thoroughly unqualified for his position at this critical juncture and, indeed, that his only "qualification" for the ambassadorship was a tireless loyalty to the Democratic Party in recent elections. With no diplomatic experience and no desire to follow Foreign Service protocol,

Florman began firing off some of the most bizarrely colorful dispatches in U.S. diplomatic history, often culminating in a sarcastic insult directed at the State Department or, more often, a quotation from Shakespeare, Cicero, a Broadway musical, or the Bible. Upon arriving in Bolivia (which he poetically described as a "country reeking with pestilence and populated with helplessly poor people, brutal overlords and shrieking beasts"), he concluded that paying more for tin and thereby "making the tin barons richer is materialistic emotionalism" that would be "palpably absurd." Although Martínez Vargas had first believed that having an old and trusted friend of President Truman as ambassador would benefit his nation and that Florman would become a "good friend of Bolivia," that belief was quickly shattered.[36]

The new U.S. ambassador despised the rosca, whom he blamed for the "poverty, imbecility, and injustice which now pervade the natives," who would "stop being human vegetables and turn into skeletons" if they were left at the mercy of the tin barons. Therefore, even if the price of tin was to "skyrocket," it would do the country and its populace no good, for the "triumvirate" with its army of "lobbyists, stooges, and other mercantile subversive elements" constituted nothing less than the "largest international racket that has ever been formed in human history." Florman nonetheless lionized President Urriolagoitia as a "resolute, unshrinking, firm of purpose, honest, admirable" leader who had defied the tin barons' "astonishingly successful" "criminal shenanigans."[37] Florman's solution for Bolivia's ills was "a special treatment of social, economic, and political hormones,'" which would "result in a physiological and therapeutic healing and rejuvenating process that will pleasantly surprise the Department and the world in general." If that was not feasible, he suggested that the importation of "carloads" of chewing gum might at least wean Bolivians away from coca chewing.[38]

Though President Urriolagoitia had Ambassador Florman's confidence and backing, he quickly lost that of the tin barons. In April 1950, he decreed that virtually all of their foreign exchange was to be handed over to the government. The decline in the price of tin had reduced government revenue by more than half during 1949, and officials insisted that complete surrender of foreign exchange was the only possible means to salvage government finances. With this one move, the president almost irrevocably "alienated the mining interests" and the newspapers they controlled. Only Carlos Aramayo and his *La Razón* remained committed to Urriolagoitia, terrified of who might succeed him if he fell. Antenor Patiño's minions immediately proclaimed the decree "unworkable" but hoped to hammer out a compromise with the government before "a more unsympathetic and vindictive group" came "into power." Florman's reaction was predictable and furious. He denounced the tin barons, "who consider themselves above the law of the land and show it with their barefaced hostility" and who "prostrate themselves with mythological grievances [and] with a mounting chorus of vilifications against their government."[39] The tin barons managed to delay implementation of the decree, but the president had made dangerous enemies.

The economic crisis was destroying President Urriolagoitia's government before his eyes. Not only had it provoked him into alienating the tin barons, but it was also costing him his credibility and authority among his supporters and the public at large. In May 1950, his ministers of government and labor went behind his back to settle a labor dispute in La Paz, essentially "double-crossing" him. Workers in La Paz, facing inflation and the wage freeze, had predictably demanded raises. When Urriolagoitia refused, the two ministers had defiantly raised wages and forced the president to demand their resignations. Unable to find competent and loyal civilians even within the PURS, he appointed a colonel and a general to their posts. Because runaway inflation continued unchecked and even Chargé Espy conceded that workers were "unquestionably justified in seeking increased wages," the appointment of reactionary, possibly incompetent, military officers to key posts virtually guaranteed labor strife in the pivotal arena of La Paz.[40]

Apparently emboldened by what Chargé Espy called President Urriolagoitia's "spineless appeasement of labor" and "vacillation," a pro-MNR "Coordination Committee" threatened a general strike unless wages were increased by 60 percent, all political prisoners were freed, and all exiles were allowed to return. When students rioted and burned the offices of *La Razón* and *Tribuna*, the president ordered the arrest of the "Coordination Committee," branding them "Communists." For the State Department, it was clear that Urriolagoitia "now stands alone" and that only his "strong and dignified bearing" was holding back the "disintegration of the situation." However dignified that bearing, the president's transparent efforts to blame the strike first on "Communism" generally and later on a "Communist-MNR alliance" showed how desperate he was. Eerily, the last days of Villarroel seemed to be playing out again; in May, Espy reported that Urriolagoitia's administration "may well be nearing its end."[41]

If the most dramatic episode was an "absurd," if not "comic-opera" coup attempt by several Falangist officers and three hundred cadets in July 1950, then a student strike in August was the most volatile. Demanding amnesty for political prisoners, La Paz students mounted machine guns on university buildings, marched on the Plaza Murillo in force, and even shot several police officers. Ambassador Florman attributed the upheaval to a laundry list of MNR, PIR, Communist, Trotskyite, and Falangist "demagogues" and believed that "the lightning is so close that it may strike at any moment and there are no lightning rods." Asserting that "narrow-minded fanatics" and "subversive, tyrannical hypocrites" were on the verge of ousting Urriolagoitia and igniting a "destructive conflagration beyond Bolivia's borders," he vaguely requested "spiritual assistance" from his superiors.[42] Although President Urriolagoitia had "at first used kid gloves, not wanting to make martyrs," he tossed them aside when the president of the Senate, Waldo Belmonte Pool, was crippled by machine gun fire, issuing a stern ultimatum that ended the strike and led to the surrender of 80 students and about 120 "professional thugs."[43]

The strike had, as others before it, a palpably anti-U.S. cast to it. On 21 August 1950, a large group of students had approached the U.S.-run Centro Cultural Boliviano-Americano shouting, "Down with Yankee imperialism!" Strike leaders had entered and "courteously" demanded the closure of the building and cancellation of classes, threatening to damage the facility if their demands were not met or if the police were called. The director had complied, and the U.S. Embassy, fearing the spread of anti-U.S. sentiment, had recommended that the tin companies evacuate the families of their U.S. employees. Secretary Acheson, "loath to yield to the pressure of anti-American minorities in Bolivia or elsewhere," had simply called for heightened security.[44]

Declaring, on the one hand, that Bolivia was "creeping to a precarious explosion," Ambassador Florman was nevertheless confident, on the other, that there had never been "such friendship from the Bolivians" toward the United States as there was at that moment. He was equally confident that this amity was all of his doing. "I reached the hearts of the innkeeper and the tailor and the miner and the priest and the farmer and the Indian and the soldier," he proclaimed, but then warned that "without immediate assistance in kind (not dollars), we will unwittingly shake the foundation of a nation and of all the good will the Ambassador has built here." Just a day after warning of a "precarious explosion," the mercurial Florman announced that "the Bolivian sordid past is in the background" and that the nation faced a "brilliant future" in which "bachelors and newlyweds in the United States will continue to enjoy life with a minimum of effort by using Bolivian tin–lined canned spaghetti with meatballs, Campbell's tomato soup and Portuguese sardines."[45] The 1950 tin negotiations would reveal a harsher reality, however: U.S.-Bolivian relations had never been worse, and Washington was not inclined to provide assistance of any kind.

The 1950 Tin Contract

As the price of tin plummeted throughout 1949 and economic chaos gripped Bolivia, President Urriolagoitia grasped at the last straw available to him, the tin contract to be renegotiated at the beginning of 1950. Ambassador Martínez Vargas's opening discussions with the Reconstruction Finance Corporation boded ill. Because the RFC now permitted private importation and natural market fluctuations, the agency would be purchasing only the quantities necessary for government use, to maintain the tin stockpile, and to supply the Longhorn smelter in Texas City. Although Ambassador Martínez Vargas was instructed to request a restoration of the 99¢ price and a decrease in Texas City smelting costs, an unsympathetic RFC announced that it was going to demand higher smelting fees.[46] All of the pieces were in place for another protracted and bitter negotiation.

The State Department understood all too well that the "long-term tin situation from Bolivia's standpoint looks bleak" and that the United States alone was to blame for keeping what controls remained in place. The Combined Tin Committee, which every producing nation now wished to disband, continued to operate, limiting Bolivian options. U.S. planners favored retention of the CTC to keep the Soviet Union from acquiring anything more than insignificant quantities of black market Asian tin and to prevent a return to "the extreme prices that would otherwise have prevailed in the past few years." Though U.S. diplomats expressed a "keen interest in Bolivian economic progress," they asserted that it was "too late" to argue for a free market, although they conceded that "this might have been done with considerable advantage to Bolivia about a year ago." U.S. stockpiling would bolster demand for a time, but the increase in the world supply meant that "prices in the future might well be considerably below current quotations."[47]

Even worse, the Reconstruction Finance Corporation was planning a new offensive. In July 1949, RFC officers acting at the behest of Patiño's general counsel, Alexander Royce, compiled a two-page list of new taxes that Hertzog had imposed on the tin industry in violation of the 1947 tin contract. RFC Chairman Harley Hise expressed "serious misgivings" about this "disregard for the quoted contractual commitment of the Bolivian government" and asked Secretary Acheson to "vigorously and promptly" bring the matter to "the attention of the Government of Bolivia."[48] Apparently, President Urriolagoitia had demanded five hundred thousand dollars from Patiño to help defray the costs of defeating the movimientistas during the civil war, and the tin baron's company was now "coming to the end of its rope." Patiño claimed that it was currently losing 3¢ per pound of exported tin and would soon be losing 8¢ per pound. With that in mind, Royce proposed that the United States exert direct pressure on the Bolivian government. Because Patiño's company was incorporated in Delaware, Royce argued that the State Department was obligated to protect it.[49] At the very moment the State Department was looking for a way to salvage the Bolivian political economy, Patiño and the RFC were urging it to court disaster by intervening directly in Bolivia's internal affairs. Government revenue had been so low that Urriolagoitia had risked openly challenging the tin barons in April, and now Patiño and the RFC sought to reduce that revenue even further.

The State Department refused to take up the gauntlet. Economic expert Willard Thorp argued that a "vigorous protest to another government" must be "based on indisputable grounds." He deftly sidestepped Chairman Hise by asserting that "further analysis is needed" and suggested a meeting between State and RFC officials to discuss the issue. Deaf to Patiño's protests, President Urriolagoitia announced a new tax of 2¢ per pound on the tin producers to finance the Cochabamba–Santa Cruz highway and the La Paz–Beni railroad in December.[50] Although the State Department was willing to stand against the tin barons and the RFC on this matter, the upcoming tin contract negotiations were for much higher stakes.

Martínez Vargas's dream of 99¢ per pound had died stillborn when the world price of tin had dropped to 78¢ a pound. The tin barons cut off shipments in the hopes of reacquiring some leverage, while Director Canedo Reyes and Ambassador Martínez Vargas launched a new barrage of eloquent appeals. Canedo Reyes argued that Bolivia was owed "preferential treatment" for its wartime sacrifices as well as compensation for the $150 million in profit that the RFC had robbed from his government in the postwar period. He expressed his confidence that Bolivia would receive "equitable treatment" because the "greatness of the United States is not only material but moral."[51] Martínez Vargas presented Assistant Secretary Miller with a detailed memorandum outlining what State Department functionaries called "the time-worn arguments that the U.S. held down the price of tin unfairly during the war and postwar years while the cost of machinery, equipment, foodstuffs, and manufactured articles Bolivia imported from the U.S. rose precipitously." The ambassador further blamed the United States for assisting in the restoration of Malay Straits tin production because Marshall Plan credits to Belgium, Holland, and Great Britain had allowed these nations to rebuild more rapidly, to Bolivia's detriment. In short, due to the "profound repercussions" of the "closing of the free market," the "very life of Bolivia was threatened."[52]

Although Assistant Secretary Miller conceded that President Urriolagoitia's government was "earnestly endeavoring to follow democratic procedures" and was perhaps as "good a Government as could be expected under the circumstances," the State Department cast diplomatic niceties aside when it responded to the Bolivians. One officer advised Ambassador Martínez Vargas not to "over-emphasize his argument that Bolivia had made great sacrifices during the war, as they could not be compared to the cost of war in lives and property to the nations which participated actively in military operations against the totalitarian forces."[53] Even the U.S. Embassy staff, ordinarily the Bolivians' best ally, was indignant, pointing out that "Bolivia was protected from Nazism without sacrificing a single soldier" or spending "one boliviano." Labeling Canedo Reyes a "strong spokesman" for "a certain sector of Bolivian opinion which either believes or finds it to its bargaining advantage" to mention a U.S. "moral obligation" to "subsidize the Bolivian tin industry," embassy officials sharply noted that the tin barons had quite likely made "the richest profits in their history during the war and immediate postwar years."⁵⁴ The Bolivians were going to get no support from the State Department this time.

Far from it. The department had approached the Munitions Board and the National Strategic Resources Board to determine whether there was indeed a "strategic interest in maintaining Bolivia as a source of tin." The Munitions Board replied that "no one tin-producing area is considered absolutely essential to the defense of the United States." Even if the Bolivian mines were closed, they could always be reopened in case of a war, and the current stockpile would last until that could occur. Therefore, even if the tin industry in Bolivia collapsed, it did not "mean that heroic efforts are necessary to sustain" it, and the Defense Department was therefore "not prepared to underwrite with stockpile funds" any subsidization. The National Strategic Resources Board concurred and hoped that the State Department's response to Ambassador Martínez Vargas would be "sufficiently blunt to awaken the Bolivians to the realization that the divine intervention of the U.S. could not be counted on to alleviate their difficulties."⁵⁵

Although President Truman was willing to meet with Urriolagoitia's personal envoy, the State Department asserted that the tin contract was not of "sufficient importance or urgency" for Secretary Acheson to discuss it further with the president. Having surveyed the Bolivian economy in 1949, the U.S. Embassy in La Paz had found the primary cause for Bolivia's shortage of foreign exchange to be the importation of "costly non-essential and semi-luxury merchandise" by elites and that if the Bolivian tin industry did indeed collapse, it would be "largely the fault of the Bolivian administration," which had failed to curb the tin producers' costs or make needed reforms. In short, the embassy concluded, "there is no reason to expect the U.S. to subsidize the industry to enable operation at an abnormal rate and continuation of current administrative chaos." Though conceding there was good "reason for aiding Bolivia if one consider[ed] only concepts of fair play and justice," the Truman administration made it abundantly clear that "our consistent policy" was not to do so.⁵⁶

Assistant Secretary Miller then "frankly" informed Ambassador Martínez Vargas that "no immediate solution or special assistance to Bolivia was in sight" and that the Munitions Board did not consider "continuous access to Bolivian tin to be of great importance." "Lacking hope of rendering effective assistance," the State Department had chosen to "startle" the Bolivians into "doing something for themselves," an approach suggested by the Defense Department and completely endorsed by the Reconstruction Finance Corporation, which believed it might "facilitate negotiations." As the agency noted tersely: "The Bolivians would be well advised to sign up with the RFC immediately and attempt to put their economic house in order rather than asking for more U.S. help."⁵⁷ The State Department was essentially abandoning President Urriolagoitia to his fate. Observing that "it is questionable whether the present pro-democratic administration could make sensible and effective reforms and remain in power," Assistant Secretary Miller declared that "time is running out" for President Urriolagoitia to make a deal with the RFC, which was planning to find an alternative source for tin if a deal was not struck soon.[58]

In December 1949, Embassy Second Secretary Richard Johnson reached the "unpalatable conclusion" that Bolivia's postwar experiment in liberal capitalist oligarchy had been "premature or even retrograde." Johnson expected the military to rise from the barracks at the first hint of any "proletarian uprising" and to form a "reasonably benevolent military dictatorship" that might well look to Washington for guidance. When this occurred, the State Department would need to embrace the new regime and "exert all of its influence" to ensure that it did not take on "a Movimientista cast." He feared that pursuing a utopian "observance of hollow democratic forms" would only "retard" Bolivia's "slow progress toward real democracy by forcing its leaders to resort to dictators of the Perón variety for comfort and aid." By the beginning of February 1950, the State Department had reconciled itself to the fact that "nothing could be done to give the Bolivian tin industry special assistance," fully cognizant that, absent such assistance, a "drastic reduction in the production of tin as well as violent political and social disturbances" would almost certainly ensue.[59]

Ambassador Martínez Vargas did not take the news well; indeed, he delayed forwarding the State Department's "frank" formal statement to his superiors for as long as possible. Even worse, the ambassador received the news just after learning that the Export-Import Bank had granted Indonesia a $100 million loan. Although he acknowledged the "wisdom" of protecting "the Asiatic front in the Cold War," he lamented that the United States was "forgetting its rear guard in Latin America."[60] When Martínez Vargas denounced U.S. tin policy as nothing less than "abuse," State Department officers could only sheepishly remind him that the British had also played a role in forcing prices down over the years. And when the ambassador mentioned the Indonesian loan, U.S. diplomats noted that Bolivia had actually received far more per capita over the years, but this was of little solace. Martínez Vargas hoped that President Truman himself could be enlisted to find a solution but was warned that this was unlikely because the tightfisted U.S. Congress would be hesitant to authorize any outlay. Nonetheless, with "his hopes high" and "counting on the support" of Ambassador Florman and the Department of State, Martínez Vargas proceeded to seek both an end to the impasse and a loan from the United States.[61]

With options dwindling rapidly, the ambassador and the tin barons again enlisted retired Assistant Secretary of State Spruille Braden in March 1950, in the hope that Braden, a former miner himself, might convince U.S. diplomats of the errors in their approach. But when Braden argued that, from a technical standpoint, it would be next to impossible to quickly reopen mines that had been closed, the State Department was unmoved. Neither was it impressed by Bolivian appeals for "fair play" or for an Export-Import Bank loan to cover food imports for the next five years. Indeed, the only concession the Bolivians were able to obtain was a reduction in shipping costs to offset the increased smelting fees the RFC hoped to impose.[62]

With no hope of compromise, the Bolivians dug in for the long haul. Antenor Patiño continued to ship his tin to Great Britain; Carlos Aramayo and Mauricio Hochschild took out loans from U.S. banks to maintain their operations and to continue paying their taxes. Without this arrangement, the U.S. Embassy observed, the "Bolivian Government would now be in much deeper waters financially than it actually is." For the State Department, the only positive aspect of this crisis was that the "actual economic hardships" that Bolivians were enduring would have a "sobering" effect and convince the political parties to "attack their problems vigorously and realistically." As it was, however, President Urriolagoitia had little choice but to hope the Bolivian saying that "often when things are at their worst, a surprising development occurs which keeps the country from falling into the abyss" would prove true once again.[63] Even as Ambassador Martínez Vargas urged his superiors to simply give in to the Reconstruction Finance Corporation, the tin barons continued to hold out for a miracle.

They got one on 25 June 1950, when North Korean forces crossed the 38th parallel to invade South Korea. Within weeks of the outbreak of the Korean War, the price of tin on the international markets rocketed from 74¢ to more than $1.00 per pound and showed no signs of stopping there. Suddenly, conditions were near perfect for a complete turnaround in Bolivia's favor. Bolivian tin production was down, the British had sold off their reserves, banditry in Malaya jeopardized production there, and accidents took several dredges out of production in Indonesia. Anticipating that the United States would be "trying to acquire tin at any price" to increase its stockpile, speculators and tin brokers responded to rumors of a return to price controls by driving the price even higher. The Munitions Board's complacency evaporated when it determined that the United States now needed to "acquire all possible tin regardless of cost." For the Bolivians, the "crisis has passed."[64]

The 1950 tin contract, signed within a month, was everything the Bolivians could have hoped it would be. The Reconstruction Finance Corporation agreed to purchase all non-Patiño tin at the current market price. The six months of Bolivian tin shipments sitting on the docks of Antofogasta would be sold at the price prevailing on the day of the signing. The Bolivians insisted that the British even pay that price to Patiño for all of his shipments over those six months. The only possible bone of contention between the negotiators was Bolivia's commercial treaty with Argentina. RFC officials were concerned that the Argentines might demand their eight thousand tons of tin concentrates under the provisions of the still-unratified pact.⁶⁵ Once assured that the treaty was "dormant" and "extremely unlikely" to ever go into effect, the RFC signed the new contract. Ambassador Martínez Vargas could not resist jabbing the imperious agency: the RFC could have had six months of Bolivian tin for less than 75¢ per pound if it had not quibbled over "three or four cents."⁶⁶

For President Urriolagoitia, the July 1950 settlement with the RFC was a welcome victory that might allow him to undo some of the damage his government had sustained over the previous six months. For all of the State Department's optimism about Urriolagoitia's ascendance and strength during the civil war, little had gone right for the new government after that. It had barely survived labor unrest and insurrections in the mines and cities. The president's policy of fiercely repressing the MNR and exiling suspected opponents while yielding to a number of labor's demands had won him few friends. Workers remained hostile to a government they considered to be a puppet of the rosca, while the tin barons lukewarmly supported it only because it was a reasonably effective bulwark against revolutionary nationalism. It had taken the outbreak of hostilities in Korea and the welcome news of a stunning triumph over the RFC to save Urriolagoitia.

Though the State Department heaped praise on the Bolivian president, it had failed to provide any meaningful support for Urriolagoitia during either the civil war of 1949 or the tin negotiations of 1950. U.S. leaders had maintained the Good Neighbor nonintervention pledge but had apparently been willing to risk both an MNR takeover and an economic collapse to do so. This became all too clear during the tin negotiations when U.S. policy makers explicitly conceded that Urriolagoitia would most likely not survive without State Department assistance. Hoping to teach the Bolivians self-reliance, U.S. diplomats had offered them only a cold shoulder, although they had done so with some remorse and trepidation. The defense planners and the RFC technocrats had no such qualms, nor had the State Department's Edward Miller, Willard Barber, and James Espy, who at times matched them in their callousness. The Korean War had brought Urriolagoitia a badly needed reprieve, but nothing more.

5

TO THE MAMERTAZO

July 1950–May 1951

In Bolivia, opposition to the mine owners is traditionally the most popular cause of all. The Government, by its repudiation of the August 11 decree and the adoption of the decree of October 30 providing a better deal for the mine owners than had existed for several years, became, in the eyes of many, supporters of the "rosca." The MNR was the only prominent party opposed to the mining interests and as such benefited from the natural tendency of these voters who also opposed the Big Three.
—*William B. Cobb, 10 May 1951*

The ray of hope has been destroyed by those who have arrogated power to themselves in the most disgraceful and illegal form possible.
—*Víctor Paz Estenssoro, 18 May 1951*

The Korean War tin boom gave President Urriolagoitia some much welcomed breathing space, energizing the populace, satisfying the tin barons, and winning his government a degree of support and confidence. Still, the president appeared to understand that its windfall profits would evaporate the day the Korean conflict ended. He therefore made his boldest move yet on 11 August 1950 by reissuing his April decree seizing the tin barons' foreign exchange. With this step, he would subjugate the Big Three to the state and greatly increase government revenues for reform. For the first time, his Partido de la Unión Republicana Socialista was poised to undertake significant reform.

Unfortunately for the president, the Reconstruction Finance Corporation and Ambassador Florman had other ideas. Acting against Secretary Acheson's explicit orders, Florman forged an alliance with the tin barons and undertook an energetic campaign to prevent the implementation of the 11 August decree.

The success of this campaign deprived Urriolagoitia of a much-needed victory. In its wake, with the support of Senator Lyndon Johnson, the RFC launched an all-out, if not entirely legal, assault on the world price of tin, driving the final nails into the coffin of liberal constitutional oligarchy and paving the way for Víctor Paz Estenssoro to win the presidential election of May 1951. Although Urriolagoitia would hand over power to yet another military junta to block Paz Estenssoro's ascension, the seeds of the National Revolution had been sown.

The 11 August Decree

Contrary to what the Argentines and Paz Estenssoro believed, President Urriolagoitia intended to make the most of the tin boom by solidifying his political and economic position. On the political front, he arrested PIR leader José Arze and made much of the Falangists' "absurd" coup attempt, which he had suppressed in July.[1] On the economic front, he resurrected his April decree confiscating the tin producers' foreign exchange. His 11 August 1950 decree demanded that the tin barons surrender all but 28 percent of their foreign exchange revenue from the first 75¢ per pound and all exchange revenue from sales above that price at a highly unfavorable conversion rate. It gave the Banco Central complete control over all foreign currency expenditures, including dividends, amortization costs, foreigners' salaries, and purchases of imported machinery. Among other things, the government planned to use the foreign exchange to fund economic diversification projects and the development of new mining facilities, as well as to stabilize the boliviano.[2] With the measures called for in the decree, the president hoped to force the tin barons to reinvest their profits within Bolivia, to develop the nation's resources, and to set its economy on a healthier footing. In short, President Urriolagoitia was bidding to launch a fundamental reform of Bolivian society that went further than anything even Major Villarroel had done.

As expected, the tin barons and their press organs rose up in defiance, proclaiming that the 11 August decree would signal the "death of the Bolivian mining industry": it would "kill all plans for further capital investment" and force mine owners to "gut" their mines by working only the richest veins, which required little imported machinery. It was, Carlos Aramayo's *La Razón* pronounced, nothing short of "totalitarianism" and a "mortal threat" to the nation. *El Diario* predictably echoed *La Razón*'s charges and leveled some of its own. Not only would Urriolagoitia's decree "kill free enterprise" and put management of the companies into the hands of an "incompetent bureaucracy," but it would also jeopardize tin shipments to the United States and thereby antagonize Bolivia's foremost ally. The tin barons' representatives in Washington scurried to the State Department with dire predictions that U.S. tin supplies were endangered. Aramayo told Ambassador Florman he was "fed up with all this nonsense" and was "going to Europe for a conference with Patiño to see what we can do to nullify this mess."³

For their part, opposition newspapers praised the 11 August decree. Owned and edited by Alfredo Alexander (who had negotiated the original Argentine-Bolivian commercial treaty), *Ultima Hora* rebutted the tin barons' polemics and commended President Urriolagoitia for finally taking this necessary step for national development. Alexander wryly pointed out that the same pro-rosca newspapers—*La Razón* and *El Diario*—that had lauded Urriolagoitia as a "democratic" leader before 11 August were now denouncing him as "totalitarian." When the tin barons tried to convince the State Department that the 11 August decree would imperil UN efforts in Korea, Alexander rallied nationalists to his cause with fierce denunciations of the rosca. *La Tribuna*, a generally pro-PURS organ, agreed with Alexander and repeated his accusations that the tin barons were conspiring to oust the government if the decree was not rescinded. The Bolivian Congress awakened from its paralysis to weigh in on the controversy: several bills to support or strengthen the decree were introduced and rapidly gained momentum.⁴

On the U.S. side, Secretary Acheson and the RFC were predictably "disturbed" by the decree and the "serious" potential it had to disrupt Bolivian tin production. State Department officers informed Ambassador Martínez Vargas's lieutenant that it would be "unfortunate" if a government that was receiving U.S. loans and other assistance were to take actions that would assail private capital and risk depressing tin production. They reminded the Bolivians of their "eloquent" appeals in January 1950 that the tin companies could not survive without 90¢ per pound and instructed Ambassador Florman to emphasize to President Urriolagoitia the need for study before implementing such a radical initiative. They also directed Florman to inform the tin barons that this was "an internal affair of Bolivia" and therefore neither the State Department nor the RFC would interfere. If asked to comment, the ambassador was to say that U.S. interest in the matter, beyond a general concern for Bolivia's economy, was confined to maintaining tin production. Florman was explicitly ordered to "avoid any indication" that the U.S. government "supports the mining industry against the Government or the Government against the industry."⁵ This admonition was probably wise in light of Florman's oft-proclaimed hostility toward the tin barons, but no one could have predicted the course he would soon take.

Alarmed at the coming confrontation, the ambassador cabled the department that, because Urriolagoitia was the "only human who can remedy [the] situation," he had decided to meet with him as soon as possible. Florman was "reasonably confident" that he would "succeed in having [the] decree modified" so that it would "suit" the mine owners so long as they refrained from "engaging in any propaganda whatever." Secretary Acheson's response was swift and decisive: reminding the ambassador of his earlier instructions, he ordered him to avoid "any indications" that the Truman administration was requesting modification of the decree. Ignoring the order, Florman promptly arranged a meeting with the foreign minister and informed him that the United States would be "deprived of its required tin needs owing to curtailed production" should the decree go into effect.[6]

The foreign minister immediately called the president, who assured him that the decree could eventually be altered to guarantee U.S. tin supplies should problems arise. Not satisfied by that assurance, Florman arranged a meeting directly with Urriolagoitia for 6 September. After spending an hour with the president, he proudly reported that the 11 August decree "is now a dead duck," that the "Presidential Palace door is wide open," and that a "qualified" group of three U.S. citizens representing the tin barons would shortly be walking through that door "for mopping up operations."[7] Florman personally ushered the three in to meet with President Urriolagoitia and the finance and foreign ministers. After hearing the tin barons' alternative, and in the ambassador's presence, the president ordered his foreign minister to "reach agreement with each" representative within forty-eight hours. According to embassy officer Thomas Maleady's account of the meeting, through these three spokesmen, the tin barons had simply "told the government it had damned well better fall in line and amend the decree as the U.S. Govt. (read Florman) desired."[8]

Florman's about-face in favor of the tin barons was remarkable and almost inexplicable. Although "an outspoken opponent of monopolistic tin cartels" in the past, he was "constrained to yield ground when the uninterrupted supply of tin to our country [was] threatened" by an "ill-timed" and "tactless" decree. The tin barons were threatening to reduce their production by half as part of a "squeeze play" on President Urriolagoitia and perhaps also on the United States. The U.S. citizens representing Antenor Patiño, Mauricio Hochschild, and Carlos Aramayo had persuaded the ambassador that the situation was dire. Florman had asked them to draft an alternative plan of their own, which they did, calling for an RFC loan to the tin barons that would both permit an "uninterrupted increased production of tin" and increase tax revenue for the Bolivian government. When Urriolagoitia rejected that plan out of hand, Florman presented their second effort, which called for a 20 percent reduction of the export tax and a 15 percent reduction of the dividend tax. The tin barons had enlisted Truman's envoy completely to their cause.[9]

Ambassador Florman's hostility to the decree was, at least in part, based on his mistaken belief that it had originated with a UN mission headed by Hugh Keenleyside of the Canadian Development and Resources Ministry. Although Keenleyside had been called in to assess and analyze the Bolivian economy and recommend changes, according to Florman, Keenleyside's real goal was not to improve conditions on the Altiplano, but "to dissolve an era of good feelings" and create an "atmosphere harmful to the U.S.A." And when Princeton professor John Lindberg, an "obviously eminent exponent of Swedish socialism" and a close friend of Albert Einstein, had disclosed on 10 August that "a tin decree with teeth will be issued tomorrow," Florman immediately inferred that Lindberg himself had authored the decree. In a dispatch to the State Department, he took the opportunity to digress into a bizarre, incoherent red-baiting critique of Einstein's political views and those of other scientists who preached nuclear disarmament. He then apparently told Bolivian officials that they "did not need to worry about the recommendations of the UN mission because the United States would take care of Bolivia."[10]

Responding to Bolivian newspapers' claims that the UN mission had called for nationalization, a reining in of capital flight, and massive infusions of foreign aid, Keenleyside reassured the State Department that it had done nothing of the sort. In fact, Keenleyside's greatest fear was that the State Department would "undermine" his work by "offering to solve Bolivia's problems for them." His mission had called for "painful adjustments," the need to "disregard ancient theories" and to "break the bonds of caste, creed and race" in order to take back the nation from "a limited class whose main interest is to retain their wealth and private privileges." In short, it had called for "a social uprising" that would bring "about a change in the distribution of income and power" to "extirpate the privileges and the flagrant inequalities" and "inspire the masses with enthusiasm for the progress which overcomes all obstacles." More important, the mission had also called for measures to attract foreign investment and shift the tax burden away from mining. Keenleyside therefore considered the 11 August decree to be "most unfortunate," even though he also believed that the tin barons had "raped Bolivia of its wealth for generations." Because Bolivia was essentially "a beggar seated on a golden chair," Keenleyside argued that the highest priority was an "overhaul" of public administration. When embassy officer Maleady later pointed out that such an overhaul would entail the United Nations "assuming trusteeship of the country," President Urriolagoitia actually agreed, at least in principle.[11]

Once Ambassador Florman, who Bolivians believed was acting with President Truman's backing, weighed in, President Urriolagoitia quickly met the tin barons' terms and issued a new decree to "supplement" the one of 11 August. Although portions of the earlier decree were retained, under the new decree, the tin barons would actually receive 14¢ more of foreign exchange per pound of tin than they had before 11 August. The Big Three would have been "more than pleased" to retain one-third of their foreign exchange, but Florman's deal allowed them to retain 42 percent. In return, the tin barons pledged to expand production over the next year, something they were obviously going to do anyway with the tin price at historic highs. Thanks to Florman, what had started as a measure to give the government greater control over foreign exchange had handed the tin barons a major victory that would drain government coffers even further. Florman boasted that his intervention had been decisive. On at least one occasion, he had prevented the finance minister from walking out in disgust over the tin barons' duplicity. *La Razón* and *El Diario* were naturally "jubilant" over the new agreement, *La Tribuna* predictably supported the government, while a furious *Ultima Hora* fumed over the suspected U.S. interference. Florman was "especially pleased" to report that the tin barons were also "jubilant" because the benefits accruing from the amended decree "exceed their fondest expectations."[12]

Florman never did truly understand the scandal, which he blamed on Alfredo Alexander, an "ambitious demagogue" who was determined to "wreck the tin agreement" and Urriolagoitia's government through his "yellow journal." He believed that he had "literally saved" Bolivia's tin-producing companies from nationalization and their personnel from deportation, quieted the "apocalyptic fears" that had arisen, and ushered in an "air of millennial hope." He further believed he had single-handedly ushered in a new era in Bolivian history in which "extreme violence," revolutions, and the "overthrow of the Bolivian government" were "a thing of the past." Thanks to him, President Urriolagoitia would serve out the remainder of his term and "outgoing and incoming Presidents will ride in an open carriage at the inaugural parade." In short, "the transition from chaos to orderliness is now a foregone conclusion in Bolivia." Declaring, however, that he would not touch "Bolivian domestic politics" with a "ten-foot pole," Florman forwarded a memorandum entitled "United States Ambassador Saved the Entire Bolivian Tin Industry from Utter Collapse, Chaos, and Revolution" in one of his dispatches to the State Department.[13]

Florman's ill-conceived intervention and bombastic, arrogant style alienated both his embassy staff and the Bolivians. "Fed up" embassy personnel, who derisively referred to the ambassador as "Oiving," "IF," or "bête noire," started sending important information to personal friends in the State Department in informal letters to avoid Florman's efforts to censor or otherwise "kill" their reports. Even Assistant Secretary Edward Miller's already low opinion of Aramayo "dropped a notch" when the tin baron spoke "effusively about Florman and what a grand ambassador he was."[14] Urriolagoitia's diplomats soon realized that they had been duped by the tin barons and Florman. Even with the record-high prices for tin, the deal Florman had brokered produced less tax revenue than the previous year, and "everyone" in Urriolagoitia's government was quite upset by "this development." Nor were they the only ones upset by the ambassador's meddling. Outside the door to Florman's office, embassy security guards extinguished the fuse on what they thought to be a "stink bomb," only to discover that it was in fact a homemade explosive device containing cement and twelve sticks of blasting gelatin. Clearly, "whoever placed it there wasn't playing," for "had it gone off there probably would have been another vacant ambassadorship."[15]

One Bolivian diplomat who had sat in on the conferences amending the 11 August decree sharply contrasted Florman, whose word was now "taken with, not a grain, but a whole bagful of salt," with his predecessor, Joseph Flack, who had been bluntly honest at all times. Unwilling to blame the U.S. ambassador, however, Urriolagoitia singled out his minister of hacienda to be a scapegoat for the fiasco. But when, before returning to Washington, Florman asked Urriolagoitia to write a letter to President Truman explaining "how much he, Florman, had done for Bolivia" and "what a masterful diplomat he, Florman, is," Urriolagoitia's response, according to embassy officer Maleady, was, "in effect, 'nuts' and IF got no letter." Florman never did understand the harm he had caused. Indeed, six months later, he went so far as to suggest that "the Department should probably publicize" his intervention "for its own benefit," rather than "stifle it."[16]

The 1951 Tin Impasse

Despite the 11 August debacle, the Bolivians had every reason to believe that their troubles with the Reconstruction Finance Corporation, for the most part, were over when negotiations opened in December 1950. Although the RFC still purchased tin for U.S. government use and the stockpile, the price of tin had been set by the London, Singapore, and New York markets for more than a year. It had soared to $1.97 per pound as a result of the Korean War and rampant speculation, leading both the RFC and the Bolivians to hope for a two-year contract. The two sides reached quick agreement that all sales would be at the prevailing world price in Singapore and London or the rate at which the RFC was selling to consumers (less smelting fees). When disputes arose over smelting fees, which the RFC hoped to increase to offset recent wage increases at the Longhorn smelter in Texas City, the two sides quickly reached a compromise that would increase smelting fees as the price rose.[17]

Before the RFC could finalize the deal, however, it had to receive approval from the Defense Production Agency (DPA), now headed by former ITT executive William Harrison. Under the Defense Production Act of 1950, the RFC could not incur financial losses (as was likely with this contract) unless it did so as part of the "defense program." In short, if DPA Director Harrison and his fellow defense planners deemed stockpiling Bolivian tin to be critical to U.S. defense, the RFC could violate its legal obligation to break even. Declaring that "the stockpile objective for tin is far from fulfilled" and that "we must endeavor to acquire all the tin that can be acquired in the foreseeable future," Director Harrison offered his tentative approval.[18] Although Ambassador

Martínez Vargas was operating under the assumption that the most serious problem the tin producers faced was the traditional 3¢ differential between the Singapore and New York prices, a far more serious problem was on the horizon. RFC Tin Division Chief Wiley F. McKinnon and Assistant Secretary Miller had both warned the ambassador in January that the RFC was developing a plan to bring the price of tin down "substantially," but no one could have anticipated how successful that plan would be.[19]

In February, Lyndon Johnson's Preparedness Subcommittee of the Senate Armed Forces Committee issued its findings on tin prices and set the tone for the next two years. The report concluded that the tin cartel was secretly still in existence, "gouging" the "weary" American taxpayer, but that the subcommittee "intends to do whatever it can to put an end" to it. It further condemned tin producers for tacitly supporting Communism, enraging the Malayans, "whose miners were being killed daily by communists." The Bolivians were perhaps the only ones who could take heart from the report: it concluded that, because of geographic factors, "we should, therefore, rightly expect the price for tin originating in Malaya and Indonesia to be lower than for tin from Bolivia."[20] Essentially, Johnson's subcommittee was giving the RFC a mandate to do whatever it could to drive down the world price of tin.

Anticipating such a mandate, the RFC technocrats and defense planners had for months been developing a plan that constituted nothing less than "an active resistance to the present market price" of tin, the "No. 1 problem in importance of the strategic materials." Spurred by the Preparedness Subcommittee's condemnation of government tin purchases at the "exorbitant prices" prevailing on world tin markets, the RFC put its new mandate to "cause a lower foreign price for tin" into effect. On 12 March 1951, with only the State Department dissenting, the Defense Production Agency ordered that the New York tin market be closed, all stockpile purchases suspended, and the RFC reestablished as the sole U.S. tin importer and distributor.[21] These steps alone brought the price of tin down almost 50¢ to $1.34 per pound, but it rose again in less than a month to $1.51. "Keenly aware of the danger," the RFC, which had traditionally sold its tin to industry for the price of tin concentrates plus smelting and processing costs in order to break even, took the radical step of selling its accumulated reserves of tin to consumers and industry for just $1.34 per pound in order to drive the world price back down.[22]

Only two constraints bound the RFC. The first was an escape clause in almost all existing tin contracts that permitted suppliers to abrogate their contracts should the United States restore price controls. Since RFC Chairman W. E. Harber acknowledged that he was "establishing an unnaturally low price" through "what is in effect a monopoly," he fully expected every supplier to exercise its escape clause should the RFC persist in selling its tin at $1.34

per pound, which, the chairman went on to say, was "indeed a serious problem" because the agency might lose up to 90 percent of its tin supply. The RFC was able to gain British support for tin price controls by promising U.S. assistance to Great Britain for its purchases of zinc, sulfur, and cotton, but other suppliers were not so easy to appease. The Bolivians, in particular, refused to ship a single pound of tin at $1.34 or to finalize their contract with the United States.[23]

The other constraint upon the RFC was its congressionally mandated obligation to break even. The RFC's tin program, which had reaped significant profits since 1946, was about to incur significant losses. Because it was still selling inventory it had acquired at a much lower price over the previous ten months, it could temporarily absorb the loss of selling at $1.34 per pound; indeed, it had actually managed to turn a $24 million dollar profit over the previous few months.[24] The RFC had not, however, been able to drive the world price below $1.50 even by selling tin at $1.34 per pound, although this "undoubtedly had been an effective drag on the upward trend." DPA Director Harrison therefore determined that, unless the Defense Production Act was amended, the RFC had to increase its selling price to at least $1.50. Though willing to countenance RFC losses when the goal was the simple but critical acquisition of tin, Director Harrison had to admit that "the Government-owned tin held by the RFC was not intended for use in controlling market prices." Moreover, "such use" represented an "untenable" policy with regard to long-term contracts and, "although unintentional," had "the appearance of being unfair."[25]

Edwin Gibson of the General Services Administration, presiding over the tin stockpile, went further, explicitly withdrawing the RFC's mandate to operate at a loss as granted by the Defense Production Agency and the Preparedness Subcommittee because it had originally been intended only to "assure the availability to the United States of overseas supplies." The RFC was exceeding its mandate and violating U.S. law in the process. RFC Chairman Harber was nonetheless eager to continue the policy, and DPA Director Harrison eventually came to agree. "The matter was left for the attorneys to decide." With their assent, the RFC policy went forward, subject to weekly review.[26] Despite its questionable legality, the policy was inarguably effective. Whenever the price of tin dropped on the Singapore market, the RFC would drop its price to match it, but when the price in Singapore rose, the RFC would hold its own price steady. Although the agency acknowledged that this was "not consistent with a sound long-range selling program," its actions worked to bring down the world tin price; indeed, within months, the RFC was effectively setting that price.[27]

When Senator Johnson met with RFC officials at the end of March, he was "emphatic" in his support of the new RFC policy and urged defense planners to spare no expense in driving the world tin price downward. The RFC proceeded to sell at a loss throughout April; though, overall, the agency was still operating in the black, problems would arise in six months when it sold the tin it had purchased at more than $1.50 per pound for the new market price, which would be far lower. Officially, the RFC pledged that it would eventually sell the tin it acquired for a profit through some yet-undeveloped formula. Unofficially, RFC Chairman Harber and Tin Division Chief McKinnon had to know full well that every step they took was calculated to ensure the world price of tin never again approached the prices they had paid since the onset of the Korean War. "We trust," Chairman Harber wrote to DPA Director Harrison, that a "solution to the problem may shortly be found which will eliminate" any discrepancies. Division Chief McKinnon tried to find such a solution in June by calculating that RFC had created "theoretical savings" of almost $75 million for a year's worth of tin concentrates.[28]

McKinnon confessed to State Department officers that the RFC directors' success in driving down prices "may have gone to their heads." A genuine fear of having to answer to Senator Johnson's subcommittee for submitting to price gouging in months past was pushing them toward belligerence and over-aggressiveness.[29] President Urriolagoitia was their first target. When the RFC pressed him to sign a long-term contract with the price set at the market level, the president refused, but so desperate was his need for foreign exchange that he agreed to a limited, short-term deal on the agency's terms. The RFC had allowed the last tin agreement to lapse when prices were at $1.80 per pound and was now able to acquire three months of Bolivian tin production at less than $1.40 per pound. The Bolivians had little choice but to sign before the RFC's underselling policy drove prices down even further.

Encouraged by the agency's early successes, Senator Johnson urged the RFC on. When RFC officers met with Preparedness Subcommittee Counsel Donald Cook in May, all agreed that, even though the "weight of this policy is just beginning to be effective," the world price of tin was "still unreasonable." They agreed to a virtual suspension of tin metal purchases from Belgium and Indonesia and planned to use Bolivian concentrates processed at Texas City to make up the difference. In this way, the United States would need no further tin purchases in 1951. Conceding this would lead to a dangerous depletion of RFC's tin stocks, an "emphatic" Counsel Cook was quick to point out that every 1¢ reduction in the world price of tin saved U.S. taxpayers $5 million. He urged the agency not to sign a long-term contract with the Bolivians for "fear that it might be an encouraging sign to other foreign tin producers" and suggested that La Paz be given only one-month extensions. Tin Division Chief McKinnon disagreed, claiming that a long-term pact would secure better terms for the RFC, although a "refusal to enter into any contract would accomplish much more."[30]

McKinnon suggested that if the United States halted all purchases, the ensuing "backup of tin concentrates would be helpful in causing a price decline" globally. Unfortunately, the demands of the Texas City smelter were too great. If tin concentrate purchases stopped for any appreciable length of time, the smelter would have to be shut down and would be difficult to restart because essential personnel would leave and be next to impossible to replace. Finally, because no other smelter was processing low-grade ore like that from Bolivia, those concentrates could not be sold at all—actually reducing the global supply of tin and driving the price upward. McKinnon therefore urged the defense planners to "undertake an aggressive policy of tin concentrate purchases."[31] As useful as it might have been to purchase no Bolivian tin, it was simply not feasible.

For the Bolivians, the RFC's new policy was nothing short of an outrage. The agency had maintained a buyer's monopoly to force down the price of Bolivian tin until world supplies increased and a free market could accomplish that result. Once prices rose on the open market, however, the RFC reestablished control over the market and abused its position by selling the tin stocks it had already acquired to drive the price down, costing the tin barons and President Urriolagoitia's government millions of dollars a month. U.S. policy makers had even canceled an intergovernmental conference to discuss the price of tin in March because it was "undesirable" to negotiate "in the face of a rising price or one following the foreign markets." Once the world tin price started to drop, U.S. planners then argued that that there was no need for such a meeting. The RFC had succeeded in creating an unprecedented unity in Bolivian politics: every organ of the Bolivian press, across the political spectrum, filled its pages with what Ambassador Florman called "mud-slinging and moronic editorials branding us as Yankee imperialists." For their part, President Urriolagoitia's diplomats were "fit to be tied." The Bolivians pleaded for a new international tin agreement to stabilize the price, but there was little hope of reaching one. Even if the United States could somehow be convinced to permit such a step, British and Dutch producers informed the State Department that they might just press for a low price simply to force "some of Bolivia's mines out of business" and thereby reduce the tin supply.[32]

Ambassador Florman regarded the "bewildered" Bolivian response to the RFC campaign with bemusement, commenting that Bolivians "take the tin business very earnestly, almost like a national sport." When, however, President Urriolagoitia's foreign minister asked Florman to act as a liaison between him and the masses to "undo the harm and alleviate the anguish," he was happy to oblige. Although he would not concede that "we caused the damage," Florman did issue two press releases suggesting that promising negotiations were under way. Such lies, he believed, would work "like magic" to ease Bolivian "lamentations" and would lead Bolivians to "become more respectable and stop pretending to be experts in international finance and mineralogy."[33] Florman's delusions aside, Urriolagoitia had become thoroughly disenchanted with his erstwhile U.S. ally and its envoy. If there was any consolation to be had, it was that the president's term was about to expire, and new elections would bequeath his problems to a successor.

The Election of 1951

The presidential election set for 6 May 1951 would ultimately reshape Bolivian history and was, in every way, an outgrowth of the selfish, intra-elite bickering that had paralyzed first Hertzog's and then Urriolagoitia's government. Still, the continuing tin impasse and the vestiges of the 11 August fiasco also guaranteed that the election would be marked by widespread anti-U.S. sentiment and a reinvigorated hostility toward the tin barons and the government they appeared to dominate. Because the Movimiento Nacionalista Revolucionario was permitted to field its own candidates, it would also be a referendum on the sexenio, conducted in a political climate exceptionally favorable to Víctor Paz Estenssoro and his nationalists.

The first to announce his candidacy was Gabriel Gosálvez of Urriolagoitia's Socialist Party. A former president of the Banco Central and a businessman, Gosálvez had resigned his post as ambassador to Argentina at the end of October 1950 to make himself eligible and appeared to have the inside track. He had not only Urriolagoitia's support but also, it was rumored, Perón's personal and financial backing.[34] Gosálvez hoped to run as the PURS candidate, but infighting predictably broke out at the party convention in January. The Republican Socialists, the single largest party of the coalition, believed one of its members should be the coalition's candidate. Because Hertzog had been a Genuine Republican and Gosálvez, like Urriolagoitia, a Socialist, they raised a valid point. Republican Socialist Party Chief Waldo Belmonte Pool would have been a natural choice, but the gunshot wounds he had suffered in 1950 forced him to seek extensive medical treatment at Bethesda Naval Hospital. When the Socialists refused to consider another Republican Socialist, Belmonte's party walked out of the convention along with a number of embittered Genuine Republicans. The PURS nomination fell to Gosálvez by default. Although the coalition held a virtual monopoly on political power, the jockeying for position among its parties had become so bitter that it splintered completely.[35]

The irony, of course, was that ideologically, all three parties were virtually identical on all major issues. Yet they appeared determined to split the vote so thoroughly that no one party or coalition would win a majority. Even as the PURS coalition disintegrated, its members contented themselves with the knowledge that the radical parties would be unable to gain more than a plurality of the vote, guaranteeing that Congress would be able to block their accession to power. This complacency would cost them dearly. Demetrio Canelas, a leader of the Genuine Republicans and probably Bolivia's most astute journalist, appeared to be the only observer who recognized the danger that the coalition parties were courting and at one point called for a united front, but to no avail. Although a number of Republican Socialists and Genuine Republicans remained with the PURS, probably to maintain their positions in Congress, the cabinet, and the party apparatus, others sought a coalition with the Liberals but refused to accept the consolation prize of vice-presidential nomination under Liberal candidate and longtime party chief Tomás Elío. The Liberals offered the vice presidency to whoever would join it in a coalition, but when no one rose to the bait, they resorted to petty regionalism by naming a Liberal cruceño to join the paceño Elío, an elder statesman who was only running because of "his duty to take part in the democratic process," on the ticket. For their part, the Falangists nominated General Bilbao Rioja, who the State Department believed had "as much chance of success as the proverbial snowball" in hell. All together, the candidates inspired little more than "tired apathy." When a U.S. diplomat asked a Bolivian girl on the street about the election, she told him it was "just the same old names."[36]

Fearful that Gosálvez would launch a "Peronist-type regime" or push forward with the nationalization of the tin mines, the tin barons recruited Guillermo "Willie" Gutiérrez as their "white hope." Supposedly financed by 2 million bolivianos of Carlos Aramayo's money, Gutiérrez, a "volatile former Chaco War hero" and "revolutionary legend," initially looked like a strong candidate. He had been a leader in the movement to oust Villarroel, an editor of *La Razón*, a secretary for Aramayo, a diplomat, and an active pirista who had abandoned the party when it toed the Communist party line. Unable to find a political party willing to sponsor his aspirations, Gutiérrez had been forced to create his own, the Acción Cívica Boliviana. Reacting to the parades of trucks adorned with "¡Viva Gutiérrez!" banners, one Bolivian wryly observed that Aramayo was the "chauffeur" of the vehicles. Indeed, ignoring the Liberals, Falangists, piristas, and members of other minor parties, the PURS used *La Tribuna* presses to print handbills denouncing Gutiérrez's new party as "Aramayo contra Bolivia." With no specific agenda, Gutiérrez seems to have spent much of his time futilely trying to dissuade voters that he was a puppet of the hated tin barons despite all evidence to the contrary. The U.S. Embassy eventually concluded that Gutiérrez "threatens neither government nor other nominees" and "looks more and more like a teen-age Don Quixote."[37]

The MNR predictably nominated Víctor Paz Estenssoro from exile. Remarkably, in early March, President Urriolagoitia granted him permission to return, or at least seemed to. Gosálvez had apparently interceded on the MNR chief's behalf, leading many to believe the two had reached a "non-aggression understanding." It was far more likely, the U.S. Embassy conjectured, that Urriolagoitia planned to have Paz Estenssoro arrested when he set foot in Bolivia. As Paz Estenssoro was preparing to board a Pan American Grace airplane in Buenos Aires, however, ten thousand supporters gathered to await his arrival in La Paz, the largest crowd seen throughout the entire presidential campaign. Most likely out of fear for the safety of the other passengers, airline executives refused to transport him. But when Paz Estenssoro then attempted to board a Braniff plane on 13 April, the Bolivian government ordered that airline not to let him. And when Braniff ignored the order, the Bolivian minister of government ordered the plane back to Paraguay just as it was about to land in Santa Cruz.[38]

Apparently, the president had had a change of heart. Two days earlier, someone, presumably a movimientista, had blown up an army ammunition dump, and the police reported rumors of a MNR coup set to coincide with Paz Estenssoro's return. One U.S. mining corporation took the threat seriously enough to evacuate all U.S. citizens on its staff and to stop all mining rather than permit the workers easy access to dynamite. Although the show of MNR strength at the La Paz airport may well have played a role, President Urriolagoitia explained to U.S. diplomats that he had barred Paz Estenssoro's return because he feared that relatives of those killed by the Villarroel government would assassinate the MNR chief and that his government would be blamed. Few believed the explanation. At any rate, police fired tear gas into the expectant crowd at the airport, killing a young boy, and arrested between fifty and one hundred MNR leaders, some of whom the government imprisoned and others of whom it exiled. Though Paz Estenssoro denied any revolutionary plans and indeed claimed that launching a revolution weeks before an election he planned to win was "inconceivable," he remained out of the country as the election campaign reached its final stages.[39]

Meanwhile, Paz Estenssoro's vice-presidential candidate, Hernán Siles Zuazo, and FSTMB leader Juan Lechín had managed to sneak back into the country to rally the movimientistas. Although they did not appear in public for fear of arrest, their presence in the country was an important boost for the party, as was President Urriolagoitia's sudden mass arrest and deportation of MNR leaders on charges of planning to overthrow the government and assassinate the president. If anything, the U.S. Embassy reported, the persecution only aroused public sympathy for the MNR.[40]

In a development almost as helpful as the split within the intra-elite parties, the Movimiento Nacionalista Revolucionario would not have to share workers' votes with the Partido de la Izquierda Revolucionaria. The PIR's march toward Soviet Communism and extinction as a party had continued unchecked throughout 1950. Once José Arze proclaimed his loyalty to the Soviet Union, his party was doomed. U.S. diplomats noted that "hardly a day passes but that word is published" of the defection of prominent piristas unable to "stomach" the party's new orientation. With many of its leaders exiled, its members facing the threat of excommunication from the Catholic Church, its meetings suppressed by the government, and the rank and file abandoning the party en masse, the PIR's position was hopeless. Though Arze was running for president and had sought an alliance with the MNR, to no avail, his impact on the election would be negligible.[41]

The "administration candidate" of an unpopular government, Gabriel Gosálvez nonetheless appeared to be the favorite, at least until a desperate diplomatic gambit just weeks before the election. In an effort to prove that the Bolivian government was a "true friend" of the United States and to win President Truman's support for a new tin contract in April, Foreign Minister Pedro Zilveti had publicly promised that a division of Bolivian troops would be sent to Korea to fight alongside U.S. forces. The backlash in Bolivia was immediate and fierce. Students, veterans groups, movimientistas, Falangists, union members, and even pro-rosca candidate Gutiérrez joined a wave of protests against the PURS in general and against Zilveti in particular. *El Diario* pronounced that "we do not have meat to eat but we offer meat for the cannons" of the North Koreans.[42]

Ambassador Martínez Vargas pleaded with the State Department for a quick resolution to the tin contract to save Zilveti and the PURS and to "show the Bolivian people that he had obtained something in return." Deputy Assistant Secretary of State Thomas C. Mann was unsympathetic. When Martínez Vargas told him of violent protests in La Paz against the government's promise of Bolivian troops, Mann suggested that the ambassador remind his people that if they were "complaining about spilling their blood for the Yankees, a lot of Yankees were also complaining about American blood already being spilled in Korea for Bolivia and other countries in this hemisphere." Foreign Minister Zilveti had expected his pledge of troops to win him friends in Washington, and he remained in the United States in the hope of getting "something to take home to show his people." He was to be disappointed, and it is quite possible that his delay in returning to La Paz was a mere pretext to avoid the violent protests that undoubtedly awaited him there.[43]

For Ambassador Florman, the 6 May 1951 election was little more than an opportunity to permit "a host of impudent illiterates under the tutelage of intellectual fakers requisite powers to push their subjects around for reasons which they deem worthy, which include the denial of personal rights to individuals whose virtuous principles make them offensive." For Bolivians, however, it was an opportunity to install Paz Estenssoro in the Palacio Quemado. With only one significant disturbance, the election was perhaps the quietest in recent Bolivian history, and U.S. observers applauded the "absolute orderliness" of the event. By 5:00 P.M. on election day, the La Paz results were in and showed that Paz Estenssoro had won almost half of the votes—more than twice as many as Gosálvez—there. That trend continued as results filtered in from Cochabamba, Oruro, Potosí, and Santa Cruz. Gosálvez only came close to

Paz Estenssoro in Sucre and Tarija, with the MNR outpolling the PURS by more than ten to one in the mining districts. In sum, of the 126,123 votes cast, Paz Estenssoro won more than 54,000, Gosálvez garnered fewer than 42,000, and Gutiérrez, Elío, and Arze won fewer than 7,000 apiece. Although the PURS retained its working majority in the Senate, Lechín and five other MNR members emerged as the Senate's second-largest faction.[44]

Gosálvez canceled his "victory parade" and conceded immediately as army district commanders flocked to La Paz, fearful that if Paz Estenssoro did indeed become president, their heads, "either figuratively or literally, would be lopped off." The army hoped that, if a final decision could be postponed until August, when Congress reconvened, the PURS could hand the election to the Falangist Bilbao Rioja, who had managed to win almost 10 percent of the vote. Liberals proposed a solution whereby Gosálvez could be installed as president over a disqualified Paz Estenssoro, while Siles Zuazo would be given the vice presidency to appease the MNR.[45] For his part, the forward-looking Liberal Luis Guachalla actually suggested that Paz Estenssoro be given the presidency so that the MNR would have to reach an accommodation with the military, the establishment parties, and Congress. If denied the fruits of his election victory, Guachalla warned, Paz Estenssoro would be forced to lean more heavily on extremists like Lechín and to launch a revolution. Guachalla's prophetic advice, which at least offered the prospect of preserving some elements of the old order, was universally ignored.[46]

President Urriolagoitia had pledged that, if Paz Estenssoro won an absolute majority, he would turn the presidency over to him, but he clearly had no intention of doing so under any circumstances and instead appealed to Washington for assistance. Foreign Minister Zilveti "laid it on thick about the MNR being Communist," reminded the State Department of its Truman Doctrine pledge to support anti-Communist governments, and claimed that the Soviets were on the verge of making Bolivia "their first satellite state" in the Western Hemisphere. Ambassador Martínez Vargas compiled a folder of documents for the State Department that he believed were "irrefutable proof" of the alliance between the "Nazi-Fascist and Communist totalitarian forces."[47]

The most interesting of these was a statement from the executive secretary of the Bolivian Communist Party that Paz Estenssoro had "never made any anti-Soviet declarations." Embassy officials concluded that "odd as it may seem," the Communists seem to have become "a tool of the administration diehards intent on putting Gosálvez into the presidency at any cost." Indeed, Assistant Secretary Miller found the ambassador's documents to be "rather flimsy" and easily discounted. Unable to convince the State Department of a Communist menace that warranted intervention, Foreign Minister Zilveti and Ambassador Martínez Vargas tried once again to blame Perón. This gambit also failed miserably: every U.S. report suggested that, if Perón supported anyone, it was

Gosálvez. Zilveti reminded the U.S. Embassy staff of Paz Estenssoro's pledge to nationalize the mines and of his supposedly "rabidly anti-Yankee" stance, hoping, in embassy officer Maleady's words, to "hang on us the onus for disqualifying Paz."[48]

Foreign Minister Zilveti's plan was simple. In theory, since no candidate had won an absolute majority, Congress would select the winner. It could deny Paz Estenssoro the presidency just by arguing that, because he was out of the country, was not registered to vote, and was still wanted for crimes committed during the Villarroel years, he was ineligible to be president. Embassy officer Maleady believed the Bolivian minister was sounding him out to see how these "anti-democratic" steps would be received in Washington and warned that "if we fail to come up with something by which to eliminate [the] MNR," the PURS would simply declare "Paz legally ineligible." The U.S. response was simply that the election was a domestic Bolivian matter and therefore not within the purview of the Department of State. As Assistant Secretary Miller put it: "Much as I detest what the MNR stands for," U.S. diplomats "could not possibly become participants even indirectly to a deal of this kind." What Zilveti did not understand was that U.S. diplomats had written off Bolivian liberal constitutional oligarchy more than a year before.[49]

The election results did not particularly surprise U.S. policy makers. Embassy officers had reported months earlier that Urriolagoitia's tireless persecution of the MNR, far from crippling the party, was producing a backlash in its favor. Assistant Secretary Miller believed that Foreign Minister Zilveti had "tried too hard to be pro-U.S." and that his promise to send Bolivian troops to Korea was "responsible in part for the defeat of the PURS." Every Bolivian and U.S. official understood the implications of the election. Either the established parties would have to conspire to deprive the clear winner of the presidency in August or Paz Estenssoro would be installed. Rejecting both possibilities, President Urriolagoitia created and exercised a unique third option, the *mamertazo*. He resigned the presidency on 15 May, handed the reins of power over to a military junta led by General Hugo Ballivián, and immediately boarded a plane for Chile.[50]

For the State Department, Urriolagoitia's departure marked an unwelcome but not unexpected transition in Bolivian history. The U.S. Embassy had anticipated both the mamertazo and the "bloodshed [that] must follow." Paz Estenssoro bluntly informed a U.S. diplomat he would have no qualms about starting a civil war if the election was stolen from him. He predicted he would be "ready to take over or revolt" by August.[51] Though the Truman administration welcomed the presence of the army as a stabilizing influence and as a buttress against the MNR, it was also certain that Paz Estenssoro and the MNR would not take the theft of their electoral victory "lying down." Anticipating immediate violence and fearing that "this may be 'it,'" the U.S. Embassy requested that airplanes in Panama be made available for the evacuation of U.S. citizens. Antenor Patiño moved more quickly and evacuated the wives and children of his managers from the mining camps. Still living in a "cheaply furnished" Buenos Aires apartment and wearing "frayed" clothing, Paz Estenssoro announced that, even though he did not blame the United States for the mamertazo (as the Peronist press did), he considered himself the rightful president of Bolivia—despite Urriolagoitia's "evident psychotic disturbance."[52]

President Urriolagoitia's farewell address, delivered from Chile, was a sad and ironic commentary. He recalled his "continual efforts to guide the political struggle into peaceful channels" but lamented that he could not "quell the existing animosities." He called upon Bolivians to "gather around the national flag" and support the junta, for only in its "patriotic" hands could "democracy and our republican institutions" be preserved from the Argentine-funded "fascist-Communist" forces.[53] For "elder statesman" Demetrio Canelas, Urriolagoitia's fall was the natural outgrowth of the PURS's "policy of vengeance" against the MNR and its unwillingness to confront the true problems of the nation. Whereas the State Department had seen Presidents Hertzog and Urriolagoitia as quixotic reformers, valiantly if futilely attempting to chart a middle course, the legendary Canelas boldly and publicly pronounced that "few governments have caused as much damage to the country" as theirs or "created such vengeful feelings." Canelas tellingly pointed out that, even though the MNR had failed to win 50 percent of the vote, candidates opposed to the Urriolagoitia government had won almost 70 percent.[54]

General Ballivián, General Antonio Seleme, and the other officers of what many critics called the "Junta Usurpadora" immediately, and predictably, promised that their stay in power would be "brief." Their first statement reiterated much of Urriolagoitia's farewell address and rehashed the oft-repeated accusations of a MNR-Communist alliance. Ballivián declared that his junta was merely a necessary step to "reestablish harmony among Bolivians" and "repress attempts [to] Sovietize" the nation.[55] Because the mamertazo had been so sudden and unexpected, the first days of military rule were quiet. Anticipating the inevitable MNR response, however, the junta declared a state of siege, outlawed strikes, imposed censorship on the newspapers (including the sympathetic *La Razón*), banned public gatherings, and established a curfew. MNR leaders, journalists, and union chiefs were rounded up and detained; U.S. managers and engineers in the mines evacuated their families. Although all of Urriolagoitia's ambassadors tendered their resignations, only two were accepted: the generals made it clear that they were not going to deviate too far from the PURS agenda.[56]

On 21 May, the junta solidified its position and ended a "situation fraught with danger" when it finally succeeded in capturing Juan Lechín and putting to rest any fears of a general strike. Although Siles Zuazo escaped into hiding, other MNR leaders were arrested daily.[57] The U.S. Embassy reported that, whereas Urriolagoitia and the PURS had been thoroughly discredited for their weaknesses, Ballivián and his compatriots had brought a "feeling of relief from political turmoil." Still, it did not take long for the junta to commit its first mistake by arbitrarily arresting Canelas. The "crotchety, at times cantankerous" Canelas had simply expressed a fairly common opinion that the MNR had earned the opportunity to govern. His arrest signaled the onset of a brand of "high-handed" and arbitrary military rule that nearly all Bolivians hoped to avoid. The United States nonetheless recognized the junta within two weeks.[58]

For the State Department, supporting the junta was a foregone conclusion. Put simply, "the only alternative to the present government in Bolivia seems to be the MNR." Since Ballivián's government was entirely friendly to the United States," supportive of private enterprise, and anti-Argentina, whereas the MNR was "intensely nationalistic," anti-U.S., and pro-Perón, "our narrow self-interest" was clear. Embassy officer William Hudson's apologia even credited the junta with the defending democracy since any weakening of it would lead to a MNR coup that would eliminate the "opportunity for the election which the junta sincerely intends to hold." General Ballivián had clearly established his authority over the nation, pledged to honor Bolivia's international obligations, and had not assumed power as a result of "external influences." Because a number of conservative regimes in South America had already seized the opportunity to repudiate the MNR, the United States had moved swiftly to accord the junta recognition.[59]

No mere caretaker, General Ballivián signed an agreement with the United Nations in October to fully implement the findings of the Keenleyside report, in what embassy officer Maleady called the most "portentous" event since Villarroel's assassination. UN technical personnel would be insinuated into the Agriculture, Finance, Labor, and Public Works Ministries to do what "no one, Bolivian or outsider" had been able to do, "give the Bolivian economy a planned overall orientation." Just as Wall Street executives of the Klein Mission were transforming General Odría's Peru, so UN technocrats hoped to transform General Ballivián's Bolivia. On the other hand, diplomatically asserting that Bolivian troops were better used defending the strategic resources of the Western Hemisphere, Ballivián quickly backed away from Zilveti's pledge to send troops to Korea.[60]

The problem faced by the junta was how to get power back into civilian hands without putting it into Paz Estenssoro's. Although some in the junta sought early elections, the complete paralysis and disunity of the established parties made it almost certain that any new election would yield another, possibly even more decisive MNR victory. The tentative solution that the army eventually settled upon was a new voter registration drive to be held in May 1952 to purge the rolls of movimientistas, followed by a congressional election that October. The newly seated Congress would select a president for the nation.[61]

Though the timeline was not what the State Department desired, the junta's proposed solution gave U.S. diplomats a pretext for continuing to call General Ballivián's regime an "American Republic."

The U.S. Embassy's epitaph for the Urriolagoitia presidency praised its "well-meaning and well-intentioned" policies but condemned the wage increases the president had mandated and his counterproductive persecution of the MNR. In the end, U.S. diplomats believed that "those people of Bolivia who value freedom and the free expression of the people's choice owe the president a debt of gratitude for his hands-off policy" regarding the election. Still, the results of that election were nothing short of a catastrophe for the traditional political parties, the United States, and Bolivian liberal constitutional oligarchy. When given the opportunity, a clear plurality of the voting public (some 43 percent) had chosen Paz Estenssoro's alternative and, in effect, granted the MNR a mandate. If President Urriolagoitia had earned praise for permitting the election to go forward, his response to it had made revolution, if not civil war, all but inevitable. U.S. diplomats also found fault with his "inability" to curb Bolivia's high inflation and especially with his campaign against the MNR, which had managed only to arouse "great sympathy" for Paz Estenssoro, "a man who had had little contact with the average Bolivian voter for almost five years."[62]

The Truman administration, however, must also bear a share of the blame for the president's failures. Urriolagoitia's one bold effort to reform the national economy and preserve the vestiges of the old social order by overturning a central aspect of the economic one had been derailed by an unlikely alliance of the tin barons and the U.S. ambassador, Irving Florman. Embassy officers believed that, when Urriolagoitia knuckled under to the rosca, his PURS lost almost all of its legitimacy with the masses, paving the way for Paz Estenssoro's remarkable electoral victory. Assistant Secretary Miller could only lament that he no longer had Ambassador Joseph Flack's "steady hand at the tiller down there" during those critical moments.[63] Moreover, the policy that the Reconstruction Finance Corporation pursued in March 1951 seemed calculated to infuriate Bolivians of all political stripes. At a time when President Urriolagoitia should have been celebrating a tin boom, earning increased government revenue to promote reform, and winning credit for both, he was instead besieged, not just by Paz Estenssoro and the tin barons but also by the United States.

6

BALLIVIÁN

May 1951–April 1952

Of course your assurances of cooperation with our program are greatly appreciated. In our opinion that cooperation will be most effective if we do not confuse the importance of tin to the American defense program with the problem of maintaining a satisfactory level of economic welfare in Bolivia.
—Stuart Symington, 6 July 1951

As is well known, Bolivia has cooperated in the past with the grand nation of the north. I know the admirable people intimately; their virtues cannot be dimmed by the activities of a minor government agency playing with pennies. I am sure that the country of Washington the unblemished; of Lincoln the liberator; of Roosevelt whose equal in the annals of Democracy must be sought in the Greek classics; of Truman the staunch opponent of Communism, understanding perfectly the scope of our problems, must perforce stop those hostile persons who would condemn us to economic starvation.
—Hugo Ballivián, 3 January 1952

General Hugo Ballivián Rojas entered office on 16 May 1951 with no clear agenda or mandate other than to forestall a takeover by the Movimiento Nacionalista Revolucionario. General Ballivián, himself a member of an upper-class family, headed a junta of officers who had been handed the reins of power by President Urriolagoitia in an act of political desperation. The army had long been the final resort of the rosca, and so it was again. Yet, speaking of the newly installed junta, the chief of the Federal Police remarked that he "never in his life had run across a more inept group politically."[1] The generals and colonels faced two nearly impossible situations, and it took less than a year to prove that they were incapable of dealing with either of them.

The first was the looming National Revolution. The movimientistas, spurred by their election victory and outraged by its theft, gained strength and momentum with each passing day. Promising new elections, Ballivián permitted most of the exiled leaders except for Víctor Paz Estenssoro to return, hoping to channel MNR discontent into at least partial restoration of liberal constitutional oligarchy. But the movimientistas would have none of it. State Department officers had years before resigned themselves to the inevitability of a military government but believed that the enlightened authoritarianism they expected from Ballivián would be preferable to the weak, vacillating democracy of the last five years. The military, at least, would be able to effectively repress the MNR and to resist the popular pressures that had so troubled Presidents Hertzog and Urriolagoitia.

General Ballivián would need the full support of the Truman administration if he was to have any hope of averting revolution. It soon became clear, however, that Senator Johnson and the new chairman of the Reconstruction Finance Corporation, W. Stuart Symington, far from supporting the new regime, were determined to beat Bolivia to its knees and impose upon it the lowest tin price they could. Ballivián would never enjoy the benefits of a true tin contract throughout his eleven months in the Palacio Quemado. By the time President Truman finally removed Chairman Symington in early 1952 and put an end to the RFC's campaign against Bolivia, it was too late. While thousands of tons of tin concentrates sat unsold and unshipped on the docks of Antofogasta and Arica and food shortages racked Bolivian cities, Paz Estenssoro and the MNR would launch the National Revolution.

Stuart Symington's RFC

In the end, RFC Chairman Stuart Symington turned out to be almost as dangerous to General Ballivián's junta as Paz Estenssoro. Appointed on 7 May 1951 to clean up the scandal-plagued agency, Symington had long been one of the most fiscally aggressive of the defense planners. He believed that overpaying for tin was nothing short of a crime. If "America is exploited in the prices it is forced to pay," he thundered, "may we not be laying the foundation for the ultimate destruction of our free enterprise system?"[2] In short, Symington took the "battle for tin" personally.

Although most of the RFC's directors had been pleased to bring the price of tin down to $1.50 per pound, by the middle of June, the agency had driven the Singapore price down to just $1.06. Chairman Symington was aiming for a pre–Korean War price of 74¢ per pound. He proudly reported that the RFC's efforts were saving U.S. taxpayers tens of millions of dollars per year and could save even more.[3] He offered the Bolivians a six-month contract for just $1.03

and deemed this to be most generous, representing as it did a 32 percent increase over the pre–Korean War price. There could be no doubt that the chairman was completely unconcerned about the impact this would have on the Altiplano. For his part, Ambassador Martínez Vargas refused even to forward the offer to his superiors.[4]

Hoping to educate the defense planners on the dire consequences of their policies, U.S. diplomats arranged for a joint State Department–RFC mission to La Paz to study the tin industry. Notably, Chairman Symington and Senator Johnson insisted that the mission's sole purpose was to "find out the true cost" of tin production, "not to study what the price of tin should be." At the end of June, State Department officer Rollin Atwood accompanied Symington's personal assistant, George Weaver, and an RFC mining engineer to La Paz, where they spent weeks meeting with government officials, bankers, the tin barons, most of the medium tin mine owners, a "large representative group" of the small mine owners, and a number of labor leaders.[5]

Atwood found the situation in La Paz to be "tense and in many ways desperate." Interruptions and fluctuations in RFC tin purchases had "left all but the largest companies hanging in thin air." As tin production slowed or even stopped, up to 50 percent of the nation's tin miners were thrown out of work. With little foreign exchange coming into the country, imported food was becoming scarce, and the prospect of a catastrophic general strike loomed larger by the day. According to State Department officer Atwood and embassy officer Thomas Maleady, nothing short of the survival of General Ballivián's government was at stake: they pleaded for a "stopgap" agreement with the RFC that would permit the small and medium mine operators to resume their normal operations. Not surprisingly, Ambassador Florman disagreed, asserting with his inimitable logic that, because "revolutions always begin against a tyrant," and "there is no tyrant in Bolivia at this time," there could be no revolution.[6]

The RFC had reached somewhat different conclusions. Whereas Antenor Patiño and Carlos Aramayo claimed that inflation had driven the costs of their imports up by 30 to 40 percent in the previous year, Symington's lieutenant, E. C. Welch, concluded that the correct figure was closer to 21 percent. Welch argued that the "average" pre–Korean War price for Bolivian tin should "probably" be 83¢ per pound and that the tin barons could only guess at what taxes and exchange restrictions would cost them for the next year. He was willing to concede the Bolivian government the right to levy export taxes but insisted that these should be "reasonable" and not subsidized by the U.S. government through an inflated tin price. The more than 100 percent tax increase that, he believed, President Urriolagoitia had imposed since the Korean War certainly did not qualify as "reasonable." Welch further suggested that if Bolivian tin producers closed the least efficient 10 percent of their mines, their average production costs would decrease by approximately 3½¢ per pound. In short, average costs of production were $1.10 per pound but should have been 99¢ if export taxes were reduced to "reasonable" levels and 10 percent of tin miners lost their jobs. It did not help the tin barons' cause when the RFC learned that they had "paid high dividends and that in some cases profits had amounted to a 100% return on the invested capital" during the previous year.[7]

Nonetheless, after conducting a close analysis of the Bolivian economy, U.S. Embassy personnel disputed Welch's conclusions. The Bolivian producers claimed that Patiño could break even at the RFC's $1.03 per pound, Aramayo and Hochschild required $1.20 per pound to do so, and the small and medium mine owners required at least $1.40. Because of global inflation, devaluation of the boliviano, and recent wage increases (most notably, a 30 percent wage hike for mine workers decreed just before the election), the producers' claims were at least plausible. Like the still-classified Keenleyside report, the embassy report attributed much of the "critical artificial exaggeration of the degree of marginality of Bolivian tin production" to the "striking tax immunity" that landowners and the wealthy enjoyed. It concluded that, at a price of $1.15 per pound, the junta might be able to keep the economy on an "even keel" but would require $1.30 per pound to gain the "elbow room" it needed to "effect necessary changes" without provoking a "political crisis caused by economic factors." The State Department and most members of the Vital Materials Coordinating Committee agreed that the price should fall somewhere between $1.10 and $1.25 per pound. On the other hand, even a price of $2.00 per pound would be meaningless unless the junta was willing to lift the tax burden on an industry that "may even now have been taxed out of existence." Ambassador Florman, of course, concluded that all Bolivian producers could profit at 80¢ per pound and that "if the price of tin were $10.00 a pound the Bolivian people would derive no benefit."[8]

Although the RFC officers in La Paz were apparently convinced by the statistical evidence that it would be "impossible" for the Bolivians to accept $1.03 per pound and that the small and medium mine owners could not operate at less than $1.30 per pound, Chairman Symington seemed determined to "pull the rug from under the mission." He met with Ambassador Martínez Vargas and made accusations that could only be described as "insulting"; he continued to publicly condemn Bolivian participation in a tin cartel he somehow believed was still in existence. The Bolivian Embassy responded by publicly denying it was a part of any cartel and by calling for "fair treatment" for the nation whose tin had been critical for the "final victory of the Allied armies," lest Symington destroy "the community of interests and the complete solidarity" between the two nations.[9]

The "only thing that is saving the situation," State Department officer Atwood reported, was a widespread "feeling" within the junta that Atwood and his fellow officers were "sincere in our endeavor to find a solution." Deputy Assistant Secretary Mann politely tried to muzzle Chairman Symington, suggesting that, in order not to "increase the risk of misunderstanding," the RFC should "refrain from making any public statements at this time." Symington countered by asking if "the Bolivians believe they will receive a more sympathetic reaction from State," might "this not be a reason they defer signing a contract on terms which would appear to be fair to both countries?"[10]

While Symington and the State Department debated, General Ballivián took matters into his own hands. He first offered to step up production of tungsten, "which [U.S.] defense agencies want[ed] badly," in return for a more reasonable tin contract. Chairman Symington considered the issues of tungsten and tin to be "unrelated," but Assistant Secretary Miller noted that, for the Bolivians, "the two cannot be dissociated." The general's second gambit was more dramatic. As the U.S. mission was preparing to return to Washington with its final report, he dispatched Alfredo Alexander, one of the original negotiators of the 1947 commercial treaty with Argentina, to Buenos Aires to finally implement the pact, which would grant Perón the right to purchase all of Bolivia's tin for 1951 and 1952. As even Ambassador Florman conceded, implementation of the treaty would be a "public relations coup." Alexander had been arguing in the pages of his newspaper, *Ultima Hora*, that negotiations with the Reconstruction Finance Corporation were hopeless and that Bolivia should turn to its neighbor Argentina. Moreover, the reopening of treaty negotiations put the issue of an Argentine loan back on the table. General Ballivián, State Department officer Atwood explained, was willing "to give consideration to any solution which might ameliorate the present desperate situation."[11]

Although Bolivian officials privately assured Atwood that they did not intend this step to be a "threat to the United States" and there was little chance that the Argentines, almost as bankrupt as the Bolivians, were in any position to implement the treaty, the very idea of Bolivia turning to the peronistas was disquieting. "There is a growing demand on the part of the public for some sort of action," Atwood reported, and State Department "assurances" could no longer be counted on to "ward off Bolivian resentment." Moreover, if Argentina did come to Ballivián's rescue, "Perón might be able to dig up enough exchange to take a large hunk of what [tin] is available." If he did, the RFC would have to "pay through the nose" to get it.[12]

Well aware that the Argentines might again throw a monkey wrench into U.S. tin procurement and that the U.S. stockpile was dwindling, the RFC softened its stance. For the RFC's Welch, "THE MOST IMPORTANT THING IS TO OBTAIN TIN," and a few cents difference no longer made that much of a difference. Since "we have already shown the producers that we will not be held up for exorbitant prices," any agreement in the "neighborhood" of $1.09 per pound would cement the world price at that level, whereas a reduction to $1.03 would be of only "psychological" value.[13]

On 9 July, urgently seeking a "stopgap" to salvage the deteriorating situation in La Paz and to replenish the U.S. tin stockpile, Chairman Symington asked Secretary Acheson to "tell him what price" the State Department "thought he ought to pay to Bolivia" and promised that "he would pay it." Symington wanted to pay just $1.03 per pound, but Atwood, Weaver, and the others who had gone to La Paz suggested that $1.20 would be more appropriate. State Department officer Winthrop Brown calculated that "mathematically the mid-point" between $1.20 and the RFC's offer of $1.03 per pound "would be about $1.12." Symington agreed on the spot to make an offer at that price to Ambassador Martínez Vargas, believing that it would "probably be satisfactory to the Johnson Committee," and Secretary Miller promised to press the Bolivian "not to adopt an arbitrary and adamant attitude."[14]

When a rumor surfaced that Carlos Aramayo, Mauricio Hochschild, and Antenor Patiño were meeting in Paris and planned to reject the U.S. offer of $1.12 per pound, U.S. diplomats moved quickly. They sought out one of Hochschild's executives in New York and informed him that "this offer was the very best that the United States could make at this time" and warned that "if it was not accepted, there might be political and economic collapse in Bolivia."[15] Of greater concern to the Bolivians were fears that the "stopgap" $1.12 price would become the permanent price.

U.S. diplomats in La Paz and Washington offered their assurances that this was not the case and that the "stopgap" would have no bearing on the long-term rate to be negotiated later, based on the reports of the mission. They reminded Ambassador Martínez Vargas that, even though the United States was "under attack throughout the world," its "highest officers" had turned their attention to Bolivia to formulate a "generous" offer. Arguing that this offer "represented a beginning" and that the price negotiated in the long-term contract would be applied retroactively to the tin delivered during the "stopgap," State Department officers asked the ambassador to "make the best of the present difficult situation by accepting the offer."[16] The Bolivian Foreign Office, "relying on [U.S.] good faith," authorized Martínez Vargas to accept the "inappropriate and impractical" price but hoped that the final agreement on price would be more "fair." The Bolivians immediately shipped seventeen hundred tons of tin concentrates, and mining resumed.[17]

The fiercest criticism of the "stopgap" proposal came from Whitehall. British officials complained that they had not been informed of the RFC's plans despite the obvious implications for them: under the U.S. proposal, British smelters processing Patiño tin would be obligated to pay at least $1.12 per pound for nearly half of Bolivia's tin. Not only would the new price be a financial drain, but the Malayans would also demand a revision of their contract with the

Ministry of Supply to match Patiño's. The *Financial Times* denounced the deal as a "desperate device to prevent Bolivian mine shutdowns" and "price discrimination." It even argued that the "stopgap" was "incompatible with normal concepts of business conduct," as if the RFC–Ministry of Supply monopoly was.[18] State Department officer Brown explained to his British counterpart that, when the Bolivians had "incontinently rejected" the offer of $1.03 per pound, the RFC had offered a higher price "to break the impasse" and "get some money moving into Bolivia" in view of its "extremely dangerous political situation." Besides, Antenor Patiño had publicly stated that he could make money at $1.03 per pound, and "it should not be too difficult for the UK" to force his price down to that level. Although Secretary Acheson conceded that "we should have told [the British] what we were doing," he was quick to note that only the "RFC's action had permitted the British to get tin" for anything less than $1.80 per pound in the first place.[19] The "stopgap" temporarily stanched the economic bleeding in Bolivia and encouraged the junta, but it soon became clear Chairman Symington and Senator Johnson intended to torpedo the deal.

The Tin Impasse of 1951

On 24 July 1951, the day the Bolivians provisionally accepted the "stopgap," RFC Chairman Symington testified before Senator Johnson's subcommittee. Symington began by boasting that, with the mandate received from the senators to drive down the world price of tin, his agency was saving U.S. taxpayers $500 million. He then explained that the goal of the joint mission to La Paz had been to "get the facts on tin production costs" and establish "their relationship to the Bolivian economy and the world tin cartel." Presenting no evidence, Symington related that "our own experience" confirmed "the findings of this committee" that a cartel still existed despite the formal dissolution of the International Tin Committee in November 1946. The United States, he declared, "will not pay any more than $1.12 a pound for tin, even if no beer or dog food is packed in tin next year."[20] For the Bolivians who had believed that $1.12 per pound was a "provisional" price that would eventually be retroactively increased in a long-term contract, this was nothing short of a betrayal. That betrayal was made all the worse, Ambassador Martínez Vargas told Secretary Miller, because all tin shipped to the United States under the provisional "stopgap" had only put the RFC "in a stronger position to sit out the fight."[21]

Chairman Symington went on to pronounce that "it probably would not help Bolivia much, even if they did receive an exorbitant tin price"; indeed, it "might perpetuate the worst handicap to a healthy Bolivian economy." He condemned the tin barons for living "outside their country," failing to "invest any foreign exchange at home unless it is necessary to do so in order to protect their Bolivian mining interests," and hoping to soak "the American taxpayer and the American consumers." Furthermore, he accused the Bolivian government of deliberately falsifying its statistics and blamed it for trying to support an entire nation on one product. The true fault lay with those Bolivians who looked to the United States for a high tin price in order to avoid facing "up to their responsibilities." If the United States "allows itself to be exploited," it might well "lose what we are fighting for in Korea—because we are laying a foundation for the ultimate destruction of free enterprise through heavy and unnecessary taxation." If the Bolivians included taxes in their computation of a "fair price," they were asking for nothing less than "a key to the United States Treasury."[22] "No monetary measure," Welch told Symington, "can be placed upon the loss of prestige which would result from a complete defeat in our effort to buy at a fair and reasonable price." Symington's tirade won bipartisan praise in the Senate but elicited a very different reaction in Jakarta, Kuala Lumpur, and especially La Paz.[23]

Anticipating the inevitable firestorm, Secretary Acheson ordered the embassy staff in La Paz to "refrain" from "any comment" to the public, producers, or the government in the wake of Symington's bombast. Even the British, who were among the beneficiaries of Symington's campaign, noted that "matters are not, of course, helped by the sort of statements" he had issued. Although embassy officer Maleady believed that the junta showed "admirable discretion" by refraining from comment, Chairman Symington had led the Bolivians to "question our bona fides" and "good faith." Ambassador Martínez Vargas deemed Symington's statements to be an "outrage."[24] The Bolivian press "damned the yanquis with one voice"; one La Paz columnist sarcastically nominated Symington for a "Stalin prize" for "brilliant anti-U.S. propaganda." Assistant Secretary Miller's feeble defense to Liberal statesman Luis Guachalla was an outright lie: Symington "had been badly misquoted by the press" and that "the people and government of Bolivia could be assured of his good faith." Guachalla, of course, believed none of it and warned that "sympathy towards the U.S. is disappearing in Bolivia, but what is more grave is that faith in American democracy may be lost."[25]

A spokesman for Carlos Aramayo openly assailed Chairman Symington's statements in *La Razón*, asserting that "it was not his place" to criticize the Bolivian political economy, while Antenor Patiño's general manager condemned the "unjust and uneconomic" pricing policies of the RFC. Tin would, he claimed, be approximately $1.40 per pound if its price had mirrored those of other metals and the RFC had not undertaken its "unilateral action." If the general manager received only $1.12 per pound, he would be forced to shut down or cut back production from all but one of the Patiño operations, which could well "cause the downfall" of the government and "bring about chaos." It was, however, easy to understand why Chairman Symington and Senator Johnson had "unfairly" targeted the tin producers, the general manager explained, since "producers of other metals are represented in the United States and have a political voice." Hochschild's vice president agreed wholeheartedly.[26]

Just a week after Chairman Symington's testimony, the junta retaliated. Its Office of Press, Propaganda, and Information released a pamphlet entitled "The Bolivian Tin Trap," a denunciation of "plutocratic" "yanqui shareholders" who "enslaved" Bolivians and sought to transform the nation into an "economic colony of Wall Street." Symington had managed to incite an ultraconservative military regime to issue official publications singing the praises of Peronist "social capitalism" and echoing Marxist denunciations of the United States. An oblivious Ambassador Florman reported that "the Bolivian Government is much pleased by the prevailing tin price established by Mr. Symington, in whom they, as well as the Bolivian people, have implicit confidence." More accurately, embassy officer Maleady reported that it was impossible to get cooperation from anyone in the Bolivian government because of what it called the "intransigent, arbitrary, unilateral depressing of the tin market by the RFC to the detriment of the interests of the Bolivian Government and producers."[27]

When approached by Ambassador Martínez Vargas, Chairman Symington did indeed privately back down from his bombastic pledge not to pay "a cent above $1.12." Still, the ambassador quickly came to understand that Symington was now determined to pay the Bolivians only their "cost of production," once he determined what that was.[28] By mid-August, however, both the RFC and Secretary Acheson were threatening to withdraw the U.S. offer because the Singapore price had fallen below $1.12 per pound. Having driven the world price below $1.00 per pound, Symington was now provoking complaints from Belgium, Great Britain, and Indonesia with his higher offer to the Bolivians. "The longer we hold open the offer," he told Secretary Acheson, "the more trouble we will have."[29]

The Bolivians eventually yielded to necessity, formally accepted the "stop-gap," and opened negotiations for a long-term contract. Chairman Symington, who had no intention of paying the Bolivians any more than $1.12 per pound, presented the findings of the joint mission to La Paz as proof that the Bolivians could produce tin at that price after all. The RFC had skewed the mission's statistical evidence by factoring the Patiño mines' ultrarich veins into its calculations for an "average" cost of production to produce a deceptively low figure that would guarantee profits for the Patiño mines but force other mines to produce at under cost or close down. The agency failed to account for inflation either in the prices of other metals or in the goods purchased by the Bolivians. It ignored the fact that Bolivia had refused to sell a single pound of tin at the RFC's "fair" price of 72¢. Worse yet, by taking early 1950, a time when Bolivia was suffering from a "severe fiscal crisis" owing to the low price of tin, as the basis for its calculations, the agency implied that the nation should exist on the brink of "economic collapse" in a perpetual state of social unrest. In other words, the RFC was attempting to impose a price that the Bolivians had never accepted and that had already caused "a severe crisis" for President Urriolagoitia.[30]

Ambassador Martínez Vargas and the tin producers still held out hope for $1.50 per pound and met in September to coordinate their strategy. In early October, they prepared a memorandum for Chairman Symington designed to dispel his misconceptions. The tin producers pointed out that in no other negotiations between any nations for any other goods were the "average production costs" the basis for negotiation. Moreover, not only were Patiño's costs much lower than all other tin producers, but also none of his tin even went to the United States. The producers claimed, falsely, that there had been no tax increases in years and, more credibly, that their labor costs had risen by 70 percent. Whereas the East Asian colonies benefited from cheaper labor, easier access to alluvial tin, and Marshall Plan funds allocated to the imperial powers, Bolivia had spent the last five years exhausting its best mines to reduce production costs. Even Senator Johnson had admitted the previous year that the Bolivians were entitled to a higher price than their East Asian rivals. In most of their memorandum, however, the producers focused on wartime and postwar inflation. Using statistics compiled by the *Bulletin of the National Association of Purchasing Agents*, they showed clearly that, since 1939, the costs of all commodities had increased by 288 percent, and those of some goods purchased heavily by Bolivia, such as livestock and coarse textiles, had increased by 400 to 500 percent. If the cost of tin had increased as much as those of other commodities, it should be priced at $1.44 per pound before transport and smelter expenses, and if it was compared directly with copper and zinc, it should be priced at $1.68 per pound. Unimpressed with the Bolivian analysis, the RFC publicly announced that it had to "unscramble the tin producers' arithmetic" before commenting further.[31]

When two days of meetings failed to budge Chairman Symington, Ambassador Martínez Vargas finally threw up his hands, informing his superiors that there was no point in any further negotiations. Symington simply ignored the Bolivian statistics and discounted the current Singapore tin price (which had risen to $1.30) as an "artificial one" resulting from manipulations of the "producers' cartel." "Any step on our part," Martínez Vargas and Guachalla agreed, "will do nothing but weaken our cause." In withdrawing from the negotiations, the Bolivians hoped that "confidential discussions" with the State Department would eventually break the logjam.[32] For his part, however, Assistant Secretary Miller "felt it important that we discourage any idea" that the Bolivians could "play us off against the RFC," if only because of the "tendency of the RFC to engage in demagogic maneuvers against us with Senator Johnson."[33]

Embassy officer Maleady openly sided with the Bolivians, protesting that "someone has to break the ice, so why the hell cannot we be the ones to do it?" and that by "being so cold-blooded and hard-hearted," the United States was encouraging revolution or even a turn toward the Soviet bloc. He reported that "extremely pro-U.S." but thoroughly "disillusioned" Bolivian leaders "are going around long-faced" and openly wondered how long it would take them to simply say "to hell with the U.S." Even worse, Bolivians were starting to see the movimientistas as "martyrs instead of tyrants." With "tin prices tobogganing," the junta and the United States were facing "vehement, even vitriolic criticism" from every segment of Bolivian society.[34]

Whatever U.S. diplomats thought, Chairman Symington and his fellow "bulls in a tin shop" had no intention of deviating from their "maddening" course. Although the chairman claimed he had to take into account "reasonable" Bolivian taxes when considering a price of tin, he deemed most to be unreasonable and insisted that taxation in Bolivia had increased by 100 percent in the previous two years. Even worse, in a radical new proposal, the chairman offered to compute the "average" cost of Bolivian tin production and allow the Bolivian government to distribute the profits to meet each company's individual costs. Symington's new proposal left the State Department aghast. Not only did it run counter to almost every tenet of U.S. foreign policy, but it would also encourage nationalization and would certainly be used against U.S. corporations across the hemisphere in the future.[35]

In many ways, Chairman Symington was taking his cues from Senator Johnson's subcommittee, which had accused tin producers of "gouging" and even "murdering" the United States. Whereas the State Department hoped to convince the chairman to find a "mutually satisfactory" price, he vowed that "his boys" could "deal with the Bolivians and could really make things tough for them." Although the Munitions Board was urging new purchases and a replenishing of the tin stockpile, Symington had concluded that the United States "could live on the present stockpile for a long time" and "should do so."[36] To soothe fears of a shortage, the chairman had publicly stated that the United States had enough tin for "seven or eight months," but, in fact, the RFC only had sufficient tin to keep the Texas City smelter in operation for that time. Meeting U.S. industrial needs would require use of the stockpile. This did not stop Symington from ceasing all RFC stockpile purchases and reintroducing conservation measures in November to bring additional pressure to bear on La Paz. At the same time, the chairman announced that, because the tin stockpile was "very large," the RFC would only make purchases in Bolivia that would be "considered reasonable by American taxpayers."[37]

The Defense and Interior Departments joined the State Department in protest: selling off the tin stockpile, as Senator Johnson and Chairman Symington proposed, "would be a perversion" of the stockpile's purpose. Not only was "the political situation in the Far East" so "serious that we cannot rely on" Malay Straits tin, but selling off the stockpile would impede any future stockpiling because producers' "fears that we will use" it "as a commercial weapon against them will be confirmed." "Nothing would please the Russians more than to have us do this," one diplomat claimed, "because they would have chapter and verse to quote against us in support of their constant propaganda theme that the United States is using its economic strength to force down the standards of living of underdeveloped peoples." Still, the State Department understood that Senator Johnson and the RFC did not take its arguments seriously and hoped that they would heed those of the Munitions Board, which also opposed Symington's plan. They did not. Tin Division Chief McKinnon argued quite simply that President Truman could legally release the stockpile "during a state of emergency," and one had already been proclaimed for the Korean War. "Between us," Chairman Symington informed Assistant Secretary Miller, Defense Mobilizer "Charlie Wilson told me that we could tap the stockpile." Symington was clearly planning to do just that, regardless of the consequences.[38]

For the State Department, it was now clear that Chairman Symington's obsession was a threat to U.S. diplomacy. His plans to raid the stockpile and essentially force the nationalization of Bolivian tin were, it turned out, only the first of his radical ideas. The chairman also intended to have his agency purchase no Bolivian tin whatsoever but purchase the entire Indonesian surplus to maintain the Texas City smelter. Even though this would thrust the RFC into competition with Dutch smelters and increase the world price of tin in the process, the State Department had no doubt that Symington would do it. Apparently, the chairman even contemplated sanctions against Malaya, Indonesia, Bolivia, or Great Britain should they not cooperate.[39] Still, U.S. diplomats remained hesitant to challenge him openly.

Symington had once blamed the State Department for Bolivian intransigence, and there were rumors that "officers of the Department were being strongly influenced by a lobbyist representing tin interests." Several of the tin barons' managers and representatives had met with State Department officers over the previous six months, as had the U.S.-born public relations expert hired by all three companies. Moreover, Assistant Secretary Miller had accepted a dinner invitation from Carlos Aramayo that virtually invited charges of corruption. Although Miller had paid for his own meal (and fourteen dollars for the tin baron's) and had warned Chairman Symington in advance, the most distressing part of the meeting was the assistant secretary's admission "that I agreed 100 percent with Aramayo in practically all respects, but I was not in a position to say so." Thus even though the State Department understood that Symington was courting disaster and engaging in what amounted to economic warfare with the Bolivians, it could not confront him directly or even openly question his desire to get the best price for U.S. taxpayers for fear of Senator Johnson's "righteous indignation" and the likelihood that his subcommittee would launch an ugly investigation.[40]

If the State Department was timid, U.S. labor unions were not. In August, Bolivian unions complained to the American Federation of Labor, the Congress of Industrial Organizations, and the United Mine Workers in the hope of enlisting them in the fight against the Reconstruction Finance Corporation. Their appeals were successful. The foreign policy leaders of all three unions, Serafino Romualdi, Ernst Schwarz, and Thomas Kennedy, sent concurrent letters to Assistant Secretary Miller, pleading for the State Department to end the impasse before it led to "the establishment, in Bolivia, of a Communist or Fascist totalitarian regime." The tin barons naturally agreed and launched their own protest. At the sixth meeting of the Tin Study Group, Carlos Aramayo and Mauricio Hochschild openly accused the U.S. representative of "economic aggression," and the meeting degenerated into a producers' assault on RFC "discrimination."[41]

When talks on the 1951 tin contract finally resumed, the price of tin on the London exchange was down to $1.20 per pound, Guachalla and Ambassador Martínez Vargas demanded $1.50 per pound, and Symington refused to budge from $1.12. And when neither side yielded an inch, negotiations broke down entirely at the end of October. The RFC proposed putting aside negotiations on the long-term price and discussing smelter fees or another "stopgap" price, but to no avail; the Bolivians were counting on a tin shortage to drive the RFC to the bargaining table in earnest. Ambassador Martínez Vargas continued his tireless efforts to show Chairman Symington the errors in his analyses, holding as a last recourse an appeal to Secretary Acheson and President Truman for the restoration of an open market. When he presented yet another refutation of RFC statistics in mid-November, hoping that Chairman Symington would see reason before "unprecedented damage to U.S.-Bolivian relations" was done, Symington and his "boys" opted instead to get tough.[42]

Speaking for the RFC, E. C. Welch gave an interview to the *New York Herald Tribune* in which he, according to Ambassador Martínez Vargas, "declared an economic war on Bolivia" in the most "inaccurate, tendentious, and unjust" terms yet. Welch condemned the U.S. banks that lent money to the tin producers to allow them to sustain their operations during their embargo and proclaimed that the "struggle over tin" was "obviously nearing a climax" because "Bolivia can't hold out indefinitely." He even questioned Bolivia's contribution to the war effort by pointing out that only half of Bolivian tin helped the U.S. war effort (while the rest, of course, went to Great Britain). When confronted, Welch claimed that he did not make several statements attributed to him and retorted that the tin producers had made distasteful comments about the United States as well. The Bolivians reminded him that, unlike the tin barons, he was a government official. Although Martínez Vargas had always been "under the impression that the problems of tin" were "located in a terrain of friendly cooperation" and "American spirit," Welch had "disgracefully" turned the negotiations into "simple extortion" and the "starvation of a small and less developed nation." "In any event," the ambassador concluded, the Bolivians now understood that they were "engaged in an economic battle" not just for "our country, but also for all" of the continent, a battle that would "make trouble for the United States throughout Latin America." Embassy officer Maleady could only lament that "it will take a long time to recover goodwill already lost."[43]

Symington's Removal and the National Revolution

By December, Assistant Secretary Miller's wing of the State Department was finally ready to move against Chairman Symington and the arguments "he has been making for months with such tiresomeness and demagoguery." "There is no problem," Miller wrote to Ambassador Claude Bowers in Chile, "that has worried me as much as the tin problem." The assistant secretary was furious that Symington, in "flagrant violations" of his agreement "to cease fighting this issue in the press," was placing Bolivia "morally behind the Iron Curtain," to the "detriment of our foreign relations." At one point, apparently unaware of the assistant secretary's sympathies, Symington had even tried to recruit Miller to convince Aramayo to accept the RFC's price. By the end of 1951, the need to break the tin impasse was becoming urgent.[44]

Also in December, the Bolivian Foreign Office started to make good on Martínez Vargas's threat: Bolivia would "make trouble" for the United States by enlisting the other nations of Latin America in its cause. The tin barons had pressed Undersecretary of Foreign Affairs Ernesto Daza Ondarza to invoke the Organization of American States (OAS) charter, but he had resisted, believing that such an appeal would only be "laughed at." When Daza Ondarza was transferred to an embassy abroad, however, his successor evidently yielded to their pressure. For its part, Ballivián's government sent an eight-chapter circular to its embassies across South America with orders to distribute it to the press and chancelleries. The purpose in highlighting the RFC's tactics was to "prepare the way" for a Bolivian complaint before the OAS charging the United States with "economic aggression." The Bolivian arguments found fertile ground. A Colombian journalist contrasted the billions the United States was spending in Europe and Asia with the "irritating stinginess" of the "little seen" Good Neighbor policy. Ecuadoran President Galo Plaza Lasso was sympathetic but thought that the Bolivians had "handled the situation very awkwardly." He found it impossible to believe that the U.S. government would permit, much less contribute to, the "total collapse" of the Bolivian government and thought the Bolivians had done "the wrong thing in trying to scare the United States into action." He nonetheless conceded that the junta was "at the end of its rope."[45]

Peronist newspapers in Buenos Aires denounced Bolivia's "being crucified by rapacious imperialism" and capitalized on this "opportunity for whipping up anti-U.S. sentiment" in one of "the most violent press campaigns against the U.S. recently." When combined with Peruvian complaints about U.S. tariff policies on tuna and "the allegedly raw deal" being given to Chilean copper, it seemed "that our government's financial chickens are coming home to roost," as this "minor but increasingly vexatious problem" was rapidly growing worse.[46] Perón, in particular, was most sympathetic to Bolivian efforts to unite the South American nations exporting raw materials. Great Britain had acted as Europe's sole purchaser for Argentine meat and wheat for years, and the Marshall Planners had punished Argentina much as the RFC was punishing Bolivia. If the Bolivians brought their case before the OAS, Perón pledged his full support against the "arbitrary" purchasing monopolies maintained by Great Britain and the United States. "Today for me," he exclaimed to the Bolivian ambassador, "tomorrow for you" would be the rallying cry for the nations of South America united against Anglo-American imperialism.[47]

The junta, understanding that it was now in an open fight for its life, proceeded on all fronts against Chairman Symington. Bolivian diplomats attempted to peddle their tin in France and Great Britain. The British firms were not interested, and the French, "mindful of their obligations to and dependency upon us," had little interest, either, embassy officer Maleady reported. The Bolivians denounced the RFC on the floor of the UN General Assembly and even cultivated allies in the U.S. Congress.[48] Two congressmen, Abraham Multer of New York and Clinton McKinnon of California, traveled to La Paz in December to meet with the tin producers and the junta. Representative Multer reported that "everywhere he had gone in Latin America he had been greeted with complaints about United States policy on tin," and he vowed to fight on Bolivia's behalf. Multer refused to meet with Chairman Symington, whom he believed to be "so intransigent that he could see no useful purpose in sitting down with him." When Senator Johnson tried to "quiet down" the congressman, Multer arranged an appointment directly with President Truman to urge him to "break the impasse on tin."[49]

As the chorus against Chairman Symington grew louder, Assistant Secretary Miller made his move. He had apparently concluded, only by bypassing Secretary Acheson, who was preoccupied with the Korean War and with McCarthyite attacks, and involving President Truman could the RFC be brought into line. To that end, Deputy Assistant Secretary Mann and State Department officer Atwood had told Truman's aide David Stowe in November that the "inability of the RFC" to reach agreement with the Bolivians was "creating ill will and resentment toward the U.S. not only on the part of government officials but with the rank and file of the Bolivian people." They had wanted to alert the president to the fact that Chairman Symington was about to raid the tin stockpile, not for defense, but "in order to drive down the price of tin" and that Bolivia, alone or in concert with other Latin American nations, might soon launch an open protest in the Organization of American States or the United Nations. Mann had avoided criticizing "any individual"; he had raised the issue "in view of the President's personal interest in good relations with the Latin American republics."[50] This first step had paved the way for the State Department's Latin American experts to bypass Secretary Acheson and to present their case directly to President Truman himself.

Assistant Secretary Miller's masterstroke, however, was enlisting Chilean president Gabriel González Videla, who had privately pledged to support a Bolivian OAS protest, to write a personal letter to President Truman in early December pleading the Bolivian case. Noting that the "Tin War" had been conducted "in an almost violent manner," the Chilean told Truman that no one doubted that the United States would win any conflict but that victory would have "very grave political" consequences. He defended the Bolivians as "only endeavoring to obtain the necessities of life" and warned that others would condemn the United States for freezing "prices when it needs to buy in times of scarcity" and for only eliminating "control in times when prices fall by themselves." González Videla's letter "had a good preliminary effect in Washington," Miller reported. Perhaps inspired by the letter from Ecuadoran President Plaza, which he had forwarded to President Truman, Miller had asked González Videla to "write a letter to a certain presidential colleague." The Chilean had agreed "at once."[51]

In the meantime, U.S. diplomats needed to convince the Bolivians they would be "doing themselves more harm than good by causing [the United States] trouble in the OAS at this juncture." They were loath to ask Ambassador Martínez Vargas to deliver the message because it might "seriously damage his position with his government," and his superiors "might not pay attention to him." Although embassy officer Maleady enjoyed "considerable personal prestige" with the Bolivian foreign minister, it "would be difficult to authorize" him "to give the Junta sufficient information to justify a suggestion that a [diplomatic] slow-down would be in Bolivia's interest." It seems that Assistant Secretary Miller found another messenger in Ecuadoran president Plaza, who told the Bolivians that, in Miller's words, "it is not going to help their situation to fight this matter out in the press or through pressure tactics which only play into the hands of our enemies (and I don't mean just the Commies)." The Bolivian diplomats agreed to "ride along a while longer before considering any step which might be distasteful to us" in the hopes that "President Truman's interest will bring about a settlement." In La Paz, embassy officer Maleady urged the Bolivians to "keep their fingers crossed" and "say a flock of Hail Marys" in hopes that the Miller's plan would produce the "long-hoped-for break."[52]

The appeal from his stalwart Cold War ally Gabriel González Videla seems to have finally spurred President Truman to get involved. He instructed Secretary Acheson to meet with Chairman Symington, and he pledged to settle the matter himself if the secretary could not reach an agreement with the chairman. When informed of the Chilean appeal, a seemingly penitent Symington rushed to meet with Acheson and promised that "if he were wrong in his stand, he wanted to do something about it."[53] When Symington and Acheson met on 20 December, however, it quickly became clear that the RFC chairman was far from repentant. After reminding the secretary of the "widespread support" he enjoyed from people like Senator Johnson, Symington reiterated that the price of $1.12 per pound he was now offering to Bolivia was "exceedingly generous." When Secretary Acheson asked what the chairman proposed to do to break the stalemate, Symington announced that he planned to convince the Malayan and Indonesian producers to accept $1.12 per pound. He would ignore the Bolivians until he had both set a world tin price and reduced the demand for Bolivian tin. Moreover, he apparently told the secretary that "only Congress could force him to change his present attitude." Acheson closed the meeting by meekly suggesting that the RFC "should approach these negotiations with some flexibility as to the price."[54]

As Secretary Acheson pondered his options, the RFC moved ahead with Symington's plan and negotiated a long-term deal with the British for twenty thousand tons of Malayan tin at a price of $1.18. The deal was a blow to the Bolivians, who might have accepted "something less than $1.50 but nothing so low as $1.25," let alone $1.18. It was obvious that the RFC had no intention of returning tin purchasing to private hands now or for years to come. Moreover, the deal with the Malayan producers stipulated that if the United States paid more to any other country's producers, the Malayans would receive the same, effectively freezing the ceiling price.[55] To persuade the British to accept $1.18 per pound for tin, Chairman Symington had to offer them a reduced price for steel from U.S. manufacturers; he refused, however, to budge from the price of $1.12 per pound he was offering the Bolivians for their tin. Senator Johnson, outraged that the tin barons seemed to be "more concerned about the prospect of future unsaleable tin surpluses than with the spectre of Communist aggression," soon pronounced from Capitol Hill that any new tin contract at a price higher than $1.18 would provoke a congressional investigation.[56] The Bolivians were furious that, yet again, their "interests had been sacrificed in a barter between the two great powers." Although Antenor Patiño could survive a tin impasse indefinitely, Mauricio Hochschild claimed that his firm was running a deficit of between fifty thousand and eighty thousand dollars per month at just one mine.[57]

By the beginning of 1952, Chairman Symington's opponents were gaining ground. Ambassador Martínez Vargas, who had since mid-December wanted a chance to explain to President Truman directly that "the RFC seems to conceive the tin problem as an economic struggle in which the United States must beat Bolivia to her knees," finally got his wish on 3 January.[58] Assistant Secretary Miller supported the ambassador wholeheartedly, helped arrange his appointment with the president, and even provided him with talking points to make his case more effectively. As Miller was briefing the ambassador, Secretary Acheson urged President Truman to inform the Bolivian that "you are giving the matter your personal attention" and that "tin purchasing policy is now under active consideration at the highest level."[59]

The president did just that. What is more, within hours of meeting with the ambassador, Truman announced that he had accepted Chairman Symington's resignation. Secretary Acheson then gave a press conference promising a successful conclusion to the tin debacle. Officially, Symington had resigned because his task of restoring public faith in the RFC had been completed. Indeed, the president publicly awarded his fellow Missourian a Distinguished Service Medal for his years of government service, but, privately, he wrote that "Stu needs to take some time off and get an objective view on things."[60] Celebrations over Symington's removal, however, turned out to be premature.

Because of a power struggle between President Truman and the Senate, Chairman Symington was allowed not only to remain in office until 14 February but also to name his own replacement for a week longer. When, on 7 January, the president appointed Securities and Exchange Commission Chairman Harry A. McDonald, a Republican under investigation by the House of Representatives, to chair the RFC, Democrats on the Senate Banking Committee refused to act on his appointment. But when the Banking Committee then suggested that the president appoint an interim chairman of the agency until McDonald's status was resolved, Truman threatened to personally take over the RFC himself, an extraordinary move that was, nonetheless, the only way in which the president could bypass the Senate's power to advise and consent. Truman's bluff, if it was in fact a bluff, succeeded in forcing the Senate's hand, and McDonald was confirmed, thus averting a truly bizarre constitutional crisis. McDonald finally took office on 20 February; senatorial foot-dragging had given Symington an extra month to inflict even more damage. As Defense Mobilizer Wilson told Ambassador Martínez Vargas, Symington "still has an influence," and paying a higher price than $1.12 per pound for Bolivian tin "might provoke a Congressional investigation."[61]

During the standoff over McDonald's appointment, President Truman had ordered Defense Mobilizer Wilson and Jess Larson of the Defense Materials Procurement Administration (DMPA) to reopen tin contract negotiations with Bolivia. Wilson met with Ambassador Martínez Vargas for more than two hours and was very sympathetic, but his hands were tied by "that damned British agreement." Wilson thought that Bolivia's tin problem could be solved if it built its own smelter, but the ambassador informed him that the Bolivians could not afford to wait. When Wilson all but agreed to pay them $1.22 per pound for their tin, Chairman Symington, a lame duck with nothing to lose, refused to obey Wilson's orders, apparently "holding out for instructions from higher up." Larson, as sympathetic and perplexed as Wilson, could only hope that the solution might be found in a subsidized reduction of smelting fees.[62] For Ambassador Martínez Vargas, the true miracle was that President Truman, Secretary of State Acheson, Secretary of Commerce Charles Sawyer, Secretary of the Treasury John Snyder, and Defense Mobilizer Wilson, some of the most powerful men in Washington, if not the world, were now actively working to salvage his government. Moreover, they were dedicating important time to this issue even as a steel strike was threatening the entire U.S. national security procurement program. Once Symington was finally out of the way and McDonald was confirmed, the only difficulty that Assistant Secretary Miller could "see ahead is that the Bolivians may make the mistake of sticking adamantly to a price of $1.50 a pound."[63]

Although Ambassador Martínez Vargas believed that the goodwill of President Truman and the defense planners boded well, his superiors had run out of patience; over the ambassador's objections, they renewed their push for a Bolivian protest before the OAS. In an appeal to the people of Peru, published by the major Peruvian newspapers, Bolivia's ambassador in Lima explicitly condemned Chairman Symington and his "hostile" and "mercantile" tactics and requested support from the Organization of American States. Ballivián's ambassador in Buenos Aires did the same. This was particularly annoying to the State Department because it gave Perón "additional damaging propaganda which will be exploited here and in the OAS." Other messages sent to Rio de Janeiro, Santiago, and Mexico City, claimed that the junta would "no longer act as a beggar at the door of the powerful" and would "put the matter before the OAS."[64]

Secretary Acheson immediately ordered his embassy to confront General Ballivián and warn him that nothing would be better calculated to make U.S. negotiators' difficult position "impossible" than "public statements playing into the hands" of Senator Johnson. The secretary was stunned by the "immoderate" language of Ballivián's envoys and surprised that the Bolivians would undertake such provocative action now that President Truman had personally intervened to find a solution in the "spirit" of "mutual respect." The Reconstruction Finance Corporation was actually contemplating elimination of "most favored nation" clauses in its contracts with other tin producers to allow Bolivia an increase in the price of tin, and Bolivian aggressiveness did not sit well with men who were now bending over backward to break the impasse over tin. Neither did Bolivian diplomat Alberto Ostria Gutiérrez's assertion that giving Bolivia a fair deal would only cost the United States "the value of two or three bombers which—painful to say—are being lost almost daily to Korea." Assistant Secretary Miller warned an "obviously embarrassed" Ambassador Martínez Vargas that the ill-conceived "campaign of continental publicity" was "prejudicial to the success of the delicate current tin negotiations."[65] When embassy officer Maleady presented the State Department's protest directly to Ballivián, the general was "exceedingly regretful" and said that no one was more "pro-U.S. than he." He blamed the move on overzealous Foreign Ministry officials and denied that he had any intention of pursuing the OAS protest now that "preliminary talks were under way." He concluded by assuring Maleady that he "will see to it" that nothing else is done to "annoy" the United States. Maleady believed that "we will have no more unwise publicity" and guessed that "several [Foreign Ministry] people will get a severe knuckle rapping" for having acted without instructions. The most notable aspect of the episode, the U.S. Embassy believed, was that, even though the Bolivian "Foreign Office realizes the affair got out of hand," not one newspaper article or editorial in Bolivia offered an apology or mentioned a need for moderation.[66]

By mid-March, understanding both that the Texas City smelter would be forced to close by May if a new supply of tin concentrates was not acquired and that the U.S. tin metal stockpile was down to 10 percent of its desired level, RFC Chairman McDonald, Defense Mobilizer Wilson, and the DMPA's Jess Larson were ready to "get down to brass tacks" and hoped that this round would be free from "any legacy of feeling from what might have happened in the past." Mauricio Hochschild, now leading the Bolivian negotiating team himself, finally abandoned his demand for $1.50 and was prepared to accept $1.35, which would cost the United States "only $20,400,000." He was willing to take less if smelting fees were reduced, but Tin Division Chief McKinnon pointed out that the RFC was already losing money on the Texas City smelter at its current rates. Hochschild's outbursts did not make a "good impression" on Larson, who expressed "great regret" that the tin baron would compromise no further at this desperate hour.[67]

If Hochschild was doing nothing to facilitate an agreement, Senator Johnson and his subcommittee seemed determined to ensure that there would be no agreement at all. During the course of the meeting, Larson received a telephone call and a "long lecture" from Johnson Subcommittee Counsel Donald Cook, demanding that the DMPA pay no more than $1.18 per pound. Cook guessed that Larson was "getting lots of heat from the State Department" and urged him "not to yield to it." Larson told him he was not "getting any heat from the State Department" that he was not also getting from President Truman or Defense Mobilizer Wilson. State Department officers promised that if Larson and Wilson could improve their offer "slightly," Assistant Secretary Miller would pressure La Paz for acceptance.[68]

When negotiations resumed the next day, however, Wilson shot down Hochschild's offer outright. Hochschild countered with a proposal to sell twelve thousand tons at $1.18 per pound, but only if the RFC restored tin purchasing to private enterprise. Wilson refused. The Bolivians were to be even more disappointed when, days later, it was announced that the Indonesians had accepted an RFC offer of $1.18 per pound for almost twenty thousand tons of tin. Senator Dennis Chavez suggested that "on the face of it," it might seem that $1.18 was, in fact, a fair price, except that the Export-Import Bank granted the government of Indonesia a $22,770,000 loan the same day. The Bolivians had suspected that the Indonesians would be offered "some special financial assistance to induce them to sign" at the RFC's price, and, despite "emphatic" State Department denials, they evidently were. This "tricky" "concealed subsidy," Senator Chavez asserted, was exactly what the RFC had resisted for years in its dealings with Bolivia. Although the Indonesian deal and a subsequent deal at the same price for nine thousand tons of tin from the Belgian Congo were a "blow" to the junta, embassy officer Maleady reported that the press and public were "waiting to see" if the Good Neighbor policy could pass the coming test. If the RFC did not make a better offer, "another continental press campaign" was likely, as was the fall of the junta.[69]

General Ballivián, too, understood how fragile his position was and wrote a direct appeal to President Truman to intervene personally in the negotiations to permit a "just and honorable understanding." The general had not launched a "campaign of wide recrimination," which many other leaders might have, embassy officer Maleady reported, and his personal appeal "obviously indicates the urgent need for immediate action." If Ballivián could not achieve a victory soon, the "position of the present weak Bolivian Government, which is friendly to us and has sought to minimize the bad effects of the tin contract disagreement, may become desperate." Maleady went on to warn that, if there was no "prompt settlement," the junta might "throw up hands" and allow the MNR to convert Bolivia into a "pro-Perón," "pro-Commie," "anti-U.S. country."[70] On 26 March, Maleady further reported that the junta wanted to settle the tin contract by "the end of the month" to "present to the people as a major accomplishment" and "strengthen its hand in slapping down two groups stirring up trouble within the armed forces."[71]

A compromise was actually available. The foreign minister had already conceded to embassy officer Maleady that, if a "few cents could be obtained" somehow, Bolivia would "sign up at $1.21½." The DMPA's Jess Larson and Defense Mobilizer Wilson were willing to do so, but Hochschild again held out, insisting on $1.30 per pound plus a reduction of smelter fees that would effectively cost the RFC more than $1.35 per pound. When Wilson asked if this was the best the tin baron could offer, Hochschild claimed that it was, and the meeting broke up. The State Department representative closed the meeting by stating that "no one should have any reason to be optimistic."⁷² Hochschild was single-handedly blocking an agreement that the U.S. government hoped would save his government from revolution and, in the end, his company from nationalization.

If there had been any cause for optimism in the face of Hochschild's obstinacy, Senator Johnson seemed determined to squelch it. On 4 April, he wrote an open letter to Chairman McDonald, Secretary Acheson, and President Truman, urging them not to pay the Bolivians any more than they were paying the British, Belgians, or Indonesians. He claimed that the United States had already acquired sufficient tin for 1952, implying that the Bolivians should again be given an ultimatum. Most important, however, he retracted his subcommittee's oft-cited conclusion that the Bolivians should be paid more for their tin than Malay Straits producers. Senator Johnson also urged President Truman to "not accept the recommendations of the State Department" to grant the Bolivians a higher price. Paying more than necessary was a waste, for there was no chance of it "trickling down to the Bolivian people." Since "there is no danger that the tin producers will espouse Communism" (although "their activities might well result in forcing the common man in Bolivia in that direction"), "we do not favor creating another crop of tin millionaires" at U.S. taxpayers' expense.⁷³

Not surprisingly, the "reversal in the position of a committee whose pronouncements had dominated U.S. tin policy caused a great furor in Bolivia." The Large and Medium Miners Associations immediately retorted that this "unprecedented" statement made it clear that Senator Johnson was acting in a "mistaken effort to spare the RFC" from "embarrassment." Although the senator may have believed he was "taking an expedient step out of a difficult situation," he had instead created "intense pressure for the Bolivian producers, labor, and government." The associations ominously warned that if the contract was not settled fairly and swiftly, "many damaging consequences may ensue."⁷⁴ Even though Ballivián's subordinates had "maintained an admirable attitude and kept their mouths shut," the U.S. Embassy reported "widespread disillusionment across Bolivia." Although RFC Chairman McDonald and the DMPA's Jess Larson "were not too worried" about Senator Johnson's bombshell, this was only because they believed they were on the verge of breaking the tin impasse themselves.⁷⁵

For Larson and McDonald, it was clear that any agreement would have to bypass Hochschild. Larson therefore contacted Ambassador Martínez Vargas, Luis Guachalla, and Enrique Peñaranda on 7 April to present a new offer. Larson had already authorized a $5.5 million loan to the government of Bolivia and, with McDonald, was prepared to go to President Truman to request an additional 2¢ per pound if this did not produce an agreement. Moreover, the Export-Import Bank was on the verge of approving more than $8 million in loans for petroleum extraction, tungsten mining, aviation development, and the construction of a meatpacking plant in Bolivia.[76] It was, of course, too late. On 9 April 1952, the day the National Revolution broke out in La Paz, Chairman McDonald was preparing to present his new offer—most likely $1.21 plus the loan packages—which he was "certain" would "have been acceptable." On the day the sexenio ended, a deal that might have saved liberal constitutional oligarchy was imminent.[77] As MNR militias stormed into the streets and Lechín's forces poured out of the mining camps to overthrow General Ballivián, U.S. policy makers could only wonder whether they could have averted the National Revolution. Hochschild might well have wondered the same.

For the State Department, Bolivian diplomats, and even the Chileans, there was no doubt that much of the blame for the revolution should be placed at the feet of Senator Johnson, RFC Chairman Symington, and the U.S. "attitude on tin." The Chilean ambassador in Washington bluntly asserted that the "failure of the tin negotiations was the principal reason for the revolution" because it "made it easy to rally the Bolivian people around this demagogic banner."[78] For the British Foreign Office, it was clear that "the principal architect of the present coup d'état was Mr. Stuart Symington." The State Department argued, and "newspaper comment" seemed to "bear out," that the revolution "may well have been tripped off by" the "chain of events" that culminated in Senator Johnson's open letter. Truman's advisors urged the president to reprimand Senator Johnson for having "complicated the task of the Executive agencies." They hoped that it might lead the senator to "give more thought to the long-range implications of his public" statements and provide a "much needed reminder" that "the Office of the President and not the Preparedness Subcommittee has the basic responsibility for implementing the policies set forth in the Acts of Congress." President Truman's reproof reflected very little of this, instead praising the "invaluable contributions" and "excellent work" of Senator Johnson's committee but asking that the senator in the future not "unnecessarily complicate the implementation of the very programs" he oversaw.[79]

Senator Chavez, too, let Johnson off the hook by accusing Chairman Symington of violating the mandate the Preparedness Subcommittee had laid down for the RFC. Nowhere in his venomous eighteen-page statement did Chavez hint at Johnson's role in fueling the conflict or spurring Symington on to his worst excesses. Just days before the onset of the National Revolution, Chavez had warned the Senate that "the possibility of crisis for the Bolivian government is a grave actuality." For this, he blamed Symington and his "overbearing and heartless," "mendacious and too-clever," "stupid and disastrous," "stubborn and asinine" campaign, "hell-bent to prove to the world that we would get what we wanted."[80]

State Department officer Brown's critique of Senator Johnson's role was, however, the most damning. The department and the Bolivians had heard Chairman Symington boast of his Senate support "again and again" and believed that his determination to raid the stockpile came straight from Senator Johnson. According to Brown, Johnson's subcommittee created an "attitude of bitterness and hostility" that never dissipated, and Senator Johnson and Subcommittee Counsel Cook's "strong support" for Chairman Symington only made him even more "inflexible." The subcommittee's report had been "cited continuously" by Symington as evidence of a tin cartel and by the Bolivians as evidence that they should be paid more than the Malay Straits producers, encouraging intransigence on both sides. Then, when Johnson retracted the report's second principal conclusion, this retraction had become one of many factors triggering the National Revolution.

The "tragedy of this whole matter," State Department officer Brown concluded, "is that we could have settled with the Bolivians at $1.21½ or less six months ago, with good feelings on both sides and without bad repercussions all over Latin America." Instead, this "tin episode has become a running sore in our entire relationship with Latin America which will not soon be forgotten."[81] Senator Johnson, of course, was thoroughly unrepentant; months later, his subcommittee fired another shot at the Bolivians, condemning them for shipping Patiño tin to Great Britain instead of the United States. Assistant Secretary Miller could offer no defense except to meekly comment that "the Executive Branch of our Government does not necessarily acquiesce in all of the points made by the Johnson Committee Report." Heedless of all criticism, Senator Johnson and his subcommittee continued to voice their accusations about a tin cartel for at least another year, outraging tin-producing nations.[82]

The final irony of the National Revolution was that the Bolivian elites and even junta members had pleaded for direct U.S. intervention against the supposedly "pro-communist and violently anti-American" MNR. They had invariably been told that any such action would be "entirely contrary to the non-intervention policy of the United States."[83] This had not stopped Senator Johnson and Chairman Symington from assailing the junta for almost a year. Although the State Department privately conceded its role in the coming of the National Revolution, it publicly resisted efforts by the tin barons to place blame at its feet by pointing out that two MNR rebellions launched when the tin difficulties were at their worst had failed, but the one that had succeeded had done so at the moment when a new contract was imminent. It is impossible to know whether a tin contract would have saved General Ballivián's government, but the financial crisis and constant pressure from Washington had certainly done nothing to help his last-ditch efforts to salvage liberal constitutional oligarchy. As Deputy Assistant Secretary Thomas C. Mann later lamented, "we felt very strongly that haggling over a few cents difference in the price of tin might set in motion forces which would lead to the overthrow of a friendly, middle-of-the-road government and precipitate nationalization." He was "not glad to say our predictions came true."[84]

7

PAZ ESTENSSORO

April 1952–January 1953

The age-old revolution [in Bolivia] is finally busting forth. This revolution—which I'm afraid has its elements of Indian racialism as well as everything else—is not something we can stop. We can ride with it and try to guide it, but we will be foolhardy indeed if we try to brake it or break it.
—*Robert Alexander, 16 May 1952*

The United States is sympathetic to the desire of the new MNR government to provide a better political, economic, and social life for its people; and relations with the new government have thus far been good, despite the numerous problems of common concern. The hardest problems remain to be solved, but it is hoped that with goodwill on both sides they can be settled in such a fashion as to prevent any damage to the traditional friendship between the two countries and to make possible an even closer relationship.
—*William Hudson, 29 September 1952*

The National Revolution of April 1952, which Demetrio Canelas called the "greatest political and material victory in all of our history" and Waltraud Quieser Morales called a "replay of the 1949 civil war but with more good fortune and fewer mistakes," was over in a matter of days, but its implications lasted for decades.[1] Although stopping the Movimiento Nacionalista Revolucionario had been the cornerstone of almost a decade of U.S. policy in Bolivia, the MNR's victory proved to be far less damaging to U.S. interests than anyone imagined. Indeed, U.S. diplomats, who had expected to find the party to be monolithic and radical, quickly discovered that it was in fact quite divided. On the one hand, Juan Lechín Oquendo headed a "leftist" wing of unionists and mine workers committed to radical syndicalism and a swift, thorough cleansing of the old order, but, on the other, Víctor Paz Estenssoro and Hernán Siles Zuazo headed a "rightist" wing of upper- and middle-class intellectuals committed to gradualist reform, compatible in many respects with the State Department's vision for Bolivia.

With the army and every other political party thoroughly discredited by the events of the sexenio, U.S. policy makers had little choice but to support Paz Estenssoro and his conservatives against Lechín's radicals. Still, President Truman's State Department never could completely reconcile itself with the MNR. The department joined forces with the Reconstruction Finance Corporation to use the tin contract as both lever and cudgel against the new government in its efforts to promote moderation, block nationalization of the tin mines, protect U.S. shareholders in the Patiño mines, and minimize the damage the National Revolution might do to U.S. interests across the hemisphere. In essence, U.S. policy drifted, its makers apparently dumbstruck by the National Revolution and nursing a seemingly ineradicable antipathy toward the MNR.

The National Revolution and Its Aftermath

By early April 1952, the economic crisis had reached a peak, thanks to the tin impasse and the incompetence of the junta. Markets in La Paz had been unable to acquire either meat or bread the week of Christmas 1951, and the situation had improved only slightly over the next several months, when the junta managed to acquire short-term loans from U.S. banks to keep at least some foodstuffs flowing into the country. General Ballivián had attempted to use these loans as "proof that the Great Democracy of the North will not let a friend die" and had released foreign exchange to luxury goods importers in the hopes of creating an illusion of financial strength.[2]

The junta urgently sought a means by which it could leave office and return power to civilians—so long as those civilians were not movimientistas. In late February 1952, the junta's General Humberto Torres Ortiz asked the MNR for a "truce," promising early elections and "strict constitutional norms" in exchange for the party's assistance in finding a "pacific solution of the nation's problems." Within days, however, the junta responded to a new round of food shortage protests by arresting movimientista leaders and organizers. When the attorney seeking habeas corpus for the victims was himself arrested, mothers and wives of MNR detainees organized a hunger strike. And when the junta then broke up the strike with tear gas, all talk of a truce ended.[3]

The harbinger of the National Revolution turned out to be the junta's General Antonio Seleme Vargas, a most unlikely revolutionary. When General Torres Ortiz had opened discussions with the MNR, General Seleme was among the fiercest opponents of any compromise. On 8 April, however, the ambitious but otherwise nondescript Seleme learned he was to be ousted from his post in the junta as part of a sweeping reorganization of Ballivián's government. The junta's finance minister had "failed miserably" in transporting food imports, its labor minister was using his post to "ape Argentina's Perón" and win the "adulation of labor," and its defense minister was old and ill. For his part, Seleme had ignored direct orders to disband most of his police units and thus undo President Urriolagoitia's efforts to maintain a force sufficient to counter the army.[4] Whereas all other ministers in the cabinet submitted their resignations to Ballivián, Seleme secretly cut a deal with the MNR's Siles Zuazo, pledging the support of his police troops in return for both military command of the revolt and the presidency until elections could be held in October. News of Seleme's imminent ouster forced the unprepared MNR to make its move on 9 April without advance planning and nearly doomed the revolution.[5]

Although Seleme was able to seize the center of La Paz, the Palacio Quemado, the army arsenal at Orkojahuira, and key radio stations, Torres Ortiz struck back quickly. The MNR broadcast early declarations of victory, claimed to have captured the members of the junta, and even asserted that the revolution had Torres Ortiz's backing. All three claims were badly mistaken. Torres Ortiz's troops in El Alto and Miraflores descended upon the MNR forces in La Paz, who fought desperately to hold off their advance. In what U.S. diplomats later came to believe was a clever ploy by Siles Zuazo to get Seleme out of the picture, the MNR leader supposedly told the general that the "fight was lost" and silenced MNR radio broadcasts for two hours to confirm it. In any event, as soon as Seleme gave up and sought asylum in the Chilean Embassy, the call went out over the MNR's radio stations: "It is today or never!"[6]

The masses of La Paz answered the call. MNR militias, union members, and disorganized workers took to the streets, joining police and sympathetic military units to battle the junta with every weapon at their disposal. They transformed Seleme's crude barracks coup into a genuine popular revolution. Siles Zuazo, supported by ex-villarroelistas, coordinated the furious MNR counterattack. Cut off by miners who seized the Oruro rail line and attacked El Alto, Torres Ortiz's forces were overwhelmed. The general surrendered the next day and fled the country, as did most of the junta's other officers. The MNR had finally triumphed.

From the failed 1949 uprising, when movimientistas had won almost every urban center in the country except La Paz but had still been beaten, they had learned that La Paz was crucial to victory. Local governments in Cochabamba, Sucre, and Potosi surrendered almost immediately. Only in Oruro did local authorities resist: their forces fired upon a crowd in the city square before capitulating. Although the Red Cross and the La Paz diplomatic corps first estimated there had been thousands of casualties, the final tallies were much lower. The junta, stripped of any legitimacy it may have once possessed, had collapsed with a speed that stunned all observers. With it went the old order based on the alliance of the landowners, tin barons, and the army. The U.S. Embassy noted that, although there had been "unquestionably a great deal of popular sympathy for the revolution, there was also a great deal of public apathy." In 1946, the masses of La Paz had risen against Major Villarroel to launch the sexenio, but, six years later, no one rose to defend the old order, which had been thoroughly discredited. Siles Zuazo's first move was to call Paz Estenssoro home from Buenos Aires with a "red carpet treatment." As embassy officer Maleady remarked with what turned out to be unjustified bitterness, that carpet would be "a much deeper red from the casualties estimated as high as ten thousand dead and wounded."[7]

Unlike in 1946, the U.S. Embassy reported no rioting or mob violence and, more important, even though the Bolivian army had abandoned U.S. citizens in the mining camps, there had been no hint of violence against them by the victorious MNR. Although the movimientistas appeared united, it quickly became clear that the very nature of the National Revolution was in dispute. So long as the MNR was a repressed opposition party, movimientistas had been able to paper over their deep ideological differences.[8] With victory, however, came the need to govern and make difficult choices. Whereas Hernán Siles Zuazo, Walter Guevara Arze, and the intellectuals who had founded the party sought stability and evolutionary changes, Juan Lechín, the miners, and the MNR militias who had bled for the revolution demanded immediate and radical restructuring of the country.

Paz Estenssoro and Siles Zuazo hoped to transform the MNR into a broad, multiclass party that would have looked much like a traditional party but with expanded yet controlled mass participation. In sharp contrast, Lechín and the MNR's labor faction aimed for a syndicalist state with the lion's share of power resting in the hands of their new, all-encompassing labor federation, the Central Obrera Boliviana (COB). Furthermore, Lechín's followers, who now included many old radicals from the Partido de la Izquierda Revolucionaria, the Partido Obrero Revolucionario, and other, smaller parties, aimed for nothing less than the immediate nationalization of the mines. They doggedly opposed any suggestion that the tin barons be reimbursed for their properties, claiming that the exorbitant profits wrested from the mountains over the decades were more than sufficient compensation. To make good on the revolution's promises, they sought to immediately grant universal suffrage and implement land reform by expropriating large fincas throughout the countryside. In short, the MNR's left wing sought to overturn every remnant of the old order before a counterrevolution could occur.[9]

Paz Estenssoro may have been president, but Lechín clearly held the fate of the new regime in his hands. Mauricio Hochschild's managers respected and feared him as a man "who cannot be bought, because they have tried to buy him"; the AFL deemed him "serious and highly intelligent," and the CIO considered him to be "just a New Dealer." The State Department, however, described Lechín as "an extremely radical, ambitious, and violent individual" and an "extremist demagogue." Where the MNR "might be able to turn out 300 people for a meeting" in the mining camps, Lechín's Federación Sindical de Trabajadores Mineros de Bolivia "could turn out a thousand." Even worse, the department believed Lechín harbored a personal vendetta against the United States, crediting an old, unsubstantiated rumor that an American mining engineer had "debauched Lechín's *chola* woman" years before.[10] The "unquestionably magnetic" and "ruthless" Lechín was so horrifying to U.S. policy makers that Richard Nixon, having received "very disturbing" reports as a junior senator on the Labor and Public Welfare Committee, asked for a State Department briefing on him.[11]

The conflicting demands of Lechín's roles as head of the COB and MNR minister of mines induced what U.S. observers would call "political schizophrenia." With the army discredited and chastened, Lechín's miners, MNR militias, and other civilians retained the almost twenty thousand rifles they had been handed during the revolution. Clearly, their voice would dictate who controlled the nation, and if their loyalty to Lechín and the COB outweighed their loyalty to Paz Estenssoro and the MNR, then the new president had a tiger by the tail. Ironically, Paz Estenssoro could probably count on the support of the same police and army that had mercilessly harassed the movimientistas for six years, for they despised Lechín above all else. To Secretary Acheson, hinting that extended nonrecognition might lie ahead, the mere presence of Lechín, let alone his "possible dominance," "creates doubts" about whether the new government could "maintain order" and "honor its international obligations."[12]

The situation was even more complicated than it first appeared. Lechín was hardly in complete control of the unions making up the Central Obrera Boliviana. He had, for years, relied on the skills, loyalty, and organizing strength of the Trotskyite POR within the FSTMB, and the *poristas'* power within the COB now equaled that of the movimientistas. Lamenting that "the Right Wing is winning out in the government," Juan Sanjines, head of the COB's railroad workers union, warned that "this government and the MNR are transitory" and that "the workers are going to take power and set up socialism." Lechín also believed that the right wing of the MNR was "not particularly friendly to the labor movement" but that it would desert the party once his "agrarian revolution" was launched in the countryside. Another labor leader all but likened Paz Estenssoro to the rosca and proclaimed that the "labor movement is a living challenge to the right-wing elements in the government." Bolivian labor leaders understood quite well that President Paz Estenssoro and Vice President Siles Zuazo sought to use the Central Obrera Boliviana to bring workers under the control of their government; indeed, the labor leaders saw the MNR as only a slightly more progressive version of the PURS.[13] Although the State Department feared Lechín might break with the MNR to launch a true social revolution, it was just as likely that, tainted by his *movimientismo*, he might lose control over his own COB if revolutionary changes did not occur rapidly enough.

Once Paz Estenssoro was installed in the Palacio Quemado, he appointed Lechín minister of mines and petroleum and Lechín's ally German Butrón labor minister. Together, Lechín and Butrón would rewrite Bolivian labor and mining laws to suit the workers. Days after the revolution, Lechín hinted he would seek to implement an FSTMB formula under which mine workers would receive an automatic raise with every cent paid for tin above the price of $1.12 per pound. Indeed, at the first meeting of the new ministers, he "pounded the cabinet table for immediate, outright nationalization" of the mines. The State Department could only hope that "cooler heads" would overrule him, and they did. Paz Estenssoro, Siles Zuazo, and other conservatives outvoted Lechín's faction 4 to 3 and opted instead to create a commission to "study" what form nationalization should take, if it should take any form at all.[14]

This good news for the State Department was somewhat offset by news that all factions of the new government had agreed to do without the moderating influence of the United Nations and the technical experts proposed by the Keenleyside mission.[15] Still, an unwillingness to yield sovereignty to the United Nations did not mean that reform was not going forward. On 21 July, as a first step toward incorporating indigenous Bolivians into the national polity, literacy requirements for voting were abolished. As for land reform, the new president suggested it should wait until nationalizing the tin mines provided the funds needed for its implementation. Justifiably suspicious of the loyalty of the Federal Police, who had helped carry the MNR to power in April, President Paz Estenssoro formed "escort regiments" in Oruro and La Paz and "Honor Groups" of MNR militias in the countryside, armed largely with weapons taken from army arsenals.[16] Although the president counted on the army to protect him from Lechín and the militias, he was not willing to risk a military counterrevolution by disarming the popular forces. For all the MNR's delicate balancing act, the early months of its rule strongly suggested that the movimientistas were not going away anytime soon.

U.S. Recognition

For the State Department, the crucial question was recognition of the new regime. U.S. pledges made at the 1948 Bogotá Conference seemed to preclude the use of nonrecognition as a weapon against a new government, but the State Department nonetheless contemplated doing just that. Indeed, there was considerable support for indefinite nonrecognition of the MNR regime, not just among the rosca, but also among Bolivia's neighbors to the west. Carlos Aramayo and Mauricio Hochschild lobbied the State Department to withhold recognition to discourage the seizure of their properties. Even as they worked to use their influence in Washington and elsewhere to erect an "Iron Curtain" around the MNR's Bolivia, the tin barons hoped the new U.S. ambassador, Edward Sparks, would be willing to act as their "intermediary" with Paz Estenssoro, as Ambassador Florman once had with President Urriolagoitia. Sparks's answer to their request was an unequivocal no.[17]

For his part, Chilean president González Videla considered the MNR to be a "combination of Nazi-communist elements." Indeed, his government and the Chilean press were convinced that some diabolical combination of Perón and the Communists had masterminded, if not bankrolled, the MNR takeover with "funds, brown and red." The Chileans even requested that U.S. banks not lend money to the MNR so that Perón "will have to feed Bolivians and put a difficult burden on Argentina." The Chilean position with the new regime grew even more strained in June when the MNR newspaper *La Marcha* somehow obtained and published copies of González Videla's 1951 appeal to President Truman. Even though Truman's formal response had been so noncommittal as to be in no way "embarrassing to us," in the minds of the MNR, González Videla had "meddled in Bolivian domestic politics" to "help maintain the Military Junta in power," just as he was now meddling to block international recognition of the new government.[18]

Branding the MNR as "leftist, Commie, and Peronist," Peruvian dictator Manuel Odría—another U.S. ally—agreed entirely with the Chileans. He believed that nonrecognition of the MNR government would cause it to collapse and be replaced by a more "moderate" one. Indeed, Odría would support recognition of the new regime only to prevent the "catastrophic contingency" of Lechín's taking over.[19] Barring that contingency, Odría and González Videla believed that recognition of the MNR government would "be fatal for Latin American governments fighting Communism" and hoped the United States would follow their example "indefinitely." Peruvian and Chilean opposition to the National Revolution was predictable. As Latin Americanist Robert Alexander would later explain, "what is going on in Bolivia is likely to be contagious." When the "Indians on one side of Lake Titicaca receive land, those on the other side are going to want it."[20]

Rumors of a Paz Estenssoro–Perón alliance had been rampant for years, but there had never been much evidence of it. U.S. diplomats in Argentina even suggested that the MNR chief was now "very cool" (if not "bitter") toward the peronistas because of their "playing along" with Presidents Hertzog and Urriolagoitia and General Ballivián over the years. On the other hand, Argentine aid, which "could be furnished immediately by Perón without strain," would be invaluable for quickly putting food on Bolivian tables. Indeed, Eva

Perón's personal airplane, carrying doctors, nurses, and medicine, landed in La Paz even before Paz Estenssoro's. Three more planes carrying propaganda, more nurses, and eight tons of food took off the next day as Argentine trucks broadcast, "Misery knows no frontiers!" through the streets of La Paz. That said, as Assistant Secretary Miller made perfectly clear, even though "adoption of too stiff a [nonrecognition] policy" by the United States "might drive Bolivia into the Argentine camp," there was simply no credible evidence of any Peronist intrigue in the National Revolution.[21]

This did not, of course, stop either Enrique Hertzog or Mamerto Urriolagoitia from approaching U.S. diplomats with dramatic warnings that Bolivia had been lost to Perón and the Communists. Secretary Acheson dismissed their claims as "inaccurate or exaggerated." Indeed, U.S. Embassy officers observed "neither communist influence nor communist tactics." There was no shouting of "Down with Yankee imperialism!" and certainly no appeal to the Soviet Union. Although COB publications did take an "anti-U.S. slant" soon after the revolution, it was "difficult to determine" whether the source was Peronism or Communism because "Perón's tactics" had become "hardly distinguishable from the communist line." Forced to choose, the embassy officers leaned toward Peronism because Argentine unionists had advised their Bolivian counterparts in the establishment of the COB, but they attached little importance even to that.[22]

For true Communists and piristas, the MNR takeover presented "something of a poser." After denouncing Paz Estenssoro and his party as a "reactionary fascist machine" for years, Latin American Communists were forced to concede that the movimientistas had successfully staged what could only be seen as a "people's revolution of liberation." According to one U.S. diplomat, "the possibility that the movement has support and guidance" from the anti-Communist Perón had only "compounded this dilemma." On the other hand, the MNR had no qualms about attacking the PIR. Movimientistas, well remembering Major Villarroel's fate and the central role piristas had played in it, violently broke up PIR rallies with shouts of "Away with the hangmen!"[23]

Even if Paz Estenssoro was clearly no Communist, the State Department did have questions about Lechín. Still in Washington, Liberal statesman Luis Guachalla observed that, even though Lechín's vision of People's Militias was an exceptionally dangerous one, the union leader's "fondness for fine clothes, big cars, and flashy women" precluded him from being a Communist. The State Department ultimately concluded that Lechín "is not a doctrinaire Marxist" but rather an opportunist who would "follow any line he thinks beneficial to the workers' interest and his own." For their part, the MNR conservatives worked to deny the Cold Warriors in Washington any fodder for red-baiting. "Without publicity or fanfare," Paz Estenssoro was discreetly replacing Lechín's followers in influential posts with conservatives. As union leader Sanjines proclaimed to U.S. Embassy officers, "we Leftists are being weeded out."[24]

On the one-year anniversary of the MNR's 1951 election victory, movimientista leaders hosted a massive rally predictably featuring "much damning of the Rosca" and praise for those persecuted during the sexenio. President Paz Estenssoro gave a speech reiterating the need for nationalization of the tin mines, but, according to the U.S. Embassy, he "left a loophole" by "failing to state just what form nationalization would take." Of greater interest were speeches by labor leaders Juan Lechín and José Lucio Quiros. Embassy officer Maleady, having somehow acquired the original drafts of the speeches, noted that someone had made changes to both in longhand. To Lechín's speech, someone had added boilerplate anti-Communist declarations, and in Lucio's, someone had revised two references to "foreign imperialist influence" to clarify that the imperialists in question were "Communism and the Stalinist PIR." Since references to foreign imperialism would "ordinarily be interpreted by the man in the street as meaning the U.S.," someone, presumably from Paz Estenssoro's wing of the party, was working to tone down whatever anti-U.S. sentiments the radicals may have held. At the May Day parade, the MNR forbade any flags other than the Bolivian and "forcibly evicted from the ranks" anyone wearing a red armband. For U.S. policy makers, the absence of the Communist clenched fist and the overwhelming presence of the two-finger "V-for-Víctor Paz" salute made clear that there was no red menace in Bolivia. In short, the State Department concluded, "the Commie and Argentine threats seem relatively remote at present."[25]

If the State Department could not present evidence of outside interference in the National Revolution to justify withholding recognition, it would have to argue that the MNR did not truly control the nation and could not keep the peace. Although certainly not anticipating a "reign of terror," the embassy conceded that "men who have been sought, persecuted, and beaten for six years are not likely to turn the other cheek." Still, no one could legitimately fault the MNR for its protection of U.S. citizens and property. When workers had plundered the home of one Hochschild manager during the revolution, Lechín sent personal representatives to the mines to ensure the safety of the property and of all foreign employees. And when embassy officer Maleady informed the minister of mines that disappointed union members at the Corocoro mine had dynamited all roads to the facility and were taking a "menacing attitude" toward company officials, Lechín, "heretofore the workers' god," intervened to send "the men back to work," at some cost to his own prestige. Just weeks after the revolution, even the State Department had to concede that the MNR had "effectively restored order in several situations" that "might have developed into bad incidents."[26]

There was also the matter of Carlos Aramayo's *La Razón*, which closed its doors during the revolution. Although Aramayo's henchmen in New York and Washington attempted to portray this as a parallel to Perón's infamous closing of *La Prensa*, and U.S. diplomats suggested that the issue "adds an authentic Perón-like touch to the situation," there were important differences. The MNR never forbade *La Razón* from publishing. Instead, the movimientistas had simply refused to furnish police protection and publicly announced that police would not fire upon anyone assaulting *La Razón*'s offices or facilities. With that in mind, Siles Zuazo had apparently "suggested that it might be in the paper's interest to refrain from controversial topics" or "postpone publication until order was assured." Because the pro-rosca newspaper had spearheaded every assault on the MNR for more than a decade, had called for the lynching of Major Villarroel, and was so intimately linked to Aramayo, Secretary Acheson chose to ignore its closing and hope the situation would "work itself out." It eventually did when President Paz Estenssoro simply converted the *La Razón* building into a new Ministry for Mines and Petroleum.[27]

The Truman administration quickly realized that, for want of any viable alternative to the MNR, it had to support and encourage Paz Estenssoro's faction in the hopes that his conservatives could rein in Lechín and avert what Washington saw as the worst excesses of revolutionary government. The Paz Estenssoro government was repeatedly compared to the Kerensky government in revolutionary Russia: "If it falls," embassy officer William B. Cobb observed, there "seems to be no alternative for Bolivia but communism," some radical variant under Lechín, or a general "disintegration through which neighboring countries might be sucked into an international conflict." Calling Paz Estenssoro the "white hope" against the indigenous masses, Assistant Secretary Miller argued that it might be necessary to "meet him half way in order to prevent his losing control over the more fanatical and hostile elements in his own party."[28] Embassy officer Maleady reported that, even though the MNR conservatives seemed to control the cabinet, there was every evidence that they did "not dare to meddle in Lechín's domain" of the COB; indeed, some of the more pessimistic conservatives had told him they were nearly "certain" that Lechín and the radicals would push the government into an anti-U.S. posture and transform the country into "an Argentine province."[29]

"Following the matter closely," Secretary Acheson and President Truman ordered the embassy to assess Paz Estenssoro's chances of remaining in control but to otherwise "avoid any action at this time which would constitute or might be interpreted as recognition of the new regime."[30] President Paz Estenssoro was well aware of the danger he faced, Maleady reported, but found himself hemmed in by armed miners and militias, many of whom were presumably loyal to Lechín. The president was cautiously working to disarm the militias, but Acheson, deeply concerned about the threat they posed, contemplated making recognition of the government contingent upon his success. Though unsure exactly what impact such a position might have on the MNR power struggle, Maleady informed the secretary that it was likely to backfire in one way or another. Acheson eventually agreed and prepared for a protracted battle between Lechín and Paz Estenssoro, "who looks better than anyone else on the horizon." The secretary concluded that "our tin policy offers the most flexible, effective, and appropriate available instrument for influencing decisions" in Bolivia.[31] As President Truman's inner circle deliberated, embassy officer Maleady was told only to remind President Paz Estenssoro of his earlier statements regarding private property and the MNR's independence from Perón. Maleady was not to "extort any anti-Peronista promises" but merely to ensure that the MNR was truly independent of Argentine influence.[32]

"Depressed and defeatist," the tin barons quickly reached much the same conclusion as the State Department. Their first inclination was to immediately sell the twelve thousand tons of Bolivian tin concentrates that had accumulated on Chilean docks to the Reconstruction Finance Corporation at whatever price necessary, but Win Nathanson, the public relations counsel for Mauricio Hochschild and Carlos Aramayo, convinced them to "do nothing for the time being" that might provoke Lechín. Nathanson hoped to explore a "profit-sharing arrangement" with the MNR regime similar to the arrangement oil companies had worked out with Venezuela. Although President Paz Estenssoro's creation of a nationalization commission suggested that expropriation was not a foregone conclusion, Nathanson made it clear to Assistant Secretary Miller that "the most important factor" in maintaining order would be the "attitude and actions of the United States government." The managers at the Patiño enterprises, fearful of the "chaos" that would follow if Paz Estenssoro faltered, also decided to cooperate with him until a more satisfactory alternative could be found. Moreover, Antenor Patiño believed he could ride out any nationalization by running his company for the government, thus protecting and maintaining his mines for the two years he expected the MNR to remain in power.[33]

Patiño's Catavi manager D. C. Deringer believed that, without the current management and staff, Minister of Mines Lechín could not hope to keep the tin industry "in the black." Although the government might be able to use selective mining of the best veins in Catavi for a year and appear to be successful, it would deplete the mine "without any hope of again resuming commercial operations." He further believed that the MNR simply did not understand how complex the operation of the tin mines truly was and seemed determined to drive off the foreign technicians and engineers who had the essential expertise. He explained that patriotism might well lead miners to work harder in the nationalized mines, but endemic Bolivian graft would more than undo any gains from that quarter. And even if Patiño employees did help run the government-owned mines, Lechín might then turn a profit, proclaim victory, and emerge even stronger.[34]

By late May, Aramayo and Hochschild, having concluded, with State Department support, that they needed to give Paz Estenssoro a "practicable alternative" to nationalization, proposed their profit-sharing scheme. Hochschild's general manager had apparently convinced himself that President Paz Estenssoro and Vice President Siles Zuazo were only going to "go through the motions of nationalization" to appease Lechín and the radicals. In fact, Foreign Minister Walter Guevara Arze, a key conservative movimientista, apparently informed a U.S. businessman in La Paz that just one Aramayo mine would be nationalized to provide a token victory for the radicals while the rest of the Big Three's mines would remain untouched. Patiño himself had taken a more realistic approach: he had been quietly preparing for nationalization since the 1951 election. He had deftly guaranteed U.S. interest in the tin mines by "quietly" selling U.S. citizens shares in his Bolivian facilities and canceling an order for a $2.5 million sink and float plant for Catavi to prevent it falling into the MNR's hands.[35]

Also by late May, the State Department had concluded that "continued nonrecognition would not assist Paz but would rather have the effect of strengthening extremist elements in the government," encouraging nationalization, and "pushing the government more in the direction of Perón." Assistant Secretary Miller had argued that "we are acting like ostriches with our heads in the sand" and that the United States would have to face the reality of Paz Estenssoro's presidency sooner or later. Since "Paz looks better than anyone else on the horizon," President Truman had agreed that recognition was "probably the right course of action." This in no way implied solidarity with the tin barons, who "are in large part responsible for their present predicament." It was instead an acknowledgment that the nationalization of the mines would be a bad precedent for the rest of South America, encouraging the Chileans to nationalize copper and the Venezuelans to nationalize oil, and would make U.S. tin purchases from expropriated properties problematic. The embassy had reported that, though the political "situation leaves much to be desired," it was not "greatly abnormal for Bolivia," and the State Department had informed U.S. allies that it would recognize the new government within a week.[36]

The Nationalization of the Big Three

Although President Truman had been compelled to recognize the MNR regime to avoid strengthening Lechín and the leftists, he was not about to give up his true leverage, a long-term tin contract, until the issue of nationalization had been resolved. Assured that the movimientistas had no significant ties with either Peronism or Communism, the State Department saw little standing in the way of rapprochement. Nationalization offered no immediate threat to the United States: the tin barons were all foreign nationals and only Patiño's company had a significant number of U.S. shareholders. Still, the department understood that if the MNR proceeded to expropriate the tin companies, it could set off a chain reaction across South America, or at least establish a dangerous precedent. For the next eight months, U.S. diplomats therefore intervened in Bolivian affairs, not to protect U.S. investments in Bolivia, but to send a message to nationalist revolutionaries across the hemisphere. In its final days, the Truman administration, if nothing else, made its goals in South America crystal clear.

Representatives of the Defense Materials Procurement Administration, Emergency Procurement Service, Reconstruction Finance Corporation, and Export-Import Bank met with State Department officers in mid-June and unanimously agreed not to make more than spot purchases of Bolivian tin until the nationalization issue was resolved. Although both the State Department and the RFC realized that such purchases would cause the flow of Bolivia's foreign exchange to be "spasmodic" and unpredictable, there was simply no alternative. Since "the only effective bargaining weapon in the hands of the United States" was the tin contract, for once, the purchasing agencies and the State Department saw eye to eye.[37]

For its part, the RFC, facing a strike at the Texas City smelter, saw no immediate need to purchase any Bolivian tin but did want to make a long-term bulk purchase to secure the stockpile against the uncertainties of the Korean War. The State Department argued that Chairman McDonald should make at least small spot purchases because, if the RFC stopped all purchasing, it would create an "impression in Bolivia that we are trying to run their economy into the ground." The Truman administration hoped to avert nationalization by exerting economic pressure, but feared doing so openly. The department explained to the Bolivians that the RFC could not sign a long-term contract until the nationalization question was resolved because doing so "might create questions of ownership of the ores involved." Victor Andrade, once again Bolivia's ambassador to the United States, apparently did not realize that the fear of lawsuits was merely a pretense.[38]

Regardless of the final outcome of the nationalization study, President Paz Estenssoro was certainly going to exert much closer control over the tin industry than his predecessors. On 2 June 1952, he decreed that all mineral exports from Bolivia would be handled by the Banco Minero. By establishing an export monopoly, the MNR would be able to more closely monitor and regulate the activities of the tin barons and funnel the profits of the mines into industrialization and rural reform projects it had so long dreamed of implementing. The 2 June decree, which contravened existing tungsten and tin contracts, would force the tin barons to apply to the government for any foreign exchange and was a clear blow to private enterprise. Secretary Acheson ordered Ambassador Sparks to tell the Bolivians that implementing the decree "would add serious complications which might tend to make" the RFC "prefer alternative sources elsewhere." Sparks was to advise the Bolivians that nationalization was unwise economically and to suggest that, if problems with the 2 June decree were "worked out satisfactorily," U.S. loans for small and medium mine owners "contemplated" in March might "still be considered."[39]

Although U.S. policy makers hoped that depriving President Paz Estenssoro of a tin contract would force him to moderate his position on nationalization, it only prodded him to seek new, disquieting methods of selling Bolivia's tin. The day after establishing the Banco Minero monopoly, the president apparently authorized two foreigners, Hanns Ditisheim and Leon Henderson, to sell all tin produced in Bolivia over the next two years at as high a price as they could negotiate. They would be given one month to do this and 20 percent of the sales revenue to purchase all food and machinery needed by the mining industry; their profits would come from whatever discounts they could arrange with foreign suppliers. In addition, 2 to 9 percent of the revenue would be funneled to the MNR Welfare Fund and the Banco Minero. Believing that the tin barons had traditionally exaggerated the costs of their purchases and thereby earned "secret rebates," the MNR hoped to sever the ties between the companies and their traditional suppliers, "damage some politically unpopular firms," and create a source of income for the government. Apparently, during the months of nonrecognition, the RFC had told the Bolivians that it would not "deal directly with the Banco Minero," and Henderson, onetime head of President Roosevelt's Office of Price Administration, had, in Ambassador Sparks's words, "seized upon this situation." He soon discovered that the RFC's reluctance had nothing to do with the Banco Minero and everything to do with the good behavior of the MNR.[40]

For the State Department, the sudden appearance of profiteers was every bit as disturbing as the Banco Minero monopoly itself. Ambassador Sparks saw no reason why the Bolivians needed private agents to sell their tin and was "disturbed" by the power these agents would wield as the sole importers for the mining industry. After consulting with his superiors, he assured Paz Estenssoro that the RFC would deal directly with the Banco Minero and that the "Henderson-Ditisheim option" had been entirely unnecessary. Indeed, the State Department found Paz Estenssoro's arrangement with Henderson and Ditisheim highly unusual, somewhat suspicious, and altogether undesirable. Not only were there tremendous opportunities for conflicts of interest, misunderstandings, and outright fraud, but also the United States might well come under fire because of Henderson. Ambassador Andrade could only hope Ambassador Sparks's assurances could be counted on: that the RFC would indeed negotiate with the Banco Minero once the Henderson-Ditisheim arrangement expired.[41]

As soon as Ditisheim and Henderson were out of the picture, Raúl Canedo Reyes, now representing the Banco Minero, offered the RFC an eighteen-month contract at $1.21 per pound for all non-Patiño tin. Although the RFC insisted upon only a spot purchase through September, the problem was going to be smelter costs. The Longhorn smelter at Texas City had sufficient tin to operate through next spring, and the stockpile was adequate. Great Britain's Capper Pass smelter was offering to pay only $1.19½ per pound; the RFC had no reason to offer more than that.[42] Canedo Reyes accepted that the RFC needed an increase in smelting fees to offset higher labor costs, and even acknowledged it as "fair," but feared "the political consequences of the increase taking effect in the first transaction" of the MNR government. He was not alone. State Department officers and even U.S. bankers associated with Mauricio Hochschild and the Banco Minero found it "politically unfortunate" that this step, which could easily breed ill will, had to be taken. Nonetheless, the RFC's first offer was just $1.17½ per pound. Ambassador Andrade protested that "it would appear to the Bolivian public that they were being discriminated against," but to no avail. In fact, since the market price of tin had already dropped below $1.17 per pound, State Department officers were surprised that the RFC had offered as much as $1.17½ and suggested that Andrade accept the offer before it was withdrawn.[43]

Though the ambassador warned his superiors that there was little or no chance for a better price, Andrade complained to U.S. diplomats that he had no option but to "appeal to the sense of equity of the United States" since no foreign banks were eager to "finance a Bolivian holdout." He asserted that the MNR would "find it hard to explain to" the Bolivian people "why they [were] not receiving fair treatment" at the hands of the United States yet continued to "combat Argentine propaganda to the effect that the U.S. was not fair to Latin America." Even though the difference between the U.S. and Bolivian offers was now only one-half cent per pound and Andrade understood that he had little choice but to accept the RFC's offer, he continued to plead for a half-cent per pound reduction in smelting charges for "political and psychological" reasons. Because Paz Estenssoro was radically cutting military spending and eliminating the tin barons as "middlemen," he could afford to "take ½ cent less" without "going into bankruptcy, but the psychological effect might be disastrous." State Department officers were unimpressed by Andrade's eloquence.[44]

With a return to the familiar "take-it-or-leave-it" days, Ambassador Andrade understood that he "had no alternative" and recommended to his superiors that they accept the RFC's offer. He had other motives, as well. He personally needed to conclude this negotiation to "freeze Ditisheim out" and to convince his government that a private businessman could not have gotten a better deal from the RFC. Within a week, however, the Bolivians had optioned their tin to a U.S. company, Mercantile Metal and Ore, this time for an unprecedented 3 percent commission. President Paz Estenssoro was clearly desperate: RFC experts had never before seen a tin sales commission larger than one-eighth of a cent per pound. Although Assistant Secretary Miller immediately sought to put an end to this sort of contracting, which would take money from the Bolivian economy and open the U.S. government to charges of discrimination or collusion, how the State Department was going to avoid giving Paz Estenssoro a tin contract yet dissuade his government from engaging in increasingly reckless efforts to get one remained unclear.[45]

Indeed, still fearful that signing a long-term tin contract would effectively give a "green light to confiscatory nationalization," the State Department was now the only obstacle to finally achieving one. After years of being ignored by the RFC, U.S. diplomats were finally able to exert their influence on the agency; only they were doing so to deny a long-term tin contract that would help stabilize the Bolivian economy. What Assistant Secretary Miller now sought was a convincing pretext for the United States to refuse such a contract "without openly admitting" it was. He could no longer use the RFC as a pretext because the defense planners had all but conceded they would have signed a long-term deal with the Bolivians if the State Department had not objected. State Department and RFC officials discussed several options but ultimately found all "transparent or ineffectual."[46]

By mid-August, Sparks thought it was time for "straight talking" about nationalization because "the present situation is likely only to deteriorate with the passage of time." He believed that President Paz Estenssoro, Vice President Siles Zuazo, Ambassador Andrade, and others had shown "sincerity and a genuine desire for close, cooperative relations with the United States." However, failure to nationalize the tin mines would be "political suicide" for the movimientistas, inevitably leading to the "downfall of the government." Sparks therefore urged the State Department to resurrect the aid package it had contemplated in the days before the revolution and to offer it to Paz Estenssoro. If U.S. assistance could help the president "step up mining, agriculture," and petroleum development, the department might bolster the conservatives and "swing the scale to a solution short of outright nationalization." Earnestly seeking to "avert actions which would be disastrous for Bolivia," "create unfortunate precedents in the Americas," and strain U.S.-Bolivian relations, Ambassador Sparks was calling for the United States to openly embrace the MNR.[47]

His superiors refused. Because of the "confused" situation in La Paz, Secretary Acheson and Assistant Secretary Miller were unwilling "to use even an implied promise" of "assistance as a bargaining point at this stage," but they did permit Sparks to inform the Bolivians that, if nationalization were handled satisfactorily, "we would be willing to work out with them a broader program of economic cooperation." Miller, Deputy Assistant Secretary Mann, and State Department officer Atwood reaffirmed to Ambassador Andrade that the United States fully supported the MNR's plans for economic diversification and would assist them in resolving the "grave problems" of Bolivia but made it clear that there would be no long-term contract until the issue of nationalization was resolved. When Secretary Acheson warned yet again that nationalization would create an environment that would discourage private investment, Ambassador Andrade could only retort that, despite the "most liberal treatment" that had been given to the tin barons for decades, there had been almost no foreign investment in his nation.⁴⁸

This was a key argument for Lechín and the radicals. Indeed, the Nationalization Study Commission Report concluded that not only had the tin barons siphoned their profits out of the country, but they had also "systematically" discouraged "fresh capital from being invested in Bolivia, lest such investments strengthen Bolivia economically and thereby weaken their own hegemony." The report went on to illustrate the countless tax evasion schemes the tin barons had used to defraud the nation. By citing the exact amounts of taxes not paid by the tin barons, the commission seemed to be laying the foundation for an argument that the amount of unpaid taxes should be deducted from the value of the mines. Vice President Siles Zuazo confirmed as much to U.S. diplomats. Although the tin barons valued their Bolivian properties at more than $60 million, the MNR considered them to be worth only $22 million, and it remained to be seen how that figure compared to the back taxes the government thought the Big Three owed.⁴⁹ It was not entirely unlikely that the tin barons might end up losing their properties and still owing the government.

In late September, Carlos Aramayo and Mauricio Hochschild proposed that the government pay them $60 million for their mines over the course of several decades. Their companies would continue to manage and operate the mines until the government finally assumed the titles for the properties in as few as ten years.⁵⁰ For his part, Antenor Patiño proposed selling his mines to the government for $5 million down and a "modest" $25 million to $35 million over time, so long as he was hired to operate them. Patiño refused to make common cause with Aramayo and Hochschild: his operations, both within Bolivia and globally, were much larger than theirs, some of his shareholders were U.S. citizens and thus protected by the U.S. government, his firm was incorporated in Delaware, and the average Bolivian despised Aramayo and Hochschild far more than they did him. Therefore, the other tin barons were, as Patiño put it, "a different breed of cat." Whereas Patiño was already confident he had the backing of the U.S. government, Aramayo and Hochschild hired former U.S. Senator Millard Tydings, recently unseated for his opposition to McCarthyism, to be their advocate in Washington.⁵¹

Tydings joined the fight at a distinct disadvantage: his new clients had no real connection with the United States. Unfamiliar with the situation in Bolivia, he met with Tin Division Chief McKinnon, "casting about" for "possible courses of effective action." Evidently, Tydings favored either an embargo on Bolivia or an appeal to the OAS to expel Bolivia, a measure he claimed already had the support of two foreign governments. Lack of support from both the RFC and the State Department did not stop him from threatening Ambassador Andrade and Vice President Siles Zuazo with a U.S. embargo. The movimientistas responded that they had survived too many far worse threats in the course of the previous six years to be cowed or dissuaded by Tydings's "childish" efforts at intimidation.[52]

Lame Duck Diplomacy

The State Department's efforts to forestall expropriation ended on 31 October 1952, when President Paz Estenssoro announced the nationalization of the Big Three's tin mines in a ceremony at María Barzola Field, site of the 1942 Catavi Massacre. The tin barons argued that the MNR was cutting off its nose to spite its face. A movimientista spokesman found a different metaphor: "When a dog has a gangrenous tail, its master has no recourse but to cut it off." As Bolivians took to the streets in celebration, however, the question of compensation remained open. When Ambassador Andrade presented the nationalization decree to the State Department, Undersecretary David Bruce informed him that the only concern of the United States was the compensation of foreign shareholders, especially U.S. citizens. According to Andrade, 2 percent of the gross return from the mines would be applied to compensation, but Carlos Aramayo, Mauricio Hochschild, and Antenor Patiño had to pay "what they owed to the Bolivian State and people." Although the MNR informed Ambassador Sparks that it might "modify some of its counterclaims sufficiently to leave the companies some balance of compensation," this was hardly encouraging.[53]

The U.S. Embassy's assessment was telling: "The amount of compensation will largely be determined by the nuisance value which the companies are able to exert." The "lower limit is that which the companies might be persuaded to accept in return for withdrawing all pressures" against the government, while the "upper limit will be that which the government finds politically tolerable." If the tin barons were "too obdurate in their demands" and successfully "harassed" the MNR through propaganda and foreign pressure, they might "price themselves out of the market and get nothing."[54] For the State Department, however, nationalization actually changed very little. Whereas the Truman administration had denied President Paz Estenssoro a long-term tin contract to dissuade him from nationalization, now it would hold out the promise of such a contract to persuade him to properly compensate the tin barons for the properties he had nationalized. If the State Department could not have a precedent that permitted liberal capitalism to flourish, it would cut its losses and settle for one that discouraged expropriation without indemnification.

Although the department was, to some extent, obligated to help Patiño's shareholders win reimbursement, Tydings had to convince it to go to bat for Aramayo and Hochschild as well. He urged that no Bolivian tin be purchased until "satisfactory progress was made" regarding compensation for his clients and begged the State Department to "put pressure" on President Paz Estenssoro to "appoint a representative to come to Washington to negotiate with him." When Assistant Secretary Miller informed him that the department could not support his appeals directly, Tydings vowed to take the matter to both outgoing President Truman and President-elect Eisenhower. He then threatened Ambassador Andrade again with a U.S. embargo if his clients were not properly compensated. Andrade told Tydings he was "surprised" that a U.S. statesman who "represented the liberal tradition could find it compatible with his conscience to represent the worst reactionaries in Bolivia."[55]

With Dwight Eisenhower's election victory in November, the State Department finally found a valid excuse for denying Bolivia a long-term tin contract. President Truman refused to make any commitment that might tie the hands of the incoming Eisenhower administration. The president-elect would "have to be consulted about any decisions in this matter and there was no machinery for such consultation." Ambassador Sparks argued, however, that the best way to guarantee the foreign exchange Bolivia so badly needed was to link the compensation of U.S. shareholders directly to a long-term tin contract.[56] Ambassador Andrade agreed, and on 9 December, he approached Deputy Assistant Secretary Mann with an urgent plea for a twelve- or eighteen-month contract. Since nationalization, the tin companies had provided no operating capital for the mines, and the government had been selling off its gold reserves to keep them in operation. Even worse, fearing that the United States would not purchase Bolivia's tin and that food imports would "therefore be severely curtailed," Bolivians had been hoarding food and creating shortages.[57]

A long-term contract, Ambassador Andrade believed, was "essential to prove to the people of Bolivia that the United States was not imposing economic sanctions for Bolivian nationalization." Although a spot purchase would be useful, concluding a long-term contract would provide the MNR with invaluable "ammunition" to use against its "Communist" critics. The ambassador promised that 5 percent of the profits from the contract could be set aside for the compensation of U.S. shareholders and suggested that the issues of compensation and the contract be negotiated simultaneously. He made it clear that only in return for such a contract would his government accept arbitration for Patiño shareholder compensation. Deputy Assistant Secretary Mann was amenable, but because such an arrangement might otherwise seem like a U.S. ultimatum, he proposed that Andrade present this "package deal" as his own idea. The ambassador agreed.[58]

Mann argued that the "package deal," which the RFC approved within days, was "our best chance" of winning "reasonably favorable terms" for U.S. shareholders and would set an important precedent for future expropriations across Latin America. Moreover, it would not cost the United States much leverage because the RFC had been prepared to make spot purchases or even sign a long-term contract anyway. Furthermore, a contract would "minimize the risk that we will be accused of economic aggression," supporting the tin barons, or "causing the economic plight of Bolivia." Mann certainly did not want to bear the "onus throughout all of Latin America for the misery that the Bolivian people are face to face with" and hoped to eliminate the "suspicion, voiced in the United Nations and elsewhere, that we were prepared to impose economic sanctions against Bolivia for nationalization" and in defense of the hated tin barons. Finally, Mann argued that, should the Bolivian economy collapse without a contract, as Ambassador Andrade predicted it would, "there is currently no hope of the present regime being replaced by more moderate elements."[59]

On the other hand, the deputy assistant secretary conceded, the "package deal" might strengthen the MNR's hand in its dealings with other shareholders and might be "interpreted as showing that the United States was not taking a sufficiently strong attitude against nationalization in general." Responding to rumors of the proposed deal, a furious Tydings demanded that the State Department act forcefully on behalf of his clients and proclaimed that, if the RFC purchased a single pound of Bolivian tin, it would be acting as an "international fence" for "stolen property." Mann agreed to continue to informally press the Bolivians to pay compensation to all shareholders but was "doubtful" that they would because of the hatred they held toward Aramayo and Hochschild.[60]

Within the week, Ambassador Andrade asked Deputy Assistant Secretary Mann to ensure that he received credit for the "package deal." Apparently, Mercantile Metal and Ore was again pressing the Bolivians to take over the sale of their tin by arguing that it "had great political power in the United States." Mann readily agreed to Andrade's request but had a favor of his own to ask of him. The United States could only involve itself in the claims of U.S. shareholders, so would the ambassador consent to meet with Tydings at his home to discuss a parallel settlement with foreign investors? Mann had no official duty to assist Tydings, but the "confiscation of anybody's property anywhere in the world was not a desirable thing," and an agreement with Tydings would clear away any obstacle to a long-term contract. Andrade was happy to oblige.[61]

Ambassador Andrade and the State Department actually drafted an agreement for arbitration of Antenor Patiño's claims. Andrade's primary concern was that Patiño might have convinced the British government to block the sale of tin concentrates from his properties to the Williams, Harvey smelter. The State Department quickly reassured him by sharing confidential British documents. Contrary to Patiño's fear mongering, the British were concerned only with continuing the flow of tin and actually took some satisfaction at the thought that Patiño was receiving a bloody nose. The State Department's only concern was that the Bolivians might not be prepared for legal challenges from the tin barons, but this, too, was unfounded: the movimientistas had hired their own former U.S. senator, John Danaher, to act as their counsel. In explaining the proposed "package deal" to Patiño's vice president, State Department officers implored him to keep "our plan a complete secret, in order to allow Ambassador Andrade to present the plan to his government in the manner he considers most politic."[62]

Even though Andrade had essentially drafted the "package deal," his superiors found it unacceptable. They rejected outright the provision calling for the United States to withhold a percentage of the tin sales revenue in a special account for the compensation of U.S. shareholders. They sought assurances that shareholders would only be paid for the portion of their stock that had been nationalized, whereas the deal made that a matter for the arbiters. Finally, they worried that selection of one arbiter by the International Court of Justice might imply that the court had jurisdiction over nationalization. Disappointed that his superiors had not trusted the good faith of the U.S. government, the ambassador feared the "package deal" might quickly evaporate if no action was taken.[63]

Secretary Acheson urged Ambassador Sparks to make "every effort," including a "full discussion with Paz," to persuade the Bolivians that the State Department was "acting in complete good faith and not trying to pressure them into hasty action." Still, because the procurement agencies were planning to end their tin stockpile purchases in June 1953, the consequences of any delay could be "extremely grave." Even worse, rumor had it that Congress was preparing to close the Texas City smelter. If either of these developments occurred before an agreement was reached, Bolivia would be without a buyer in a glutted tin market, and the United States would lose its major source of leverage. When the Bolivians told Secretary Acheson they wanted another stopgap agreement to give them time to contemplate the "package deal," the secretary warned that the one-year contract offer would be off the table in days if it was not accepted.[64]

President Paz Estenssoro seemed content to await the Eisenhower administration. He ordered Ambassador Andrade to offer Deputy Assistant Secretary Mann a five-thousand-ton spot purchase contract for the tin that had piled up since September, but the president refused to even discuss the establishment of a compensation fund for the transaction.[65] The deal was quickly concluded, if only to avoid the perception that the United States would not purchase nationalized tin and to meet Bolivia's immediate need for foreign exchange. On 19 January 1953, now authorized to accept the "package deal," Ambassador Andrade met with Deputy Assistant Secretary Mann and again requested a long-term contract. A regretful Mann told the ambassador it would simply "not be practical" to resume contract talks on the eve of President Eisenhower's inauguration. Mann could only lament that the "package deal" could have been made to work had the process been started "two or three weeks earlier."[66]

Instead, President Truman appropriately left office with the tin contract in limbo, where indeed it had remained for much of his presidency. By the time a new contract was signed, the world price of tin had dropped from $1.21 to 78¢ per pound. President Paz Estenssoro did finally concede to some compensation for the tin barons but made sure that everyone understood he had done so only because "the United States told us that they could not buy tin from us on a long-term contract unless we made an agreement with the North American stockholders." Although U.S. diplomats faulted the president for his dalliance with Ditisheim, Henderson, and Mercantile Metal and Ore and his reluctance to compensate the tin barons for their expropriated properties, they conveniently overlooked their own role in blocking a tin contract.[67]

Embassy officer William Hudson tried to put the best possible face on the events of 1952. Acknowledging that "our accomplishments" were "all negative," he explained that the United States "rescu[ed] what we could from a tidal wave of nationalism." He proudly proclaimed that "it was due entirely to United States efforts that the inevitable nationalization of most of the country's mining industry took the form which recognized the principle of compensation" and noted that, despite the "rising xenophobia among the ignorant masses of Bolivia," no U.S. citizens lost their lives. On the other hand, Hudson was forced to concede that the difficulties over the tin contract had "probably contributed in some degree to the success of the revolution," which Robert Alexander has called the "most profound Latin American unrest since the Mexican Revolution." For Alexander, the "politically alert" of Latin America were watching to see whether the Movimiento Nacionalista Revolucionario could "for the first time in four hundred years" manage to integrate "the Indian into the life of the country" and how the United States would respond.[68]

For its part, the Truman administration, despite acknowledging the need to cooperate with Paz Estenssoro, could not overcome its visceral hostility toward the MNR. Although low- to mid-level officers of Truman's State Department made one last-ditch effort to secure a tin contract that might have provided some assistance to conservative movimientistas, it was far too little, far too late. Not surprisingly, the MNR mistrusted what appears to have been Deputy Assistant Secretary Mann's genuine effort to arrive at a mutually advantageous solution to several problems. In the end, however, and thanks in part to a hostile Truman administration, Bolivians appeared to have finally rid themselves of liberal constitutional oligarchy. The incoming Eisenhower administration, free from the prejudices of the Truman years, would openly embrace the MNR and the National Revolution and attempt to steer both in Washington's direction.[69]

CONCLUSION

We know that since 1946, the present and the future of the tin industry depended on the goodwill of the North American Administration.
—R. Querejazu Calvo, 18 February 1950

If the owners of the mining properties, the Patiños, the Aramayos, and the Hochschilds, had spent a reasonable part of the wealth taken from Bolivia's mines on the development of the country's resources and on the improvement of the living standards of the masses, they would still have the mines. For over a half century the tin mines of Bolivia have remained in private hands and the result has been great fortunes for men like the late Simon Patiño. Other results have been one of the lowest standards of living in the world for Bolivian workers and a primitive and backward country.
—Victor Andrade, 19 November 1952

In the end, the Truman administration's dealings with Bolivia must be considered a failure on almost every level. They were, however, an instructive failure, exposing many of the flaws of the early Cold War policies of the United States in South America. Although individual State Department officers often showed an exceptionally perceptive understanding of events on the Altiplano, they rarely managed to implement effective policies. They correctly understood that there was, for all practical purposes, no Communism in Bolivia and perceived that the Movimiento Nacionalista Revolucionario was the greatest potential threat to their conception of liberal capitalism. They also understood that the rosca's liberal constitutional oligarchy was in its final days, barring a concerted effort at reform, but were unable to provide any meaningful assistance to those embarking on such an effort.

Indeed, even though the United States had the political, economic, and military power to push one of the weakest, poorest nations in the hemisphere in the direction it desired, it lacked both the will and the diplomatic acumen to apply that power consistently and effectively. The behavior and actions of the Reconstruction Finance Corporation illustrate this point perfectly. Defense planners quite understandably sought to dismantle the onerous tin cartel and to secure a resource vital to U.S. national security; they were able to do both with ease. Those planners gave almost no consideration, however, to the diplomatic implications of their actions and the long-term complications their single-minded approach risked, much less to the creation of a balanced, cohesive U.S. strategy. Indeed, between the entirely unnecessary and provocative bluster of the FEA's Alan Bateman and RFC Chairman Stuart Symington, the ignorant and stubborn blundering of Senator Lyndon Johnson, and the willingness of President Harry Truman to tolerate a confused, vacillating policy until days before the National Revolution, it is a small miracle that U.S. policy did not end in disaster. This is not to exonerate U.S. diplomats. Ambassador Irving Florman's incompetence and insubordination made short work of his superiors' attempts at diplomatic restraint and balance, U.S. diplomats persisted in both foolishly and stubbornly branding the MNR as "Nazi," "Peronist," or "Communist" rather than developing a more sophisticated, realistic analysis, and State Department officers rarely presented their analyses forcefully enough to challenge their superiors' inertia or the defense planners' recklessness. Not surprisingly, when Dwight Eisenhower and the Republicans took over the White House, they quickly reversed most of Truman's policies toward Bolivia.

Eisenhower and the MNR

The Bolivian mess landed on the new president's desk almost immediately after he took office on 20 January 1953. Millard Tydings wasted no time in appealing to Secretary of State John Foster Dulles and the Republicans on behalf of his clients, Carlos Aramayo and Mauricio Hochschild. He asked again that the U.S. government refuse to purchase Bolivian tin until his clients were satisfactorily reimbursed for their expropriated properties, lest it "contribute to the climate of moral decay and outright thievery" that would eventually "come home to plague us." He warned that the "day after" the United States signed a tin agreement, the leftist Juan Lechín would oust Paz Estenssoro from power. Deputy Assistant Secretary Mann, in a noncommittal response, suggested that, though the State Department was still in favor of spot purchases by the RFC, "it would be a mistake to try to force the issue [of compensation] with the Bolivians at this time." Still, the Eisenhower administration at first seemed supportive of Tydings when, in early March and with Secretary Dulles's approval, the RFC announced that it was no longer interested in signing a long-term tin contract. The agency had been warning Bolivians for three months that if it filled its annual quota before securing a contract with La Paz, there would be no long-term deal. With the tin stockpile almost full, tin prices unlikely to rise again in the near future, and the Texas City smelter losing money, the Republicans decided that, as Kenneth Lehman has put it, for "both economic and philosophical reasons . . . it was time the government got out of the tin business."[1]

Meanwhile, the Bolivian government and economy were, once again, on the verge of total collapse. The economy, already strained by the revolution and years of conflict with the RFC, came under intense pressure when a Chilean judge, at the behest of the tin barons, ordered a virtual embargo on all goods in Antofagasta destined for the Bolivian mines. Moreover, the tension between the Lechín and Paz Estenssoro factions of the MNR had intensified on nearly every issue. Even as Lechín's faction demanded no compromise with or compensation for the tin barons, immediate confiscation of the fincas, and the dissolution of the military, President Paz Estenssoro reached a preliminary accommodation with Patiño, pursued more gradual agrarian reform, and rebuilt the army. The president delivered on one key promise of the National Revolution, universal suffrage, but appeared to be moving too slowly for some on the others.

In late August, the U.S. Embassy predicted that, "without outside help," the Bolivian economy would be in "a complete state of chaos by the end of 1953," and "the MNR party would be torn apart." U.S. policy makers had little doubt which faction would emerge triumphant, especially after MNR militias and the petroleum syndicates put down an uprising by the Falangists in November even before the Federal Police or the army could take to the field.[2] Acting independently or in conjunction with militants of the Central Obrera Boliviana, indigenous groups were organizing and, at times, lashing out violently at the hacendados. In the last weeks of the Truman presidency, the militias and unions had quickly dealt with rightist MNR civilians and military officers when they attempted a coup by kidnapping labor leaders Juan Lechín, Ñuflo Chávez, and German Butrón, but it had taken all of Paz Estenssoro's legendary skill to paper over the fundamental divisions between the party's two factions and maintain some semblance of unity. And that "unity" had come at a price: the president had been forced to enact agrarian reform that tilted toward the "radical" position.[3]

The January 1953 coup attempt was an excellent reminder of the fragility of the political situation in La Paz. Lechín's supporters took the occasion to denounce the United States for its "economic aggression." President Paz Estenssoro made "demagogic, dishonest, and malicious" speeches threatening to sell his tin behind the Iron Curtain, although Lechín's speeches were "even worse, both in tone and content." Deputy Assistant Secretary Mann and Ambassador Andrade agreed that the MNR was rapidly reaching the point where "it would be unable to convince its people of the desirability of cooperating with the United States."[4]

Whereas Ambassador Sparks believed that Paz Estenssoro was threatened by Lechín and the radicals, the AFL believed that Lechín's position was both crucial and tenuous. Without a tin contract to restore financial stability, both Lechín and Paz Estenssoro would be "steamrollered" by the "overwhelmingly nationalistic" rank and file of the COB. Indeed, the AFL believed that, by allying himself so forcefully with the MNR, Lechín would be the first casualty of a Bolivian economic collapse. In short, the AFL concluded, neither Lechín nor the MNR would "maintain their position for many more weeks if the United States will not buy tin."[5] With MNR and union militias as the dominant military force in the nation, indigenous Bolivians beginning an unprecedented mobilization, the position of MNR conservatives imperiled, and the agrarian and labor movements mutating in ways that the United States could not understand, the political situation was rapidly deteriorating.

To "resist communist attempts to undermine" the government, embassy counselor Edward Rowell argued, and to "keep this tinder box, which might set off a chain reaction in Latin America, from striking fire," it was "urgent" that the United States "seize the initiative" and offer all "financial and other aids that may be necessary." According to Rowell, the "uninformed consensus" in Bolivia was that the current crisis had been "consciously induced by the United States" and that, if Paz Estenssoro's government fell "as a result of the tin situation, Latin American nationalism will count it as one more triumph of 'Yankee imperialism' over the 'revolutionary forces' striving for the 'economic liberation' of South America." The MNR's "propaganda Blitzkrieg" blaming the United States for the "consequences of its own incompetence and irresponsibility," which had "already seriously damaged our position in Bolivia," was in fact little more than a "smokescreen to divert public attention from the economic chaos and political disunity prevailing in Bolivia."[6]

Although Ambassador Sparks reported that "neither the MNR Party in the mass, nor its most important leaders, are communist or crypto-communist in spite of some obvious Marxist ideological taints" and an "ingrained suspicion of the United States and its motives," there was still cause for great concern.[7] Embassy staff believed that, since Villarroel had been overthrown by a "coalition of the extreme left and the extreme right," the MNR was reluctant to antagonize either extreme until "it was sure enough of its own strength to withstand simultaneous attack on both fronts." A sharp warning from Sparks temporarily stopped top MNR leaders from fanning the flames of anti-U.S. sentiment, but the economic crisis grew worse by the day. Milton Eisenhower, serving as advisor to his brother on Latin American affairs, entered the fray in June. He quickly came to support State Department assertions that action had to be taken to prevent a counterrevolution in Bolivia—either by the "exceedingly tyrannical" Falange or by leftists "of some kind or another." Proclaiming that the movimientistas were "not Communists" and that even their controversial land reform program was "the only way to avert violent revolution," Milton became an open advocate for Paz Estenssoro.[8]

By August, the Eisenhower administration had opted for a full diplomatic embrace of President Paz Estenssoro to protect him from Lechín, the left-wing militias, and the prospect of Bolivia becoming a "focus of Communist infection" as a result of "our apparent indifference." Embassy officers, convinced that "any collapse in Bolivia will be widely believed to be the result of pressure by 'American imperialism,'" believed that the MNR, "for all of its foolishness, corruption, and other faults," was "preferable to any successor which is in sight." Since it was a "distinct possibility" that Communists might be that successor, Eisenhower's State Department opted for full support of the MNR. It decided to resume spot purchases of Bolivian tin until alternate markets could be found. Even so, as a result of recent drops in the international price of tin to 78¢ per pound and a decline in agricultural production in the aftermath of President Paz Estenssoro's agrarian reform decree of 2 August 1953, Bolivia was facing a shortfall of $10 million to $15 million between "exchange earnings" and "requirements for absolutely essential imports" for the year. Because there was no prospect for repayment, both the Treasury Department and the International Monetary Fund opposed a direct loan. Milton Eisenhower, wishing his government had a "slush fund for which it would not have to make a very explicit accounting," proposed to his brother that Paz Estenssoro be given grants under the Famine Relief and Mutual Security Acts. In the short term, the grants would avert starvation in Bolivia, and, in the long term, their funds could be used to encourage Bolivia's agricultural development and thus reduce its crippling dependency on tin mining. The president approved. Tydings did not.[9]

When the aid package was delayed, President Paz Estenssoro feared that Washington was stalling in the hopes that he would be "overthrown by a rightist group." His fears were entirely misplaced. Although U.S. policy makers would most certainly have welcomed a "rightist" coup, even Tydings conceded that there was no credible group capable of pulling one off, so the MNR conservatives won U.S. support by default. Though heaving "a sigh of relief" at word of impending assistance—the United States would send $9 million of famine relief aid by December, with another $1.3 million soon to follow—Paz Estenssoro's foreign minister requested additional developmental loans, without which "Bolivia would be able only to keep afloat and never extricate itself from the economic mire in which previous governments had sunk it."[10] In October, Ambassador Sparks had informed the Bolivians that his superiors expected to "see more clearly established the dominance of the moderate elements in the Government" as well as a humble written request for aid from President Paz Estenssoro to President Eisenhower. He had received both in short order.[11]

With unintended irony, the ambassador declared that the U.S. aid had provided the MNR with "some independent security for the first time since it took power" and had quieted "much of the latent mistrust that has existed heretofore." It took less than a month for the Eisenhower administration's diplomatic about-face to "pay dividends." President Paz Estenssoro revamped his cabinet strongly in favor of the right wing and clamped down on the Communist Party, suppressing its newspapers and purging suspected Communists from Bolivian government posts at the behest of the U.S. Embassy; he also supported the U.S. case against Guatemala's Marxists in the Organization of American States. In COB elections, the movimientistas' slogan, "Out with the Communists!" delivered huge victories. By November 1953, Bolivian Communists, who had once been ambivalent about the National Revolution, were denouncing it as vigorously as they ever had the rosca, much to Washington's satisfaction. Although Ambassador Sparks could not have been happier with the developments of the previous four months, Assistant Secretary of State John Moors Cabot made it clear to Ambassador Andrade and Foreign Minister Walter Guevara Arze that aid in 1954 would be contingent upon the MNR's continued cooperation.[12]

Ambassador Sparks also made it clear that at no time did he or his staff believe that "an overt Communist Government would take power in Bolivia in the foreseeable future" but that the MNR's own "more extreme elements supported by armed workers and peasants might assume power and effect a much wider collaboration with the existing Communist parties." Alternatively, "the right might take control of the principal urban centers but would have to endure a long period of belligerency in the rural areas and mining centers which would destroy much of the remaining human values in Bolivia."[13] Still, President Eisenhower's approach represented nothing less than a complete reversal of President Truman's. Professing support for a series of relatively moderate oligarchs who represented the last hope of the old order, Truman's diplomats had betrayed them to the RFC agenda time and time again. The Eisenhower administration, by contrast, had fully embraced the radical Movimiento Nacionalista Revolucionario, in the hopes of forestalling a worse radicalism. In other words, explicitly anticapitalist, implicitly anti-U.S. revolutionaries, who, in the words of a thoroughly disenchanted Demetrio Canelas, had "provoked racial belligerence," "supplanted a conscientious and cultivated citizenry of European extraction with an illiterate indigenous electorate," and "ruined the vital forces of the Bolivian economy through nationalization," had received more support in President Eisenhower's first year than pro-U.S. conservatives had received during all of Truman's seven.[14]

In retrospect, Presidents Hertzog and Urriolagoitia, the Partido de la Union Republicana Socialista, and the other traditional parties were all but doomed from the start. But even though their internecine fighting would probably have ruined their efforts to preserve liberal constitutional oligarchy in any case, the

United States government and its insatiable hunger for cheap tin had made that a grim certainty. They hoped to rein in the power of the formidable Big Three without directly challenging them. And, at the same time, they also hoped to deradicalize the miners and other workers, to draw them away from the Movimiento Nacionalista Revolucionario, the Partido Obrero Revolucionario, and the Partido de la Izquierda Revolucionaria and into the existing political structure through incremental bread-and-butter reform. In short, they were trying to thread a needle. Whereas Tomás Monje, Enrique Hertzog, Mamerto Urriolagoitia, and Hugo Ballivián only rarely showed flashes of the skill that would have been necessary to do so, partisan infighting and RFC economic pressure were persistent, crippling distractions.

To ensure that Bolivian tin continued to feed the Allied war machine, the Truman administration had from its first days been loath to confront Villarroel, Paz Estenssoro, and the movimientistas. Even Assistant Secretary of State Spruille Braden, who was fixated on ridding the hemisphere of the "fascism" he saw in Perón and Villarroel, trod lightly in Bolivia despite his certainty that the MNR was a Peronist, if not Nazi, puppet. U.S. diplomats were more than willing to endanger U.S. engineers, businessmen, and their families by leaving them in harm's way in the mining camps to maintain the flow of tin. Even as Villarroel hung lifeless from a lamppost and militant miners painted the names of U.S employees on lampposts in the mining camps, the State Department urged U.S. citizens to remain in place.

That the Truman administration would endeavor to destroy the international tin cartel after the war was understandable, but the evolution of that goal into a U.S. policy to monopolize the tin industry in the postwar period spelled disaster for the PURS governments. Although there was only the slightest chance that Hertzog or his compatriots would have effectively used higher tin prices to diversify the Bolivian economy and wean the nation from its dependence on tin exports and food imports, the Reconstruction Finance Corporation eliminated whatever chance may have existed. The RFC mandate ensured that weak Bolivian governments would annually face the economic might of the United States at its peak. Ambassadors Andrade and Martínez Vargas and the tin barons employed every "weapon of the weak" that they could find—and even succeeded in bringing the RFC to bay on several occasions—but this was a battle they knew they were doomed to lose and lose badly.

The irony, of course, was that the cornerstone of the Truman administration's policy toward Latin America was a fierce opposition to economic nationalism, ostensibly in favor of liberalized multilateral commerce. In theory, U.S. policy makers sought the elimination of cartels and monopolistic practices to prevent the onset of another depression and a catastrophic third world war. In practice, however, as U.S. relations with Bolivia and the retention and expansion of the RFC monopoly so clearly revealed, they were willing to countenance the very practices they so often condemned in the name of U.S. national security, to discard their supposedly cherished principles in the service of crass opportunism, and to exploit their privileged position at the end of the war. An emergency wartime measure evolved first into a postwar lever to extort low prices from a virtually helpless nation and later into a means to manipulate global markets to the advantage of U.S. military and commercial interests. There may have been no Communist threat in Bolivia, but the global Communist threat that spawned the U.S. national security apparatus ensured that the Cold War would leave its imprint on the Altiplano nonetheless.

The State Department cannot be held entirely responsible for these developments. Its efforts to promote the Good Neighbor policy, shepherd Bolivia through a critical transition, and assist governments that were, from the U.S. perspective, almost ideal were effectively crushed by the juggernaut of the emerging national security apparatus. U.S. Embassy assessments of Bolivian events were often perceptive and sometimes almost prescient. If diplomats like Joseph Flack and Edward Sparks were, from time to time, unduly optimistic in their assessments of Monje's junta, Hertzog, Urriolagoitia, and even Ballivián's junta, it was a reflection of their desire to see a pro-U.S. Bolivian democratic variant emerge and stabilize a deeply troubled nation. Although policy makers like Spruille Braden, Edward Miller, and Dean Acheson periodically worked to intercede on behalf of the Bolivians, they were easily and regularly cowed by the RFC and other procurement agencies. It took the combined efforts of several South American presidents, congressional leaders, the major U.S. labor unions, and the State Department to finally goad President Truman into removing RFC Chairman Symington. Even so, Symington and his senatorial allies were able to stymie the president, Defense Mobilizer Wilson, and the other defense planners for months. It is little wonder that the State Department's Office of Inter-American Affairs had no success in challenging the RFC alone.

The bizarre interactions of the RFC monopoly and the weak governments of the sexenio put U.S. diplomats into an extremely uncomfortable, if not untenable, position. They found themselves fighting against elements of their own government to fill the wallets of the corrupt and decadent tin barons at U.S. taxpayers' expense in the hopes that the Bolivian government, through higher taxes and restrictions on trade, could translate a small percentage of those ill-gotten gains into a modicum of reform. That the State Department could not commit itself wholeheartedly to this contradictory and counterproductive course is hardly surprising. U.S. diplomats also found themselves on the same side as the tin barons on a number of occasions, but it is to their credit that most deeply resented being there and harbored no illusions about them.

On the other hand, however, the State Department cannot be entirely exonerated. The process that led to Irving Florman being sent to Bolivia in the first place was a fundamentally flawed one. That it permitted him to remain the U.S.

CONCLUSION

ambassador in La Paz for nearly two years only underscores the point. Perhaps even worse, five months after the National Revolution, embassy counselor Rowell confessed that "the Ambassador has talked to Lechín only once," and he "doesn't know how to go about making contact with the left-wing group."[15] Although Truman's State Department may not have been preoccupied with the dim prospects of Communism in South America, the department's Cold War focus on Europe and Asia permitted the Bolivian situation to deteriorate until the National Revolution was inevitable. Indeed, the Bolivians tried repeatedly to win Washington's attention and evoke a knee-jerk response with ill-conceived and transparent stories of Communist penetration of the Altiplano, understanding that so long as tin was flowing into Texas City, the Truman administration was satisfied. Because any Bolivian government, no matter how radical, would be forced to sell its tin to the Reconstruction Finance Corporation, there was no good reason to divert resources to the remote heart of South America. Put simply, Washington did not have a large enough stake in Bolivia to be overly concerned by any development there until the Eisenhower presidency.

Although the State Department faulted first Hertzog and then Urriolagoitia for using the salad days of high prices to decree wage increases almost monthly, the Partido de la Unión Socialista understood better than anyone that revolution was simmering in the mines. Infighting between and within the established parties prevented both PURS presidents from ever enjoying enough security to launch genuine reform, not that they were especially inclined to. Indeed, even as Ambassador Flack sang the praises of Tomás Monje and his junta in 1946, Flack's assistant, Douglas Henderson, knew that their efforts were doomed. Henderson warned that "the underlying current which is molding public opinion and forcing it into action in Bolivia is directed against the feudal structure of Bolivian society, against the oligarchy which has arbitrarily ruled the country without reference to the will of the people." He further warned that the "pseudo-revolutionary programs, whether of the right or left, are not going to satisfy Bolivians today" because their "basic program is to protect privilege."[16]

As Washington told any Bolivian who would listen, the price of tin was going to drop cataclysmically at some point after the war. La Paz would no longer be able to count on the tin cartel to maintain high prices or on taxation of the tin barons to preserve the government. Still, at no point was there any serious discussion of reforming the tax structure, imposing a significant income tax on the landowners, redistributing land, or undertaking any sort of fundamental economic reform. Instead, Presidents Hertzog and Urriolagoitia simply raised wages and saddled the tin barons with ever higher taxes. The worst symptom of this, U.S. observers repeatedly noted, was that luxury items constituted an ever greater share of Bolivian imports with each passing year of the sexenio. Indeed, the RFC and Ambassador Florman might well have been correct in arguing that no tin price would have led the PURS to make the needed changes.

During the economic crisis of 1949, Embassy Second Secretary Richard Johnson offered a pessimistic explanation of what had gone wrong: the "apathy of the general public" had combined with "the selfish attitude taken by organized minorities" and "regional and class selfishness and splinter-party politics" to paralyze the governments.[17]

Politically aware Bolivians understood all too well that their economy was hopelessly and fundamentally flawed and that the tin barons' empire was at the root of its flaws. Every dollar the Big Three funneled overseas was a dollar not being used to improve the lot of impoverished and malnourished Bolivians, develop national resources, or take any step that might avert the National Revolution. This colossal capital drain amounted to hundreds of millions of dollars. To permit greater taxation and secure greater government revenue, the regimes of the sexenio thus found themselves alongside the tin barons battling the RFC for a higher price. That this situation was untenable in the long term was clear even to the PURS. Indeed, even the timid Enrique Hertzog, before taking office, contemplated nationalizing the tin mines and had Demetrio Canelas sound out U.S. diplomats regarding that possibility. This was no passing fancy: Hertzog would later urge General Ballivián's "Junta Usurpadora" to nationalize the mines—if only to "steal the thunder" of the MNR. Even Waldo Belmonte Pool, a longtime leader of the PURS, apparently said of nationalization, "I do not believe there is a person with a contrary opinion on the subject."[18]

It is not enough to label the regimes of the sexenio governments of the "gran minería" or Urriolagoitia a servant of "patiñismo," as the movimientistas and some historians have done.[19] They certainly owed their position to the tin barons and the landed elite and gave the rosca far more benefits than the Villarroel or Paz Estenssoro governments. They also sought to preserve the essence of the old oligarchic system: feudalism in the countryside, the complete exclusion of indigenous Bolivians from the political process, the reliance of the national economy upon tin exports, and a narrow version of liberal constitutional oligarchy that obeyed democratic forms. Still, Hertzog and Urriolagoitia recognized that, for that system to endure, urban and mining camp radicalism had to be defused through a combination of repression and appeasement, and the government needed to establish its ascendancy over the tin barons, win a greater share of their foreign exchange, and possibly even nationalize the tin industry. As a result of government decrees and regulations, miners' wages rose 129 percent between 1944 and 1948 and continued to increase rapidly until the National Revolution. Moreover, according to Manuel Contreras, the cost of social welfare measures was almost half the value of those wages.[20] Although these social advances never kept pace with postwar inflation, most could be traced back to the Villarroel government. Hertzog and Urriolagoitia had kept them in force and even, at times, augmented them. Indeed, until Paz Estenssoro enacted universal suffrage and agrarian reform, his policies were not all that different from those of his predecessors, much to the chagrin of the president's more militant followers. MNR radicals never forgot that, in the days before Paz Estenssoro's triumphal return from exile, Siles Zuazo had warned that nationalization and agrarian reform were not necessarily inevitable.

Assistant Secretary of State John Moors Cabot may have provided the most appropriate epitaph for the sexenio and the role of U.S. tin policy in its demise. Speaking to his fellow citizens in Columbus, Ohio, in December 1953, Cabot noted that the Bolivian tin miner, whose "job notably contributes to your wife's convenience when she prepares your supper" and "also contributes an element essential to war production," had "twice in the past fifteen years" been asked to "produce a vital ingredient to keep the free world free." As a result, the price of tin "soared to fantastic heights despite our efforts to control it." Then, after World War II and again after the Korean War, "we stopped buying," and "tin dropped as precipitously in price as it had risen." "Even the wisdom of Solomon," the assistant secretary declared, "would not suffice to direct Bolivian economic affairs under such circumstances." Cabot had implicitly offered a small vindication of the postwar liberal constitutional oligarchs.[21] None had ever displayed anything resembling the "wisdom of Solomon," but even with such wisdom, they could not have coped with U.S. tin purchasing policy, much less with the centuries-old problems of their nation.

EPILOGUE

The State Department [is] in many respects only a switchboard operator; its power to assist the Bolivians in attacking their economic problems [is] limited, since many of the means for doing this rested in the hands of other Government agencies or even of private agencies.
—*Edward Miller, 5 April 1951*

When you need help overthrowing another president, just call us!
—*Miners and peasants leaving La Paz, October 2003*

The events of the sexenio are often understandably overlooked by historians, bookended and overshadowed as they were by the controversies of World War II and the major upheaval of the National Revolution of April 1952. Still, those events shed light on several larger trends in diplomatic, Bolivian, and U.S. history, and the forces that shaped the sexenio continued to affect U.S.-Bolivian relations for decades. The "battle for tin" of the postwar period highlights the decline of Franklin Roosevelt's noninterventionist Good Neighbor approach to Latin America. That a Republican administration more than willing to engage in heavy-handed intervention elsewhere managed to reach accommodation with the National Revolution is telling. So, too, is the inability of the Movimiento Nacionalista Revolucionario to solve most of their nation's (and the tin industry's) fundamental problems. Indeed, its failure gave rise to another revolution fifty years later, which at once paralleled and repudiated the National Revolution.

Implications for the Good Neighborhood

Simply put, the "battle for tin" must be seen as one of many steps that the Truman administration took that effectively ended Franklin Roosevelt's Good Neighbor policy. Articulated in the 1930s, Roosevelt's Good Neighbor pledge was, in its most basic form, a U.S. renunciation of intervention in the internal affairs of Latin American states in the hope that cooperation might replace the bitter confrontations and "big stick" policies of the past. On a deeper level, Roosevelt was committing the United States to a more cooperative, multilateral relationship with the other nations of the hemisphere by disavowing unilateralism and interventionism. The reality of the Good Neighbor policy never truly lived up its lofty rhetoric and was always more style than substance, as U.S. wartime relations with Argentina and Bolivia illustrated clearly. Still, this did not stop Latin Americans as disparate as Argentine populist Juan Perón, Dominican despot Rafael Trujillo, and Peruvian revolutionary Víctor Haya de la Torre from venerating its architect.[1]

It did not take South Americans long to recognize that the Truman administration was presiding over nothing less than what Bryce Wood has called the "dismantling" of Roosevelt's approach.[2] Although Spruille Braden's Blue Book was the most obvious manifestation of U.S. interventionism and perhaps a symbolic end of the Good Neighbor policy, the arbitrary unilateralism manifested in the tin negotiations was, in some ways, even more troubling in the long term. After all, the publication of German documents to influence an election seem almost tame when compared to the devastating impact of the Reconstruction Finance Corporation's policies in Bolivia, let alone the "big stick" invasions and interventions that Caribbean and Central American nations had endured in the past. Although President Truman's diplomats continued to mouth the platitudes of the Good Neighbor policy, these rang hollow when contrasted with the brutal realities of the tin contract negotiations. *La Razón* frankly stated in 1947 that "Mr. Truman has apparently forgotten Mr. Roosevelt's policy" since "Uncle Sam has become again a hard trader," taking "the best chestnuts for himself and leaving the waste for his neighbor." Even Secretary Acheson, in one of his rare discussions of the hemisphere, acknowledged that "unfavorable comparisons were drawn with the days when Cordell Hull and Sumner Welles were so preoccupied with Latin America's problems."[3] He did not dispute them.

Indeed, U.S.-Bolivian relations illustrate clearly that the Good Neighbor policy had become a hollow shell by 1946. Truman's diplomats may have had no real response to Bolivian accusations of "economic aggression," but they did steadfastly attempt to maintain the appearance of nonintervention on a number of occasions. Most notably, rather than take any action that might be considered intervention, U.S. policy makers were apparently prepared to accept a MNR victory in the 1949 civil war, President Urrioagoitia's 11 August 1950 decree seizing the tin barons' foreign exchange, and Foreign Minister Pedro Zilveti's frenzied attempts to deny Víctor Paz Estenssoro the presidency in 1952.

Openly taking a side in Bolivia's internal disputes (as Braden had done in Argentina) would have opened a Pandora's box, leading every government, faction, and revolutionary movement in the hemisphere to seek U.S. approval for itself and condemnation of its rivals. Given the volatility and fluidity of

South American politics, this would have produced resentment toward and endless complications for Washington. As it was, U.S. silence was viewed as tacit approval or hostility, even when the State Department was attempting to adhere to a policy of strict neutrality. Indeed, convinced that not purchasing Bolivian tin after the National Revolution would be perceived as intervention, Deputy Assistant Secretary Thomas Mann did his best to arrange a purchase the United States did not even need. Of course, "strict neutrality" did not stop U.S. diplomats from building international support for the junta that ousted Villarroel or expressing their displeasure at the National Revolution by withholding recognition for more than a month and a tin contract for much longer. Washington could easily have taken far more decisive action at any point but understood all too well that doing so would have been counterproductive in the long term. However expedient and prudent it may have been for the State Department to attempt to rise above the fray of local politics in the name of "nonintervention," this narrow interpretation of the Good Neighbor policy stripped it of much of its original spirit.

U.S. diplomats well understood how hollow U.S. declarations of "nonintervention" rang in the face of increasingly aggressive and decidedly interventionist RFC policies. Yet they also understood just how much Washington was neglecting the hemisphere. If the ultimate goal of the Good Neighbor policy had been to assist in the orderly development of a liberal capitalist hemispheric order featuring progressive democracies (or at least liberal constitutional oligarchies), that goal had been quickly subordinated to reconstruction and the containment of Communism in Europe and Asia. Indeed, as the United States preoccupation with Europe and Asia grew, Latin American leaders and diplomats in the postwar period constantly lamented its inattention to the Western Hemisphere. U.S. neglect is perfectly illustrated by Irving Florman's continued presence as its ambassador in La Paz at the critical moments before the National Revolution and Rowell's inability to even find the very visible Lechín in the months after it.[4]

Although historians have examined in some detail both the wavering U.S. commitment to nonintervention in Latin America and its growing inattention to what they called the "Inter-American System," there is a third aspect to the failure of U.S. diplomacy in the hemisphere. State Department proponents of the Good Neighbor policy simply did not have enough control over U.S. foreign policy to actually implement it. Throughout the postwar period, U.S. diplomats were frustrated by domestic actors who, in service to the growing national security apparatus, fiscal conservatism, or protectionism, consistently undercut the delicate balancing of nonintervention and benevolent guidance promised by the Good Neighbor policy.

Thus Senator Johnson's unwillingness to pour U.S. taxpayers' dollars into the tin barons' pockets added legitimacy and strength to RFC Chairman Symington's vendetta, which undermined all attempts by the State Department to assist the governments of the sexenio. In 1950, protectionists in the U.S. Senate threatened to restrict the importation of Venezuelan oil, spawning a crisis in the Venezuelan economy that could easily have endangered major U.S. investments there. In Peru, the State Department was unable to prevent the Federal Bureau of Narcotics from recklessly maligning the name and endangering the life of the revolutionary Haya de la Torre. It took U.S. diplomats months of intense backroom negotiations and bureaucratic wrangling to prevent this early manifestation of the War on Drugs from causing an explosive diplomatic crisis.[5] And in Argentina, the State Department's quiet, subtle campaign to destabilize and redirect Peronism was almost derailed by the crass, unauthorized proclamations of the Economic Cooperation Administration.[6]

President Truman's diplomats may well have abandoned the Good Neighbor policy, as their critics so often claimed, but they also lost the ability to implement it. The policy may never have been the truly collaborative venture between the United States and Latin American countries that its architects envisioned, but these and other steps undercut even its last vestige, the veneer of nonintervention. Indeed, by the end of the Truman presidency, it became clear that the United States had no coherent policy toward Latin America, but rather a chaotic jumble of sometimes contradictory policies authored by any number of individuals and agencies.

Eisenhower and Revolution

Ironically, it took the election of a Republican to undo some of the damage done by the last of the Democratic "Good Neighbors" and find a more pragmatic approach to at least the National Revolution. On one level, it is not surprising that President Eisenhower and Secretary of State Dulles opted to "brake" and not "break" the MNR's efforts to reform Bolivian society. The Republicans enjoyed several advantages. First, they did not have the Democrats' long and troubled history with the party. Once suspicions of collusion with Peronist Argentina caused the MNR to be labeled "fascist" during World War II, it became almost impossible for any member of the Roosevelt or Truman administration to see any redeeming value in anything Paz Estenssoro, Lechín, or the other movimientistas did or said. Even those U.S. officials who on occasion praised Paz Estenssoro's personal merits or attempted to explain the appeal of the MNR did so apologetically or prefaced their remarks with some sort of disclaimer. Although the rosca's accusations that the movimientistas were "Communists" came only late in the Truman presidency and never really eclipsed older perceptions, those accusations made it almost impossible for President Truman or Secretary Acheson to backtrack and even consider cooperation with the MNR.

Of course, up until the National Revolution, Truman's diplomats saw almost no need to accept the MNR. Indeed, ever since the revolution of 21 July 1946, U.S. policy makers had been convinced that every faction of every Bolivian regime, from the Communist PIR to the reactionary Liberals, was irrevocably opposed to its return. Fully expecting the Bolivian army to serve as a backstop for any failure of civilian government, they did not take even the instability of the liberal constitutional oligarchic governments very seriously, especially after the purge of villarroelistas in 1946. The ascension of General Hugo Ballivián's junta was therefore predictable and not unwelcome. The indecision, floundering, and paralysis of U.S. policy makers toward Bolivia in Truman's last year was the result of their failure to grasp the unforeseen, and to them shocking, new reality of the National Revolution of 1952 and their almost complete inability to even contemplate a more pragmatic approach to that reality. Taking just such an approach would not be a problem for the Republicans.

Although Eisenhower's diplomats shared their predecessor's concern about the rising tide of economic nationalism, they were able to use U.S. aid effectively to "brake" the National Revolution, as Cole Blasier, Kenneth Lehman, Stephen Rabe, James Siekmeier, Laurence Whitehead, and others have illustrated. U.S. financial assistance was explicitly calculated to ensure that the MNR conservatives "become increasingly inclined to accept United States viewpoints" on fundamental issues like trade liberalization and foreign investment. According to Whitehead, Washington hoped to ensure that the National Revolution evolved into "another banal instance of merely political change reflecting elite opportunism and manipulation." Thus, in 1954, Communists were removed from Bolivia's government. In 1955, Bolivian petroleum reserves were opened to U.S. corporations when U.S. threats to withhold food aid (inadvertently, perhaps) impeded movimientista plans for agricultural diversification. And, in 1956, redrawing Bolivian tax codes and tariffs, U.S. planners imposed rigid austerity on the nation.[7] U.S. policies may have failed to create a "showcase" for U.S.–Latin American economic growth through collaboration in Bolivia, but they did stave off chaos that might have unleashed greater radicalism. If, by 1960, Eisenhower's planners were disappointed in the results of their venture into Bolivia, it was only because they had forgotten the prospects they faced eight years earlier. To borrow from William Hudson's remarks in the closing days of the Truman presidency, Eisenhower's accomplishments were "negative" in that they helped prevent the National Revolution from taking a more radical turn.

Still, the failure of the Truman administration to prevent or come to grips with the National Revolution had other critical implications for the Eisenhower administration. One of the more interesting controversies of the Eisenhower years was his decision to at once embrace the government of Víctor Paz Estenssoro in Bolivia and overthrow the government of Jacobo Arbenz Guzmán in Guatemala.

On the surface, the two governments had much in common. According to Lehman, "both advanced similar modernizing reform programs," "drew support from analogous coalitions," and "rejected the political elitism, sociological Eurocentrism, and export-oriented economic liberalism of the oligarchies that traditionally ruled their countries," seeking "instead to enfranchise newly rising classes, further integrate native peasants into national society, and empower the state to redirect economic development." U.S. policy makers feared that both revolutions would become models for neighboring nationalists, be they Andean or Central American. Because, however, the Eisenhower administration perceived the two regimes quite differently, it arrived at two quite different policies.[8] These perceptions were directly bequeathed to the Eisenhower from the Truman State Department through holdovers like Thomas Mann, Edward Sparks, and John Cabot.[9]

Indeed, Ambassador Sparks and Deputy Assistant Secretary Mann had been among the earliest voices for accommodation with the MNR conservatives after the National Revolution. They understood that, after the nationalization of the tin mines, U.S. policy makers needed a carrot as well a stick to be effective. Lehman has described the process by which low-level State Department officials led by Sparks convinced the Eisenhowers that accommodation with the MNR was preferable to any alternative. Not only did President Eisenhower's diplomats have no viable alternative to Paz Estenssoro, but they also had superiors willing and able to take decisive action in Latin America. Truman's diplomats had argued fruitlessly against the RFC's policies for years before Assistant Secretary Miller conspired to bring his president into the fray. The depth of the Bolivian economic crisis and the fear that the National Revolution might suddenly take an even more radical, if not Communist, turn convinced Eisenhower to become involved in just months. Indeed, as Lehman had noted, for ardent Republican Cold Warriors, the perception of the MNR as "fascist" and "Peronist" may actually have facilitated accommodation by undercutting any argument that it was also "Communist."[10] If Truman's diplomats had been more concerned with Communism, perhaps they might have reached the same conclusions as their Republican successors.

Although it is significant that Eisenhower inherited lower-level diplomats from the Truman administration, he also assumed the Democrats' long-term analyses of problems in Guatemala and Bolivia: the first based on a justified fear of Communism and a hostility toward the United Fruit Company; the second on serious concerns about Bolivia's "poverty and dependency on tin."[11] It did not take a Communist to understand that Bolivia's political economy, which Carter Goodrich has described as "that of a mining camp," was hopelessly warped and desperately in need of reform. When U.S. diplomats lamented that the tin industry was overtaxed, they were not simply repeating laissez-faire platitudes. They recognized that the Bolivian governments were placing their primary export into an untenable competitive position that would eventually lead to disaster.

The Truman administration, despite its philosophical discomfort, seemed willing to tolerate the seizure of all of the tin barons' foreign exchange provided President Urriolagoitia could channel the proceeds into constructive projects. U.S. policy makers may not have endorsed the immediate incorporation of indigenous Bolivians into the national polity, but they understood quite well that Bolivia's feudal agricultural system was holding back national development, and they encouraged its diversification. For years, they had gone to great pains to finance the construction of a Cochabamba–Santa Cruz highway to assist in the development of Bolivian resources and to facilitate that diversification. The Truman administration had only hoped that the white or mestizo liberal constitutional oligarchs of the sexenio would be able to carry out these necessary reforms at a conservative pace and with Washington's guidance. In short, Truman's policy makers were sympathetic to a number of the movimientistas' goals so long as these could be divorced from the MNR itself. That option, of course, was not open to Eisenhower either.

Still, it helped that the MNR program did not directly threaten any vital U.S. interest. The landowners affected by agrarian reform were not U.S. citizens, as they were in Guatemala, where the United Fruit Company was a primary target. Of the nationalized tin companies, only Patiño's could claim to have a significant number of U.S. shareholders, although this may well have been legalistic legerdemain. Certainly no one mistook Patiño's company for a U.S. corporation, despite its Delaware incorporation papers. United Fruit, on the other hand, enjoyed powerful advocates in the United States, including Spruille Braden, Henry Cabot Lodge, Thomas Corcoran, and public relations master Edward Bernays, all of whom forcefully pressed the case that Arbenz was Communist and advocated decisive action.[12] In Bolivia, the primary "victims" of the National Revolution were the profiteering tin barons, who were mistrusted by policy makers as disparate as Irving Florman, Lyndon Johnson, Edward Miller, Stuart Symington, and Harry Truman. Indeed, there were few less sympathetic figures in the hemisphere than the Big Three, and RFC Chairman Symington's public campaign had only cemented U.S. public hostility toward them. Ironically, the "battle for tin," which had so embittered Bolivians against Washington and the tin barons that it facilitated the National Revolution, had also turned the rosca's greatest potential allies in the United States into enemies or, at best, largely indifferent observers.

Lehman has identified the movimientistas' willingness to accommodate themselves to dependency on the United States as another key factor in the U.S. decision to embrace President Paz Estenssoro's regime. Indeed, Lehman has argued that the president and even Lechín, at times, adroitly sought a U.S. alliance to bolster their control of the revolution against their more radical challengers.¹³ This argument has considerable merit, and Laura Gotkowitz's recent assessment of the National Revolution and "the popular uprising it restrained" only bolsters it. Whereas older histories have focused on the roots of the revolution in La Paz, the other major cities, and the tin mines, Gotkowitz's account emphasizes the growing agitation among the rural, indigenous population that at once contributed to and threatened the MNR vision. It asserts that the National Revolution was nothing less than a "reaction against indigenous mobilization and thus a product of the liberal oligarchic project itself," even though the revolution also "engendered a more inclusive political culture."¹⁴ Paz Estenssoro and the MNR conservatives were threatened not only by Juan Lechín's Central Obrera Boliviana and its leftist syndicalism, but also by a rising tide of agrarian mobilization that threatened to overturn the political order entirely. The urban intellectuals of the MNR, and even Lechín, had no more interest in the complete destruction of the social and racial order than did U.S. policy makers, preoccupied with the armed peasant and worker militias of the immediate postrevolutionary era. In this context, it becomes even easier to discern the common ground that Paz Estenssoro and the Eisenhower administration managed to find.

Gotkowitz's assessment clearly illuminates the real limits of the National Revolution. Although MNR conservatives hoped to eradicate the most inhumane aspects of the feudal hacienda system, they sought to do so without unleashing "a revolutionary transformation of society that augured the end of a state perceived to be ruled by landlords."¹⁵ Though they went well beyond the oligarchs of the sexenio to promote reform and to salvage what they could of the traditional order, they were willing to go only so far. It should not be forgotten that in the wake of the 1951 election, Luis Guachalla and Demetrio Canelas were amenable to a Paz Estenssoro presidency, and even the reactionary Liberals were apparently willing to hand the vice presidency over to Siles Zuazo. In this respect, Paz Estenssoro and the MNR conservatives might have had more in common with both the liberal constitutional oligarchs and Washington than they did with the Quechua- and Aymara-speaking masses of the Bolivian countryside. Paz Estenssoro had argued since World War II that both his party and his nation required U.S. support to prosper. It just took him more than a decade to convince Washington.

In this regard, Lehman's and Blasier's comparisons of the Mexican and Bolivian revolutions are pertinent. Lehman has asserted that, unlike Venustiano Carranza, "the most stubbornly resistive to U.S. meddling" of the Mexican revolutionaries, both Paz Estenssoro and Lechín "understood the need to come to terms with the United States" and "sought a patron in Washington" from the outset. Blasier has shown how Carranza exploited and benefited tremendously from a fierce U.S.-German rivalry before World War I to gain critical room to maneuver and permit his revolution to find its own course. This was not an option for President Paz Estenssoro, as Blasier has pointed out. Given both his domestic position and the nature of the Cold War, the president could neither threaten nor even contemplate a move toward the Soviet bloc.

Indeed, Jacobo Arbenz's experience in Guatemala illustrates well that, in all likelihood, such a move would have been nothing short of disastrous. Eisenhower may not have given much credence to old accusations that the MNR was Communist, but it certainly would not have taken much to change his mind. Whereas Carranza could shelter "Mexico's revolution at its most vulnerable stage," because of the need for a tin contract, financial assistance, and support against popular forces in the mines and countryside, Paz Estenssoro was forced to turn almost immediately to the United States. Lehman has concluded that "the Bolivian Revolution was not broken" by Eisenhower "because ultimately, it proved too malleable to make that necessary." In other words, if Eisenhower did help slow the National Revolution, it was only because Paz Estenssoro wanted or needed it slowed as well. That malleability may well have saved Paz Estenssoro from Arbenz's fate, but the cost was the MNR's continued dependency on and obedience to the United States.[16]

The Decline of Tin and the "Third Bolivian Revolution"

Just as U.S. policy toward Bolivia was shaped for a decade by the events of the sexenio, the ramifications of "battle for tin" endured. In 1956, the United States, having finally filled its stockpile and acknowledged the consequences of market instability, was now amenable to a new International Tin Agreement. But even though it would tolerate a new ITA with export control mechanisms and buffer stocks, not needing to be a member of the resurrected prewar cartel to influence world tin markets, it would not join until 1976 and even then only for five years. The U.S. stockpile, which amounted to roughly two years of world consumption, would serve for decades as a vehicle to keep tin prices from rising too high. The stockpile may have been conceived as insurance in case of a third world war, but it was always available, as the Bolivians understood all too well, to serve U.S. political and economic peacetime ends as well. The RFC monopoly and campaign to lower tin prices were, in this respect, stopgap measures until the stockpile was ready to assume its functions. The U.S. decision to stockpile led to higher prices for Bolivian tin in the years after World War II, but it also gave U.S. policy makers a whip hand over the international tin markets of Europe and Asia for decades.[17]

If President Paz Estenssoro envisioned using tin sales to finance the economic transformation of his nation, he, too, was to be disappointed. Bolivian tin production, which had peaked during the war at more than forty thousand tons, fell to less than thirty thousand tons at the time of the National Revolution

EPILOGUE

and continued to decline to less than twenty thousand tons by 1960. At the same time, the workforce in the mines grew by more than 50 percent. The decline of the tin industry represents the confluence of several trends. To take advantage of the high prices the tin barons had at times enjoyed during the sexenio, they had overworked the best veins of their mines, neglected technological improvements, and failed to find new deposits to exploit. The MNR regime and its successors did much the same with their nationalized mines, sustaining Bolivia's economy by squeezing profit from them and diverting it to other areas. Any gains the MNR might have made by expropriating the tin barons' share of profits were erased by the demands of an enlarged, militant workforce that the party could challenge only at great risk to itself. Mismanagement of the state-run tin company, COMIBOL, only exacerbated these deficiencies, especially because the world price of tin remained low. Even when tin prices did rise in the 1970s, COMIBOL still suffered from what John Thoburn has called "a mode of corporate behavior in which the maintenance of output took precedence over the urgent need to innovate." The government invested just $3 million into COMIBOL before 1960 and just $10 million on exploration from 1965 to 1975, ensuring that Bolivian tin remained among the least competitive in the world and completely dependent on the International Tin Agreement.[18]

Even thirty-three years after the National Revolution brought the movimientistas to power, the U.S. tin stockpile was influencing events in Bolivia. In 1985, President Siles Zuazo handed control of the nation over to Paz Estenssoro, much as he had in 1952. Once again, Paz Estenssoro faced an agricultural crisis, an economy teetering on the brink of collapse, and falling tin prices resulting from the demise of the latest incarnation of the ITA. Although tin generated just 35 percent of Bolivian foreign exchange by this point, national export earnings dropped by more than 40 percent when the price of tin fell from $7.61 to $2.43 per pound. Once again, U.S. policy makers had a hand in the decline. Not only had the U.S. withdrawal from the ITA in 1981 been one of many factors in its demise, but, mirroring what the Reconstruction Finance Corporation had done under President Truman, the Reagan administration dumped tin from the U.S. stockpile onto the market and defeated producers' attempts to stabilize the price. And, once again, in response to an economic crisis, Paz Estenssoro undertook a U.S.-sponsored austerity program. Because "closing the mines and leaving the tin in the ground," according to Lehman, would "now save the country money," COMIBOL laid off almost three-quarters of its miners.[19] The dire predictions of the 1940s had at last come true.

The odd symmetry of the events of the 1950s and 1980s serves, if nothing else, to underscore how, even without massive investments in Bolivia or great effort, the United States cast a long shadow. The U.S. decision to stockpile tin, welcomed by Bolivians during the war, should have been a boon for the tentative reformers of the sexenio at least, but instead it became yet another means to exercise U.S. power and authority. But the United States bears only a small part of the blame for the decline of Bolivian tin. If, for generations, the tin barons drained the resources of the Altiplano to enrich themselves, the MNR and subsequent Bolivian governments did much the same to finance national development. Neither secured the future through reinvestment nor solved the fundamental problems in either the industry or national economy. Under the prewar International Tin Agreement, the International Tin Committee (ITC) had permitted old patterns to persist, and sometimes even to flourish, but the dissolution of the ITA in 1946 ultimately paved the way for the National Revolution. Similarly, under the ITA resurrected in 1956, a re-formed ITC (renamed the "International Tin Council"), though weakened considerably, allowed the state-run Bolivian tin industry to stave off complete collapse for almost three decades. Perhaps not entirely coincidentally, the end of the primacy of tin occurred as Bolivia became what Forrest Hylton and Sinclair Thomson have called a "shining trophy in the global showcase of neoliberalism" and a "model for free-market capitalist reforms."[20] With the decline of tin, coca and cocaine rose to assume its place as the focus of U.S.-Bolivian relations.

Therefore, in the context of a U.S.-, World Bank–, and International Monetary Fund–supported neoliberal economy and a U.S.-mandated War on Drugs, what James Dunkerley and others have called the "Third Bolivian Revolution" started in 2000. The Bolivian "neoliberal experiment" that was launched in the 1980s started to collapse in 2000 with the Cochabamba "water war," when popular forces arose to prevent a World Bank–mandated Bechtel Corporation takeover of the city's water services. Popular protests against the "Washington consensus" and the establishment's political parties that espoused and maintained it spread and worsened. Spurred on by backroom deals that promised to deliver Bolivia's newfound hydrocarbon wealth into the hands of foreigners, the "water war" soon became a "gas war." As dissent spread and escalated, coca growers opposed to eradication schemes joined the ranks of urban protestors. Despite violent repression, local, peasant, and indigenous protestors staged hunger strikes and marches and formed blockades. Together, in October 2003, the protestors ousted the government of Gonzalo Sánchez de Losada. In the wake of the October disturbances, the only remaining political organization with any real claim to legitimacy was former coca grower Evo Morales's Movimiento al Socialismo— an organization that, like the Movimiento Nacionalista Revolucionario in 1952, had risen to prominence through its fierce denunciations of both the corrupt, ineffectual political system of vendepatria elites and free market capitalism. Morales won a sweeping victory in the 2006 election, promising, as Paz Estenssoro once had, nothing short of the transformation of his country.[21]

There are other parallels between 1952 and 2006. The "reforms" and privatizations of the 1980s had undone a number of the achievements of the National Revolution and created a climate, like that of the 1940s, where Bolivia's natural resources were again being exploited largely for the benefit of elites and is not an unfamiliar pattern in Bolivian history. Just as Spaniards and white creoles were enriched by the silver of Potosí, the nitrates of Atacama were ceded to Chile in the nineteenth century, and tin made Simón Patiño one of the richest men on the planet, so, too, did Bolivian oil and natural gas seem destined to create wealth for others rather than for the people of Bolivia. If a major impetus of the National Revolution was to lay claim to the nation's tin wealth, Evo Morales's movement clearly aimed to seize control of its hydrocarbons. Just as Paz Estenssoro and Lechín hoped that nationalized tin mines would provide the wealth needed to modernize Bolivian society in the 1950s, so Morales and followers hope that control over the nation's hydrocarbon wealth might uplift the masses and break centuries-old patterns of poverty, exploitation, and underdevelopment.

The images of truckloads of workers descending on La Paz to join the uprising and blockades of 2003 evoke obvious parallels with the revolution of 1952. Nevertheless, they are more an indication of the MNR's ultimate failure. In Dunkerley's words, the National Revolution "can now almost be thought a cause of [the revolution of] 2000–2006 by virtue of its insufficiencies." Or, as Hylton and Thomson have observed, the National Revolution failed to "reverse patterns of internal colonialism," to produce "democratized, egalitarian forms of political representation," and to expand "the domain of communal autonomy and indigenous sovereignty."[22] It is perhaps appropriate that Paz Estenssoro, who, with U.S. support, had "braked" the National Revolution, reopened Bolivia's oilfields to foreign exploitation, and blocked the aspirations of the "radicals" in the 1950s, was a central figure in imposing the U.S.-backed neoliberal austerity plan of the 1980s—a principal target of Morales and the popular forces. The movimientista leaders, as U.S. diplomats understood as early as World War II, sought to incorporate the indigenous masses into Bolivian society, but within carefully prescribed limits; they had no interest in overturning the social order. Paz Estenssoro and his MNR may have hoped to substantially loosen liberal constitutional oligarchy, but, as Gotkowitz has pointed out, they simply "recreated colonial divides in modern institutions and idioms."[23]

The protestors who toppled Sanchez de Lozada's government and put Evo Morales into power clearly envisioned the creation of a more inclusive and just society for the indigenous masses, fulfilling and surpassing the promises of the National Revolution. Indeed, the first major projects Morales undertook were nationalization of hydrocarbons, agrarian reform, and the increased democratization of Bolivian politics through a new constitutional convention. The National Revolution, in leaving those projects uncompleted (or later undoing what it had originally done), made the "Third Bolivian Revolution" necessary.[24]

In retrospect, it is all too easy to see parallels between the bankrupt political coalitions of the neoliberal decades preceding Morales's election and the desperate flailings of the PURS during the sexenio. If the "battle for tin" provoked by the Reconstruction Finance Corporation exposed the flaws and weakness of liberal constitutional oligarchy in the 1940s, elite adherence to neoliberalism and the War on Drugs at the end of the twentieth century did much the same. The Movimiento Nacionalista Revolucionario, harnessing bottom-up popular forces to promote its own top-down revolution, may well have been as much the harbinger of the "Third Bolivian Revolution" as Villarroel was of the National Revolution. Indeed, it might be fair to argue that the battle being waged today by the Movimiento al Socialismo is the next stage of the battle against liberal constitutional oligarchy waged in the 1940s and 1950s.

NOTES

ABBREVIATIONS

AMRECA	Archivo del Ministerio de Relaciones Exteriores y Culto (Argentina)
AMRECB	Archivo del Ministerio de Relaciones Exteriores y Culto (Bolivia)
ARG	Argentina
ASF	Administrative Subject Files
COB	Central Obrera Boliviano
DGAP	Dean G. Acheson Papers
DPA	Defense Production Agency
EEUU	Estados Unidos (United States)
ELP	U.S. Embassy La Paz
GMMA	George Meany Memorial Archives
GRBT	Gran Bretaña (Great Britain)
HSTPL	Harry S. Truman Presidential Library
JLP	Jay Lovestone Papers
MC	Memorandum or Memoranda of Conversation
MNR	Movimiento Nacionalista Revolucionario
MRC	Metals Reserve Company
MSP	Mutual Security Program
NAII	National Archives of the United States II
ORIT	Organización Regional Interamericana de Trabajadores
PIR	Partido de la Izquierda Revolucionario
PURS	Partido de la Unión Republicana Socialista
RA	Robert Alexander
RASSLAA	Records of the Assistant Secretaries of State for Latin American Affairs
RD	Research Department
RFC	Reconstruction Finance Corporation
RG	Record Group
SRP	Serafino Romualdi Papers
TP	Tin Program
WHCF	White House Central Files

INTRODUCTION

The first epigraph to this chapter is drawn from Espy to Department, 10 February 1950, NAII, RG 59, 724.00; the second, from Paz Estenssoro, Memorandum del Movimiento Nacionalista Revolucionario de Bolivia para la IV Reunión de Ministros de Relaciones Exteriores, Marzo de 1951, GMMA, RG 18-009, SRP, Bolivia. Translations from Spanish-language sources throughout volume are mine unless otherwise noted.

1. Dunkerley, *Bolivia*, 12; see also Gamarra, "The United States and Bolivia," 177–206; Kohl and Farthing, *Impasse in Bolivia*, 11–33; Stefantoni and Do Alto, *Evo Morales*, 35–52.
2. Spruille Braden, Speech before the Inter-American Council, 24 April 1952, Columbia University Rare Book and Manuscript Library, Spruille Braden Papers, Miscellaneous, 1950s; see also Acheson, "Memorandum for the President," 22 May 1952, NAII, RG 59, RASSLAA, 1949–53, Bolivia; Dunkerley, *Bolivia*, 241.
3. Rabe, *Eisenhower and Latin America*.
4. For example, U.S. Ambassador Harold Tittmann noted that Peruvian dictator Manuel Odría "used the words 'Communist' and 'Peronist' interchangeably" when describing his opponents, depending on which group was further out of favor with the United States at the moment. Tittmann to Miller, 29 April 1952, NAII, RG 59, RASSLAA, 1949–53, Peru.
5. Latin American Intelligence Conference, "Report of Committee," 13–17 January 1947, NAII, RG 84, ELP, Classified, 891; Burgin, "Survey of Communism in Bolivia," 30 March 1950, NAII, RG 59, 724.001; Alexander interview with Moller, 10 July 1953; Alexander to Lovestone, 21 July 1953, both in GMMA, JLP, RA; see also, Lehman, *Bolivia and the United States*, 95.
6. Bethell and Roxborough, "The Postwar Conjuncture in Latin America," 1–33; see also Gilderhus, *The Second Century*, 126–27, 133; Parkinson, *Latin America, the Cold War, and the World Powers, 1945–1973*; Schwartzberg, *Democracy and U.S. Policy in Latin America During the Truman Years*; Smith, *Talons of the Eagle*, 123–34.
7. Burgin, "Survey of Communism in Bolivia," 30 March 1950, NAII, RG 59, 724.001; Alexander, "Totalitarianism and Democracy in Latin America," 22 April 1952, GMMA, JLP, RA; see also Lehman, *Bolivia and the United States*, 95.
8. Ríos Gamboa, *Bolivia*, 28–33.
9. Although the U.S. entente with General Manuel Odría in Peru has generally been described as a "Cold War alliance" (and it did eventually become one), anti-Communism had almost nothing to do with its formation in 1949–50. Dorn, "'Exclusive Domination' or 'Short-Term Imperialism,'" 81–102.
10. Green, *The Containment of Latin America* and "The Cold War Comes to Latin America," 149–95; Grow, *The Good Neighbor Policy and Authoritarianism in Paraguay*; Siekmeier, *Aid, Nationalism, and Inter-American Relations*, 83–130.
11. Dorn, *Peronistas and New Dealers*; Escudé, *Estados Unidos, Gran Bretaña, y la declinación argentina, 1942–1949*; MacDonald, "The U.S., the Cold War, and Perón," 405–14.
12. Ewell, *Venezuela and the United States*, 152–61; Lewis, *Paraguay Under Stroessner*, 38–48; Oddone, *Vecinos en discordia*; Rabe, *The Road to OPEC*, 94–137; Randall, *Colombia and the United States*, 192–95.
13. Siekmeier, *Aid, Nationalism, and Inter-American Relations*; Child, *Unequal Alliance*; Pach, "The Containment of U.S. Military Aid to Latin America, 1944–1947," 225–43; Trask, "The Impact of the Cold War on United States–Latin American Relations," 271–85.
14. Eisenhower, as quoted in Rabe, *Eisenhower and Latin America*, 79; see also Lehman, *Bolivia and the United States*, 60–95, and Kenneth Lehman's insights on Eisenhower's comment in "Revolutions and Attributions," 205–6.
15. Latin American Intelligence Conference, "Report of Committee," 13–17 January 1947, NAII, RG 84, ELP, Classified, 891; see also Bethell and Roxborough, "The Postwar Conjuncture," 1–33.
16. United Nations, *Report of the United Nations Mission of Technical Assistance to Bolivia*, 2 (hereafter "Keenleyside Report").
17. Maleady, "Bolivian Dilemma," 2 April 1952, NAII, RG 59, 824.00; see also ORIT Research Department, "Bolivia: Portrait of a Retarded Country," February–March 1952, GMMA, SRP, RD, 1951–53; "Keenleyside Report," 29–33; Gallardo Lozada, *La nación postergada*, 260–63.
18. Espy to Department, 10 February 1950, NAII, RG 59, 724.00; see also Alexander interview with Chavez, 11 July 1953, GMMA, JLP, RA; Gallo, *Taxes and State Power*, 55–74.
19. Malloy, *Bolivia*, 191.
20. Knudson, *Bolivia*, 8; see also Albarracín Millán, *Bolivia*, 187–89; Gallo, *Taxes and State Power*.
21. Guzman, *Historia de Bolivia*, 254; Albarracín Millán, *Bolivia*, 187–89; see also Thoburn, *Tin and the World Economy*, 70.

22. Thoburn, *Tin in the World Economy*, 31.

23. Ibid., 28–32, 38–40; see also Contreras, *The Bolivian Tin Industry*, 8–12, 16–17.

24. Bolivian statement to ECOSOC, n.d., NAII, RG 84, ELP, General, 350; Mills to Miller, 20 October 1949, NAII, RG 59, 711.24; see also Lehman, *Bolivia and the United States*, 100.

25. According to the Organización Regional Interamericana de Trabajadores (ORIT), 74 percent of miners earned less than 60¢ per day and one-fifth earned less than 20¢. ORIT Research Department, "Bolivia: Portrait of a Retarded Country," February–March 1952, GMMA, SRP, RD, 1951–53; Florman to Department, 14 April 1950, NAII, RG 59, 724.00; Alexander interview with De Tuddo, n.d., GMMA, JLP, RA; see also Dunkerley, *Rebellion in the Veins*, 6–25.

26. Goodrich, "The Economic Transformation of Bolivia," GMMA, SRP, Bolivia; ORIT Research Department, "Bolivia: Portrait of a Retarded Country," February–March 1952, GMMA, SRP, RD, 1951–53; Alexander interview with De Tuddo, n.d., GMMA, JLP, RA; see also Contreras, *The Bolivian Tin Industry*, 16.

27. Mier y Leon and Reyes, "Memorandum," 11 January 1947, NAII, RG 59, 824.6354.

28. Espy to Department, 10 February 1950, NAII, RG 59, 724.00; see also Canelas, *Dictadura y democracia en Bolivia*, 210, 283–4.

29. Gamarra Zorrilla, *Liberalismo y neoliberalismo*; Roque Bacarreza, *Los años del condor*, 25.

30. A May 1951 ORIT survey pointed out that a tin miner had to work more than a day to earn enough money to purchase a chicken or a kilogram of Argentine butter. A man's suit cost more than a month's salary. ORIT Research Department, "Bolivia: Portrait of a Retarded Country," February–March 1952, GMMA, SRP, RD, 1951–53; Goodrich, "The Economic Transformation of Bolivia," GMMA, SRP, Bolivia; Andrade, Address Before the Pan-American Women's Association, 15 November 1952, AMRECB, EEUU-1-R-56/116; see also "Keenleyside Report," 89.

31. Quieser Morales, *Bolivia*, 56–57.

32. Malloy, *Bolivia*, 98–101; Quieser Morales, *Bolivia*, 61–65.

33. Quieser Morales, *Bolivia*, 62; Lema Pelaez, *Con las banderas del movimiento nacionalista revolucionario*, 37–39; Bonsal to Hull, 7 January 1944, NAII, RG 59, 824.00; see also Gallardo Lozada's excellent synopsis of the MNR's strategy as a "coherent and fitting mechanism to destroy the hated oligarchic enemy" in *La nación postergada*, 302–7.

34. Malloy, *Bolivia*, 144–47.

35. Canelas, *Dictadura y democracia*, 251; Murillo Cárdenas and Larrea Bedregal, *Razón de Patria*, 8–18; see also Malloy, *Bolivia*, 101–10.

36. Malloy, *Bolivia*, 33–113.

37. Lehman, *Bolivia and the United States*, 75–82.

38. Ibid., 80.

39. Abecia Baldivieso, *Las relaciones internacionales en la historia de Bolivia*, 116–18; see also Gallardo Lozada, *La nación postergada*, 305.

40. Malloy, *Bolivia*, 112–18; see also Abecia Baldivieso, *Las relaciones internacionales*, 120–21; Ostria Gutiérrez to Bowers, 12 April 1944, NAII, RG 59, 824.00; Whitehead, "Bolivia," 127–31.

41. Paz Estenssoro conceded that there had once been traces of anti-Semitism in the MNR but explained that this was "not a racial matter but an economic one." Roughly eight thousand Jews had fled Hitler's Europe to Bolivia, but five thousand had been admitted through what U.S. diplomats called a "passport racket scheme" that netted its perpetrator $2 million. They had entered Bolivia on agricultural visas but, even Jewish leaders in La Paz conceded, promptly used financial assistance from a New York relief agency to establish businesses that "dislodged" Bolivian shopkeepers. The State Department interpreted the MNR's 1942 call for the "absolute prohibition on Jewish immigration" to mean that "the party is infected with Nazi ideas of racial exclusivism" despite its "faith in the people of Bolivia of Indian and mixed blood." Bennett to Duggan and Lyon, 16 June 1944; Rockwell to Duggan and Lyon, 2 June 1944; Bonsal to Hull, 7 January 1944, all in NAII, RG 59, 824.00; Knudson, *Bolivia*, 106–13; MNR newspaper quotation on pp. 121–22; Adam to Secretary, 5 July 1945, NAII, RG 59, 824.00.

42. Gallardo Lozada, *La nación postergada*, 307–9; Lema Pelaez, *Con las banderas*, 39; Knudson, *Bolivia*, 148; Alexander, *Bolivia*, 79; Bedregal, *Víctor Paz Estenssoro, el politico*, 133–35; Mitchell, *The Legacy of Populism in Bolivia*, 20.

43. Stines to Ambassador, 24 January 1944, NAII, RG 59, 824.00.

44. Gonzalez Torres and Iriarte Ontiveros, *Villarroel*, 68; see also Stines to Ambassador, 24 January 1944, NAII, RG 59, 824.00.

45. Lieutenant Colonel Marion Hardesty was justifiably fearful that he would be labeled a "wide-eyed and gullible schoolboy" for this assessment. Hardesty to Military Intelligence Service, 24 December 1943NAII; "Summary of Dispatch dated January 12, 1944 from British Legation at La Paz to the Foreign Office covering the revolution in Bolivia," n.d.; Bonsal to Hull, 1 January 1944; Duggan to Hull, 10 January 1944, all in NAII, RG 59, 824.00.

46. Roosevelt to Hull, 14 January 1944; Bonsal to Hull, 7 January 1944; see also Hull to Embassy La Paz, 26 January 1944, all in NAII, RG 59, 824.00.

47. Bennett to Duggan and Lyon, 16 June 1944; see also State Department Memorandum, "Bolivian Situation," 13 June 1946; Ostria Gutiérrez and Bonsal, MC, 11 May 1944, de Zengotita to Secretary, 20 December 1945, all in NAII, RG 59, 824.00; Lehman, *Bolivia and the United States*, 80–86.

48. United Kingdom Delegation to the Tin Study Group, Memorandum, April 1947, AMRECB, GRBT-1-R-50/64; Tidwell, "The Government's Tin Program, 1940–1950," RG 234, Office of the Secretary, Administrative Histories of the RFC's Wartime Programs, 1943–54, Metals Reserve Company, Box 6 (hereafter "The Government's Tin Program"); Thoburn, *Tin in the World Economy*, 67–83.

49. Leonard, "Trade Controls on Tin," 30 July 1945, NAII, RG 234, MRC, TP, ASF, 1942–54; Thoburn, *Tin in the World Economy*, 75–83.

50. Dunkerley, *Rebellion in the Veins*, 11–13; "The Government's Tin Program," 22–24.

51. "The Government's Tin Program," 1; Thoburn, *Tin in the World Economy*, 86–89.

52. Goodloe to Eckler, 22 April 1947, NAII, RG 234, MRC, TP, ASF, 1942–54; "The Government's Tin Program."

53. "The Government's Tin Program," 29–52.

54. Ibid., 27–36, 47–50.

55. Hillman, "Bolivia and British Tin Policy, 1939–1945," 314.

56. "The Government's Tin Program," 32–44, 111; see also Hillman, "Bolivia and British Tin Policy," 296–99; Navia Ribera, *Los Estados Unidos y la revolución nacional*, 38–9.

57. "The Government's Tin Program," 58–61.

58. John Hillman has illustrated quite well that this "opportunity" was almost entirely illusory. Hillman, "Bolivia and British Tin Policy, 1939–1945," 291–315.

59. "The Government's Tin Program," 94, 104; Hillman, "Bolivia and British Tin Policy," 299–301; Whitehead, "Bolivia," 133–35.

60. "The Government's Tin Program," 99.

61. British Treasury, as quoted in Hillman, "Bolivia and British Tin Policy," 306; see also "The Government's Tin Program," 101–10.

62. Strong to Hull, 23 December 1943, NAII, RG 59, 824.00; see also "The Government's Tin Program," 168–70.

63. Vogelsang to Douglas, 24 August 1945; see also Fortas to Snyder, 3 October 1945, both in NAII, RG 234, MRC, TP, ASF, 1942–54.

64. Vogelsang to Douglas, 24 August 1945, NAII, RG 234, MRC, TP, ASF, 1942–54; see also Thoburn, *Tin in the World Economy*, 95.

65. Martínez Vargas a Gutiérrez, 28 de abril de 1948, AMRECB, EEUU-1-R-51/98; Martínez Vargas a Ministro, 13 de octubre de 1946, AMRECB, GRBT-1-R-49/63; Martínez Vargas a Ministro, 26 de setiembre de 1946, AMRECB, EEUU-1-R-49/9; see also Martínez Vargas a Gutiérrez, 28 de abril de 1948, AMRECB, EEUU-1-R-51/98.

66. Martínez Vargas a Hertzog, 13 de diciembre de 1947, AMRECB, EEUU-1-R-50/96; Martínez Vargas a Ministro, 30 de setiembre de 1946, AMRECB, EEUU-1-R-49/92; Querejazu Calvo a Ministro, 28 de febrero de 1950, AMRECB, GRBT-1-R-50/64.

67. Moeller Speech, 15 de abril de 1947, AMRECB, GRBT-1-R-50/64; Martínez Vargas a Ministro, 13 de diciembre de 1947, AMRECB, EEUU-1-R-50/96; McKinnon Memorandum, 21 June 1949, NAII, RG 234, MRC, TP, ASF, 1942–54.

68. Orloski to Secretary, 13 June 1947, NAII, RG 59, 824.63; Romero a Ministro, 3 de junio de 1946, AMRECB, GRBT-1-R-49/63; see also Querejazu a Ministro, 14 de junio de 1947, AMRECB, GRBT-1-R-50/64.

69. Espy reported that one Bolivian firm capitalized at 33 million bolivianos made an annual profit of 150 million bolivianos, but declared only 30 million to the government and quietly paid out the remainder to stockholders. Apparently, stories such as this one were common, if unconfirmed. Espy to Department, 10 February 1950, NAII, RG 59, 724.00; Interdepartmental Technical Committee on Tin Subcommittee on Trade Controls, "Trade Controls on Tin," 30 July 1945, NAII, RG 234, MRC, TP, ASF, 1942–54; "Keenleyside Report," 29.

70. Johnson to Goodloe, 26 May 1947, NAII, RG 234, MRC, TP, ASF, 1942–54.

71. *Financial Times*, 9 January 1948, 4; McKinnon Memorandum, 19 August 1949, NAII, RG 234, MRC, TP, ASF, 1942–54.

72. Querejazu Calvo a Ministro, 28 de febrero de 1950, AMRECB, GRBT-1-R-50/64.

CHAPTER 1

The first epigraph to this chapter is drawn from Paz Estenssoro, as quoted in Boal to Secretary, 24 December 1943, NAII, RG 59, 824.00; the second, from Thurston to Secretary, 13 February 1945, NAII, RG 59, 824.504.

1. Sarmiento to Editor, *Herald Tribune*, 22 May 1946, AMRECB, EEUU-1-R-49/91.

2. Adam to Secretary, 5 July 1945; Wright to Spaeth, 11 October 1944; de Zengotita to Secretary, 20 December 1945, all in NAII, RG 59, 824.00.

3. Stettinius to Embassy Santiago, 2 January 1945; de Zengotita to Secretary, 20 December 1945; Thurston to Espy, 29 September 1945, all in NAII, RG 59, 824.00.

4. De Zengotita to Secretary, 20 December 1945; Thurston to Espy, 29 September 1945, both in NAII, RG 59, 824.00; Thurston to Secretary, 28 August 1945, NAII, RG 59, 824.6354.

5. MNR, as quoted in Thurston to Secretary, 3 September 1945, NAII, RG 59, 824.00.

6. De Zengotita to Secretary, 20 December 1945, NAII, RG 59, 824.00; see also Thurston to Secretary, 28 August 1945, NAII, RG 59, 824.6354; Ramsey, "Banco Minero Threatens to Undermine the Ckaccha System of the Compañia Minera Unificada del Cerro de Potosí," 13 June 1945; Halle to Wells, Lockwood, and McClintock, 23 June 1945, both in NAII, RG 59, 824.6354; Thurston to Secretary, 22 January 1945, NAII, RG 59, 824.00; Thurston to Secretary, 31 March 1945, NAII, RG 59, 824.63; Thurston to Secretary, 25 September 1945, NAII, RG 59, 711.24; Murillo Cárdenas and Larrea Bedregal, *Razón de Patria*, 147–53; Malloy, *Bolivia*, 122–23.

7. Mitchell, *The Legacy of Populism in Bolivia*, 22–33.

8. Gotkowitz, *A Revolution for Our Rights*, 192–232.

9. Thurston to Secretary, 23 April 1945; Thurston to Secretary, 27 April 1945, both in NAII, RG 59, 824.00; see also Gallo, *Taxes and State Power*, 90–91; Gotkowitz, *A Revolution for Our Rights*, 192–232; Hylton and Thomson, *Revolutionary Horizons*, 73–74.

10. Andrade, *My Missions for Revolutionary Bolivia*, 113; Hoover to Lyon, 31 July 1945, NAII, RG 59, 824.00; see also Byrnes, Andrade, and Rockefeller, MC, 14 June 1945, NAII, RG 59, 824.6354; Thurston to Secretary, 3 September 1945, NAII, RG 59, 824.00.

11. De Zengotita to Secretary, 20 December 1945, NAII, RG 59, 824.00; Murillo Cárdenas and Larrea Bedregal, *Razón de Patria*, 153; Ríos Gamboa, *Bolivia*, 58.

12. Mitchell, *The Legacy of Populism in Bolivia*, 22–33; quotation on p. 24; Gallo, *Taxes and State Power*, 140–43.

13. McConaughy to Secretary, 22 September 1944; see also Adam and Paz Estenssoro, MC, 26 January 1945, both in NAII, RG 59, 824.00; Knudson, *Bolivia*, 109.

14. MNR newspapers, as quoted in de Zengotita to Secretary, 17 July 1945, NAII, RG 59, 824.63.

15. De Zengotita to Secretary, 17 July 1945, NAII, RG 59, 824.63; Thurston to Secretary, 8 March 1945, NAII, RG 59, 824.50; Neathery to Secretary, 13 March 1945; Halle to Welles, Butler and Flournoy, 23 March 1945, both in NAII, RG 59, 824.504.

16. Thurston even went so far as to call upon German Monroy Block's Labor Ministry to "engage in a little pro-American propaganda among the miners, especially since its influence over mine labor was so marked." Thurston, Monroy Block, and de Zengotita, MC, 14 September 1945, NAII, RG 59, 824.6352; Thurston to Secretary, 6 July 1945, NAII, RG 59, 824.63; Thurston to Secretary, 4 September 1945, NAII, RG 59, 711.24.
17. Thurston to Secretary, 25 July 1945, NAII, RG 59, 824.504.
18. Adam to Secretary, 1 January 1946, NAII, RG 59, 824.00.
19. Lechín Oquendo, as quoted in de Zengotita to Secretary, 8 January 1946, NAII, RG 59, 824.504; see also Adam to Secretary, 1 February 1946, NAII, RG 59, 824.00.
20. Paz Estenssoro, as quoted in Espy to Flack, 21 January 1945, NAII, RG 59, 824.00.
21. Espy to Flack and Wells, 30 November 1945; Espy to Flack, 21 January 1946; Stines to Ambassador, 24 January 1944, all in NAII, RG 59, 824.00.
22. Torres Gigena a Ministro, 10 de abril de 1946, AMRECA, Bolivia 1946, 1, 1; Stuart to Secretary, 5 November 1945, NAII, RG 59, 824.00.
23. Stuart to Secretary, 5 November 1945, NAII, RG 59, 824.00; Adam and Paz Estenssoro, MC, 26 January 1945, NAII, RG 59, 824.00; Espy to Wells and Flack, 31 October 1945, NAII, RG 59, 824.00.
24. Thurston to Secretary, 18 October 1945; Thurston to Secretary, 22 October 1945, both in NAII, RG 59, 824.00; Espy to Flack, 24 January 1946, NAII, RG 59, 711.24.
25. Thurston to Secretary, 25 September 1945, NAII, RG 59, 711.24; Thurston to Secretary, 3 September 1945; Adam to Secretary, 11 February 1946, both in NAII, RG 59, 824.00; see also Thurston to Secretary, 7 September 1945, NAII, RG 59, 711.24.
26. Adam to Secretary, 19 February 1946, NAII, RG 84, ELP, Classified, 800.
27. Adam to Secretary, 4 January 1946; Adam to Secretary, 11 February 1946, both in NAII, RG 59, 824.00; see also Torres Gigena a Ministro, 10 de abril de 1946, AMRECA, Bolivia 1946, 1, 1; Adam to Secretary, 21 January 1946, NAII, RG 59, 824.00; Knudson, *Bolivia*, 125.
28. Andrade a Ministro, 9 de abril de 1946, AMRECB, EEUU-1-R-49/91; see also Frank, *Juan Perón vs. Spruille Braden*; Rapoport, *Gran Bretaña, Estados Unidos, y las clases dirigentes argentinos, 1940–1945*.
29. Andrade a Ministro, 9 de abril de 1946, AMRECB, EEUU-1-R-49/91; Whitehead, "Bolivia," 121; see also Knudson, *Bolivia*, 138–39.
30. Espy to Flack, 12 February 1946, NAII, RG 59, 824.00; see also U.S. Department of State, *Consultation Among the American Republics with Respect to the Argentine Situation*, 1–133; Knudson, *Bolivia*, 114–17.
31. Abecia Baldivieso, *Las relaciones internacionales*, 122–23.
32. Villarroel replied, "That's why I appointed you." Whitehead, "Bolivia," 129.
33. De Zengotita to Secretary, 20 December 1945; Burrows to Secretary, 16 November 1944, both in NAII, RG 59, 824.00.
34. Embajada en La Paz, "Sobre la situacion de Bolivia," 2 de setiembre de 1946; Torre Gigena a Ministro, 10 de abril de 1946, both in AMRECA, Bolivia 1946, 1, 1; Embajada Buenos Aires a Ministro, 1 de abril de 1946, AMRECB, ARG-1-R-74/141; see also Carles, "Sobre infiltración brasileña en Santa Cruz de la Sierra," 9 de noviembre de 1946, AMRECA, Bolivia 1946, 2, 11.
35. Embajada Buenos Aires a Ministro, 26 de marzo de 1946, AMRECB, ARG-1-R-74/141; de Zengotita to Secretary, 20 December 1945, NAII, RG 59, 824.00; Embajada Buenos Aires a Ministro, 12 de Julio de 1946, AMRECB, ARG-1-R-74/144; Thurston to Secretary, 22 March 1945, NAII, RG 84, ELP, Classified, 800.
36. Tewksbury to Secretary, 4 September 1945, NAII, RG 59, 835.6176; Andrade a Ministro, 6 de febrero de 1946, AMRECB, EEUU-1-R-49/91; Embajada Buenos Aires a Ministro, 13 de abril de 1946, AMRECB, ARG-1-R-74/142; Thurston to Secretary, 22 March 1945, NAII, RG 84, ELP, Classified, 800; Dorn, *Peronistas and New Dealers*, 44–46; Lehman, *Bolivia and the United States*, 83.
37. Adam to Secretary, 25 March 1946, NAII, RG 59, 711.24; Adam and Paz Estenssoro, MC, 26 January 1945, NAII, RG 59, 824.00.
38. Andrade a Ministro, 9 de abril de 1946, AMRECB, EEUU-1-R-49/91; Espy to Flack, 21 February 1946, NAII, RG 59, 824.6354.

39. Espy to Flack, 12 Febuary 1946, NAII, RG 59, 824.00; see also Adam to Secretary, 19 February 1946, NAII, RG 84, ELP, 800; Adam to Secretary, 6 February 1946, NAII, RG 59, 824.00.

40. For example, even *El Diario*, in its 25 July 1941 issue, had conceded that the incriminating 1941 letters were in all likelihood forgeries. This did not, of course, stop Braden from using them as a centerpiece for his case. Knudson, *Bolivia*, 113–15; Adam to Secretary, 21 February 1946, NAII, RG 84, ELP, Classified, 800; Espy to Flack, 7 March 1946, NAII, RG 59, 824.00.

41. Torres Gigena a Ministro, 22 de abril de 1946, AMRECA, Bolivia 1946, 1, 1; Andrade a Ministro, 9 de abril de 1946, AMRECB, EEUU-1-R-49/91.

42. Adam to Secretary, 21 February 1946; Espy to Flack, 12 February 1946, both in NAII, RG 59, 824.00.

43. Espy to Flack, 7 March 1946; Adam to Secretary, 22 March 1946; Acheson to Embassy La Paz, 22 March 1946; Espy to Flack, Briggs, Spaeth, and Braden, 6 May 1946, all in NAII, RG 59, 824.00.

44. Hochschild and Ramsey, MC, 8 August 1945, NAII, RG 59, 824.6354; Andrade, *My Missions for Revolutionary Bolivia*, 32, 60; Andrade and Ramsey, MC, 3 August 1945, NAII, RG 59, 824.6254; Whitehead, "Bolivia," 131; see also Espy to Flack, Butler, Briggs, and Braden, 22 October 1945, NAII, RG 59, 824.6354.

45. Grew to Crowley, 13 July 1945, NAII, RG 59, 824.6354.

46. Ramsey to White, Wells, Espy, Brundage, and Lipkowitz, 29 August 1945; Grew to Crowley, 13 July 1945; see also Barnett to Kennedy, 10 July 1945, all in NAII, RG 59, 824.6354; Andrade, *My Missions for Revolutionary Bolivia*, 68.

47. Andrade and Ramsey, MC, 6 August 1945, NAII, RG 59, 824.6354; see also "The Government's Tin Program," 182–85.

48. Hochschild and Ramsey, MC, 8 August 1945; Hochschild, Wilcox, Kennedy, Espy, and Barnett, MC, 14 September 1945; Hochschild, Kennedy, Espy, and Barnett, MC, 19 December 1945 all in NAII, RG 59, 824.6354.

49. Andrade, *My Missions for Revolutionary Bolivia*, 70–73; see also Ramsey to White, Wells, Espy, Brundage, and Lipkowitz, 29 August 1945, NAII, RG 59, 824.6354; Hobson to Levinson, 2 October 1946, NAII, RG 234, MRC, TP, ASF, 1942–54.

50. Thurston to Secretary, 28 August 1945; Hochschild, Kennedy, Espy, and Barnett, MC, 19 December 1945 both in NAII, RG 59, 824.6354; Andrade, *My Missions for Revolutionary Bolivia*, 72–73; Espy to Wells and Flack, 1 October 1945, NAII, RG 59, 824.6354.

51. Adam to Secretary, 28 January 1946, NAII, RG 59, 824.6354; see also Andrade a Ministro, 22 de enero de 1946, AMRECB, EEUU-1-R-49/91.

52. Ramsey to White, Wells, Espy, Brundage, and Lipkowitz, 29 August 1945; Andrade and Clayton, MC, 10 July 1946 both in NAII, RG 59, 824.6354.

53. Thurston to Secretary, 20 February 1945, NAII, RG 59, 824.00.

54. Andrade a Ministro, 23 de enero de 1946; Andrade a Ministro, 4 de enero de 1946, both in AMRECB, EEUU-1-R-49/91.

55. Andrade a Ministro, 1 de abril de 1946, AMRECB, EEUU-1-R-49/91; Andrade, *My Missions for Revolutionary Bolivia*, 114.

56. Braden, Wright, Thurston, Jewett, Johnson, et al., MC, 21 March 1946; Andrade, Quiroga, Canedo Reyes, Sanchez, Hochschild, Kemper, Jewett, Johnson, et al., MC, 22 March 1946 both in NAII, RG 59, 824.6354; Andrade, *My Missions for Revolutionary Bolivia*, 114; Espy, "Supplemental Memorandum," 9 April 1946, NAII, RG 59, 824.6354.

57. Hochschild, Gruenebaum, and Quiroga Rico, "Memorandum," AMRECB, EEUU-1-R-49/91.

58. Espy, "Supplemental Memorandum," 9 April 1946; Canedo Reyes, Rovira, Jewett, Johnson, Espy, et al., MC, 25 April 1946 both in NAII, RG 59, 824.6354.

59. Andrade, *My Missions for Revolutionary Bolivia*, 114–21; Andrade a Ministro, 9 de junio de 1946, AMRECB, EEUU-1-R-49/92; Andrade a Ministro, 15 de mayo de 1946, AMRECB, EEUU-1-R-49/91; see also Navia Ribera, *Los Estados Unidos*, 55–56.

60. Andrade a Ministro, 15 de mayo de 1946, AMRECB, EEUU-1-R-49/91; Bedderson a Andrade, junio de 1946; see also Andrade a Ministro, 9 de junio de 1946, both in AMRECB, EEUU-1-R-49/92.

61. Braden, Andrade, and Espy, MC, 20 May 1946, NAII, RG 59, 824.6354; Barber to Webb, 9 March 1950, NAII, RG 59, 824.2544; see also Andrade a Ministro, 15 de mayo de 1946, AMRECB, EEUU-1-R-49/91.
62. Clayton, Braden, Wright, Briggs, and Espy, MC, 10 April 1946 NAII, RG 59, 824.6354; see also Andrade a Ministro, 9 de abril de 1946, AMRECB, EEUU-1-R-49/91; Braden, Wright, Thurston, et al., MC, 21 March 1946, NAII, RG 59, 824.6354.
63. Andrade, Braden, and Briggs, MC, 17 July 1946 NAII, RG 59, 824.6354.
64. Espy to Wells, Braden, and Briggs, 3 October 1946, NAII, RG 59, 824.6354; Andrade, *My Missions for Revolutionary Bolivia*, 121; see also Andrade a Ministro, 15 de mayo de 1946; Andrade a Ministro, 28 de febrero de 1946, both in AMRECB, EEUU-1-R-49/91.
65. Mesa Gisbert, *Historia de Bolivia*, 562–63; see also Lema Pelaez, *Con las banderas*, 56–57; Quieser Morales, *Bolivia*, 68.
66. Neathery to Secretary, 14 June 1946; Adam to Secretary, 6 June 1946; Adam to Secretary, 14 June 1946, all in NAII, RG 59, 824.00; see also Galarza, "The Case of Bolivia," GMMA, SRP, Bolivia.
67. Andrade and U.S. labor leader Ernesto Galarza actually attempted to blame the strike on "economic causes" arising "from the uncertainty and delay in the conclusion of the new tin contract." The State Department forcefully rejected this as a rather transparent ploy. Galarza, "The Case of Bolivia," GMMA, SRP, Bolivia; Espy to Wells, Braden, Butler, and Briggs, 13 July 1946, NAII, RG 59, 824.6354.
68. Flack to Secretary, 22 July 1946, NAII, RG 59, 824.00; see also Mesa Gisbert, *Historia de Bolivia*, 563–64; Ostria Gutierrez, *The Tragedy of Bolivia*, 64.
69. Flack to Secretary, 27 October 1949, NAII, RG 59, 711.24; Espy to Armour, 7 July 1947, NAII, RG 84, ELP, Classified, 800; see also Navia Ribera, *Los Estados Unidos*, 57–58.

CHAPTER 2

The first epigraph to this chapter is drawn from Canelas, *Dictadura y democracia*, 260; the second, from Gosálvez a Ministro, 3 de septiembre de 1949, AMRECB, ARG-1-R-77/183.
1. Messersmith to Secretary, 29 October 1946, NAII, RG 59, 824.6354; Mann to Braden, 29 October 1946, NAII, RG 59, 824.5018; Adam to Secretary, 31 May 1946, NAII, RG 84, Embassy Buenos Aires; see also Espy to Flack and Briggs, 13 May 1946, NAII, RG 59, 824.00.
2. Flack to Secretary, 1 August 1946, NAII, RG 84, ELP, Top Secret; Acheson to Flack, 1 August 1946, NAII, RG 59, 824.00.
3. Flack to Secretary, 25 September 1946, NAII, RG 59, 824.00; Galarza, "The Case of Bolivia," May 1949, GMMA, SRP, Bolivia.
4. Flack to Corrigan, 12 September 1946, Franklin Delano Roosevelt Presidential Library, Frank Corrigan Papers, Correspondence; Flack to Braden, 22 July 1946; Flack to Secretary, 25 September 1946, both in NAII, RG 59, 824.00.
5. Flack to Braden, 22 July 1946, NAII, RG 59, 824.00; Orloski, "Mineral Trade Notes for the Third Quarter of 1946," 8 November 1946, NAII, RG 84, ELP, Classified, 863; see also Lehman, *Bolivia and the United States*, 94.
6. Flack to Secretary, 2 August 1946; Flack to Secretary, 7 August 1946, both in NAII, RG 59, 824.00.
7. Braden described the new ambassador, whom he had known since 1919, as "one of the highest-calibre Bolivians it has been my pleasure to know." As quoted in Braden to Lovett and Armour, 27 June 1947, NAII, RG 84, ELP, Classified, 800; Martínez Vargas, as quoted in ibid.; see also Acheson to Flack, 1 August 1946, NAII, RG 59, 824.00.
8. Pinto Escalier a Ministro, 12 de agosto de 1946, AMRECB, ARG-1-R-74/145; Adam to Secretary, 9 August 1946; Flack to Secretary, 12 August 1946, both in NAII, RG 59, 824.00.
9. Flack to Secretary, 12 August 1946, NAII, RG 59, 824.00; Memorandum for the President, 9 August 1946, HSTPL, WHCF, State Department Correspondence.

10. Messersmith to Braden, 23 August 1946, NAII, RG 84, Embassy Buenos Aires; "The Lampposts of La Paz," *Time*, 7 October 1946; Ostria Gutierrez, *The Tragedy of Bolivia*, 75; Lema Pelaez, *Con las banderas*, 79; Mesa Gisbert, *Historia de Bolivia*, 564.

11. Flack to Secretary, 22 July 1946, NAII, RG 59, 824.00.

12. Acheson to Embassy Buenos Aires, 30 August 1946, NAII, RG 59, 824.00; Flack to Secretary, 14 October 1946, NAII, RG 59, 824.5018; see also Daza Ondarza a Ministro, 6 de agosto de 1946, AMRECB, ARG-1-R-74/145; Daza Ondarza a Ministro, 10 de agosto de 1946, AMRECB, ARG-1-R-74/175.

13. Daza Ondarza a Ministro, 20 de agosto de 1946, AMRECB, ARG-1-R-74/146; Pinto a Ministro, 14 de agosto de 1946, AMRECB, ARG-1-R-74/145; Embajada Buenos Aires a Ministro, 14 de diciembre de 1946, AMRECB, ARG-1-R-74/150.

14. Daza Ondarza a Ministro, 13 de agosto de 1946, AMRECB, ARG-1-R-74/145; Daza Ondarza a Ministro, 19 de agosto de 1946, AMRECB, ARG-1-R-74/146; see also Embajada Buenos Aires a Ministro, 12 de julio de 1946, ARG-1-R-74/144.

15. Daza Ondarza a Ministro, 23 de agosto de 1946, AMRECB, ARG-1-R-74/146; Espy to Briggs, 31 October 1946, NAII, RG 59, 824.6354.

16. Daza Ondarza a Ministro, 20 de agosto de 1946; Daza Ondarza a Ministro, 19 de agosto de 1946, both in AMRECB, ARG-1-R-74/146.

17. Rios Marmol a Bramulgia, 31 de agosto de 1948, AMRECA, Bolivia 1948, 1, 2; Peñaranda a Ministro, 8 de octubre de 1946, AMRECB, ARG-1-R-74/148.

18. Linville to Hall, 19 May 1947, NAII, RG 59, 824.5018; Martínez Vargas, Diez de Medina, Braden, and Espy, MC, 14 August 1946, NAII, RG 59, 824.6354; see also Solares a Flack, 12 de agosto de 1946, NAII, RG 84, ELP, Classified, 800; Wells to Braden, 23 July 1946, NAII, RG 59, 824.00.

19. Bolivian diplomats requesting wheat from the United States were explicitly told, "DO NOT MENTION" price, for this would "undoubtedly produce an unfavorable result." Bedoya a Guachalla, 29 de agosto de 1947, AMRECB, ARG-1-R-75/159; Smith to Cale, 25 October 1946, NAII, RG 59, 824.5018; see also Martínez Vargas a Ministro, 28 de agosto de 1946, AMRECB, EEUU-1-R-49/92; Flack to Secretary, 10 January 1947, NAII, RG 59, 824.5018.

20. Daza Ondarza a Ministro, 19 de agosto de 1946; see also Daza Ondarza a Ministro, 23 de agosto de 1946; Daza Ondarza a Ministro, 24 de agosto de 1946, all in AMRECB, ARG-1-R-74/146.

21. Peñaranda a Ministro, 28 de octubre de 1946, AMRECB, ARG-1-R-74/148; Orloski to Secretary, 16 January 1947, NAII, RG 59, 624.3531; see also Messersmith to Secretary, 29 October 1946, NAII, RG 59, 824.6354; Peñaranda a Ministro, 11 de octubre de 1946; Peñaranda a Ministro, 28 de octubre de 1946, both in AMRECB, ARG-1-R-74/148.

22. Orloski to Secretary, 4 November 1946, NAII, RG 59, 824.6354; Flack to Secretary, 19 May 1948, NAII, RG 59, 824.00.

23. Paz Estensorro, as quoted in Burrows to Secretary, 15 November 1946, NAII, RG 59, 824.00.

24. Galbraith, "Political Parties and Political Agroupments in Bolivia," November 1946, NAII, RG 59, 824.00; Henderson to Flack, 15 August 1946, NAII, RG 84, ELP, Classified, 800.

25. Galarza, "The Case of Bolivia," May 1949, GMMA, SRP, Bolivia.

26. Malloy, *Bolivia*, 128.

27. Hoover to Neal, 22 July 1946, NAII, RG 59, 824.00.

28. Flack to Secretary, 6 February 1947, NAII, RG 59, 824.00; Flack to Secretary, 26 February 1947, NAII, RG 59, 824.6354.

29. Flack to Secretary, 4 December 1946, NAII, RG 59, 824.00.

30. Anaya, as quoted in Flack to Secretary, 15 August 1946; Flack to Secretary, 25 July 1946, both in NAII, RG 59, 824.00.

31. Dearborn to Hall, Wells, and Braden, 9 September 1946; Flack to Secretary, 24 June 1947, both in NAII, RG 59, 824.00.

32. Flack to Secretary, 13 August 1946, NAII, RG 59, 824.00; Flack to Secretary, 28 August 1946, NAII, RG 59, 824.01; Henderson to Flack, 3 October 1946, NAII, RG 84, ELP, 800.

33. Scherer to Secretary, 21 February 1947; Donnelly to Secretary, 9 January 1948; Flack to Secretary, 20 January 1947, all in NAII, RG 59, 824.00; see also Ostria Gutierrez, *The Tragedy of Bolivia*, 79.

34. Malloy, *Bolivia*, 136–50.
35. Flack, as quoted in Galbraith, "Communism in Bolivia," 23 February 1947, NAII, RG 59, 824.00B.
36. Mier y Leon and Canedo Reyes, "Memorandum," 11 February 1947, NAII, RG 59, 824.6354.
37. NAII, RG 59, 824.6354.
38. Flack to Secretary, 26 February 1947; Flack to Secretary, 24 February 1947, both in NAII, RG 59, 824.6354.
39. Martínez Vargas a Ministro, 15 de enero de 1947, AMRECB, EEUU-1-R-50/95; Espy to Flack, 10 January 1947, NAII, RG 84, ELP, 863.5; Martínez Vargas, Braden, Espy, and Wright, MC, 7 February 1947; see also Braden, Wright, Espy, Anderson, and Lipkowitz, MC, 5 February 1947 both in NAII, RG 59, 824.6354.
40. Braden, Wright, Espy, Anderson, and Lipkowitz, MC, 5 February 1947; Smith to Braden and Wright, 3 January 1947, both in NAII, RG 59, 824.6354; "The Government's Tin Program"; Espy to Flack, 10 January 1947, NAII, RG 84, ELP, Classified, 863.5.
41. Malaya produced only eighty-five hundred tons of tin in 1946, in stark contrast to British projections of forty thousand tons. Querajazo a Ministro, 25 de marzo de 1946; Querajazo a Ministro, 7 de mayo de 1947; Houwert, Report to Plenary Session of the International Tin Conference, 17 April 1947, all in AMRECB, GRBT-1-R-50/64; Johnson to Goodloe, 26 May 1947, NAII, RG 234, MRC, TP, ASF, 1942–54.
42. Johnson to Goodloe, 26 May 1947, NAII, RG 234, MRC, TP, ASF, 1942–54; Martínez Vargas a Ministro, 15 de enero de 1947, AMRECB, EEUU-1-R-50/95.
43. Espy and Johnson, MC, 18 February 1947, NAII, RG 59, 824.6354; see also Espy to Flack, 10 January 1947, NAII, RG 84, ELP, Classified, 863.5.
44. Martínez Vargas a Ministro, 15 de enero de 1947, AMRECB, EEUU-1-R-50/95.
45. Orloski to Secretary, 14 February 1947, NAII, RG 59, 824.6354; Espy to Flack, 10 January 1947, NAII, RG 84, ELP, Classified, 863.5.
46. Braden, as quoted in Wells to Wright and Braden, 14 March 1947, NAII, RG 59, 824.6354; Orloski to Secretary, 13 June 1947, NAII, RG 59, 824.63; see also Solares a Ministro, 28 de febrero de 1947, AMRECB, GRBT-1-R-50/64.
47. Martínez Vargas a Ministro, 8 de mayo de 1947, AMRECB, EEUU-1-R-50/95; Martínez Vargas, Diez de MediNAII, Braden, Wright, Smith, and Wells, MC, 11 March 1947 NAII, RG 59, 824.6354; see also Martínez Vargas a Ministro, 8 de marzo de 1947, AMRECB, EEUU-1-R-50/95.
48. Alvéstegui a Ministro, 1 de abril de 1947, AMRECB, ARG-1-R-75/155; see also Dorn, *Peronistas and New Dealers*.
49. Flack to Secretary, 27 December 1947, NAII, RG 59, 724.35; Buitrago Carrillo, "Memorandum," n.d., AMRECA, Bolivia 1947, 1, 10, especial; Rios Marmol, "Informe sobre la situacion de Bolivia durante los meses de mayo y junio de 1949," 28 de junio de 1949, AMRECA, Bolivia 1949, 1, 1; n.a., "Situación política de Bolivia," n.d., AMRECA, Bolivia 1949, 1, 1, 2; Perón, as quoted in Gosálvez a Ministro, 20 de agosto de 1947, AMRECB, ARG-1-R-75/157.
50. Flack to Secretary of State, 4 March 1947; Orloski to Secretary, 16 January 1947, both in NAII, RG 59, 624.3531; Abecia Baldivieso, *Las relaciones internacionales*, 128.
51. Alvéstegui a Ministro, 1 de abril de 1947, AMRECB, ARG-1-R-75/155; Flack to Secretary, 27 February 1947, NAII, RG 59, 624.3531; see also Dorn, *Peronistas and New Dealers*, 185–86.
52. Flack to Secretary, n.d.; Flack to Messersmith, 14 April 1947, both in NAII, RG 84, ELP, Classified, 531.
53. "Movimiento Revolucionario de Bolivia," 21 de julio de 1946, AMRECA, Bolivia 1946, 1, 1; Martínez Vargas, Diez de Medina, Braden, Wright, Smith, and Wells, MC, 11 March 1947, NAII, RG 59, 824.6354; Hertzog, as quoted in James to Flack, 24 March 1947, NAII, RG 84, ELP, Classified, 891.
54. Miranda, as quoted in Alvéstegui a Ministro, 1 de abril de 1947, AMRECB, ARG-1-R-75/155; Marshall to Bugbee, 28 April 1947, NAII, RG 59, 824.6354.
55. Alvéstegui a Ministro, 1 de abril de 1947, AMRECB, ARG-1-R-75/155; Peñaranda a Ministro, 8 de octubre de 1946, AMRECB, ARG-1-R-74/50; see also Alvéstegui a Ministro, 27 de enero de 1947, ARG-1-R-75/151; Flack to Messersmith, 20 March 1947, NAII, RG 84, ELP, Classified, 531.

56. Alvéstegui a Ministro, 23 de diciembre de 1946, AMRECB, ARG-1-R-74/150; Espy to Wells, 7 January 1947, NAII, RG 59, 624.3531; Flack to Secretary, n.d., NAII, RG 84, ELP, Classified, 531; Flack to Secretary of State, 9 June 1948, RG 59, 724.35. The Combined Food Board (CFB) was another of the international agencies created by the Allies to facilitate coordination, maximize production, and allocate scarce resources during and immediately after the war. For more on Perón's circumventing the CFB, see Dorn, *Peronistas and the New Dealers*, 65.

57. Paz Estenssoro, as quoted in Robert J. Alexander, *The Bolivarian Presidents*, 16–17; Esparue Becerra, "Memorandum secreto," 16 de octubre de 1948, AMRECA, Bolivia 1948, 1, 1, 3a.

58. Alvéstegui a Ministro, 7 de marzo de 1947, AMRECB, ARG-1-R-75/154; Alvéstegui a Ministro, 21 de enero de 1947; Alvéstegui a Ministro, 20 de enero de 1947, both in AMRECB, ARG-1-R-75/151; Martínez Vargas a Ministro, 8 de abril de 1947, AMRECB, EEUU-1-R-50/95.

59. Martínez Vargas, Diez de Medina, Braden, Wright, Smith, and Wells, MC, 11 March 1947; Espy to Wells, 3 January 1947, both in NAII, RG 59, 824.6354; see also Martínez Vargas a Ministro, 22 de marzo de 1947, AMRECB, EEUU-1-R-50/95.

60. Wells to Smith, 7 March 1947; Martínez Vargas, Diez de Medina, Braden, Wright, Smith, and Wells, MC, 11 March 1947; Espy to Wells, 3 January 1947, all in NAII, RG 59, 824.6354.

61. Wright, Smith, Wells, Hall, Anderson, Dorr, and Jewett, MC, 18 March 1947; Flack to Secretary, 24 March 1947, both in NAII, RG 59, 824.6354.

62. Braden, Martínez Vargas, Wright, Briggs, Wells, and Hall, MC, 17 March 1947, NAII, RG 59, 824.6354; "The Government's Tin Program," 216; Martínez Vargas a Ministro, 22 de marzo de 1947, AMRECB, EEUU-1-R-50/95.

63. Espy, "Bolivia," 21 April 1947, NAII, RG 59, 824.6354; "Statement by the Bolivian Delegation," 15–16 April 1946, AMRECB, GRBT-1-R-50/64; see also Acheson to Bugbee, 20 March 1947, NAII, RG 59, 824.6354; Martínez Vargas a Ministro, 22 de marzo de 1947, AMRECB, EEUU-1-R-50/95; Martínez Vargas, Diez de Medina, Briggs, Wright, and Hall, MC, 24 March 1947, NAII, RG 59, 824.6354.

64. Orloski to Secretary, 13 June 1947, NAII, RG 84, ELP, Classified, 863.5.

65. Flack to Secretary, 31 October 1946; Flack to Espy, 21 October 1947, both in NAII, RG 59, 824.6354; Flack to Secretary, 25 April 1947, NAII, RG 84, ELP, Classified, 800.

66. Flack to Secretary, 6 February 1947, NAII, RG 59, 824.00; Flack to Secretary, 16 January 1947, NAII, RG 84, ELP, 800.

CHAPTER 3

The first epigraph to this chapter is drawn from Daniels to Armour, 22 December 1947, NAII, RG 59, 824.6354; the second, from Hertzog, as quoted in "Man in the Middle," *Newsweek*, 16 May 1949.

1. Flack to Secretary, 28 May 1947, NAII, RG 59, 824.00.
2. Galbraith, "First Year of the Hertzog Government," May 1948, NAII, RG 59, 824.00.
3. Espy to Wells, Woodward, and Briggs, 14 May 1947; Flack to Secretary, 9 April 1947; Galbraith, "First Year of the Hertzog Government," May 1948, all in NAII, RG 59, 824.00.
4. Alexander, *Bolivia*, 76–77.
5. Flack to Secretary, 30 April 1947; Flack to Secretary, 28 April 1947, both in NAII, RG 59, 824.00.
6. Flack to Secretary 1 July 1947, NAII, RG 59, 824.00; *Camarada*, as quoted in Flack to Secretary, 17 July 1947, and in Flack to Secretary, 8 July 1947, both in NAII, RG 59, 711.24; Anaya, as quoted in Galbraith to Secretary, 19 December 1947, NAII, RG 84, ELP, Classified, 800.
7. Arze, as quoted in Flack to Secretary, 8 July 1947, NAII, RG 59, 711.24; Anaya, as quoted in Espy to Wells and Woodward, 18 July 1947, NAII, RG 59, 824.00.
8. Embassy Memorandum, "Communism in Bolivia," 23 March 1947, NAII, RG 84, ELP, Classified, 800; Flack to Secretary, 14 July 1947, NAII, RG 59, 711.24; King, "Fourth National Congress of the Bolivian Mine Workers," June 1947, NAII, RG 84, ELP, Classified, 850.4.
9. Flack to Secretary, 8 July 1947, NAII, RG 59, 711.24; see also Flack to Secretary, 19 September 1947; Galbraith, "First Year of the Hertzog Government," May 1948, both in NAII, RG 59, 824.00; Malloy, *Bolivia*, 132–33.

10. Paz Estenssoro believed that the PIR-PURS split would "indirectly have to benefit us" on several levels. As quoted in Lema Pelaez, *Con las banderas*, 99; Flack to Secretary, 12 August 1947, NAII, RG 59, 824.00; Flack to Secretary, 21 March 1947, NAII, RG 84, ELP, Classified, 800.

11. Hertzog, as quoted in Galbraith to Secretary, 19 December 1947, NAII, RG 84, ELP, Classified, 800.

12. Galbraith to Secretary, 2 March 1948, NAII, RG 84, ELP, Classified, 800.

13. Galbraith, "First Year of the Hertzog Government," May 1948; see also Galbraith to Secretary, 2 March 1948, both in NAII, RG 59, 824.00.

14. Flack to Secretary, 28 May 1947, NAII, RG 59, 824.00; Flack to Secretary, 24 May 1948, NAII, RG 84, ELP, Classified, 800.

15. Galbraith, "First Year of the Hertzog Government," May 1948, NAII, RG 59, 824.00; Galbraith to Secretary, 2 March 1948, RG 84, ELP, Classified, 800.

16. Although Hertzog pursued a somewhat sophisticated and nuanced approach in the mining camps, his policies toward agriculture, land reform, the landed elite, and the "Indian Problem" effectively repudiated even the tentative steps taken under Villarroel and permitted a return to a "climate of tension, fear, and abuse." Gotkowitz, *A Revolution for Our Rights*, 233–67; see also Galarza, "The Case of Bolivia," GMMA, SRP, Bolivia.

17. Galbraith, "First Year of the Hertzog Government," May 1948, NAII, RG 59, 824.00.

18. Ibid.; King to Flack, 27 May 1947, NAII, RG 59, 824.504; see also Galarza, "The Case of Bolivia," GMMA, SRP, Bolivia.

19. Galbraith, "First Year of the Hertzog Government," May 1948, NAII, RG 59, 824.00.

20. Ibid.; Flack to Secretary, 30 July 1948; see also Orloski to Secretary, 8 January 1948, both in NAII, RG 59, 824.6354; Flack to Secretary, 10 October 1947, NAII, RG 59, 824.504.

21. Malloy, *Bolivia*, 133–35.

22. Indeed, according to the U.S. Embassy, 1948 was a "year of unprecedented labor peace," in which workers and unions not affiliated with the MNR would win "almost every concession they sought." As quoted in Eaton, "Annual Labor Report—Bolivia—1949," n.d., NAII, RG 84, ELP, General, 680.

23. Martínez Vargas, Diez de Medina, Armour, and Espy, MC, 18 November 1947, NAII, RG 59, 824.6354; Goodloe to Thorp, 2 December 1947, NAII, RG 84, ELP, Classified; see also Martínez Vargas a Ministro, 22 de agosto de 1947, AMRECB, EEUU-1-R-50/96; *American Metal Market*, 26 June 1947.

24. Gosálvez a Ministro, 15 de agosto de 1947, AMRECA, ARG-1-R-75/157; Gosálvez a Ministro, 14 de febrero de 1948, AMRECB, ARG-1-R-76/163; see also Gosálvez a Ministro, 2 de setiembre de 1947, AMRECB, ARG-1-R-75/159.

25. Orloski to Secretary, 24 October 1947, NAII, RG 84, ELP, Classified, 531, emphasis in original; Gosálvez a Ministro, 14 de febrero de 1948, AMRECB, ARG-1-R-76/163; Espy to Mills and Woodward, 14 November 1947, NAII, RG 59, 824.6354; see also Gosálvez a Ministro, 16 de setiembre de 1947, AMRECB, ARG-1-R-75/159.

26. Gosálvez a Ministro, 14 de febrero de 1948, AMRECB, ARG-1-R-76/163; see also Espy to Mills and Woodward, 14 November 1947, NAII, RG 59, 824.6354.

27. Orloski to Secretary, 24 September 1947, NAII, RG 59, 824.6354; see also Calvo Linares a Ministro, 8 de julio de 1947, AMRECB, EEUU-1-R-50/94.

28. Malthus Hoyos a Ministro, 25 de abril de 1947, AMRECB, ARG-1-R-75/155; Perón, as quoted in Gosálvez a Ministro, 9 de enero de 1947, AMRECB, ARG-1-R-76/163; Canedo Reyes, as quoted in Espy to Mills and Woodward, 14 November 1947, NAII, RG 59, 824.6354.

29. Espy to Mills and Woodward, 14 November 1947NAII,; Orloski to Secretary, 24 October 1947, both in NAII, RG 59, 824.6354.

30. Orloski to Secretary, 24 October 1947; Orloski to Secretary, 28 November 1947, both in NAII, RG 59, 824.6354; Martínez Vargas a Ministro, 22 de agosto de 1947, AMRECB, EEUU-1-R-50/96.

31. "The Government's Tin Program," 222; Johnson and Espy, MC, 17 November 1947, NAII, RG 59, 824.6354

32. Canedo Reyes to King, 3 November 1947, NAII, RG 59, 824.6354.

33. Ibid.
34. Daniels to Armour, 19 December 1947; Daniels to Armour, 22 December 1947, both in NAII, RG 59, 824.6354.
35. Espy to Mills, Flack, Woodward, Daniels, and Armour, 8 December 1947; Flack to Espy, 21 October 1947; Espy to Daniels, 16 December 1947, all in NAII, RG 59, 824.6354.
36. Flack to Espy, 21 October 1947; Flack to Secretary, 25 July 1947, both in NAII, RG 59, 824.6354; see also *American Metal Market*, June 24, 1947; Lehman, *Bolivia and the United States*, 97.
37. Martínez Vargas Speech, n.d., AMRECB, EEUU-1-R-51/98.
38. Martínez Vargas a Ministro, 22 de agosto de 1947, AMRECB, EEUU-1-R-50/96; Braden to Lovett and Armour, 27 June 1947, NAII, RG 84, ELP, Classified, 800.
39. Johnson and Espy, MC, 17 November 1947, RG 59. 824.6354.
40. Espy to Mills and Daniels, 9 December 1947, NAII, RG 59, 824.6354.
41. Marshall to Embassy Hague, 11 August 1947; Douglas to Secretary, 24 July 1947; Baruch to Secretary, 21 August 1947, all in NAII, RG 59, 824.6354.
42. Marshall to Embassy Hague, 21 August 1947; see also Espy to Kennedy, 22 October 1947, both in NAII, RG 59, 824.6354.
43. The British, although "anxious not to give the appearance of collusion," had informed the State Department that the Bolivians would accept 85¢ per pound and asked to be kept informed of the status of negotiations in Washington. As quoted in Douglas to Secretary, 28 November 1947; Espy to Daniels, 3 December 1947, both in NAII, RG 59, 824.6354; "The Government's Tin Program," 223–27; Espy to Mills, Flack, Woodward, Daniels, and Armour, 8 December 1947; Lovett to Embassy London, 12 December 1947, both in NAII, RG 59, 824.6254.
44. Solares a Ministro, 30 de diciembre de 1947; Solares a Ministro, 24 de diciembre de 1947; see also Solares a Martínez Vargas, 20 de diciembre de 1947, all in AMRECB, GRBT-1-R-50/64.
45. The New York price of tin was traditionally 2 to 3¢ per pound higher than London or Singapore price. Mills to Daniels, Lyon, and Anderson, 31 December 1947, NAII, RG 59, 824.6354; see also Solares a Ministro, 10 de enero de 1948, AMRECB, GRBT-1-R-51/65.
46. Martínez Vargas a Ministro, 12 de febrero de 1948; see also Jewett to Martínez Vargas, 5 February 1948, both in AMRECB, EEUU-1-R-51/97.
47. Johnson and Espy, MC, 17 November 1947, NAII, RG 59, 824.6354; see also Martínez Vargas a Ministro, 23 de diciembre de 1948, AMRECB, EEUU-1-R-51/99.
48. Johnson, "Probable Economic and Political Consequences of Recent Price Increases for Bolivian Tin," 23 July 1948, NAII, RG 234, MRC, Restricted and Confidential Materials, 1.
49. Martínez Vargas, "Notas complementarias al memorandum," 19 de abril de 1948, AMRECB, EEUU-1-R-51/91; Martínez Vargas a Ministro, 17 de mayo de 1948, AMRECB, EEUU-1-R-51/98; Memorandum for Flack, 22 April 1948, NAII, RG 59, 824.00.
50. Querejazu a Ministro, 5 de noviembre de 1948, AMRECB, GRBT-1-R-51/65; Martínez Vargas a Gutiérrez, 28 de abril de 1948, AMRECB, EEUU-1-R-51/98.
51. Querejazu a Ministro, 5 de noviembre de 1948, AMRECB, GRBT-1-R-51/65; see also Martínez Vargas, Armour, and Espy, MC, 17 May 1948, NAII, RG 59, 824.6354; Johnson, "Probably Economic and Political Consequences of Recent Price Increases for Bolivian Tin," 23 July 1948, NAII, RG 234, MRC, Restricted and Confidential Materials, 1.
52. Embajada Bolivia, "Memorandum," 13 de mayo de 1948, AMRECB, EEUU-1-R-52/102; Orloski to Secretary, 8 January 1948, NAII, RG 59, 824.6354.
53. Galbraith to Secretary, 2 March 1948, NAII, RG 59, 824.00; Johnson, "Bolivian International Economic Relations in 1948," NAII, RG 84, ELP, Classified, 850.
54. Flack to Secretary, 16 June 1948, NAII, RG 84, ELP, Classified, 800; Espy to ARA (Office of American Republics Affairs, until 1949), 9 July 1948, NAII, RG 59, 824.00.
55. Galbraith to Secretary, 19 December 1947, NAII, RG 59, 824.00.
56. Flack to Secretary, 20 April 1948; Flack to Secretary, 3 May 1948; Byington to Secretary, 5 August 1948, all in NAII, RG 59, 824.00.
57. Flack to Secretary, 28 July 1948, NAII, RG 59, 824.00; see also Flack to Secretary, 22 November 1948, NAII, RG 84, ELP, Classified, 800.

58. Martínez Vargas and Espy, MC, 28 August 1948, NAII, RG 59, 824.00; Espy to Neal, 13 April 1948, NAII, RG 84, ELP, Classified, 851.

59. Flack to Secretary, 22 November 1948, NAII, RG 84, ELP, Classified, 800.

60. Espy to Secretary, 4 October 1949; Flack to Secretary, 8 October 1948; Flack to Secretary, 4 June 1948, all in NAII, RG 59, 824.00.

61. The State Department viewed the MNR victory as a positive development: "It is hard to believe that the PURS and its associates and supporting parties will fail to heed the lesson of the MNR showing." As quoted in Galbraith to Secretary, 19 December 1947; Flack to Secretary, 19 May 1948; see also Flack to Secretary, 9 April 1947, all in NAII, RG 59, 824.00.

62. Galbraith, "First Year of the Hertzog Government," May 1948, NAII, RG 59, 824.00.

63. Embassy La Paz, "Interview with President Hertzog," n.d., NAII, RG 84, ELP, Classified, 851; Martínez Vargas a Ministro, 9 de julio de 1948, AMRECB, EEUU-1-R-51/98; see also Flack to Secretary, 30 September 1948; Johnson, "Bolivian International Economic Relations in 1948," both in NAII, RG 84, ELP, Classified, 850.

64. Johnson, "Bolivian International Economic Relations in 1948," NAII, RG 84, ELP, Classified, 850.

65. Gosálvez a Ministro, 6 de julio de 1948, AMRECB, EEUU-1-R-76/169; Formichelli a Ministro, 3 de febrero de 1948, AMRECA, Bolivia 1948, 1, 1; see also Galbraith to Secretary, 30 January 1948, NAII, RG 59, 824.6354.

66. Bruce to Secretary of State, 22 April 1948, RG 59, 711.35; Hertzog, as quoted in Gosálvez a Ministro, 18 de mayo de 1948, AMRECB, ARG-1-R-76/167; Formichelli a Ministro, 8 de junio de 1948, AMRECA, Bolivia 1948, 1, 2.

67. Gosálvez a Ministro, 6 de julio de 1948; Gosálvez a Ministro, 3 de julio de 1948, both in AMRECB, ARG-1-R-67/169.

68. Gosálvez a Ministro, 25 de setiembre de 1948, AMRECB, ARG-1-R-76/171; Gosálvez a Ministro, 21 de enero de 1949; Gosálvez a Ministro, 11 de enero de 1949, both in AMRECB, ARG-1-R-77/175.

69. Gosálvez a Ministro, 3 de julio de 1948, AMRECB, ARG-1-R-76/169; Gosálvez a Ministro, 11 de enero de 1949, AMRECB, ARG-1-R-77/175; Espy to Flack, 3 January 1949, NAII, RG 84, 851.

70. The Argentines believed that Hertzog's dire personal problems "broke his morale," but his "patriotic devotion to save his country from a crisis of gravest consequences" led him to remain in office. Mujica Garmendia a Ministro, 13 de setiembre de 1948, AMRECA, Bolivia 1948, 1, 1, 2a; Galbraith to Secretary, 14 April, 1949, NAII, RG 59, 824.00; Argentine Embassy, as quoted in Flack to Secretary, 1 September 1948, NAII, RG 84, ELP, Classified, 800.

71. King to Mills and Woodward, 9 May 1949; Flack to Secretary, 3 December 1948, both in NAII, RG 59, 824.00.

72. Hertzog, as quoted in Flack to Secretary, 25 October 1948, NAII, RG 59, 824.00.

73. Flack to Secretary, 15 February 1949, NAII, RG 59, 824.00

74. Ibid.; King to Mills, Woodward, and Oakley, 30 March 1949, NAII, RG 59, 824.00.

75. Hertzog, as quoted in Flack to Secretary, 18 April 1949, NAII, RG 84, ELP. Classified, 500.

76. King to Mills and Woodward, 9 May 1949, NAII, RG 59, 824.00.

77. Ibid.

78. Flack to Secretary, 21 December 1948, NAII, RG 59, 824.00.

79. Flack to Espy, 21 October 1947, NAII, RG 59, 824.6354; Galbraith, "First Year of the Hertzog Government," May 1948, NAII, RG 59, 824.00; see also Gosálvez a Ministro, 14 de febrero de 1948, AMRECB, ARG-1-R-76/173.

CHAPTER 4

The first epigraph to this chapter is drawn from Barber to Webb, 9 March 1950; the second, from Barber to O'Gara, 10 April 1950, both in NAII, RG 59, 824.2544.

1. King to Miller, 15 September 1949, NAII, RG 59, 824.00; Eaton, "Annual Labor Report—Bolivia—1949," n.d., NAII, RG 84, ELP, General, 680.

2. Eaton, "Annual Labor Report—Bolivia—1949," n.d.; Eaton, "Monthly Labor Report," December 1949, both in NAII, RG 84, ELP, General, 680.

3. King to Barber and Mills, 5 August 1949; see also Espy to Secretary, 27 August 1949; Espy to Secretary, 30 August 1949, all in NAII, RG 59, 824.00.

4. Embajada en La Paz, "Situación política de Bolivia," n.d., AMRECA, Bolivia 1949, 1, 1; Espy to Secretary, 30 August 1949; Tittmann to Secretary, 4 September 1949; see also Bowers to Secretary, 6 September 1949, all in NAII, RG 59, 824.00.

5. Espy to Secretary, 27 August 1949; see also Acheson to Miller, 28 August 1949, both in NAII, RG 59, 824.00; Ríos Gamboa, *Bolivia*, 89–90.

6. Barber to Webb and Rusk, 30 August 1949; Martínez Vargas, Gutierrez, Rusk, and King, MC, 30 August 1949, both in NAII, RG 59, 824.00; see also Flack to Secretary, 25 April 1947, NAII, RG 84, ELP, Classified, 800.

7. Barber to Rusk, 30 August 1949, NAII, RG 59, 824.00; Martínez Vargas, Miller, and King, MC, 6 September 1949, NAII, RG 84, ELP, Classified, 350; see also Acheson to Miller, 30 August 1949, NAII, RG 59, 824.00.

8. Barber to Rusk, 30 August 1949; Martínez Vargas, Gutierrez, Rusk, and King, MC, 30 August 1949; Espy to Secretary, 1 September 1949, all in NAII, RG 59, 824.00.

9. Bowers to Secretary, 30 August 1949; Bowers to Secretary, 30 August 1949; Bowers to Secretary, 1 September 1949; Nieto, Barber, and Krieg, MC, 1 September 1949, all in NAII, RG 59, 824.00.

10. Gosálvez a Ministro, 3 de septiembre de 1949, AMRECB, ARG-1-R-77/103; Dunkerley, *Bolivia*, 245; Mallory to Secretary, 2 September 1949; see also Acheson to Embassy Buenos Aires, 14 September 1949, both in NAII, RG 59, 824.00.

11. Remorino, Quiros, Miller, and Tewksbury, MC, 13 September 1949, NAII, RG 59, 824.00; Miller, Shay, Adams, and Mills, MC, 4 October 1949, NAII, RG 84, ELP, Classified, 350.

12. Martínez Vargas a Ministro, 12 de septiembre de 1949, AMRECB, EEUU-1-R-52/101; Kreig to Barber 6 September 1949, NAII, RG 59, 824.00; Martínez Vargas a Ministro, n.d., AMRECB, EEUU-1-R-52/102.

13. Tewksbury to Barber, 6 September 1949, NAII, RG 59, 824.00. Even the 9 September statement was too much for the CIO's Martin Kyne, who thought that "silence would have been better." Declaring that Urriolagoitia's antilabor activities had "deprived" his government of "any legitimate connection with democracy" and "justified" the "current MNR insurrection," Kyne believed it would be "more merciful to shoot the labor leaders than to deny them the right to walk in the sun of freedom." Kyne, Schwartz, Swayzee, Horowitz, Fishburn, and King, MC, 13 September 1949, NAII, RG 59, 824.00.

14. Espy to Secretary, 8 November 1949; Barber to Rusk, 30 August 1949, both in NAII, RG 59, 824.00; Miller to Dreier, 13 October 1949, NAII, RG 59, RASSLAA, 1949–53, Bolivia.

15. King to Barber, 31 August 1949; Martínez Vargas, Miller, and King, MC, 6 September 1949; see also Espy to Secretary, 27 September 1949, all in NAII, RG 59, 824.00.

16. Espy to Secretary, 4 October 1949; see also King to Barber, Krieg, and McGinnis, 12 September 1949, both in NAII, RG 59, 824.00.

17. Espy to Secretary, 4 October 1949, NAII, RG 59, 824.00; Flack to Secretary, 27 October 1949, NAII, RG 59, 711.24.

18. Flack to Secretary, 27 October 1949, NAII, RG 59, 711.24; Espy to Department, 10 February 1950, NAII, RG 59, 724.00; Espy to Secretary, 9 November 1949, NAII, RG 59, 824.00.

19. Miller to Espy, 29 September 1949, NAII, RG 59, 824.00.

20. U.S. officials did break their silence once to refute claims that the United States had taken a hand in the revolt. Apparently, Bolivian government warplanes still bearing U.S. insignia had fallen into the hands of "treacherous and treasonous" rebel military leaders who employed them for bombing the Cochabamba airport. Espy to Secretary, 30 August 1949; Espy to Secretary, 4 October 1949, both in NAII, RG 59, 824.00.

21. Blocking Soviet access to tin also played a role in the decision to maintain the RFC monopoly. McKinnon Memorandum 19 August 1949, NAII, RG 234, MRC, TP, ASF, 1942–54; see also McGinnis to Secretary, 26 September 1949, NAII, RG 59, 824.6354.

22. McKinnon to Croston, 21 September 1950; Harber, "Pricing Notes," 15 April 1951; McKinnon to Directors, 21 November 1949; see also McKinnon Memorandum 19 August 1949, all in NAII, RG 234, MRC, TP, ASF, 1942–54.

23. Martínez Vargas a Ministro, 27 de enero de 1948, AMRECB, EEUU-1-R-51/97; see also Martínez Vargas a Ministro, 11 de mayo de 1949, AMRECB, EEUU-1-R-52/101.

24. Espy to Department, 10 February 1950, NAII, RG 59, 724.00; see also Espy to Secretary, 2 December 1949, NAII, RG 59, 824.00; Espy to Secretary, 12 December 1949, NAII, RG 59, 824.6354.

25. Embassy La Paz to Department of State, 13 January 1950, NAII, RG 59, 724.00; Miller to Acheson, 26 January 1950, NAII, RG 59, 824.2544; Johnson to Espy, 28 December 1949, NAII, RG 59, 724.00.

26. Embassy La Paz to Department, 21 December 1949, NAII, RG 59, 824.00; Espy to Department, 26 January 1950, NAII, RG 59, 724.00.

27. Embassy La Paz to Department, 13 January 1950; Espy to Department, 18 February 1950, both in NAII, RG 59, 724.00.

28. Espy to Department, 10 February 1950, NAII, RG 59, 724.00; see also Embassy La Paz to Department, 21 December 1949, NAII, RG 59, 824.00; Urriolagoitia and Gorman, MC, 12 July 1949; Johnson to Secretary, 17 December 1949, both in NAII, RG 59, 824.5017.

29. Espy to Department, 10 February 1950, NAII, RG 59, 724.00; Espy to Secretary, 4 October 1949, NAII, RG 59, 824.00.

30. Martínez Vargas, Miller, King, MC, 19 October 1949, NAII, RG 59, 711.24; Martínez Vargas, Ostria Gutierrez, Miller, and King, MC, 12 October 1949, NAII, RG 84, ELP, Classified, 360. Martínez Vargas also tried to persuade his superiors that he had received prompt and effective assistance from President Truman and the State Department. Martínez Vargas a Ministro, 20 de octubre de 1949, AMREC, EEUU-1-R-52/102.

31. Ostria Gutiérrez, as quoted in Martínez Vargas a Ministro, 29 de octubre de 1949, AMRECB, EEUU-1-R-52/102; Espy to Department, 10 February 1950, NAII, RG 59, 724.00;

32. Espy to Secretary, 6 February 1950, NAII, RG 59, 724.001; Martínez Vargas and King, MC, 13 February 1950; Ingraham to Department, 28 March 1950; Hall to Secretary, 20 April 1950, all in NAII, RG 59, 724.00; see also Martínez Vargas a Ministro, 8 de junio de 1950, EEUU-1-R-53/104.

33. Ingraham to Department, 28 March 1950; Florman to Secretary, 28 March 1950; Espy to Department, 18 February 1950; Martínez Vargas and King, MC, 13 February 1950, all in NAII, RG 59, 724.00; see also Martínez Vargas a Ministro, 3 de marzo de 1950; Embajada Bolivia, "Memorandum," 21 de febrero de 1950, both in AMRECB, EEUU-1-R-53/103.

34. Florman to Secretary, 6 April 1950, NAII, RG 59, 824.00; Florman to Barber, 19 May 1950, NAII, RG 59, 824.2544. Florman originally declared that "the Communist problem in Bolivia is nil" and the government's opponents "cannot be called Communist by any stretch of the imagination." By May, however, he had expended a "great deal of work" to "compile and collate" his bizarre theory. Florman to Secretary, 23 March 1950, NAII, RG 59, 724.001; Florman to Barber, 19 May 1950, NAII, RG 59, 824.2544.

35. Martínez Vargas, Barber, and King, MC, 23 February 1950, NAII, RG 59, 724.001; Espy to Department, 5 April 1950; Espy to Department, 18 May 1950, both in NAII, RG 59, 724.00.

36. Florman to Department, 14 July 1950, NAII, RG 59, 824.2544; Martínez Vargas a Ministro, 21 de enero de 1950, AMRECB, EEUU-1-R-53/103; see also Miller to Florman, 7 August 1950, NAII, RG 59, RASSLAA, 1949–53, Bolivia; "Idea Man," *Time*, 6 November 1950.

37. Florman to Secretary, 12 April 1950, NAII, RG 59, 724.00; Florman to Secretary, 14 July 1950, NAII, RG 59, 824.2544; Florman to Secretary, 13 April 1950, NAII, RG 59, 724.00; Florman to Department, 28 July 1950, NAII, RG 59, 824.2544.

38. Florman to Department, 29 May 1950, NAII, RG 59, 724.00; "Idea Man," *Time*, 6 November 1950; see also Florman to Secretary, 23 March 1950, NAII, RG 59, 724.001.

39. Johnson to Department, 11 May 1950, NAII, RG 59, 824.2544; Florman to Department, 12 April 1950; see also Florman to Secretary, 5 April 1950; Espy to Department, 5 May 1950, all in NAII, RG 59, 724.00 .

40. Espy to Department, 18 May 1950; Espy to Department, 5 May 1950, both in NAII, RG 59, 724.00.

41. Espy to Department, 18 May 1950; King to Barber and Atwood, 19 May 1950; Espy to Department, 5 May 1950, all in NAII, RG 59, 724.00.
42. Espy to Department, 24 July 1950; Florman to Secretary, 10 September 1950; Florman to Department, 14 September 1950, all in NAII, RG 59, 724.00.
43. Maleady to Department, 17 October 1950, NAII, RG 59, 724.00.
44. Crandall to Department, 22 August 1950; Acheson to Embassy La Paz, 22 August 1950, both in NAII, RG 59, 724.00. New U.S. Embassy Counselor Thomas Maleady found the tension "greatly disturbing" and sensed that "some spark may cause catastrophe." To him, it was even more disturbing that others seemed to consider the situation routine and "more or less normal in politically abnormal Bolivia." Maleady to Department, 29 August 1950, NAII, RG 59, 724.00.
45. Florman to Department, 14 June 1950, NAII, RG 59, 724.00; Florman to Barber, 19 May 1950, NAII, RG 59, 824.2544; Florman to Department, 15 June 1950, NAII, RG 59, 724.001.
46. Martínez Vargas, Miller, and King, MC, 21 October 1949 NAII, RG 59, 824.6354; McKinnon to Directors, 13 March 1951, NAII, RG 234, MRC, TP, ASF, 1942–54.
47. Mills, McGinnis, King, Hamilton, and Getzin, MC, 24 February 1949, NAII, RG 59, 824.6354; McKinnon Memorandum, 23 May 1949, NAII, RG 234, MRC, TP, ASF, 1942–54.
48. Hise to Acheson, 6 July 1949, NAII, RG 59, 824.6354. The State Department calculated that the new taxes imposed by President Hertzog amounted to approximately 7¢ per pound. Johnson to Secretary, 26 April 1949, NAII, 824.6354.
49. Rovensky, Royce, Caverly, Mills, and King, MC, 7 June 1949; Royce, Miller, King, and McGinnis, MC, 14 September 1949, both in NAII, RG 59, 824.6354; see also Espy to Secretary, 26 July 1949, NAII, RG 59, 824.50; Linz, Miller, and King, MC, 12 October 1949, NAII, RG 59, 824.7354.
50. Thorp to Hise, 6 July 1949, NAII, RG 59, 824.6354; see also Johnson to Secretary, 4 January 1950, NAII, RG 59, 824.2544.
51. Canedo Reyes, as quoted in Johnson to Secretary, 4 January 1950, NAII, RG 59, 824.2544.
52. Martínez Vargas, "Memorandum para el Departamento de Estado," 20 de enero de 1950, AMRECB, EEUU-1-R-53/103; Martínez Vargas, Miller, Mills, Getzin, and King, MC, 25 January 1950; Martínez Vargas, Miller, and King, MC, 26 January 1950, both in NAII, RG 59, 824.2544; Martínez Vargas a Ministro, 11 de mayo de 1949, AMRECB, EEUU-1-R-52/101.
53. Royce, Miller, King, and McGinnis, MC, 14 September 1949; Martínez Vargas, Miller, Mills, Getzin, and King, MC, 25 January 1950 both in NAII, RG 59, 824.2544.
54. Johnson to Department, 9 February 1950, NAII, RG 59, 824.10; Johnson to Secretary, 4 January 1950, NAII, RG 59, 824.2544.
55. Miller, McCormick, Bramble, and Getzin, MC, 18 January 1950; Costin, Curtis, Getzin, and King, MC, 18 January 1950, both in NAII, RG 59, 824.2544.
56. Barber to Acheson, 31 October 1949, NAII, RG 59, 824.00; Barber to Webb, 9 March 1950, NAII, RG 59, 824.2544.
57. Martínez Vargas, Miller, and King, MC, 26 January 1950; King to Mills, 3 February 1950; McKinnon and Getzin, MC, 1 March 1950; Mills to Miller, 24 January 1950, all in NAII, RG 59, 824.2544; see also Martínez Vargas a Ministro, 27 de enero de 1950, AMRECB, EEUU-1-R-53/103.
58. Miller to Acheson, 26 January 1950; Mills to Miller, 24 January 1950, both in NAII, RG 59, 824.2544.
59. Johnson to Espy, 28 December 1949, NAII, RG 59, 724.00; Martínez Vargas, Terrazas, and King, MC, 8 March 1950; Thorp, Kenney, Getzin, and King, MC, 3 February 1950, both in NAII, RG 59, 824.2544.
60. Martínez Vargas a Ministro, 27 de enero de 1950, AMRECB, EEUU-1-R-53/103; Martínez Vargas, Terrazas, and King, MC, 8 March 1950; see also Martínez Vargas, Peñaranda, Atwood, Spaulding and King, MC, 22 June 1950, both in NAII, RG 59, 824.2544.
61. Martínez Vargas, Barber, Mills, and King, MC, 20 March 1950, NAII, RG 59, 824.2544; Martínez Vargas a Ministro, 27 de enero de 1950; see also Martínez Vargas a Acheson, 27 de enero de 1950, both in AMRECB, EEUU-1-R-53/103; Martínez Vargas a Ministro, 23 de junio de 1950, AMRECB, EEUU-1-R-53/104.

NOTES TO PAGES 115–122

62. Martínez Vargas, Peñaranda, Atwood, Spaulding, and King, MC, 22 June 1950; see also Barber to Webb, 9 March 1950; Barber to O'Gara, 10 April 1950, all in NAII, RG 59, 824.2544.

63. Johnson to Department, 9 March 1950, NAII, RG 59, 824.2544; Embassy La Paz, "Six Month Economic Report," 9 August 1950, NAII, RG 59, 824.00; Espy to Department, 5 May 1950, NAII, RG 59, 724.00.

64. McKinnon to Directors, 23 February 1951; McKinnon to Croston, 21 September 1950, both in NAII, RG 234, MRC, TP, ASF, 1942–54; Querejazu Calvo a Ministro, 23 de agosto de 1950, AMRECB, GRBT-1-R-52/66; see also Embassy La Paz, "Six Months Economic Report," NAII, RG 84, ELP, General, 500.

65. McKinnon and King, MC, 3 July 1950; see also Acheson to Embassy La Paz, 3 July 1950; Hudson to Secretary, 31 July 1950, all in NAII, RG 59, 824.2544; Martínez Vargas a Ministro, 23 de junio de 1950, AMRECB, EEUU-1-R-53/104.

66. Florman to Department, 5 July 1950; Martínez Vargas, Peñaranda, Barber, Spalding, and King, MC, 17 July 1950, both in NAII, RG 59, 824.2544.

CHAPTER 5

The first epigraph to this chapter is drawn from Cobb to Department, 10 May 1951; the second, from Paz Estenssoro, as quoted in Bunker to Secretary, 18 May 1951, both in NAII, RG 59, 724.00.

1. Espy to Department, 24 July 1950, NAII, RG 59, 724.00.

2. Florman to Secretary, 14 August 1950; Hudson to Department, 17 August 1950, both in NAII, RG 59, 824.2544.

3. Hudson to Department, 17 August 1950; Acheson to Embassy La Paz, 25 August 1950, both in NAII, RG 59, 824.2544; Florman to Secretary, 16 August 1950, NAII, RG 59, 724.00.

4. Hudson to Department 17 August 1950; Hudson to Department, 18 September 1950, both in NAII, RG 59, 824.2544.

5. Acheson to Embassy La Paz, 25 August 1950, NAII, RG 59, 824.2544; McKinnon Statement Before Preparedness Subcommittee, 26 September 1950, NAII, RG 234, MRC, Restricted and Confidential Material; Webb to Embassy La Paz, 25 August 1950, NAII, RG 59, 824.2544.

6. Florman to Secretary, 27 August 1950; Acheson to Embassy La Paz, 28 August 1950; Florman to Secretary, 29 August 1950, all in NAII, RG 59, 824.2544.

7. Florman to Secretary, 29 August 1950; Florman to Secretary, 6 September 1950, both in NAII, RG 59, 824.2544.

8. Florman to Secretary, 3 October 1950; Maleady to Atwood, 4 September 1951, both in NAII, RG 59, 824.2544.

9. Florman to Department, 25 August 1950; Maleady to Department, 10 October 1950; see also Florman to Department, 3 October 1950, all in NAII, RG 59, 824.2544.

10. Miller could only express "surprise" at Florman's outburst and disavow it. Keenleyside, Hickerson, Bennett, Miller, et al., MC, 27 June 1951, NAII, RG 59, RASSLAA, 1949–53, Bolivia. Florman to Department, 25 August 1950; see also Florman to Secretary, 29 August 1950, both in NAII, RG 59, 824.2544.

11. Miller to King, 14 December 1950; Keenleyside, Miller, and King, MC, 1 September 1950, both in NAII, RG 59, RASSLAA, 1949–53, Bolivia; Maleady, "Bolivian Dilemma," 2 April 1952, NAII, RG 59, 824.00; "Keenleyside Report," 1, 32–44; see also Bolivian Statement in ECOSOC, n.d., NAII, RG 84, ELP, General, 350; Rovensky to Miller, 22 August 1950; Atwood to Rovensky, 22 August 1950, both in NAII, RG 59, 611.24.

12. Embassy La Paz to Department, 3 November 1950, NAII, RG 59, 824.2544; Florman to Secretary, 11 October 1950, NAII, RG 59, 724.00.

13. Florman to Department, 20 October 1950; Florman to Department, 13 October 1950, both in NAII, RG 59, 824.2544; Florman to Department, 2 February 1951, NAII, RG 59, 724.00; Florman to Department, 2 January 1951, NAII, RG 59, 824.2544.

14. Maleady to Hudson, 19 February 1951, NAII, RG 59, 4.2544; Maleady to Miller, 10 December 1951, NAII, RG 59, RASSLAA, 1949–53, Bolivia; Maleady to Hudson, 7 March 1951, NAII, RG 59, 824.2544; Miller to Maleady, 4 December 1951, NAII, RG 59, RASSLAA, 1949–53, Bolivia.

15. Maleady to Hudson, 19 March 1951, NAII, RG 59, 824.2544; Maleady to Department, 27 October 1950; Maleady to Department, 3 November 1950, both in NAII, RG 59, 724.00.

16. Maleady to Hudson, 19 March 1951; Florman to Mann, 9 September 1951, both in NAII, RG 59, 824.2544.

17. "Summary of 1951 Bolivian Tin Negotiations," n.d., NAII, RG 234, MRC, Restricted and Confidential Material; Lehman, *Bolivia and the United States*, 97.

18. Harber to Harrison, 1 March 1951; Harrison to Harber, 16 March 1951, both in NAII, RG 234, MRC, Restricted and Confidential Material; Harrison to Harber, 5 April 1951, NAII, RG 234, MRC, TP, ASF, 1942–54.

19. Martínez Vargas a Ministro, 19 de enero de 1951; see also Martínez Vargas a Ministro, 12 de febrero de 1951; Martínez Vargas a Ministro, 25 de enero de 1951, all in EEUU-1-R-54/107.

20. Brown to Kayle, n.d., HSTPL, WHCF, State Department Trade Agreements.

21. McKinnon to Directors, 21 February 1951, NAII, RG 234, MRC, TP, ASF, 1942–54; Symington, "New Concepts of the RFC," 4 December 1951, AMRECB, EEUU-1-R-54/111; McKinnon to Directors, 12 March 1951; McKinnon to Directors, 13 March 1951; see also Gibson to Larson, 23 February 1951, all in NAII, RG 234, MRC, TP, ASF, 1942–54.

22. McKinnon to Directors, 23 February 1951; McKinnon to Directors, 17 April 1951; see also McKinnon to Directors, 11 April 1951, all in NAII, RG 234, MRC, TP, ASF, 1942–54.

23. Harber to Harrison, 22 March 1951; McKinnon to Oberfell, 11 December 1950, both in NAII, RG 234, MRC, TP, ASF, 1942–54; see also DPA, "Tin," 14 May 1951, NAII, RG 234, MRC, Restricted and Confidential Material.

24. McKinnon to Administrator (Chairman), 10 July 1952; Shannon to Symington, 22 July 1951, both in NAII, RG 234, MRC, TP, ASF, 1942–54.

25. McKinnon to Directors, 29 March 1951; Harrison, as quoted in McKinnon to Directors, 3 April 1951; see also Statement of Wylie F. McKinnon, Chief of the Tin Division, Reconstruction Finance Corporation, 12 June 1950, all in NAII, RG 234, MRC, TP, ASF, 1942–54.

26. Gibson to Larson, 23 February 1951, NAII, RG 234, MRC, Restricted and Confidential Material; Harber to Harrison, 22 March 1951, NAII, RG 234, MRC, TP, ASF, 1942–54; McKinnon Memorandum for the Directors, 21 February 1951, NAII, RG 234, MRC, TP, ASF, 1942–54, 4; see also Gibson to Larson, 15 March 1951, NAII, RG 234, MRC, Restricted and Confidential Material.

27. McKinnon to Directors, 17 April 1951; see also McKinnon to Directors, 11 April 1951; RFC, "Report on Tin Operations for Six Months Ending December 31, 1951," all in NAII, MRC, TP, ASF, 1942–54.

28. McKinnon to Directors, 29 March 1951; Harber to Harrison, 16 April 1951, both in NAII, RG 234, MRC, TP, ASF, 1942–54; McKinnon to Administrator (Chairman), 12 June 1951, NAII, RG 234, MRC, TP, ASF, 1942–54, 4; see also McKinnon to Barrows, 14 November 1951, NAII, RG 234, MRC, TP, ASF, 1942–54.

29. Atwood to Miller, 13 March 1951, NAII, RG 59, 824.2544.

30. Cook, as quoted in McKinnon Memorandum to the Administrator (Chairman), 29 May 1951, NAII, RG 234, MRC, TP, ASF, 1942–54.

31. McKinnon Memorandum to the Administrator (Chairman), 16 May 1951, NAII, RG 234, MRC, TP, ASF, 1942–54.

32. Harber to Harrison, 22 March 1951, NAII, RG 234, MRC, TP, ASF, 1942–54; Florman to Department, 9 March 1951, NAII, RG 59, 824.2544; O'Gara, Schaetzel, Malenbaum, et al., MC, 11 August 1950, NAII, RG 59, 824.00.

33. Florman to Department, 9 March 1951; Florman to Department, 12 March 1951, both in NAII, RG 59, 824.2544. Florman also somehow concluded that the British were "obviously" using millions of Marshall Plan dollars to purchase Bolivian tin that they then shipped to the Soviets. Florman to Department, 24 March 1950, NAII, RG59, 824.2544.

34. Florman to Department, 29 December 1950, NAII, RG 59, 724.00; see also Navia Ribera, *Los Estados Unidos*, 98–100. The Argentine Embassy considered Gosálvez to be a "master of Machiavellianism" whose "traditional *altoperuano* attitude is pervaded by the subtlety of the psychology of insincerity." Rios Marmol, "Informe sobre la situacion de Bolivia durante los meses de mayo y junio de 1949," 28 de junio de 1949, AMRECA, Bolivia 1949, 1, 1.

35. Maleady to Department, 16 January 1951; Maleady to Department, 7 March 1951, both in NAII, RG 59, 724.00.

36. Maleady to Department, 7 March 1951; Cobb to Department, 19 April 1951; King to Krieg and Warren, 8 November 1950, all in NAII, RG 59, 724.00.

37. Maleady to Department, 16 January 1951; Cobb to Department, 29 January 1951; King to Kreig and Warren, 8 November 1950; Florman to Secretary, 26 January 1951; Maleady to Department, 7 March 1951, all in NAII, RG 59, 724.00.

38. Cobb to Department, 19 April 1951; see also Maleady to Department, 7 March 1951; Maleady to Department, 16 April 1951, all in NAII, RG 59, 724.00.

39. Cobb to Department, 19 April 1951; see also Maleady to Department, 16 April 1951; Maleady to Department 23 April 1951, all in NAII, RG 59, 724.00.

40. Maleady to Department, 23 April 1951; Maleady to Department, 11 May 1951, both in NAII, RG 59, 724.00.

41. Maleady to Department, 7 March 1951, NAII, RG 59, 724.00; see also Prado Salmon, *Poder y fuerzas armadas, 1949–1982*, 15. The MNR was the primary beneficiary of the PIR's downward spiral as former piristas who, in James Dunkerley's words, preferred "direct action to earnest reading groups" defected to Paz Estenssoro's or Lechín's camp. Dunkerley, *Bolivia*, 219.

42. Cobb to Department, 14 April 1951, NAII, RG 59, 724.00; Florman to Secretary, 7 March 1951, NAII, RG 59, 824.2544; *El Diario*, as quoted in Cobb to Department, 11 April 1951; see also Cobb to Department, 12 April 1951, both in NAII, RG 84, ELP, General, 350.

43. Martínez Vargas, Peñaranda, Loza, Atwood, and Hudson, MC, 10 April 1951; Martínez Vargas, Mann, Atwood, and Hudson, MC, 10 April 1951; Zilveti, Martínez Vargas, Romero, Miller, Atwood, and Hudson, MC, 5 April 1951, all in NAII, RG 59, 824.00.

44. Florman to Department, 2 February 1951; Cobb to Department, 7 May 1951, both in NAII, RG 59, 724.00; Cobb to Department, 14 May 1951, NAII, RG 84, ELP, General, 361.2.

45. Maleady to Department, 15 May 1951, NAII, RG 59, 724.00; see also Mesa Gisbert, de Mesa, and Gisbert, *Historia de Bolivia*, 570–71.

46. Guachalla, Miller, and Hudson, MC, 25 April 1952, NAII, RG 59, 724.00; see also Cobb to Department, 8 May 1951, NAII, RG 59, 714.00.

47. Maleady to Department, 15 May 1951, NAII, RG 59, 724.00; Martínez Vargas a Ministro, 1 de junio de 1951, AMRECB, EEUU-1-R-54/109.

48. Maleady to Department, 15 May 1951; Martínez Vargas, Peñaranda, Miller, and Hudson, MC, 9 May 1951; see also Bunker to Secretary, 18 May 1951, all in NAII, RG 59, 724.00.

49. Maleady to Department, 7 May 1951; Maleady to Secretary, 8 May 1951, both in NAII, RG 59, 724.00; Miller to Bowers, 21 May 1951, NAII, RG 59, RASSLAA, 1949–53, Bolivia; see also Acheson to Embassy La Paz, 7 May 1951, NAII, RG 59, 724.00.

50. Miller to Flack, 15 May 1951, HSTPL, Edward G. Miller Papers, Joseph Flack File; Cobb to Department, 8 June 1951; Hall to Department, 25 May 1951, both in NAII, RG 59, 724.00; see also Prado Salmon, *Poder y fuerzas armadas*, 20–22.

51. Cobb to Department, 8 May 1951; Neathery to Department, 14 May 1951, both in NAII, RG 59, 724.00; see also Prado Salmon, *Poder y fuerzas armadas*, 25.

52. Maleady to Secretary, 15 May 1951; Pool to Department, 24 May 1951; Pool to Department, 28 May 1951, all in NAII, RG 59, 724.00.

53. Hall to Department, 18 May 1951; Hall to Department, 25 May 1951, both in NAII, RG 59, 724.00.

54. Maleady to Department, 20 November 1950; see also Pool to Department, 31 May 1951, both in NAII, RG 59, 724.00.

55. Maleady to Department, 22 May 1951; Ballivián, as quoted in Cobb to Secretary, 16 May 1951, both in NAII, RG 59, 724.00.

56. Prado Salmon, *Poder y fuerzas armadas*, 28; Cobb to Department, 8 June 1951; see also Maleady to Secretary, 16 May 1951, both in NAII, RG 59, 724.00.

57. Maleady to Department, 17 May 1951; see also Maleady to Department, 1 June 1951, NAII, RG 59, 724.00.

58. Cobb to Department, 8 June 1951; Maleady to Department, 11 June 1951, both in NAII, RG 59, 724.00; see also Maleady to Department, 7 June 1951, NAII, RG 84, ELP, General, 350.

59. Hudson was nonetheless confident that "the MNR would almost certainly win an election held today." Hudson to Sparks, 28 February 1952, NAII, RG 59, 724.00. Miller to Acheson, 29 May 1951, NAII, RG 59, 611.24.

60. Maleady to Department, 5 October 1951, NAII, RG 59, 724.00; see also Kofas, *Foreign Debt and Underdevelopment*, 123–28; Maleady to Department, 22 October 1951, NAII, RG 59, 724.00.

61. Hudson to Barall, Bernbaum, Bennett, Atwood, Miller, and Mann, 6 March 1952, NAII, RG 59, 724.00.

62. Cobb to Department, 10 May 1951, NAII, RG 59, 724.00.

63. Miller to Flack, 15 May 1951, HSTPL, Edward G. Miller Papers, Miller, F.

CHAPTER 6

The first epigraph to this chapter is drawn from Symington to Mann, 6 July 1951, NAII, RG 59, 824.2544; the second, from Ballivián, as quoted in Cobb to Department, 3 January 1952, NAII, RG 84, ELP, General, 350.

1. Maleady to Department, 7 December 1951, NAII, RG 59, 724.00.

2. Symington, "New Concepts of the RFC," 4 December 1951, AMRECB, EEUU-1-R-54/111; see also Olson, *Stuart Symington*, 226.

3. Statement of Mr. W. Stuart Symington before the Preparedness Subcommittee of the Senate Armed Forces Committee, 24 July 1951, NAII, RG 59, 824.2544; *New York Times*, 19 June 1951, 41; McKinnon to Administrator (Chairman), 12 June 1951, NAII, RG 234, MRC, TP, ASF, 1942–54.

4. Symington to Mann, 6 July 1951; Symington, Warren, Atwood, and Mann, MC, 15 June 1951, both in NAII, RG 59, 824.2544.

5. The State Department apparently resisted the idea of sending Weaver because he was African American, but Chairman Symington insisted. Olson, *Stuart Symington*, 229. Symington to Mann, 20 June 1951; Atwood and Maleady to Miller and Warren, 1 July 1951, both in NAII, RG 59, 824.2544; see also Navia Ribera, *Los Estados Unidos*, 65–66.

6. Atwood and Maleady to Miller and Warren, 1 July 1951, NAII, RG 59, 824.2544; Florman to Department, 2 August 1951, NAII, RG 59, 724.00.

7. Welch, "Analysis of Costs and Prices: Bolivian Tin," 28 August 1951, NAII, RG 234, MRC, Restricted and Confidential Material; ORIT, "Memo on the Bolivian Tin Prices," 7 May 1952, GMMA, SRP, RD, 1951–53.

8. De Lima to Department, 19 June 1951, NAII, RG 59, 824.2544; De Lima to Department, 10 July 1951; Florman to Mann, 9 August 1951; Florman to Department, 29 August 1951, all in NAII, RG 59, 824.2544; see also McKinnon to Administrator (Chairman), 10 July 1951, NAII, RG 234, MRC, TP, ASF, 1942–54; Navia Ribera, *Los Estados Unidos*, 67.

9. Warren to Mann and Miller, 5 July 1951, NAII, RG 59, 824.2544; Embajada Bolivia, "Press Release," 11 de junio de 1951, AMRECB, EEUU-1-R-54/109; see also Atwood to Miller, 8 June 1951, NAII, RG 59, 824.2544.

10. Atwood, as quoted in Warren to Mann and Miller, 5 July 1951; Mann to Symington, 27 June 1951; Symington to Mann, 6 July 1951, all in NAII, RG 59, 824.2544.

11. Miller to Acheson, 9 July 1951, NAII, RG 59, RASSLAA, 1949–53, Bolivia; Florman to Department, 24 August 1951, NAII, RG 59, 724.00; Atwood, as paraphrased by Hudson, 9 July 1951,

NAII, RG 59, 824.2544; see also Calvo Linares a Ministro, 4 de diciembre de 1951, AMRECB, ARG-1-R-79/203.

12. Atwood, as paraphrased by Hudson, 9 July 1951; Maleady to Atwood, 29 October 1951, both in NAII, RG 59, 824.2544; see also Miller to Acheson, 9 July 1951, NAII, RG 59, RASSLAA, 1949–53, Bolivia.

13. Welch to Symington, 5 July 1951; Shannon to Symington, 11 July 1951, both in NAII, RG 234, MRC, TP, ASF, 1942–54.

14. Acheson, Symington, McKinnon, Allen, Miller, and Brown, MC, 9 July 1951, HSTPL, DGAP, MC; Acheson, "Paraphrase of Telegram," 7 July 1951, NAII, RG 234, RFC, Restricted and Confidential Cables through 6/30/1952.

15. Warren and Gamper, MC, 13 July 1951, NAII, RG 59, 824.2544.

16. Martínez Vargas, Warren, Krieg, and Hudson, MC, 10 July 1951, NAII, RG 59, 824.2544.

17. Maleady to Secretary, 18 July 1951; Martínez Vargas, Miller, and Hudson, MC, 20 July 1951, both in NAII, RG 59, 824.2544; see also Embassy La Paz to Department, 29 May 1952, NAII, RG 84, ELP, General, 500.

18. *Financial Times*, as quoted in Gifford to Secretary, 31 July 1951, NAII, RG 59, 824.2544; see also Querejazu Calvo a Ministro, 17 de agosto de 1951, AMRECB, GRBT-1-R-53/67.

19. Knollys and Brown, MC, 20 July 1951, NAII, RG 59, 824.2544; Acheson and Symington, MC, 10 August 1951, HSTPL, DGAP, MC.

20. Statement of Mr. W. Stuart Symington Before the Preparedness Subcommittee of the Senate Armed Forces Committee, 24 July 1951, NAII, RG 59, 824.2544; see also Daniel, "Sellers' Strike on Tin," *Washington Daily News*, 21 December 1951, 4.

21. Miller to Maleady, 4 December 1951, NAII, RG 59, RASSLAA, 1949–53, Bolivia; see also Martínez Vargas a Ministro, 20 de julio de 1951; Martínez Vargas a Ministro, 25 de julio de 1951, both in AMRECB, EEUU-1-R-54/109.

22. Statement of Mr. W. Stuart Symington Before the Preparedness Subcommittee of the Senate Armed Forces Committee, 24 July 1951, NAII, RG 59, 824.2544.

23. Welch to Symington, 26 November 1951, NAII, MRC, TP, ASF, 1942–54; see also Symington to Mann, 6 July 1951, NAII, RG 59, 824.2544; Olson, *Stuart Symington*, 230.

24. Acheson to Embassy La Paz, 24 July 1951; Gifford to Secretary, 31 July 1951; Maleady to Department, 30 July 1951, all in NAII, RG 59, 824.2544; Martínez Vargas a Ministro, 11 de junio de 1951; see also Martínez Vargas a Acheson, 12 de junio de 1951, both in AMRECB, EEUU-1-R-54/109.

25. "Tin, Taxes, and Tears," *Time*, 2 July 1951; Martínez Vargas, Guachalla, Miller, Atwood, and Bernbaum, MC, 16 August 1951; Hudson to Bernbaum, Atwood, Mann, and Miller, 29 October 1951, both NAII, RG 59, 824.2544.

26. De Lima to Department, 8 August 1951; Maleady to Department, 2 August 1951, both in NAII, RG 59, 824.2544.

27. "The Bolivian Tin Trap," as quoted in Cobb to Department, 3 August 1951; Florman to Mann, 9 August 1951; Maleady to Hudson, 30 November 1951, all in NAII, RG 59, 824.2544.

28. Martínez Vargas a Ministro, 14 de agosto de 1951; Martínez Vargas a Ministro, 20 de julio de 1951; Martínez Vargas a Ministro, 21 de agosto de 1951, all in AMRECB, EEUU-1-R-54/109.

29. Symington to Martínez Vargas, 31 de agosto de 1951, AMRECB, EEUU-1-R-54/110; Acheson and Symington, MC, 8 August 1951, HSTPL, DGAP, MC; see also Martínez Vargas a Ministro, 3 de agosto de 1951, AMRECB, EEUU-1-R-54/109; Acheson and Symington, MC, 21 August 1951, HSTPL, DGAP, MC.

30. Martínez Vargas, Memorandum para Symington, 14 de octubre de 1951, AMRECB, EEUU-1-R-54/111; La Delegación de Productores Bolivianos, "Memorandum," 5 de octubre de 1951, AMRECB, EEUU-1-R-54/110; Embajada de Bolivia, "Notes on Tin," 3 January 1952, AMRECB, EEUU-1-R-55/112.

31. La Delegación de Productores Bolivianos, "Memorandum," 8 de octubre de 1951; Martínez Vargas a Ministro, 12 de octubre de 1951, both in AMRECB, EEUU-1-R-54/110; "Tin Truce," *Time*, 30 July 1951; see also España, Kemper, Frankel, Hochschild, Sánchez Peña, and Rovira, MC, 24 de septiembre de 1951, AMRECB, EEUU-1-R-54/110.

32. Martínez Vargas a Ministro, 27 de octubre de 1951, AMRECB, EEUU-1-R-54/110.

33. Miller did, however, agree with Symington that "we simply cannot accept the right of Bolivia to impose a constant series of new taxes on the tin industry and to require us to treat those taxes as legitimate cost items." Miller to Maleady, 9 November 1951, NAII, RG 59, RASSLAA, 1949–53, Bolivia.

34. Maleady to Atwood, 29 October 1951, NAII, RG 59, 824.2544; Maleady to Secretary, 18 June 1951, NAII, RG 59, 724.00.

35. "Bulls in a Tin Shop," *Engineering and Mining Journal*, December 1951, RG 234, RFC, Restricted and Confidential Cables through 6/30/1952; see also State Department Position Paper on Bolivian Tin Negotiations, 2 November 1951, NAII, RG 59, 824.2544; "Embajada Bolivia," "Notes on Tin," 3 de enero de 1952, AMRECB, EEUU-1-R-55/112; Dunkerley, *Bolivia*, 240.

36. Symington, Shannon, Welch, Weaver, Webb, Johnson, Linder, and Brown, MC, 25 October 1951, NAII, RG 59, 824.2544; see also McKinnon to Administrator (Chairman), 9 October 1951, NAII, RG 234, MRC, TP, ASF, 1942–54.

37. McKinnon to Administrator (Chairman), 6 November 1951, NAII, RG 234, MRC, TP, ASF, 1942–54; *New York Times*, 10 October 1951, 1; see also Martínez Vargas a Ministro, 9 de noviembre de 1951, AMRECB, EEUU-1-R-54/111; *Wall Street Journal*, 9 November 1951.

38. Brown to Acheson, Webb, and Linder, 23 October 1951; State Department Position Paper on Bolivian Tin Negotiations, 2 November 1951, both in NAII, RG 59, 824.2544; Brown to Kayle, n.d., HSTPL, WHCF, State Department Trade Agreements; McKinnon to Administrator (Chairman), 19 November 1951, NAII, RG 234, MRC, TP, ASF, 1942–54; Miller, "Approximately Verbatim Notes of Telephone Conversation with Symington," 28 November 1951, NAII, RG 59, RASSLAA, 1949–53, Bolivia.

39. State Department Position Paper on Bolivian Tin Negotiations, 2 November 1951; Brown to Acheson, Webb, and Linder, 23 October 1951, both in NAII, RG 59, 824.2544.

40. Miller to Webb, 6 September 1951, NAII, RG 59, 824.2544; Miller to Maleady, 4 December 1950; Miller to Maleady, 11 January 1952; see also Miller, "Approximately Verbatim Notes of Telephone Conversation with Symington," 28 November 1951, all in NAII, RG 59, RASSLAA, 1949–53, Bolivia.

41. Schwarz to Miller, 17 August 1951, NAII, RG 59, 824.2544; Querejazu Calvo a Ministro, 27 de octubre de 1951, AMRECB, GRBT-1-R-53/67; see also Kennedy to Miller, 16 August 1951; Romualdi to Miller, 15 August 1951, both in NAII, RG 59, 824.2544.

42. Martínez Vargas, Peñaranda, Atwood, and Hudson, MC, 8 November 1951, NAII, RG 59, 824.2544; see also Martínez Vargas a Ministro, 16 de noviembre de 1951, AMRECB, EEUU-1-R-54/111; Hudson to Miller and Atwood, 29 October 1951, NAII, RG 59, 824.2544; Miller, "Approximately Verbatim Notes of Telephone Conversation with Symington," 28 November 1951, NAII, RG 59, RASSLAA, 1949–53, Bolivia; Welch and Hudson, MC, 16 October 1951, NAII, RG 59, 824.2544.

43. Martínez Vargas a Ministro, 27 de noviembre de 1951, AMRECB, EEUU-1-R-54/111; Peñaranda, Atwood, and Hudson, MC, 6 December 1951; Martínez Vargas, Peñaranda, Atwood, and Hudson, MC, 26 November 1951; Maleady to Hudson, 6 December 1951, all in NAII, RG 59, 824.2544.

44. Miller to Acheson, 29 December 1951; Miller to Bowers, 26 December 1951; Miller, "Approximately Verbatim Notes of Telephone Conversation with Symington," 28 November 1951, all in NAII, RG 59, RASSLAA, 1949–53, Bolivia.

45. Maleady to Department, 11 December 1951; Campen to Department, 10 January 1952, both in NAII, RG 59, 824.2544; Plaza to Miller, 15 January 1952, HSTPL, WHCF, State Department Correspondence.

46. Pool to Department, 3 March 1952, NAII, RG 59, 824.2544; Miller to Battle, 3 January 1952, NAII, RG 59, RASSLAA, 1949–53, Bolivia; Campen to Department, 10 January 1952, NAII, RG 59, 824.2544.

47. Embajada Buenos Aires a Ministro, 24 de diciembre de 1951, AMRECB, ARG-1-R-79/203; see also Dorn, *Peronistas and New Dealers*, 249–62; Escudé, *Estados Unidos, Gran Bretaña*, 215–20, 322–30.

48. Maleady to Hudson, 6 December 1951, both in NAII, RG 59, 824.2544. The State Department could find "nothing helpful" to assist U.S. delegates at the United Nations by way of "rebuttal in either a formal speech or informal conversation." Hudson to Bernbaum, Atwood, Mann, and Miller, 14 November 1951, NAII, RG 59, 824.2544.

49. Maleady to Hudson, 6 December 1951; Multer and Brown, MC, 23 January 1952, both in NAII, RG 59, 824.2544.

50. Stowe, Mann, and Atwood, MC, 29 November 1951, NAII, RG 59, 824.2544.

51. González Videla to Truman, 6 December 1951, HSTPL, Office File, 429; Miller to Bowers, 26 December 1951, NAII, RG 59, RASSLAA, 1949–53, Bolivia.

52. Atwood to Miller, 12 December 1951, NAII, RG 59, 824.2544; Miller to Bowers, 26 December 1951; Miller to Plaza, 24 January 1952; Maleady to Miller, 31 December 1951; Maleady to Miller, 10 December 1951, all in NAII, RG 59, RASSLAA, 1949–53, Bolivia.

53. Acheson and Truman, MC, 17 December 1951; Acheson and Symington, MC, 19 December 1951, both in HSTPL, DGAP, MC.

54. Symington, Acheson, and Thorp, MC, 20 December 1951, HSTPL, DGAP, MC; Maleady to Miller, 31 December 1951, NAII, RG 59, RASSLAA, 1949–53, Bolivia.

55. Maleady to Secretary, 11 January 1952, RG 234, RFC, Restricted and Confidential Cables through 6/30/1952; see also Martínez Vargas a Ministro, 21 de enero de 1952, AMRECB, EEUU-1-R-55/112.

56. Whitehead, *The United States and Bolivia*, 6; see also Martínez Vargas, Peñaranda, Atwood, and Hudson, MC, 13 February 1952, NAII, RG 59, 824.2544; Martínez Vargas a Ministro, 24 de enero de 1952; Martínez Vargas a Ministro, 21 de enero de 1952, both in AMRECB, EEUU-1-R-55/112; see also Martínez Vargas, Peñaranda, Miller, Brown, et al., MC, 14 January 1952, NAII, RG 59, RASSLAA, 1949–53, Bolivia.

57. Hudson to Miller, 21 January 1952, NAII, RG 59, 824.2544; Maleady to Department, 4 January 1952, RG 234, RFC, Restricted and Confidential Cables through 6/30/1952.

58. Martínez Vargas a Ministro, 26 de diciembre de 1951, AMREC, EEUU-1-R-54/111; Acheson to Truman, 2 January 1952, NAII, RG 59, 824.2544.

59. Acheson to Truman, 2 January 1952; see also Martínez Vargas, Miller, and Hudson, MC, 21 December 1951 both in NAII, RG 59, 824.2544; Martínez Vargas a Ministro, 4 de enero de 1952, AMRECB, EEUU-1-R-55/112.

60. Truman, as quoted in Olson, *Stuart Symington*, 231; see also *New York Times*, 5 January 1952.

61. Martínez Vargas, Atwood, and Hudson, MC, 5 February 1952, NAII, RG 59, 824.2544; Martínez Vargas a Ministro, 20 de febrero de 1952, AMRECB, EEUU-1-R-55/112; *New York Times*, 14 February 1952; *New York Times*, 20 February 1952.

62. Martínez Vargas, Atwood, and Hudson, MC, 5 February 1952, NAII, RG 59, 824.2544; Miller to Maleady, 11 January 1952, NAII, RG 59, RASSLAA, 1949–53, Bolivia; see also Martínez Vargas, Peñaranda, Sparks, Atwood, and Hudson, MC, 21 February 1952, NAII, RG 59, 824.2544.

63. Miller to Plaza, 24 January 1952, NAII, RG 59, RASSLAA, 1949–53, Bolivia; see also Martínez Vargas a Ministro, 14 de marzo de 1952, AMRECB, EEUU-1-R-55/113.

64. Tittmann to Department, 29 February 1952, NAII, RG 59, 824.2544; Aide Memoire, 28 de febrero de 1952, AMRECB, ARG-1-R-80/204; Bunker to Department, 29 February 1952, NAII, RG 59, 824.2544; Pool to Department, 3 March 1952, RG 234, RFC, Restricted and Confidential Cables through 6/30/1952.

65. Acheson to Embassy La Paz, 29 February 1952; Hall to Department, 14 March 1952; Martínez Vargas, Peñaranda, Miller, Sparks, Atwood, and Hudson, MC, 3 March 1952, all in NAII, RG 59, 824.2544; see also Bramble and Tyson, MC, 13 March 1952, NAII, RG 59, 856D.2544.

66. Maleady to Secretary, 7 March 1952; Cobb to Department, 5 March 1952, both in NAII, RG 59, 824.2544.

67. Martínez Vargas, Guachalla, Hochschild, Larson, McDonald, Wilson, McKinnon, et al., MC, 13 March 1952, NAII, RG 59, 824.2544; Martínez Vargas a Ministro, 14 de marzo de 1952, AMRECB, EEUU-1-R-55/113.

68. Martínez Vargas, Guachalla, Hochschild, Larson, McDonald, Wilson, McKinnon, et al., MC, 13 March 1952, NAII, RG 59, 824.2544; see also McKinnon to MacDonald, 28 February 1952, NAII, RG 234, MRC, TP, ASF, 1942–54.

NOTES TO PAGES 157–165

69. Address of Senator Dennis Chavez, "What Has Happened to the Good Neighbor Policy?" 4 April 1952, Center for Southwest Research, University of New Mexico, Dennis Chavez Papers, MSS 394 BC, Box 74, Folder 26; Peñaranda, Atwood, and Hudson, MC, 15 February 1952; Maleady to Secretary, 21 March 1952, both in NAII, RG 59, 824.2544; see also Johnson, Coerr, Ali, and Darmawan, MC, 3 March 1952, NAII, RG 59, 856D.2544; Hochschild, Wilson, Rovira, McKinnon, Brown, et al., MC, 14 March 1952, NAII, RG 59, 824.2544.

70. Ballivián to Truman, 22 March 1952; Maleady to Secretary, 27 March 1952; Acheson to Truman, 31 March 1952, all in NAII, RG 59, 824.2544.

71. Maleady to Secretary, 26 March 1952, NAII, RG 59, 824.2544.

72. Maleady to Secretary, 27 March 1952; Hochschild, Rovira, Wilson, McKinnon, Brown, et al., MC, 31 March 1952, both in NAII, RG 59, 824.2544.

73. Johnson to Truman, 4 April 1952, HSTPL, WHCF, State Department.

74. Statement by the Large and Medium Miners Associations of Bolivia in Answer to Senator Lyndon Johnson's Recent Statement, 4 April 1952, HSTPL, WHCF, State Department Trade Agreements.

75. Embassy La Paz to Department, 4 April 1952, RG 234, RFC, Restricted and Confidential Cables through 6/30/1952; Atwood to Miller, 7 April 1952, NAII, RG 59, 724.00; see also Kayle to Stowe, 16 April 1952, HSTPL, WHCF, State Department Trade Agreements.

76. Atwood to Miller, 7 April 1952, NAII, RG 59, 724.00; Bennett to Miller, 11 April 1952, NAII, RG 59, 824.10.

77. Kempff a Ministro, 23 de abril de 1952; Kempff a Ministro, 26 de abril de 1952, both in AMRECB, EEUU-1-R-55/113.

78. Nieto del Rio, Atwood, and Barall, MC, 19 April 1952; see also Bowers to Secretary, 9 April 1952, both in NAII, RG 59, 724.00; Sparks to Miller, 21 April 1952, NAII, RG 59, 724.02. For his part, a dissenting Paz Estenssoro stated that blaming the revolution on the tin impasse demonstrated a "shallow and superficial understanding of Bolivian problems." As quoted in Blasier, "The United States and the Revolution," 63.

79. Knight, "The Domestic Dynamics," 83; Kayle to Stowe, 16 April 1952; Truman to Johnson, 17 April 1952, both in HSTPL, WHCF, State Department Trade Agreements.

80. Chavez Statement, 4 April 1952, Center for Southwest Research, University of New Mexico, Dennis Chavez Papers, MSS 394 BC, Box 74, Folder 26.

81. Brown to Kayle, n.d., HSTPL, WHCF, State Department Trade Agreements.

82. Waite and Miller, MC, 15 August 1952, NAII, RG 59, 824.2544; see also Bell to Department, 8 August 1952, NAII, RG 59, 856D.2544.

83. Vicenti, Mann, and Hudson, MC, 17 January 1952; Belmonte, Miller, Bennett, Bernbaum, et al., MC, 4 April 1952, both in NAII, RG 59, 724.00.

84. Mann to Messersmith, 30 December 1952, NAII, RG 59, Records of the Deputy Assistant Secretaries of State for Inter-American Affairs, 1945–56, Messersmith.

CHAPTER 7

The first epigraph to this chapter is drawn from Alexander to Miller, 21 May 1952, NAII, RG 59, RASSLAA, 1949–53, Bolivia; see also Lehman, "Braked but Not Broken." The second is drawn from Hudson to Sayre and Bennett, 29 September 1952, NAII, RG 59, 611.24.

1. Canelas, *Dictadura y democracia*, 279; Quieser Morales, *Bolivia*, 72.

2. Maleady to Department, 4 January 1952, RG 234, RFC, Restricted and Confidential Cables through 6/30/1952; see also Vicenti, Mann, and Hudson, MC, 17 January 1952, NAII, RG 59, 724.00.

3. Cobb to Department, 7 March 1952, NAII, RG 59, 724.00.

4. Maleady to Department, 2 April 1952, NAII, RG 59, 724.00.

5. Dunkerley, *Rebellion in the Veins*, 1–3; Ríos Gamboa, *Bolivia*, 94–96.

6. Bowers to Secretary, 18 April 1952; Wade to Department, 12 April 1952, both in NAII, RG 59, 724.00; Dunkerley, *Rebellion in the Veins*, 4–5.

[235]

7. Wade to Department, 12 April 1952; Maleady to Department, 12 April 1952, both in NAII, RG 59, 724.00; see also Dunkerley, *Rebellion in the Veins*, 38–40.

8. Wade to Department, 12 April 1952, NAII, RG 59, 724.00; Mitchell, *The Legacy of Populism in Bolivia*, 40–49.

9. Blasier, "The United States and the Revolution," 66–87; Dunkerley, *Rebellion in the Veins*, 40–54; Malloy, *Bolivia*, 158–87; Siekmeier, *Aid, Nationalism, and Inter-American Relations*, 232–37.

10. De Zengotita to Secretary, 8 January 1946, NAII, RG 59, 824.504; Jackson, Galarza, Fishburn, and Hudson, MC, 23 April 1953, NAII, RG 59, 824.00; Mitchell, *The Legacy of Populism in Bolivia*, 45; Hudson to Miller, Mann, Atwood, et al., 5 May 1952, NAII, RG 59, 724.00.

11. Rowell to Department, 25 July 1952, NAII, RG 59, 824.06; Nixon to McFall, 20 May 1952, NAII, RG 59, 724.00; see also Roque Bacarreza, *Los años del condor*, 83.

12. Rowell to Department, 25 July 1952, NAII, RG 59, 824.06; Acheson to Embassy Caracas, 22 April 1952, NAII, RG 59, 724.02; see also Zalles, Stebbins, Bennett, and Hudson, MC, 29 April 1952; Maleady to Secretary, 27 April 1952, both in NAII, RG 59, 724.00.

13. Alexander interview with Sanjines, n.d.; Alexander interview with Lechín, 14 August 1952; Alexander interview with Perez, 14 August 1952; see also Alexander interview with Salazar, 13 August 1952, all in GMMA, JLP, RA.

14. De Lima to Department, 16 April 1952; Maleady to Department, 25 April 1952, both in NAII, RG 59, 824.2544; see also Navia Ribera, *Los Estados Unidos*, 129.

15. Although the MNR did resent the presence of foreigners, according to Carter Goodrich, the UN team managed to find a viable formula for cooperation by simply offering suggestions and advice to their Bolivian counterparts. By making any project "really a Bolivian enterprise" that just employs the "special skills of the foreign experts," the UN team was able to make some progress, and even Lechín requested more experts. Alexander interview with Goodrich, 15 August 1952, GMMA, JLP, RA; see also Maleady to Department, 6 June 1952, NAII, RG 59, 724.00.

16. Rowell to Department, 26 August 1952, NAII, RG 59, 824.00.

17. Rowell to Department, 14 September 1952, NAII, RG 84, ELP, General, 360; Nathanson and Hudson, MC, 25 June 1952, NAII, RG 59, 824.2544; see also Rosen and Hudson, MC, 20 May 1952, NAII, RG 59, 824.2544; Tower and Hudson, MC, 9 May 1952, NAII, RG 59, 724.00; Navia Ribera, *Los Estados Unidos*, 74–75; Blasier, "The United States and the Revolution," 63–65.

18. Smith to Department, 17 April 1952; Bowers to Secretary, 25 April 1952; Hudson to Miller, 13 June 1952, all in NAII, RG 59, 824.2544; see also Roque Bacarreza, *Los años del condor*, 72–73.

19. Tittmann to Secretary, 11 April 1952; Tittmann to Secretary, 2 May 1952; Tittmann to Secretary, 22 April 1952, all in NAII, RG 59, 724.00; see also Navia Ribera, *Los Estados Unidos*, 93.

20. Tittmann to Secretary, 27 April 1952; Tittmann to Secretary, 26 April 1952, both in NAII, RG 59, 724.00; Alexander to Lovestone, 28 July 1953, GMMA, JLP, RA see also Roque Bacarreza, *Los años del condor*, 73–74.

21. Hudson to Miller, Mann, Atwood, Bennett, Bernbaum, and Barall, 5 May 1952; Mallory to Secretary, 12 April 1952; Maleady to Secretary, 15 April 1952, all in NAII, RG 59, 724.00; Goodrich, "Bolivia in Time of Revolution," 13; Nathanson, Miller, and Hudson, MC, 17 April 1952, NAII, RG 59, 824.2544; see also Mallory to Secretary, 17 April 1952, NAII, RG 59, 724.00; Lehman, *Bolivia and the United States*, 101.

22. Acheson to Wilson, 15 April 1952; Cobb to Department, 14 April 1952; Cobb to Department, 9 May 1952; see also Wilson to Secretary, 15 April 1952, all in NAII, RG 59, 724.00; Navia Ribera, *Los Estados Unidos*, 103–10.

23. Smith to Department, 5 May 1952; Cobb to Department, 9 May 1952, both in NAII, RG 59, 724.00; see also Blasier, "The United States and the Revolution," 68–69.

24. Guachalla, Miller, and Hudson, MC, 25 April 1952; Cobb to Department, 14 April 1952; Cobb to Department, 9 May 1952, all in NAII, RG 59, 724.00.

25. Maleady to Department, 6 May 1952; Maleady to Department, 7 May 1952; Cobb to Department, 9 May 1952; Hudson to Miller, Mann, Atwood, et al., 30 April 1952, all in NAII, RG 59, 724.00.

26. Cobb to Department, 14 April 1952, NAII, RG 59, 724.00; Maleady to Department, 25 April 1952, NAII, RG 59, 824.2544; see also Acheson to Truman, 22 May 1952, NAII, RG 59, RASSLAA, 1949–53, Bolivia.
27. Hudson to Miller, Mann, Atwood, et al., 5 May 1952; Maleady to Department, 27 April 1952, both in NAII, RG 59, 724.00; Acheson to Truman, 27 May 1952, NAII, RG 59, 611.24; Malloy, *Bolivia*, 235. Jerry Knudson points out a curious irony. After Villarroel's fall, *La Razón* had boasted of its role in mobilizing the public by claiming that his government "committed an error that eventually was to become fatal. It gave temporary liberty to the press." Knudson, *Bolivia*, 134.
28. Cobb to Department, 14 April 1952, NAII, RG 59, 724.00; Whitehead, *The United States and Bolivia*, 9; Nathanson, Miller, and Hudson, MC, 17 April 1952, NAII, RG 59, 824.2544.
29. Cobb, as quoted in Embassy La Paz to Department, 15 July 1952, NAII, RG 59, 824.06; Maleady to Secretary, 12 April 1952, NAII, RG 59, 724.00.
30. Acheson to Embassy La Paz, 12 April 1952, NAII, RG 59, 724.00; see also Roque Bacarreza, *Los años del condor*, 29–33.
31. Pan-American Union official Ernesto Galarza had a rather different view. When Bolivian peasants asked his advice on whether they should hand in their guns, as President Paz Estenssoro asked, he replied that "they should keep their guns, since there had been too many cases of popular revolutions which had been on the verge of final success but had been ruthlessly suppressed once the people had been beguiled by their former masters into laying down their weapons." Jackson, Galarza, Fishburn, and Hudson, MC, 23 April 1953, NAII, RG 59, 824.00. Acheson to Embassy La Paz, 27 April 1952; Acheson to Fleming, 27 May 1952; see also Maleady to Secretary, 27 April 1952, NAII, RG 59, 724.00.
32. Acheson and Miller to Maleady, 17 April 1952, NAII, RG 59, 724.02.
33. Sparks to Miller, 27 June 1952, NAII, RG 59, RASSLAA, 1949–53, Bolivia; Nathanson, Miller, and Hudson, MC, 17 April 1952, NAII, RG 59, 824.2544.
34. Patiño threatened to revoke his employees' pensions if they worked for the government in his mines after nationalization. At least one former Patiño manager got around this by working at a former Aramayo property. Alexander interview with Goodrich, 7 July 1953, GMMA, JLP, RA. Deringer, Atwood, Hudson, Evans, et al., MC, 7 August 1952, NAII, RG 59, 824.2544.
35. Rosen and Hudson, MC, 20 May 1952, NAII, RG 59, 824.2544; Tower and Hudson, MC, 9 May 1952; Zalles, Shea, Stebbins, Miller, Mann, et al., MC, 20 May 1952, both in NAII, RG 59, 724.00; Rovensky and Hudson, MC, 29 April 1952; see also Deringer, Atwood, Hudson, Evans, et al., MC, 7 August 1952, both in NAII, RG 59, 824.2544.
36. Acheson to Truman, 22 May 1952, NAII, RG 59, RASSLAA, 1949–53, Bolivia; Miller to Tittmann, 7 May 1952, NAII, RG 59, RASSLAA, 1949–53, Peru; Truman and Acheson, MC, 22 May 1952, HSTPL, DGAP, MC; Alexander interview with Rowell, 15 August 1952, GMMA, JLP, RA; Maleady to Secretary, 23 May 1952, NAII, RG 59, 724.00.
37. Nichols to Brown, 25 July 1952; Evans, Bramble, Getzin, Atwood, Hudson, Larson, Shannon, McKinnon, et al., MC, 17 June 1952, both in NAII, RG 59, 824.2544.
38. Mann to Sparks, 14 July 1952; Andrade, Miller, and Hudson, MC, 31 July 1952, both in NAII, RG 59, 824.2544; see also Andrade a Ministro, 29 de agosto de 1952, AMRECB, EEUU-1-R-55/114.
39. Acheson to Embassy La Paz, 19 June 1952; Acheson to Embassy La Paz, 5 June 1952, both in NAII, RG 59, 824.2544.
40. Galambos to Sparks, 11 July 1952; Sparks to Mann, 14 July 1952; see also Henderson, Mann, Atwood, and Hudson, MC, 2 July 1952, all in NAII, RG 59, 824.2544; Roque Bacarreza, *Los años del condor*, 104–5.
41. Sparks to Mann, 14 July 1952; see also Sparks to Hudson, 15 July 1952; Thorp, Henderson, Nichols, and Hudson, MC, 14 July 1952, all in NAII, RG 59, 824.2544.
42. Ditisheim and Henderson claimed they still had "verbal authorization" from La Paz to sell Bolivian tin for months after their deadline but were ignored by every purchasing agency. Shannon, McKinnon, Evans, Atwood, Hudson, et al., MC, 31 July 1952, NAII, RG 59, 824.2544; see also Andrade a Ministro, 16 de agosto de 1952, AMRECB, EEUU-1-R-55/114; Andrade, Miller, and Hudson, MC, 31 July 1952, NAII, RG 59, 824.2544.

43. Nichols to Brown, 25 July 1952; Brennan, Mann, and Hudson, MC, 17 July 1952; Andrade, Evans, Getzin, Atwood, and Barrall, MC, 20 August 1952, all in NAII, RG 59, 824.2544.
44. Andrade, Evans, Getzin, Atwood, and Barrall, MC, 20 August 1952; Brennan, Mann, and Hudson, MC, 17 July 1952, both in NAII, RG 59, 824.2544; see also Andrade a Ministro, 29 de agosto de 1952, AMRECB, EEUU-1-R-55/114.
45. Andrade, Evans, Getzin, Atwood, and Barrall, MC, 20 August 1952; Andrade and Atwood, MC, 18 August 1952, both in NAII, RG 59, 824.2544; see also Andrade a Ministro, 16 de agosto de 1952, AMRECB, EEUU-1-R-55/114; Shannon, McKinnon, Miller, Mann, et al., MC, 5 September 1952, NAII, RG 59, 824.2544.
46. Acheson to Embassy La Paz, 8 September 1952; Shannon, McKinnon, Miller, Mann, et al., MC, 5 September 1952, both in NAII, RG 59, 824.2544; see also Roque Bacarreza, *Los años del condor*, 118–23, 139–40.
47. Sparks to Mann, 18 August 1952, NAII, RG 59, 824.2544.
48. Acheson to Embassy La Paz, 8 September 1952, NAII, RG 59, 824.2544; Andrade a Ministro, 23 de septiembre de 1952, AMRECB, EEUU-1-R-55/114; Siles Zuazo, Andrade, Acheson, and Bennett, MC, 7 October 1952, HSTPL, DGAP, MC; see also Miller to Andrade, 9 October 1952; Sparks to Secretary, 9 September 1952, both in NAII, RG 59, 824.254; Miller to Acheson, 7 October 1952, NAII, RG 59, 724.12.
49. Rowell to Department, 15 October 1952; Siles Zuazo and Hudson, MC, 8 October 1952; Shillock to Department, 27 January 1953, all in NAII, RG 59, 824.2544.
50. Nathanson and Hudson, MC, 24 September 1952, NAII, RG 59, 824.2544.
51. Rovensky, Miller, and Hudson, MC, 25 September 1952, NAII, RG 59, 824.2544; see also Roque Bacarreza, *Los años del condor*, 129–31.
52. Hudson to Miller, 24 September 1952, NAII, RG 59, RASSLAA, 1949–53, Bolivia; Memorandum de la Entrevista, Miller, Hudson, and Andrade, 6 de octubre de 1952, AMRECB, EEUU-1-R-55/114.
53. Shillock to Department, 27 January 1953; Andrade, Bruce, and Hudson, MC, 21 November 1952; Bruce to Certain American Diplomatic Officers, 12 November 1952, all in RG 59, NAII, RG 59, 824.2544.
54. Rowell to Department, 17 November 1952, NAII, RG 59, 724.00.
55. Tydings, Sparks, and Hudson, MC, 18 November 1952; Tydings, Nathanson, Miller, and Hudson, MC, 19 November 1952; Andrade and Mann, MC, 18 December 1952, all in NAII, RG 59, 824.2544.
56. Andrade, Bruce, and Hudson, MC, 21 November 1952; see also Sparks, Mann, Hudson, et al., MC, 10 November 1952, both in NAII, RG 59, 824.2544. Eisenhower's electoral victory also took Assistant Secretary Miller out of the tin negotiations. Miller prepared to return to his old job at Cromwell and Sullivan, a law firm currently employed by the Bolivian government on a debt readjustment issue. To prevent the appearance of a conflict of interest, Miller handed off Bolivian affairs to Deputy Assistant Secretary Mann for the remainder of President Truman's term. Miller to Mann, 20 November 1952, NAII, RG 59, RASSLAA, 1949–53, Bolivia.
57. Andrade, Mann, and Hudson, MC, 9 December 1952, NAII, RG 59, 611.24.
58. Ibid.; Mann to Bruce, 17 December 1952, NAII, RG 59, 824.2544.
59. Mann to Bruce, 17 December 1952, NAII, RG 59, 824.2544; Mann to Messersmith, 30 December 1952, NAII, RG 59, Records of the Deputy Assistant Secretaries of State for Inter-American Affairs, 1945–56, Messersmith.
60. Mann to Bruce, 17 December 1952; Mann to Tydings, 30 January 1953; Tydings to Dulles, 30 January 1953, all in NAII, RG 59, 824.2544.
61. Andrade and Mann, MC, 18 December 1952, NAII, RG 59, 824.2544; see also Andrade a Ministro, 22 de diciembre de 1952; Andrade a Ministro, 22 de diciembre de 1952, both in AMRECB, EEUU-1-R-55/114.
62. Andrade, Perez, Mann, Evans, Atwood, and Hudson, MC, 22 December 1952; Atwood to Mann, 22 December 1952, both in NAII, RG 59, 824.2544.
63. Acheson to Embassy La Paz, 7 January 1953; Andrade. Mann, and Atwood, MC, 14 January 1953, both in NAII, RG 59, 824.2544; Andrade a Ministro, 31 de enero de 1953, AMRECB, EEUU-1-R-56/116.
64. Acheson to Embassy La Paz, 7 January 1953, NAII, RG 59, 824.2544.

65. Andrade and Mann, MC, 12 January 1953; Andrade, Mann, Atwood, and Hudson, MC, 14 January 1953, both in NAII, RG 59, 824.2544; see also Roque Bacarreza, *Los años del condor*, 218–21.
66. Andrade, Mann, Atwood, and Hudson, MC, 19 January 1953; see also Mann to McDonald, 15 January 1953; Dulles to Embassy La Paz, 16 January 1953; Tydings and Mann, MC, 19 January 1953, all in NAII, RG 59, 824.2544.
67. Paz Estenssoro, as quoted in Mitchell, *The Legacy of Populism in Bolivia*, 55; Navia Ribera, *Los Estados Unidos*, 134–38; Alexander interview with Rowell, 8 July 1953, GMMA, JLP, RA.
68. Hudson to Atwood, 14 January 1953, NAII, RG 59, 724.00; Alexander to Lovestone, 17 August 1952, GMMA, JLP, RA.
69. Stuart to Department, 17 April 1952, NAII, RG 59, 724.00.

CONCLUSION

The first epigraph to this chapter is drawn from Querejazu Calvo a Ministro, 18 de febrero de 1950, AMRECB, GRBT-1-R-52/66; the second, from Andrade a Ridder, 19 de noviembre de 1952, AMRECB, EEUU-1-R-55/114.

1. Tydings to Dulles, 30 January 1953; Tydings, Smith, and Hudson, MC, 12 February 1953; Tydings and Mann, MC, 19 January 1953, all in NAII, RG 59, 824.2544; Lehman, *Bolivia and the United States*, 104; see also Dulles to Embassy La Paz, 5 March 1953, NAII, RG 59, 824.2544.
2. Rowell to Department, 28 August 1953; see also Rowell to Department, 2 October 1953; Rowell to Department, 10 November 1953, all in NAII, RG 59, 724.00; Lehman, *Bolivia and the United States*, 103–13; Prado Salmon, *Poder y fuerzas armadas*, 31.
3. Malloy, *Bolivia*, 231–34.
4. Andrade, Mann, and Hudson, MC, 29 April 1953; Hudson to Cabot, Mann, and Atwood, 11 May 1953, both in NAII, RG 59, 611.24; see also Rowell to Department, 26 January 1953, NAII, RG 59, 724.00; Rowell to Department, 30 April 1953, NAII, RG 59, 611.24.
5. Romualdi to Andrade, 25 August 1953, GMMA, SRP, 1952–55; AFL Memorandum, "Bolivia— The Labor Movement Relations with the ORIT," 21 April 1953, GMMA, SRP, Bolivia. The American Federation of Labor, hardly a bastion of radicalism, never shared U.S. government fears about Lechín and even invited the COB leader to address the 1953 AFL Convention in St. Louis.
6. Rowell to Department, 30 April 1953, NAII, RG 59, 611.24; Rowell to Department, 21 April 1953, NAII, RG 59, 724.00; Hudson to Cabot, Mann, and Atwood, 11 May 1953, NAII, RG 59, 611.24; Rowell to Department, 26 May 1953, NAII, RG 59, 724.00.
7. Sparks to Department, 23 October 1953, NAII, RG 59, 724.00.
8. Rowell to Department, 24 November 1953, NAII, RG 59, 724.00; (Milton) Eisenhower, Andrade, and Bennett, MC, 17 June 1953, NAII, RG 59, 611.24; Alexander interview with Rowell, 8 July 1953, GMMA, JLP, RA; (Milton) Eisenhower, as quoted in Blasier, "The United States and the Revolution," 73; see also Navia Ribera, *Los Estados Unidos*, 144–53.
9. Hudson to Atwood, 30 April 1953, NAII, RG 59, 824.00; Cabot to Dulles, 28 August 1953, NAII, RG 59, 724.5-MSP; Alexander interview with Rowell, 8 July 1953, GMMA, JLP, RA; see also Tydings and Hudson, MC, 7 October 1953, NAII, RG 59, 724.5-MSP; Roque Bacarreza, *Los años del condor*, 359–80.
10. Sparks to Department, 6 October 1953, NAII, RG 59, 724.5-MSP; see also Sparks to Hudson, 27 November 1953; Andrade, Jara, Barall, MC, 17 September 1953, both in NAII, RG 59, 611.24.
11. Ambassador Andrade delivered the letter from President Paz Estenssoro, "made a strong plea for further U.S. purchases of tin," and spent the rest of his ten-minute conversation with President Eisenhower discussing golf. Eisenhower, Andrade, Cabot, MC, 14 October 1953, HSTPL, John Moors Cabot Papers, Reel 14; Sparks to Department, 6 October 1953, NAII, RG 59, 724.5-MSP.
12. Sparks to Department, 23 October 1953, NAII, RG 59, 724.00; Rowell to Department, 4 November 1953, NAII, RG 59, 724.13; Rowell to Department, 24 November 1953, NAII, RG 59, 724.00; see also Guevara Arze, Andrade, Cabot, and Hudson, MC, 4 November 1953, NAII, RG 59, 611.24.
13. Sparks to Department, 23 October 1953, NAII, RG 59, 724.00.

14. Canelas's fierce opposition to land reform had led to the burning of the printing plant of his newspaper, *Los Tiempos*. Canelas, *Dictadura y democracia*, 301–3; see also Knudson, *Bolivia*, 8; Blasier, "The United States and the Revolution," 78–94.
15. Alexander interview with Rowell, 15 August 1953, GMMA, JLP, RA.
16. Henderson to Flack, 3 October 1946, NAII, RG 84, ELP, Classified, 800.
17. Johnson, "Annual Economic Review—Bolivia—1949," 3 February 1950, NAII, RG 59, 824.00.
18. Orloski to Secretary, 17 January 1947, NAII, RG 59, 824.5034; Dunkerley, *Bolivia*, 240; Andrade, Address before the Pan-American Women's Association, 15 November 1952, AMRECB-1-R-56/116.
19. Albarracín Millán, *Bolivia*, 107–8; Bedregal, *Víctor Paz Estenssoro*, 233.
20. Contreras, *The Bolivian Tin Industry*, 22–23.
21. Cabot Speech Before the Export-Import Club of Columbus, 16 December 1953, HSTPL, John Moors Cabot Papers, Reel 15.

EPILOGUE

The first epigraph to the epilogue is drawn from Zilveti, Martínez Vargas, Romero, Miller, Atwood, and Hudson, MC, 5 April 1951, NAII, RG 59, 824.00; the second, from Hylton and Thomson, *Revolutionary Horizons*, 14.

1. See Irwin F. Gellman, *Good Neighbor Diplomacy*; Gerald K. Haines, "Under the Eagle's Wing," 370–88; Wood, *The Making of the Good Neighbor Policy*.
2. See Wood, *The Dismantling of the Good Neighbor Policy*.
3. *La Razón*, as quoted in Flack to Secretary, 28 May 1947, NAII, RG 59, 711.24; Acheson, *Present at the Creation*, 496.
4. Perhaps the most disturbing aspect of Ambassador Florman's tenure was that he was lionized in some quarters for his ignorance. *Time* magazine lauded his flouting of diplomatic protocol and curt disregard for the advice of his aides. It claimed the "delighted Bolivian press" not only printed his "flowery prose" and historical commentaries, but also "begged for more." His intervention in the foreign exchange fiasco was deemed to be "just what was needed." "Idea Man," *Time*, 6 November 1950.
5. See Dorn, "The American Reputation for Fair Play," 1083–101; Gootenberg, "Reluctance or Resistance," 69–70; Rabe, *The Road to OPEC*, 121–24.
6. See Dorn, *Peronistas and New Dealers*, 250–63; Escudé, *Gran Bretaña, Estados Unidos*, 323–28.
7. Burgin, as quoted in Siekmeier, *Aid, Nationalism, and Inter-American Relations*, 241; Whitehead, "The Bolivian National Revolution," 25; see also Siekmeier, *Aid, Nationalism, and Inter-American Relations*, 244–50; Blasier, "The United States and the Revolution," 76–95; Lehman, *Bolivia and the United States*, 103–26; Rabe, *Eisenhower and Latin America*.
8. Lehman, "Braked but Not Broken," 97–103; see also Siekmeier, *Aid, Nationalism, and Inter-American Relations*, 226–27.
9. Although Cabot was not directly involved in Truman's policies toward Bolivia, he had in 1946 been the first U.S. diplomat to call for rapprochement and accommodation with Perón in the wake of the Blue Book fiasco. Dorn, *Peronistas and New Dealers*, 84–85.
10. Lehman, "Revolutions and Attributions," 197–98.
11. Ibid., 200.
12. See Cullather, *Secret History*, 14–20; Immerman, *The CIA in Guatemala*, 101–18; Schlesinger and Kinzer, *Bitter Fruit*, 80–97.
13. Lehman, "Braked but Not Broken," 93, 98–103.
14. Gotkowitz, *A Revolution for Our Rights*, 286–89.
15. Ibid., 2–7.
16. Lehman, "Braked but Not Broken," 95–106; see also Blasier, *The Hovering Giant*, 101–16.
17. Thoburn, *Tin in the World Economy*, 90–92, 174.
18. Robert Alexander is more forgiving of the MNR, arguing that the issue of compensation, which was not resolved until 1961, prevented the government from securing the foreign loans necessary

to maintain and expand the mines. Alexander, *Prophets of the Revolution*, 207; see Thoburn, *Tin in the World Economy*, 92–95, 119–21: quotation on p. 120.

19. See Thoburn, *Tin in the World Economy*, 151–56; Lehman, *Bolivia and the United States*, 194–98: quotation on p. 198.

20. Hylton and Thomson, *Revolutionary Horizons*, 3.

21. See Dunkerley, *Bolivia*, 3–44.

22. Ibid., 27; Hylton and Thomson, *Revolutionary Horizons*, 13.

23. Gotkowitz, *A Revolution for Our Rights*, 289; see also Dunkerley, *Bolivia*, 31–32.

24. See Hylton and Thomson, *Revolutionary Horizons*, 133–43.

SELECTED BIBLIOGRAPHY

ARCHIVES

Argentina

Archivo del Ministerio de Relaciones Exteriores y Culto, Buenos Aires
    Departamento Político

Bolivia

Archivo del Ministerio de Relaciones Exteriores y Culto, La Paz
    Embajada en Buenos Aires; Embajada en Washington; Legación en London

United States of America

Center for Southwest Studies, University of New Mexico
    Dennis Chavez Papers
Columbia University Rare Book and Manuscript Library
    Spruille Braden Papers
George Meany Memorial Archives, Silver Spring, Maryland
    Jay Lovestone Papers; Serafino Romualdi Papers
National Archives of the United States II, College Park, Maryland
        Record Group 59, General Records of the Department of State
            Decimal Files; Records of the Assistant Secretary of State for Latin American Affairs, 1949–53; Records of the Deputy Assistant Secretaries of State for Inter-American Affairs, 1945–56; Records of the Office of American Republics Affairs, Its Predecessors, and Its Successors; Records of the Office of Intelligence and Research
        Record Group 84, Records of the Foreign Service Posts of the Department of State
            Post Files, U.S. Embassy Buenos Aires; Post Files, U.S. Embassy La Paz
        Record Group 234, Records of the Reconstruction Finance Corporation
            Office of the Secretary, Administrative Histories of the RFC's Wartime Programs, 1943–54
Franklin Delano Roosevelt Presidential Library, Hyde Park, New York
    Frank Corrigan Papers
Harry S. Truman Library, Independence, Missouri
    Dean G. Acheson Papers; Merwin Bohan Papers; John Moors Cabot Papers; Edward G. Miller Papers; W. Stuart Symington Papers; Harry S. Truman Papers

PUBLISHED SOURCES

Abecia Baldevieso, Valentin. *Las relaciones internacionales en la historia de Bolivia.* Tomo 3. La Paz: Editorial Amigos del Libro, 1986.

Abel, Christopher, and Colin Lewis, eds. *Economic Imperialism and the State: The Political Economy of the External Connection from Independence to the Present*. London: Athlone, 1985.
Acheson, Dean G. *Present at the Creation: My Years in the State Department*. New York: Norton, 1954.
Albarracín Millán, Juan. *Bolivia: El desentrañamiento del estaño*. La Paz: Ediciones AKAPANA, 1993.
Alexander, Robert J. *The Bolivaran Presidents: Conversations with Presidents of Bolivia, Peru, Ecuador, Colombia, and Venezuela*. Westport, Conn.: Praeger, 1994.
———. *Bolivia: The Past, Present and Future of Its Politics*. New York: Praeger, 1982.
———. *Prophets of the Revolution: Profiles of Latin American Leaders*. New York: Macmillan, 1962.
Andrade, Victor. *My Missions for Revolutionary Bolivia, 1944–1962*. Pittsburgh: University of Pittsburgh Press, 1976.
Baily, Samuel L. *The United States and the Development of Latin America*. New York: New Viewpoints, 1976.
Bedregal, Guillermo. *Víctor Paz Estenssoro, el politico: Una semblanza crítica*. Mexico City: Fondo de Cultura Económica, 1999.
Bernstein, Barton J., ed. *Politics and Policies of the Truman Administration*. Chicago: Quadrangle, 1970.
Bethell, Leslie, and Ian Roxborough, eds. *Latin America Between the Second World War and the Cold War, 1944–1948*. Cambridge: Cambridge University Press, 1992.
———. "The Postwar Conjuncture in Latin America: Democracy, Labor, and the Left." In *Latin America Between the Second World War and the Cold War, 1944–1948*, edited by Leslie Bethel and Ian Roxborough, 1–32. Cambridge: Cambridge University Press, 1992.
Blasier, Cole. *The Hovering Giant: U.S. Responses to Revolutionary Change in Latin America*. Pittsburgh: University of Pittsburgh Press, 1976.
———. "The United States and the Revolution." In *Beyond the Revolution: Bolivia Since 1952*, edited by James M. Malloy and Richard S. Thorn, 53–110. Pittsburgh: University of Pittsburgh Press, 1971.
Braden, Spruille. *Diplomats and Demagogues*. New Rochelle, N.Y.: Arlington, 1971.
Bulmer-Thomas, Victor, and James Dunkerley, eds. *The United States and Latin America: The New Agenda*. Cambridge, Mass.: Harvard University Press, 1999.
Cabot, John Moors. *Toward Our Common American Destiny*. Medford, Mass.: Metcalf, 1955.
Canelas, Demitrio. *Dictadura y democracia en Bolivia*. Cochabamba: Editorial Canelas, 1992.
Chávez Ortiz, Ñuflo. *Recuerdos de un revolucionario boliviano*. La Paz: CEPBOL, 1988.
Child, John. *Unequal Alliance: The Inter-American Military System, 1938–1978*. Boulder: Westview, 1980.
Collier, David, ed. *The New Authoritarianism in Latin America*. Princeton: Princeton University Press, 1979.
Contreras, Manuel E. *The Bolivian Tin Industry in the First Half of the Twentieth Century*. London: Institute of Latin American Studies, 1993.
Cullather, Nick. *Secret History: The CIA's Classified Account of Its Operations in Guatemala, 1952–1954*. Stanford: Stanford University Press, 1999.
Dorn, Glenn J. "'The American Reputation for Fair Play': Víctor Haya de la Torre and the Federal Bureau of Narcotics." *Historian* 65 (Fall 2003): 1083–1101.
———. "'Exclusive Domination' or 'Short Term Imperialism': The Peruvian Response to U.S.–Argentine Rivalry, 1946–1950." *Americas* 61 (July 2004): 81–102.
———. *Peronistas and New Dealers: U.S–Argentine Rivalry and the Western Hemisphere, 1946–1950*. New Orleans: University Press of the South, 2005.
Dunkerley, James. *Bolivia: Revolution and the Power of History in the Present*. London: Institute for the Study of the Americas, 2007.
———. *Rebellion in the Veins: Political Struggle in Bolivia, 1952–1982*. London: Verso, 1984.
Escudé, Carlos. *Estados Unidos, Gran Bretaña, y la declinación argentina, 1942–1949*. Buenos Aires: Editorial Belgrano, 1983.
Ewell, Judith. *Venezuela and the United States: From Monroe's Hemisphere to Petroleum's Empire*. Athens: University of Georgia Press, 1996.
Frank, Gary. *Juan Perón vs. Spruille Braden: The Story Behind the Blue Book*. Lanham, Md.: University Press of America, 1980.

Frontaura Argandoña, Manuel. *La Revolución Nacional*. Cochabamba: Editoral Los Amigos del Libro, 1974.

Gallardo Lozada, Jorge. *La nación postergada*. La Paz: Editorial Los Amigos del Libro, 1984.

Gallo, Carmenza. *Taxes and State Power: Political Instability in Bolivia, 1900–1950*. Philadelphia: Temple University Press, 1991.

Gamarra, Eduardo A. "The United States and Bolivia: Fighting the Drug War." In *The United States and Latin America: The New Agenda*, edited by Victor Bulmer-Thomas and James Dunkerley, 177–206. Cambridge, Mass.: Harvard University Press, 1999.

Gamarra Zorilla, José. *Liberalismo y neoliberalismo: Breve interpretación de la historia de Bolivia*. La Paz: Editorial Los Amigos del Libro, 1993.

Geddes, Charles F. *Patiño: The Tin King*. London: Robert Hale, 1972

Gellman, Irwin F. *Good Neighbor Diplomacy: United States Policies in Latin America, 1933–1945*. Baltimore: Johns Hopkins University Press, 1979.

Gilderhus, Mark T. "An Emerging Synthesis? U.S.–Latin American Relations Since the Second World War." *Diplomatic History* 16 (Summer 1992): 429–452.

———. *The Second Century: U.S.–Latin American Relations Since 1889*. Wilmington, Del.: Scholarly Resources, 1999.

González Torres, René, and Luis Iriarte Ontiveros. *Villarroel: Mártir de sus ideales y el atisbo de la revolución nacional*. La Paz: Tallares-Escuela de Artes Gráficas del Colegio Don Basco, 1982.

Goodrich, Carter. "Bolivia in Time of Revolution." In *Beyond the Revolution: Bolivia Since 1952*, edited by James M. Malloy and Richard S. Thorn, 3–24. Pittsburgh: University of Pittsburgh Press, 1971.

Gootenberg, Paul. "Reluctance or Resistance: Constructing Cocaine (Prohibitions) in Peru, 1910–1950." In *Cocaine: Global Histories*, edited by Paul Gootenberg, 46–82. London: Routledge, 1999

Gotkowitz, Laura. *A Revolution for Our Rights: Indigenous Struggles for Land and Justice in Bolivia, 1880–1952*. Durham: Duke University Press, 2007.

Green, David. "The Cold War Comes to Latin America." In *Politics and Policies of the Truman Administration*, edited by Barton Bernstein, 149–195. New York: Quadrangle, 1970.

———. *The Containment of Latin America: Myths and Realities of the Good Neighbor Policy*. Chicago: Quadrangle, 1971.

Grindle, Merilee, and Pilar Domingo, eds. *Proclaiming Revolution: Bolivia in Comparative Perspective*. Cambridge, Mass.: David Rockefeller Institute of Latin American Studies, Harvard University 2003.

Grow, Michael. *The Good Neighbor Policy and Authoritarianism in Paraguay: United States Economic Expansion and Great-Power Rivalry in Latin America During World War II*. Lawrence: Regents Press of Kansas, 1981.

Guzmán, Augusto. *Historia de Bolivia*, 7th ed. Cochabamba: Editorial Los Amigos el Libro, 1990.

Haines, Gerald K. "Under the Eagle's Wing: The Franklin Roosevelt Administration Forges an American Hemisphere." *Diplomatic History* 1 (Fall 1977): 370–88.

Hillman, John. "Bolivia and British Tin Policy, 1939–1945." *Journal of Latin American Studies* 22 (May 1990): 291–315.

Hogan, Michael J. *Cross of Iron: Harry S. Truman and the Origins of the National Security State, 1945–1954*. Cambridge: Cambridge University Press, 1998.

Hylton, Forrest, and Sinclair Thomson. *Revolutionary Horizons: Past and Present in Bolivian Politics*. London: Verso, 2007.

Immerman, Richard H. *The CIA in Guatemala: The Foreign Policy of Intervention*. Austin: University of Texas Press, 1982.

Knight, Alan. "The Domestic Dynamic of the Mexican and Bolivian Revolutions Compared." In *Proclaiming Revolution: Bolivia in Comparative Perspective*, edited by Merilee Grindle and Pilar Domingo, 54–90. Cambridge, Mass.: David Rockefeller Institute of Latin American Studies, Harvard University, 2003.

Knudson, Jerry K. *Bolivia: Press and Revolution, 1932–1964*. Lanham, Md.: University Press of America, 1988.
Kofas, Jon V. *Foreign Debt and Underdevelopment: U.S.–Peru Economic Relations, 1930–1970*. Lanham, Md.: University Press of America, 1996.
Kohl, Benjamin, and Linda C. Farthing. *Impasse in Bolivia: Neoliberal Hegemony and Popular Resistance*. London: Zed Books, 2006.
LaFeber, Walter. "Thomas C. Mann and the Devolution of Latin American Policy." In *Behind the Throne: Servants of Power to Imperial Presidents, 1898–1968*, edited by Thomas McCormick and Walter LaFeber, 166–203. Madison: University of Wisconsin, 1993.
Leffler, Melvyn P. *A Preponderance of Power: National Security, the Truman Administration, and the Cold War*. Stanford: Stanford University Press, 1992.
Lehman, Kenneth D. *Bolivia and the United States: A Limited Partnership*. Athens: University of Georgia Press, 1999.
———. "Braked but Not Broken: The United States and Revolutionaries in Mexico and Bolivia." In *Proclaiming Revolution: Bolivia in Comparative Perspective*, edited by Merilee Grindle and Pilar Domingo, 91–116. Cambridge, Mass.: David Rockefeller Institute of Latin American Studies, Harvard University, 2003.
———. "Revolutions and Attributions: Making Sense of Eisenhower Administration Policies in Bolivia and Guatemala." *Diplomatic History* 21 (Spring 1997): 185–213.
Lema Peláez, Raúl. *Con las banderas del Movimiento Nacionalista Revolucionario: El sexenio, 1946–1952*. La Paz: Editorial Amigos del Libro, 1979.
Lewis, Paul H. *Paraguay Under Stroessner*. Chapel Hill: University of North Carolina Press, 1980.
MacDonald, Callum A. "The U.S., the Cold War, and Perón." In *Economic Imperialism and the State: The Political Economy of the External Connection from Independence to the Present*, edited by Christopher Abel and Colin Lewis, 405–14. London: Athlone, 1985.
Malloy, James M. *Bolivia: The Uncompleted Revolution*. New York: Oxford University Press, 1970.
Malloy, James M., and Richard S. Thorn, eds. *Beyond the Revolution: Bolivia Since 1952*. Pittsburgh: University of Pittsburgh Press, 1971.
McCormick, Thomas J., and Walter LaFeber, eds. *Behind the Throne: Servants to Power to Imperial Presidents, 1898–1968*. Madison: University of Wisconsin Press, 1993.
McCullough, David. *Truman*. New York: Simon and Schuster, 1992.
Mesa Gisbert, Carlos D., José de Mesa, and Teresa Gisbert. *Historia de Bolivia*. La Paz: Editorial Gisbert, 1997.
Ministerio de Relaciones Exteriores y Culto de Bolivia. *Memoria, 21 de julio de 1946–6 de agosto de 1947*. La Paz: n.p., 1947.
———. *Memoria, 7 de agosto de 1947–6 de agosto de 1948*. La Paz: n.p., 1948.
———. *Memoria, 7 de agosto de 1948–6 de agosto de 1949*. La Paz: n.p., 1949.
Mitchell, Christopher. *The Legacy of Populism in Bolivia: From MNR to Military Rule*. New York: Praeger, 1977.
Murillo Cárdenas, Elidoro, and Gustavo Larrea Bedregal. *Razón de Patria: Villarroel y nacionalismo revolucionario*. La Paz: Metodista, 1988.
Navia Ribera, Carlos. *Los Estados Unidos y la revolución nacional: Entre el pragmatismo y el sometimiento*. Cochabamba: CIDRE, 1984.
Oddone, Juan. *Vecinos en discordia: Argentina, Uruguay y la política hemisférica de los Estados Unidos Seleccion de documentos, 1945–1955*. Montevideo: Universidad de la República, 2007.
Olson, James C. *Stuart Symington: A Life*. Columbia: University of Missouri Press, 1973.
Ostria Gutiérrez, Alberto. *The Tragedy of Bolivia: A People Crucified*. New York: Devin-Adair, 1958.
Pach, Chester. "The Containment of U.S. Military Aid to Latin America, 1944–1947." *Diplomatic History* 6 (Summer 1982): 225–43.
Parkinson, Francis. *Latin America, the Cold War, and the World Powers, 1945–1973: A Study in Diplomatic History*. Beverly Hills, Calif.: Sage, 1978.
Pike, Fredrick B. *The United States and the Andean Republics: Peru, Bolivia, and Ecuador*. Cambridge, Mass.: Harvard University Press, 1977.

Prado Salmon, Gary. *Poder y fuerzas armadas, 1949–1982*. La Paz: Editorial Amigos del Libro, 1983.
Quieser Morales, Waltraud. *Bolivia: Land of Struggle*. Boulder: Westview, 1992.
Rabe, Stephen G. *Eisenhower and Latin America: The Foreign Policy of Anticommunism*. Chapel Hill: University of North Carolina Press, 1988.
———. "The Elusive Conference: United States Relations with Latin America, 1945–1952." *Diplomatic History* 2 (Summer 1978): 279–294.
———. *The Road to OPEC: United States Relations with Venezuela, 1919–1976*. Austin: University of Texas Press, 1982.
Rabinowitz, Francine F., and Felicity M. Trueblood, eds. *Latin American Urban Research*. Vol. 3. Beverly Hills, Calif.: Sage, 1973.
Randall, Stephen J. *Colombia and the United States: Hegemony and Independence*. Athens: University of Georgia Press, 1992.
Rapoport, Mario. *Gran Bretaña, Estados Unidos, y las clases dirigentes argentinos, 1940–1945*. Buenos Aires: Editorial Belgrano, 1980.
Ríos Gamboa, Walter. *Bolivia: Hacia la democracia*. La Paz: Empresa Editora, 1979.
Romualdi, Serafino. *Presidents and Peons: Recollections of a Labor Ambassador*. New York: Funk and Wagnalls, 1970.
Roque Bacarreza, Francisco. *Los años del condor: Sesenta crónicas del triunfo revolucionario boliviano en plena Guerra Fria*. La Paz: Mundy Color, 1995.
Schlesinger, Stephen, and Stephen Kinzer. *Bitter Fruit: The Untold Story of the American Coup in Guatemala*. Garden City, N.Y.: Anchor Books, 1982.
Schwartzberg, Stephen. *Democracy and U.S. Policy in Latin America During the Truman Years*. Gainesville: University of Florida Press, 2003.
Siekmeier, James. *Aid, Nationalism, and Inter-American Relations: Guatemala, Bolivia, and the United States, 1945–1961*. New York: Mellen, 1999.
Smith, Gaddis. *The Last Years of the Monroe Doctrine, 1945–1993*. New York: Hill and Wang, 1993.
Smith, Peter H. *Talons of the Eagle: Dynamics of U.S.–Latin American Relations*. New York: Oxford University Press, 1996.
Stefantoni, Pablo, and Hervé Do Alto. *Evo Morales: De la coca al Palacio; Una oportunidad para la izquierda indígena*. La Paz: Malatesta, 2006.
Thoburn, John T. *Tin in the World Economy*. Edinburgh: Edinburgh University Press, 1994.
Trask, Roger R. "The Impact of the Cold War on United States–Latin American Relations, 1945–1949." *Diplomatic History* 1 (Summer 1977): 271–285.
Truman, Harry S. *Memoirs*. 2 vols. Garden City, N.Y.: Doubleday, 1955.
United Nations. *Report of the United Nations Technical Assistance Mission to Bolivia*. ("Keenleyside Report"). New York: United Nations, 1951.
U.S. Department of State. *Consultation Among the American Republics with Regard to the Argentine Situation*. Washington, D.C.: GPO, 1946.
———. *Bulletin*. Washington: GPO, 1946–1950.
———. *Foreign Relations of the United States of America: Diplomatic Papers, 1945*. Vol. 9. Washington: GPO, 1969.
———. *Foreign Relations of the United States of America: Diplomatic Papers, 1946*. Vol. 9. Washington: GPO, 1969.
———. *Foreign Relations of the United States of America: Diplomatic Papers, 1947*. Vol. 7. Washington: GPO, 1969.
———. *Foreign Relations of the United States of America: Diplomatic Papers, 1948*. Vol. 9. Washington: GPO, 1969.
———. *Foreign Relations of the United States of America: Diplomatic Papers, 1949*. Vol. 7. Washington: GPO, 1969.
———. *Foreign Relations of the United States of America: Diplomatic Papers, 1950*. Vol. 2. Washington: GPO, 1976.
———. *Foreign Relations of the United States of America: Diplomatic Papers, 1951*. Vol. 2. Washington: GPO, 1979.

Welles, Sumner. *Where Are We Heading?* New York: Harper, 1946.
Whitehead, Laurence. "Bolivia." In *Latin America Between the Second World War and the Cold War, 1944–1948*, edited by Leslie Bethell and Ian Roxborough, 120–145. Cambridge: Cambridge University Press, 1992.
———. "The Bolivian National Revolution: A Comparison." In *Proclaiming Revolution: Bolivia in Comparative Perspective*, edited by Merilee Grindle and Pilar Domingo, 25–53. Cambridge, Mass.: David Rockefeller Institute of Latin American Studies, Harvard University, 2003.
———. "National Power and Local Power: The Case of Santa Cruz de la Sierra, Bolivia." In *Latin American Urban Research*, vol. 3, edited by Francine F. Rabinowitz and Felicity M. Trueblood, 23–46. Beverly Hills, Calif.: Sage, 1973.
———. *The United States and Bolivia: A Case of Neocolonialism*. London: Haslemere, 1967.
Wood, Bryce. "The Department of State and the Non-National Interest." *Inter-American Economic Affairs* (Autumn 1961): 5–24.
———. *The Dismantling of the Good Neighbor Policy*. Austin: University of Texas Press, 1985.
———. *The Making of the Good Neighbor Policy*. New York: Columbia University Press, 1961.

PERIODICALS

Bolivia

El Diario
La Razón
La Tribuna
Ultima Hora

Great Britain

Financial Times

United States of America

American Metal Market
Engineering and Mining Journal
Newsweek
New York Times
Time
Wall Street Journal
Washington Daily News

INDEX

Acción Cívica Boliviana, 129
Acción Democrática, 5, 7
Acheson, Dean, 3, 37, 104, 110, 192, 198
   non-intervention and, 40, 98–99, 119–20
   tin negotiations of 1951–52, and, 143–45, 152–56, 158
   Paz Estenssoro government and, 170, 172, 175, 178, 183
Adam, Hector, 28, 33, 38, 40, 49–50
Alexander, Alfredo, 119, 141
Alexander, Robert, 3–4, 163, 184, 240 n. 18
Alianza Popular Revolucionaria Americana, 5, 7
Alvéstegui, David, 65–67
American Federation of Labor, 149, 167, 188
Anaya, Ricardo, 12, 58, 73–74, 93
Andrade, Víctor, 36, 42–47, 191, 218 n. 67, 239 n. 11
   tin negotiations of 1952–53 and, 177–78, 180–83, 185, 187
Aramayo, Carlos, 47, 108, 115, 129
   nationalization and, 169, 173, 179, 182, 186
   La Razón and, 9, 69, 118–20, 171
   tin negotiations of 1951–52 and, 139–40, 142, 144, 148, 149
Arbenz Guzman, Jacobo, 201, 205
Argentina, 5–7, 53–56, 64–69, 99–100, 151, 169–70, 200
   Villarroel Government and, 28, 36–40
Argentine-Bolivian Commercial Agreement 64–69, 79–81, 84, 90–91, 115–16, 141
Armour, Norman, 86
Arze, José Antonio, 14, 36, 38, 47, 56, 93, 97, 118
   Communism and, 12, 58–59, 73–75, 87–88, 130–32
Associated Press, 47
Atwood, Rollin, 139–142, 151, 178

Ballivián Rojas, Hugo, 2, 133–38, 141, 155–57, 164–65, 191, 194
Banco Minero, 175–76
Barber, Willard, 95
Bateman, Alan, 43, 186
Batlle Berres, Luis, 97

Bechtel Corporation, 207
Belgian Congo, 17
Belmonte Pool, Waldo, 57, 110, 128, 194
Billiton Mastschappij, 19, 22
Blue Book, 36–40, 198
Board of Trade, 64
Bogotá Conference, 104, 168
Bohan, Merwin, 14
Bolivia
   agriculture, 8–9, 187
   mining, 9–12, 174–80
   taxation policy, 8, 24, 44, 60–61, 108, 112, 118–23, 139–40, 201
Bonsal, Phillip, 16
Bowers, Claude, 16, 150
Braden, Spruille, 51, 55, 61, 63, 191–92, 198, 203
   post-retirement, 2, 83, 114
   Villarroel government and, 36–41, 45–46
Brazil, 52, 65, 67
Brown, Winthrop, 142–43, 160
Bruce, David, 180
Buitrago, Mariano, 64
Butron, German, 187

Cabot, John Moors, 190, 195, 202
Canedo Reyes, Raúl, 60–61, 63, 68–69, 80–82, 96, 112, 176
Canelas, Demetrio, 49, 128–29, 134–35, 163, 190, 194
Capper Pass, 84, 177
Carranza, Venustiano, 204–5
Catavi, 15, 47, 74, 77, 92, 96–97, 174, 180
Central Obrera Boliviana, 166–67, 187–88, 190, 204
Centro Cultural Boliviano-Americano, 110
Chaco War, 12
Chavez, Dennis, 157, 159
Chavez, Nuflo, 187
Chacón, Gustavo, 34–35
Chile, 65, 98–100, 151, 169
China, 18, 22
Clayton, Will, 42, 44
Cobb, William, 117, 172

[248]

INDEX

Cochabamba, 9, 15, 47, 74, 89, 97, 102, 105, 107
Cochabamba–Santa Cruz Highway, 112, 203
Cold War, 3–8
Combined Food Board, 66, 221 n. 56
Combined Tin Committee, 23, 86, 111
Commerce Department, 103
Congress of Industrial Organizations, 149
Connally, Tom, 46
Consolidated Tin Smelters, 9, 18
Cook, Donald, 126, 156, 160
Corcoran, Thomas, 203
Corporación Minera de Bolivia, 206
Costa du Rels, Adolfo, 86

Danaher, John, 182
Daniels, Paul, 71, 82
Daza Ondarza, Ernesto, 53–55, 150
Defense Materials Procurement Administration, 154, 156–58, 175
Defense Production Agency, 123–26
Deringer, D. C., 173
Ditisheim, Hans, 176, 237 n. 42
Duggan, Laurence, 16
Dulles, John Foster, 186, 200
Dutch East Indies, 17–18, 20

Economic Cooperation Administration, 200
Einstein, Albert, 121
Eisenhower, Dwight D., 7, 181, 186, 189, 200, 239 n. 11
Eisenhower, Milton, 188
El Diario, 9, 118–19, 122, 217, n. 40
Elío, Tomás, 129, 132
Emergency Procurement Service, 175
enganche, 11
Enguino, Jorge, 52
Escobar, José, 52
Espy, James, 1, 8, 36, 82, 84, 88, 105–7, 109
  Civil War of 1949 and, 98, 101–2
  tin contract of 1947 and, 62–63, 68
Export-Import Bank, 114, 158, 175

Falange Socialista Boliviana, 12, 109, 118, 129, 187–88
Famine Relief Act, 189
Federación Sindical de Trabajadores de Bolivia, 30, 33, 74–78, 88–89, 92, 96–97
Federal Bureau of Narcotics, 200
Feis, Herbert, 19
Flack, Joseph, 36, 48, 102, 123, 136, 192–93
  Hertzog government and, 71, 75–76, 82, 87, 92
  revolutionary junta and, 50–52, 58, 61, 69
Florman, Irving, 107–10, 131, 139, 141, 145, 186, 199, 226 n. 34, 229 n. 33
  11 August Decree and, 119–27
Foreign Economic Administration, 41–43

Frente Democrático, 56–57
Frente Democrático Antifascista, 35–36, 47–48

Gaitán, Jorge, 6
Galarza, Ernesto, 57, 218 n. 67, 237 n. 31
General Tin Industries, 9
Genuine Republican Party, 35, 56
González, Natalicio, 6
González Videla, Gabriel, 97, 99, 169
Goodloe, John, 79
Good Neighbor Policy, 27, 43, 68, 116, 197–200
Goodrich, Carter, 202
Gosálvez, Gabriel, 49, 79, 99, 152–53, 230 n. 34
  election of 1951 and, 128, 132–33
Great Britain, 18–25, 44, 68, 79, 103–4, 115, 125, 142–43, 151, 182
Guachalla, Luis, 57–59, 61, 132, 146, 149, 158, 170
Guatemala, 190, 201–3
Guevara Arze, Walter, 166, 174
Guillén Olmos, Néstor, 50
Gutiérrez, Guillermo, 92, 127, 132

Harber, W. B., 124–26
Hardesty, Marion, 214 n. 45
Harrison, William, 123, 125–26
Haya de la Torre, Víctor, 198, 200
Henderson, Douglas, 193, 237 n. 42
Henderson, Leon, 176
Herrera, Jorge, 6
Hertzog Garaizábal, Enrique, 2, 57–59, 61, 71–86, 94, 190–95, 224 n. 70
Hise, Harley, 111
Hochschild, Mauricio, 9, 15, 37–38, 63, 68, 83, 97, 115, 120
  nationalization and, 169, 171, 173, 177, 179, 182, 186
  tin contract of 1946 and, 41–47
  tin negotiations of 1951–52 and, 140, 142, 149, 153, 156–59
Hoover, Herbert, 2
Hoover, J. Edgar, 3
Hudson, William, 135, 163, 184, 201
Hull, Cordell, 16, 37, 198

Indian Congress, 30–31
Indonesia, 62, 114–15
International Court of Justice, 183
International Monetary Fund, 1, 189, 207
International Tin Agreement, 205–6
International Tin Committee, 18–24, 62, 76, 83, 207
International Trade Organization, 23–24

Jewett, George, 45
Johnson Committee. *See also* Preparedness Subcommittee

[249]

INDEX

Johnson, Jesse, 45, 62–63
Johnson, Lyndon B., 124–26, 186, 203
   tin negotiations of 1951–52 and, 144, 146, 148, 151, 153, 155, 158–60
Johnson, Richard, 114

Keenleyside, Hugh, 120–21
Keenleyside Mission, 120–21, 140
Kennedy, Donald, 23, 86
Kennedy, Thomas, 149
Klein Mission, 135
Korean War, 115, 139
Kyne, Martin, 225 n. 13

La Marcha, 169
La Paz, 9, 47–8, 50–52, 55–6, 92–3, 98, 104, 165
La Prensa, 172
La Razón, 9, 69, 108, 118–19, 122, 171–72, 198
La Tribuna, 119, 122
Lagomarsino, Rolando, 54
Larsen, Jess, 154–58
Lechín Oquendo, Juan, 30, 130, 132, 134, 159, 163, 192, 204
   FSTMB and, 30, 74, 76–78, 88, 89, 96–97
   Paz Estenssoro government and, 166–68, 170–74, 179, 186–89
Liberal Party, 35, 40, 57, 59, 72–75, 88, 91, 93, 201
Lindberg, John, 121
Loaiza Beltran, Fernando, 92
Lodge, Henry Cabot, 203
London Tin Corporation, 18
Longhorn Tin Smelter, 18–22, 68, 79, 110, 123, 175–77, 187
Lucio Quiros, José, 171

Malaya, 17–18, 20, 22, 44, 62–63, 84, 115, 153, 220 n. 220
Maleady, Thomas, 120, 123, 139, 146–47, 150–51, 156–57, 172–73, 227 n. 44
Mann, Thomas C., 131, 141, 151, 160–61, 202, 238, n. 56
   tin negotiations of 1951–52 and, 178, 181–83, 186–87
María Barzola Field, 180
Marshall, George, 64, 84, 89
Marshall Plan, 92, 107, 146, 151
Martínez Vargas, Ricardo, 23, 51–52, 55, 61–68, 78, 98–101, 104, 106–7, 132
   tin contract of 1948 and, 78, 81–86
   tin contract of 1950 and, 110, 112–16, 119
   tin negotiations of 1951–52 and, 139–40, 142–43, 145–46, 149–50, 154, 158
McDonald, Harry, 154–55, 158–59, 175
McKinnon, Clinton, 151
McKinnon, Wiley, 124, 126–27, 148, 156, 179
Mercantile Metal and Ore, 177, 182

Messersmith, George, 49
Metals Reserve Company, 18
Mexican Revolution, 204–5
Mier y León, Manuel, 60–61
Miller, Edward, 100–101, 104, 112–14, 124, 133, 136, 192, 197, 238 n. 56
   Paz Estenssoro government and, 172, 174, 177–78, 181
   tin negotiations of 1951–52 and, 141–42, 148, 151–56
Ministry of Supply, 25, 84, 86, 103–4
Miranda, Miguel, 64–67, 79–81, 85, 90
mitanaje, 8
Monje Gutiérrez, Tomás 2, 50, 56, 191, 193
Monroy Block, German, 216 n. 16
Morales, Evo, 1, 207–9
Movimiento al Socialismo, 207–9
Movimiento Nacionalista Revolucionario, 1, 5, 12–15, 191, 204–6, 209
   anti-Semitism, 213, n. 41
   anti-U.S. sentiment, 32–34, 188–89
   efforts to return to power, 89–90, 93, 97–100, 129–33
   Nazism and Peronism, accusations of, 14–17, 28–29, 36–40, 132–33, 169–70, 200–201
   Paz Estenssoro government and, 164–73
   Villarroel government and, 29–32, 34
Multer, Abraham, 151
Munitions Board, 113, 115, 147
Mutual Security Act, 189

Nathanson, Win, 173
National Lead Company, 9
National Revolution, 1–2, 159, 164–66, 207–9
National Strategic Resources Board, 113
Nigeria, 17–18
Nixon, Richard, 167
Nogales, Edmundo, 16
North American Aviation Corporation, 101

Oblitas, Luis, 52
Odría, Manuel 98, 135, 169, 212 n. 4, 9
Organización Regional Interamericana de Trabajadores, 213 n. 25
Organization of American States, 150, 152, 155–56, 179
Oruro, 29, 34, 47, 165
Ostria Gutiérrez, Alberto, 106, 155
Otazo, Rafael, 34

Partido Comunista, 4
Partido Izquierda Revolucionaria, 12–14, 35, 56–60, 97, 102, 130–31
   Hertzog government and, 87–88, 91
   Paz Estenssoro government and, 166, 170

[250]

INDEX

Partido Obrero Revolucionario, 12, 30, 47–48, 56–57, 72–76, 166, 191
Partido de la Unión Republicana Socialista, 57, 65, 71–75, 87–92, 105, 109, 128–34, 190–94
Patiño, Antenor, 9, 76, 79, 96–97, 108, 111, 115, 120
   nationalization and, 179–82
   tin negotiations of 1951–52 and, 139–40, 142–43, 153
Patiño, Simon, 9–10, 15, 17, 19–22, 45
Paz Estenssoro, Víctor, 1, 12–13, 22, 59, 117, 208, 213 n. 41
   activities in exile, 54–56, 67
   election of 1951 and, 129–34
   presidency of, 166–68, 170–78, 180, 183, 187–90, 201–6
   Villarroel government and, 27, 33–34, 38–39, 42
Peñaranda del Castillo, Enrique, 13–16, 19–22, 28
Perón, Eva, 169–70
Perón, Juan Domingo, 5–7, 54–55, 65, 80, 90, 155, 174
   accusations against, 36–37, 39, 53, 99–100, 165, 169–72, 191
Peru, 151, 169, 200
Pinto, José Celestino, 34–36, 40, 44
Pinto Parada, Melchor, 75
Plaza Lasso, Galo, 150, 152
Ponce, Antonio, 16
Pongueaje, 8
Potosí, 8–9, 24, 97, 105
Preparedness Subcommittee, 124, 126, 143–44, 147
Prestes, Luis, 106
Provisional Junta of Government, 49

Querejazu Calvo, R., 185

Razón de Patria, 13–15, 30, 34–35, 40
Reconstruction Finance Corporation, 2–3, 38, 45–47, 103–4, 191
   tin contract of 1947 and, 61–69
   tin contract of 1948 and, 79–86
   tin contract of 1950 and, 110–6
   tin negotiations of 1951–52 and, 123–27, 138–60
   tin negotiations of 1952–53 and, 175–78, 181
Republican Socialist Party, 35, 56
Rioja, Bilbao, 129, 132
Rockefeller, Nelson, 59
Rodríguez, Angel, 15
Romualdi, Serafino, 149
Roosevelt, Franklin D., 2, 16, 197–98
Rovira, German, 45
Rowell, Edward, 188, 192
Royce, Alexander, 111
Sánchez de Losada, Gonzalo, 207–8
Sanjines, Juan, 167, 170
Sawyer, Charles, 155

Schwarz, Ernst, 149
Seleme Vargas, Antonio, 134, 164–65
Siam, 17
Siles Zuazo, Hernan, 33, 165
   election of 1951 and, 130, 132, 134
   vice presidency of, 166–68, 172, 174, 178–79, 190
Snyder, John, 155
Socialist Party, 35, 56, 128
Soviet Union, 3, 24, 87, 106–7, 111, 148, 171
Sparks, Edward, 175–76, 178, 180, 183, 188–89, 192, 202
Standard Oil, 14
Stettinius, Edward, 28
Stowe, David, 151
Sucre, 9
Superior Oil, 89
Symington, W. Stuart, 137–54, 186, 192, 203

Tamayo, José, 37
Texas City smelter. *See also* Longhorn tin smelter
Thorp, Willard, 111
Thurston, Walter, 27, 29, 31–33, 35, 44
Tin Study Group, 23, 104, 149
Tittmann, Harold, 212 n.4
Torres Ortiz, Humberto, 164–65
Treasury Department, 189
Treaty of Economic, Financial and Cultural Cooperation. *See* Argentine-Bolivian Commercial Agreement
Tripartite Committee, 50, 52, 57
Trujillo, Rafael, 198
Truman Doctrine, 3, 52, 100
Truman, Harry S., 2, 100, 113, 172, 174, 181, 183, 186, 192, 198, 203
   tin negotiations of 1951–52 and, 152, 154–55, 157–58, 160
Tydings, Millard, 179–82, 186, 189

Ultima Hora, 9, 119, 122, 141
Unión Civica Femenina, 35
United Fruit Company, 202–3
United Mine Workers, 149
United Nations, 47, 120–21
United Press, 47
United States of America
   recognition policy, 16–17, 51–53, 168–174
   tin purchasing policy, 17–25, 41–47, 60–69, 78–86, 110–16
Urriolagoitia Harriague, Mamerto, 2, 93–98, 100–110, 116–23, 130, 133–34, 190–91
Uruguay, 97
Vandenberg, Arthur, 46
Venezuela, 200
Villarroel López, Gualberto, 15–17, 22, 28–30, 34–41, 46–48, 191, 194

[251]

INDEX

Vital Materials Coordinating Committee, 140
Vogelsang, Erwin, 22

War on Drugs, 209
War Production Board, 22
Weaver, George, 139, 142
Welch, E. C., 139, 141, 144, 149
Welles, Sumner 18, 198

Williams, Harvey Smelter, 9, 84, 182
Wilson, Charles, 148, 154–58, 192
World Bank, 1, 207
Wright, James, 45–46

Yacimientos Petrolíferos Fiscales Bolivianos, 89

Zilveti, Pedro, 131–33, 198

www.ingramcontent.com/pod-product-compliance
Lightning Source LLC
Chambersburg PA
CBHW021358290426
44108CB00010B/298